PYTHAGORAS
OF SAMOS

Also by Marisa Calvi with Kuthumi Lal Singh
"You Don't Have Problems, You're Just Bored!"
"Pharaoh Thutmose III (Let's Go For A Walk; Book One)"
available at www.newenergywriting.com

Let's Go For a Walk
Book Two

PΨTHΔGΩRΔS
ΩΓ SΔMΩS

A life adventure of
Ascended Master
Kuthumi Lal Singh
as told to
Marisa Calvi

BCC Publishing
GLENORIE, AUSTRALIA

First published in 2010 by
Marisa Calvi
20 Pinus Avenue
Glenorie NSW 2157
AUSTRALIA

A CIP catalogue record for this book is available
from the National Library of Australia

ISBN; 978-0-9803506-3-0 (paperback)
978-0-9803506-4-7 (e-book)

Artwork; Moth motif taken from
"J'Encore" by Jessica Simanowski
www.js-artist.com

Editor; Eva Smarda Carney
newenergyexpression@gmail.com

For the students of the mystery schools

and those that now teach the new energy.

 INTRODUCTION

Welcome to the next episode of my writing adventures with Kuthumi, as we continue sharing some of his life adventures.

My time with Pythagoras began just after I had completed the story of Pharaoh Thutmose but before it was published. Knowing that I was reluctant to leave Thutmose and his family, Kuthumi offered me a glimpse and a taste of his next story to help me let go. It worked, helping ease me from Ancient Egypt to Ancient Greece.

It was not just the people of Thutmose's story that enamoured me, making it hard to let go. My time with Thutmose was like sitting by a warm fire with a friend, swapping stories as we sipped on a brandy. If I had time to sit and write, then this aspect of Kuthumi had time to talk. He even loved to chat between our writing sessions. I could get lost in writing for hours at a time, as though I was there in the very scene I was writing. I needed complete silence for my writing and in the beginning I would even need to shower when I finished to pull myself back to the present. It was intense but wonderful.

Writing with Pythagoras was completely different. I received downloads in short bursts and could not write for more than an hour at each sitting. Unlike Thutmose he *did* want me to research his history and led me to Iamblichus' biography of him, telling me that should be my guide for major events of his life.

Some days I would sit before my computer and Pythagoras just would not show up to write with me. This was especially so as we got into the details of his time at the mystery schools. Frustrated one day at the lack of progress I was making, I openly asked Pythagoras what was happening. Pythagoras confessed he felt he should not share the particulars of the mystery schools. These were sacred places that he had been privy to and even now he still felt compelled to honour their codes of secrecy.

In ancient times you proved yourself worthy to attend these schools and some schools were so hidden that just finding them showed your merit. So I argued that in the same way, if someone found their way to his book then they too were worthy to know of his experiences at the schools. Thankfully this made sense to his pragmatic nature and we moved on.

I still missed the warmth of writing with Thutmose though. I even joked that Thutmose was emotional while Pythagoras was informational.

Every now and then I like to check in with Kuthumi to see how we are doing. After all these are his stories and it's nice to know that he is happy in how they are being told. We were having one of these meetings when I made my confession.

"I don't like Pythagoras," I said.

"It's okay. He doesn't like you either," was Kuthumi's reply.

As bizarre as it sounds this somehow cleared the last block between us and from then our work together moved much faster.

There were still days when I felt I should not write and I let go of the timeline I had decided to tie myself to for this book's release. I knew our readers would rather wait another month or two for something genuine than something forced. This release opened my writing even more. I could now write with noise in the house. Even getting up from my desk to get a glass of water did not break the flow. It seemed Pythagoras' practicalities were rubbing off onto me and I did not complain.

I generally don't review my writing as I go, saving this process for when the book is complete. Kuthumi recommended this when I started writing with Thutmose and it was the best advice he gave me. When the story is done then I take off my writer hat and put on my editor hat.

When it came time to do this with Pythagoras I did so with some trepidation. The writing had happened in fits and starts over eighteen months and I really did not have a sense of the book as a whole. I was honestly scared I was going to read a mess. Instead I delighted in reading Pythagoras' story as a whole.

I read parts that I had completely forgotten I had written with him and found much more humour than I had given him credit for. Each review of the book took me even deeper into his story.

Once again I thanked myself for letting go of my expectations and for having dived into the experience of writing with Kuthumi.

Balthasar, one of the three magi who travelled to see Yeshua, is our next story. While we have not started that book yet, he is already floating around nearby. His energy and personality is something different yet again, and I know writing with him will be a new, unique experience even though it will be my fourth book with Kuthumi.

I cannot wait to start again!

Oh, and just so you know, Pythagoras and I quite like each other now!

Welcome back my dear friends!

Welcome back to the odyssey that is the retelling of my experiences.

I have to be honest and say that it has been some time since even I have revisited these stories and stepping into the remembrance is not always so easy. There are just some parts of lives that you wish you could forget. This cannot happen though when you choose to be an ascended master!

In revisiting my stories I am once again living these lives and in doing so it sometimes does become easy to forget who I am now. So I step back, and I observe the aspect of me that tells the story. I feel the depth in which that part of me is connected to the experience of that lifetime and I honour all they did in being part of my collective experience.

During my last days as a human, I pondered writing these stories myself before I left the physical realm but I knew that could not happen. I knew I needed to stand back to tell them with the compassion that would do them justice. I knew that would only happen once I surrendered into my pure essence.

Therein lies the catch; once you are complete and have called all parts of you back to the one, how then do you revisit just one part of you and not let it once again consume you?

This was the question I asked myself as I sat at my writing desk in India. The answer found me immediately. I felt it call to me in the breeze and I knew it was not a voice from within me. It was a voice I knew well though and it repeated a promise made to me before time existed and before the human realm came to be.

"We will tell your stories and we will read them ...."

It was a whisper with the strength of a tornado. It was my spirit family reminding me of the promise made before I separated from all that is, to become a sovereign being.

I knew these stories would once again be told when the time was right. But then is time ever wrong? These stories would find their way when the readers were ready.

How wonderful you have found them. How wonderful of you to join me and fulfil an ageless promise made with love.

So my dear, dear friend, when you are ready, let's go for a walk....

"And above all things, respect thyself"

from The Golden Verses of Pythagoras of Samos

CHAPTER ONE

The time of this life was just over five hundred years before the birth of Christ. Ancient Egypt still existed as it did when I ruled as Thutmose III but without the majesty and strength that it had known. Greece was a burgeoning power and pushing into the west, however it was kept in check by the growth of Persia. There was change happening slowly but steadily beneath the surface of humanity. This era saw the birth of the great age of Greek philosophy and science. To the east in Nepal and Northern India, Buddhism emerged while in China the hundred schools of thought sprung up independently, resulting in the birth of Taoism and Confucianism, amongst many others.

Even if one was not aware of the political processes in play or the new religions and philosophies being born there was still the palpable sense that change was on its way.

My physical time as Pythagoras was begun upon the island of Samos, which despite being just off the coast of modern day Turkey was, and still is considered one of the Greek Isles. At this time Samos was complete and self-sufficient with a full working economy, cultural pursuits, and a steady pulsing population. Samos was a crossroad for trade from the Orient to Europe and as such was a kaleidoscope of locals and travellers carrying their wares.

My mother's family had been upon Samos for four generations. They had originated from mainland Greece to resettle here when my great-grandfather, Anatolius arrived to build boats. He brought with him his new wife, who spent the boat ride vomiting with the nausea of her first pregnancy. When they got off the boat Anatolius stood on the shore looking over his new home and grinned as he pictured the prosperous life he would now start here. Meanwhile his pregnant wife sat on the ground, fighting one last retch of her stomach before bursting into tears.

"This island may sound and smell the same as home, but I may as well be another world away," she thought to herself.

Anatolius' ship building skills were well revered and matched by his ambitions. He worked endlessly and passionately knowing that one day he would step out of the shadow of his employer and he did. He had been upon Samos for ten years when a trader from Babylon knowing of his skills, approached him with the offer of a contract.

"Build me a fleet to carry me across the Mediterranean Sea. If they prove worthy then I shall make you my ships' master," the trader offered.

It was simple. All Anatolius had to do was build five ships to the trader's expectations and not only would he be paid for the construction but then he would continue on, overseeing their maintenance. The trader would gain a loyal tradesman on this foreign island while Anatolius would gain self-employment with guaranteed continued income. It was just what Anatolius had been working for.

Anatolius sent for his younger brothers from the mainland as they too now could benefit from his business. Besides he could hardly afford to pay full wages to the amount of men that he needed to complete the contract. His brothers crammed into his small home along with his wife and three children.

When his wife would cry to Anatolius that they could not afford meat or that she was sick of the piles of laundry they all left her he would just laugh and say, "My darling, enjoy the mess and poverty while you can. Soon you will have maids and cooks. Then you will miss all this!" He would finish by laughing.

His wife would not laugh though. "Stupid man! I will show you how much I will enjoy spending your money then we will see if you miss being poor," she spat back at him one day.

Anatolius never did miss being poor though.

A year later the boats for the trader were complete and they were magnificent. Anatolius inspected every nail and join in the wood and he would smile when he saw that each man had worked as diligently as he would have himself. When the trader walked their decks and then examined their hulls from a smaller boat Anatolius watched the trader's every gesture and expression. The trader stepped back upon the dock, clapped his hands and yelled something out to his assistants in his native tongue. They ran to the cart they had travelled upon and re-appeared with a small trunk, placing it at the trader's feet. He clapped again and they opened the trunk to reveal the gold pieces within that glistened as the sun hit them.

Anatolius could have fainted as he looked at the gold. Here was his reward for all the exhaustion, the stress and the promises to his wife, brothers and the men who had worked for next to nothing. It was sitting there before him, only a step away.

"Well done!" beamed the trader, "They are even more magnificent than I hoped. You have outdone your reputation."

Anatolius just nodded still mesmerised by the gold but he looked up at the trader, "It was an honour. I hope they serve you well."

"I am sure they will. All will know my grandeur before I even dock at their shores," the trader said laughing. "Here, take your payment and know it is well earned," he continued and pointed to the chest. "I will see you in four weeks when they have completed their first voyages."

The trader left upon his cart to begin to make plans for the boats and the goods that would travel upon them while Anatolius knelt on the dock before the trunk of gold. His brothers appeared by his side and they too were hypnotised by what they saw.

"That looks like more than he promised, Brother," one murmured and Anatolius nodded.

"Call the men," Anatolius said without looking up. "It is time they were paid."

Right there upon the dock before he took one piece for himself, Anatolius paid each and every one of his workers all that he owed them. When he was finished the gold looked as though it was hardly diminished and he realised that the trader had indeed been generous with his payment. His three brothers waited until the end, recording for him each salary paid and then Anatolius turned to them.

"I thank you for your loyalty and trust," he began, finally lifting himself to his feet before them. He then reached down and gathered more gold. In each of his brother's hands he placed all that he owed them then three times more.

"Now, go buy your own homes and find your own wives!" he said and they all laughed.

They made their way back home carrying the chest between them, still laughing as they walked. As they passed by each of the suppliers that were owed money they stopped to clear their debts, throwing in an extra gold piece as a thank you. When they were finally home Anatolius looked once more into the chest and when he saw that it was still half full he smiled and called out to his wife. She came to him with her arms crossed, expecting his usual request for wine when he entered the home but her curiosity piqued as she saw the chest before him.

"Ah, my patient and wonderful wife, come close and see that all I have promised you has finally arrived," he beamed.

His wife walked to the chest, looked in and then sighed, "And what shall be left, if any, once you have paid your debts?" she sulked.

"My debts are paid! This is ours," Anatolius said still grinning.

Then for the first time since they had arrived upon Samos he saw his wife smile.

The trader returned to Samos even faster than he should have and

Anatolius' heart sank as he saw two of the boats approach, picturing them in need of serious maintenance due to some fault in his work. Anatolius braced himself and scanned the boats for damage as the trader stepped down the gangway. He could see none and then he saw the smile upon the trader's face.

"Ah my loyal boat builder!" the trader cried out as he walked to Anatolius, grabbed his shoulders and kissed each of his cheeks in turn. "This was the fastest voyage ever and all thanks to you. I have sailed in similar conditions but never as efficiently as this. The other boats already make their way upon their second journey as we speak. I will make thrice my money this year at this speed and next year I wish to make thrice that again!" With that he commissioned another five boats and presented Anatolius with another chest of gold. "This time I will pay you in advance and perhaps this might help you work even faster!"

Which of course it did. Anatolius hired even more men and the boats were finished in six months by which time the first boats were so well-known that another twenty boats had been commissioned by other business men. The staff soon grew to two hundred and they became the largest ship building company of the region. His wife finally had her grand home filled with maids and cooks, and not once did she miss her chores.

The wealth that Anatolius created never diminished and his two sons took over the trade, keeping steady its prosperity and reputation for skilled work. Each generation carried on this tradition so that when my mother was born not only was it still a successful business but the family had amassed property and possessions that could have fed another four generations if no other boats were ever built or repaired.

So my mother, Pythia, was born into comfort and this was all that she knew. Her life was carefree and her days full of simple pleasures. As she turned fifteen her parents began to speak of marriage and she looked forward to this but she did not look forward to what Samos had to offer by way of men.

Pythia did not want any of the men who worked at the shipyards. She had grown up listening to talk of different lumbers, the new curves of a hull or the latest price for the canvas of the sails. The last thing she wanted was to have a married life full of this talk as it bored her rigid. Neither did she fancy any of the sons of the other Samos wealthy. As far as she could tell they were all just spoiled boys with no ambitions or interests beyond their families or the Samos shores.

The men who did excite her were the foreign traders that travelled to Samos and who often met with her father. Not a week went past that one didn't sit at their dinner table sharing stories of their travels and the things they had seen.

Pythia would sit listening, completely intrigued with their stories and picturing in her mind what they described. It was not that my mother wanted to travel; she just wished for a man who could speak about more than the limited little place that she believed Samos to be. Of course most of these men were far too old for my mother and even those that were within a reasonable age range were already married, however many did bring with them their sons. Unfortunately none so far had shown interest in my mother despite her beauty.

My father, Mnesarchus, was different in all respects from the droves of traders that arrived on Samos. Though he had found his trade through his family and was well-established he certainly was not like the big game traders who arrived with an entourage and a fleet of boats. My father arrived upon Samos alone, carrying his satchels of gems over his shoulders.

Mnesarchus was born in Tyre which like Samos was a city state consisting of a small island as well as some area of the adjacent mainland. It lay within the region known as Phoenicia that lies now within the land you call Lebanon. His father, Ruben, was certainly not rich and lived as a simple farmer, raising goats for their wool, their milk for cheeses and, when the herd was plentiful, their meat. Ruben's father and brothers all earned their living in this way, working together on a huge farm in the open plains on the mainland of Phoenicia. While far from the wealth of my mother's family they never needed for anything. There was one of Ruben's brothers though who broke from the tradition.

This brother found favour with a man of the village, Alexander, who worked buying and selling gems throughout the Middle East. This trade had made Alexander quite wealthy but he was now aging and he knew it would soon become difficult to travel. Alexander had no son to pass on his business to and while he could have simply ended his work, his heart ached to hand down his knowledge and expertise. He began to look at the men around him, sizing them up and evaluating their suitability in readiness to approach someone with his offer to mentor them in his trade. Alexander knew of my grandfather and uncles as they were well regarded within business by anyone who had traded with them. So one day Alexander travelled out to their farm and with the bleating of goats to greet him he asked my great-grandfather, Mikael, if he could sit with him to discuss business.

"Alexander, I thought you dealt with things much smaller and quieter than goats?" my great-grandfather joked.

"Yes, and with less stench about them too," Alexander answered as he waved his hand full of rings before his face.

My great-grandfather was curious as to why the gem trader sought him and Alexander alleviated this immediately. A man of business knew not to waste the time of another.

"Mikael, my end years are fast approaching and it makes my heart ache that I have no son to pass my trade on to. You are so blessed to have six sons," Alexander said simply. Mikael raised his eyebrow but when he saw tears form in the old man's eyes he lowered it as Alexander continued, "I have come to you today to see whether you would consider allowing one of your sons to work with me. I will give him ample wage and then when I am gone he will continue on his own."

Mikael knew this offer was a true gift and he sighed as he thought of the blessings this man now offered to one of his sons and wondered just which son he would pass this offer on to.

Alexander took his hesitancy the wrong way though. "Please Mikael, I do not wish to steal any of them away or to infer that you do not offer them as much as I could. I just know that your family are hard workers and intelligent. I can think of no others who are worthy or who will make of this as much as is possible," he begged.

Mikael raised his hand to slow the old man, "I know. I know, Alexander. I am truly flattered and I now wonder who is the most worthy of my sons."

Mikael did hesitate but it was quite clear which of his sons should go with Alexander. His three eldest sons were now married and starting families. While this didn't rule them out he knew they were comfortable and happy as they were. My grandfather, Ruben, the youngest, was far from ready for such travel and the fifth son only a year older than him did not have the business mind that he knew was needed. His fourth son though was another matter altogether.

Antonius was now eighteen years old and while he should have been settled into manhood, his father knew he was far from knowing the stability that his older three brothers had chosen. Of all his sons, Antonius was the only one that Mikael would hesitate to send to the markets to trade as the few times that he did his son could not resist the urge to squander some of the money at a taverna on the way home. Antonius was always the quickest to spend his wage with no interest in saving.

While Antonius showed no interest in choosing a wife, Mikael knew that his son was familiar with many women of the village and he feared for the day some cuckold or dishonoured father would appear at the farm with a knife in his hand, ready for vengeance. Mikael lectured his son about his behaviour, he even begged him to change his ways. Antonius would curb himself for some time but then he would return to his old habits.

Mikael had prayed that something would happen that would help Antonius change and suddenly he realised that Alexander and his offer was what he had asked for. Mikael smiled at Alexander. Perhaps the old man could succeed where he had failed in helping Antonius to find some discipline and direction. Also, quite frankly, he would be relieved to have him away from the farm and his impressionable younger sons. So what at first had seemed like a big decision in fact turned out to be quite simple.

"Alexander, I would be happy to for you to mentor my son Antonius," Mikael said as he smiled.

Coincidentally this was just the son that Alexander had in mind. The eldest of the remaining single boys and known for his lively personality, Alexander knew Antonius' charisma made him ideal for bargaining and selling. Thankfully he did not know of the more excessive aspects of his character.

For Antonius, bored with farm life and the predictability of Tyre and Phoenicia, Alexander's invitation along with his father's blessing was the ticket he had been looking for. He could stop smelling like a goat, would have more money and hopefully more women. He accepted so wholeheartedly that Alexander knew he had made the right decision. You can then imagine the old man's disappointment when, only days into their first trip, his young protégé started getting drunk regularly and returned to their inn room later each night smelling of wine and whores.

The final insult came on the last day of their initial trip. As they approached Tyre, Alexander saw that Antonius' purse lay flat against the young man's side where it hung from his belt. Alexander grabbed at the small leather pouch and immediately felt that it was empty.

"Where is your wage?" he cried out to the young man.

"It is gone in celebration of my new vocation!" Antonius finished with a smile, his eyes hazy from the previous night's rough drinking.

Alexander pulled the reigns of the donkeys that dragged their cart along so that they stopped in the middle of the road. "How am I supposed to send you back to your father with an empty purse after what I promised him?" Alexander implored.

Antonius just shrugged for indeed he didn't care and this made Alexander's blood boil. The old man suddenly forgot his age and grabbed at Antonius' shirt pulling him close and yelled into his face.

"You ungrateful brute! I could have chosen anyone but I chose you and this is the respect you return to me and your family!" He pushed Antonius back in his seat and shook his head. "What am I to do?" he said aloud to no-one.

Alexander flicked the reigns and the donkeys once again started walking. They had only an hour to reach Tyre and they were quiet the rest of the way except for Alexander who occasionally turned to give Antonius a dirty look as he grunted. When they arrived at the small road which led to the goat farm Alexander stopped the cart again.

"You can make the rest of the way on foot. Hopefully the walk will clear your hangover some more before you greet your parents," he said through gritted teeth. "I wish you luck telling them that our agreement is no more. Here," he handed Antonius a few coins. "So that you may have some scrap of dignity to return home with." With that Alexander left Antonius on the dusty road to make his way home.

It was a long walk at the best of times but today for Antonius it was not only long but incredibly hard. The sun bore down on his sore head, his back ached from hours of bouncing in the donkey cart and the coins in his purse seemed to weigh much more than they should have. Antonius had much time to think of what he would say to his father and he smirked once more because he truly did not care how his father would respond.

As he walked closer to his home the smell of the goats suddenly wafted towards him and his heart sank. It had only been a few weeks away but they smelt worse than ever and within hours this is how he would smell again also. Antonius suddenly remembered just why he had accepted Alexander's offer and then he recalled the excitement of travelling. Now when he thought of telling his father that he had failed he felt the sting of tears in his eyes.

Antonius did not tell his father of his failure that day when he returned, nor did he tell him the next day. He acted as though all had been successful and entertained the whole family with stories from the journey. He even spoke of when he would next leave with Alexander. Then on the third day Mikael was due in town with some bales of wool for a market. Antonius stepped up, offering to make the delivery, insisting that he save his father the time by doing so. Mikael believing his son to be reformed and wishing to encourage him more, allowed him.

Antonius, true to his word for the first time in his life, made his way to market to sell the wool and amazed himself that he pulled the highest price that he ever had. Ironically this was due to some of the bargaining that he had watched Alexander do on their journey. He finished up at market and stashed the money in his purse, tucking it within his clothes to keep it safe. Then he should have made his way home but he didn't. Instead he made his way to Alexander's home.

Antonius was the last person Alexander expected that day and yet he still wasn't so surprised to see him. Alexander assumed that Mikael had sent him to apologise so when Antonius threw himself at the old man's feet and begged forgiveness he grunted and nodded. What he did not expect was when Antonius continued on pleading for another chance, promising anything to the old man so that he could continue to work with him.

"You will stop the drunkenness?" Alexander asked and Antonius nodded fervently. "The womanising?" he also asked and Antonius nodded again. "Mmph!" grunted Alexander, "I will take you on again young man, but let it be known that one night of ill behaviour and I will leave you upon whatever road it is that we are travelling at that time."

"Thank you Alexander. I won't disappoint you," Antonius said, relieved beyond words.

Antonius was true to his word and even though he had to fight every last instinct within himself he conformed to the behaviour he knew Alexander asked of him no matter how much he hated to do it. Every time he saw a goat he was reminded why he changed his ways.

There was still the odd night that Antonius would slip away to a taverna but he would stop after two drinks and be back to their lodgings in a reasonable time so that Alexander had nothing to truly lecture him on. Antonius soon understood for himself the importance of heading to a business meeting with a clear head and calm stomach. The lines under his eyes disappeared and his skin glowed. He walked beside Alexander as a dynamic young man ready to take on the world.

As the years passed he took part more and more during business transactions so that when Alexander grew too frail to travel, their clients and traders were more than happy to interact with Antonius on his own. When Alexander passed away ten years after Antonius' training began, Antonius was more than ready and able to carry on the gem trade. By this time he had also settled into a marriage with a local girl of Tyre and Antonius had indeed become the model of a man that his father had hoped he would.

Ironically though Antonius had also followed in Alexander's footsteps in more ways than he planned and he too had no son to pass on his trade to. His wife had given birth to six healthy daughters, who now needed dowries. While he was more than able to provide these, in turn attracting a son-in-law to become his business heir, he looked to his family instead.

My grandfather, Ruben, had continued on at the goat farm. The farm had grown with the family but while it could support the families of six sons my grandfather knew that it would struggle to support the four or five sons that each contributed to the next generation of men and the families they would one day have. He was not the only one who thought this and some of this next generation had already moved on to other work, creating their own farms or beginning a trade.

Ruben had four sons, of which my father was the eldest. They were living modestly but my grandfather felt a sting of jealousy when he watched his brother Antonius arrive home from a journey. Ruben knew it had been merely his age that had stopped himself from being chosen by their father but he also knew of Antonius's behaviour before he left the farm and couldn't help but be angry that such disrespect and selfishness had somehow been rewarded. He hated the way his brother now dressed and the way Antonius always seemed to sneer when he now visited the farm as though the very scent of his family offended him.

So on the day that Antonius rode onto the farm and asked that he might speak in private with my grandfather, Ruben merely sighed with annoyance. The annoyance was soon replaced though as his brother sat and repeated the very conversation that Alexander had with their father just over twenty years before. Antonius was far from aging but he did not see why he should wait until he was in order to have this matter organised. Antonius also saw his nephews were becoming men and establishing their lives so his options to choose amongst them were diminishing. It was only my father and his brothers who were still young enough to consider for this role.

My father, Mnesarchus, had just turned thirteen. He was on the edge of manhood, a hard worker and fast learner. Even if he had not been the eldest my grandfather would have chosen him anyway due to these qualities.

"My eldest is the most worthy," Ruben said plainly and without hesitation when Antonius finished his proposition and they both nodded in agreement. Indeed it had been my father that Antonius had in mind all along.

Mnesarchus did not leave with Antonius until he turned fifteen.

Ruben and Antonius both agreed this was a more suitable age for a son to leave his home for such things. In the meantime though, when Antonius was in Tyre, he would have my father travel to his home. This was close to the town centre and far from the smell of goats. My father would be greeted by Antonius's wife who, although receiving him warmly, would then look him over from head to toe with pitiful eyes. My father hated this but he soon learned to ignore it.

Mnesarchus would then sit with Antonius who would begin to tell him about the basics of trade. Antonius unfurled maps and taught Mnesarchus the geography of the Middle East, Mediterranean and Northern Africa. Antonius would empty a bag of gems upon the table and then pick them up one by one, reciting what they were, and the different styles in which they were cut. In those two years my father learnt all this, as well as what gems came from which area and where they sold the best. Most importantly he soon knew what each gem was worth. Antonius quizzed him over and over until he could name a region, its gems and their value in his sleep.

My father though grew bored with this. Mnesarchus just wanted to start travelling and put all this into action. It seemed his fifteenth birthday was taking forever to arrive. As excited as he was though there was something within him that might never have cared if he didn't ever leave Tyre with this man. There was a feeling about Antonius that never felt right to my father. He could not put his finger on it but it was as though he was watching a performance whenever his uncle spoke and this seemed even more so if his wife was present.

It was only hours into their first journey when all that my father suspected was confirmed. They were bouncing along on their cart and had just left the very outskirts of Tyre when Antonius looked up to the sky and shrieked like a jackal before bursting into laughter. He turned to my father. "Ah, that wretched city is finally behind us," he said as he laughed. Then he slapped his hand down hard upon my father's thigh making Mnesarchus wince with pain.

"Now my young nephew, your true tutelage will begin," Antonius said with a grin.

Antonius certainly did put on a performance as soon as he rode into the city limits. Within Tyre he was a devoted husband and father, an upstanding member of the community, wise and sober, always beyond reproach. However once he left, most of those attributes fell away. He spoke as coarse as any farmer did and my father blushed continuously as he insisted upon speaking of sex at every opportunity.

Alexander had done much to curb Antonius' uncouth behaviour, however as soon as the old man was gone then my uncle was free to be himself once again. Although this time Antonius had some maturity and wealth to balance things. Antonius still knew that he needed to be clean and sober to do business. He also knew that he needed to arrive home with the money to support a luxurious lifestyle that he was now addicted to.

The callings of his desires pulled at him with the strength that they always did even though he had denied them for over ten years while the old man was around. So without his chaperone and tutor Antonius would still enact business with the dignity that he always did, but when all transactions and work were complete for the journey then he let those urges loose. It was then that he would book into a comfortable inn and spend a day or two drinking the local tavernas dry and sampling the local prostitutes.

Mnesarchus discovered this last vice with quite a lasting effect when he walked into their lodgings one evening after dinner to find Antonius grunting and heaving on top of a woman. My father may have been inexperienced but he had seen the goats mate enough times to know what was happening. Mnesarchus also knew that a man should only do this with his wife. Now when he walked into Antonius' home he could well match and return the pitiful stares of Antonius' wife.

It only took that one incidence for my father to never enter their inn rooms without first pressing his ear against the door to listen for the animalistic sounds his uncle made when with a woman. Even just having to hear him was as stomach turning as that one time he had seen Antonius in action.

Mnesarchus would sit in the hallway, just far enough away so that he didn't have to hear the grunting but where he could see the woman leave, signalling that he could make his way to bed to sleep. Mnesarchus would enter the room without so much as looking at Antonius, who most times would be lying naked and spread-eagled upon his bed, drifting fast into sleep.

One day, after such a night, they began their ride home. They travelled in silence for almost an hour when Antonius suddenly burst out laughing, "Am I to be treated to these scowls and silence at the end of every journey?"

Mnesarchus looked up and shook his head, but they had indeed fallen into a very regular pattern during their time together. It always began well; Mnesarchus could even deal with bawdy talk now as they left Tyre. They would attend all the markets and meet with other traders and this part of the journey always was fine too. Then Antonius would say the words my father dreaded.

"Our work is done!"

Antonius would always say this as he clapped his hands and grinned, but my father would groan inside and drop his head, for now the drinking and whoring would begin.

Mnesarchus would now be subject to two days of Antonius' drunken rudeness and then bragging about his conquests, even though the women had been paid for like a jug of wine. My father would have to find ways to amuse himself while their room was occupied and he did so quite profitably, often crossing paths with men they had dealt with upon their journeys who would invite him to their homes for meals or sit with him in a taverna and share some knowledge. However no matter how pleasant an evening he had with someone he would still have to return to his uncle and whatever state he was in by that hour.

My father had been travelling with Antonius for a year and their routine was well-established. It was once again that horrible two days before they journeyed home. Mnesarchus and Antonius had just eaten dinner and were making way to their room at the inn. Mnesarchus was so relieved that his uncle somehow seemed intent on actually retiring for the night that he did not even notice the smirk upon Antonius' face as they walked up the stairs to their room. Mnesarchus opened the door to find a woman lying naked upon his bed. He rolled his eyes and turned to his uncle.

"I'll come back later," Mnesarchus said bluntly.

Antonius grabbed Mnesarchus' arm as he tried to walk past him and turned my father to face the woman.

"This is my sixteenth birthday present for you," he said while grinning and not taking his eyes off the woman for a second while my father in turn kept his eyes to the floor. "Perhaps if you taste the delights of a woman then you will understand why I enjoy them so much. Maybe then I will not have to suffer your scowls after treating myself to one."

Before my father could refuse Antonius was gone, slamming the door behind him and my father heard him chuckling as he walked away down the corridor. Mnesarchus stood in place with his eyes down wondering what to do.

"We won't achieve much with you standing over there," the woman called out softly.

Mnesarchus looked up and saw that the woman had raised herself up on one elbow and was holding her other hand out to him. He drew in a sharp breath as he had never seen a woman naked before and her details intrigued him. Then he found his voice, albeit trembling.

19

"I—I cannot madam," he stammered.

"Really?" she said and the hand that was out held now pointed to his groin. "Because your loins tell me otherwise," she said and giggled.

My father pulled his hardness against himself, covering it with his hands, blushing madly. "Madam, this is wrong," he reasoned, "This should only be for a man and his wife."

"Urgh!" groaned the whore and threw herself back upon the mattress. "He didn't tell me you were a priest!" she cried to the ceiling.

"I am not a priest!" exclaimed my father, "I just do not wish to do—this—with you."

There was redness in Mnesarchus' face still but it was no longer from embarrassment but frustration. He would not be drawn into this, no matter how commonplace the whore and his uncle made it seem. It was revolting to think that a woman would do this for money and that men felt they needed it so much that they would pay her for it.

The woman sat up once more. "If you send me away then Antonius will not pay me and my father will beat me if I return home without money," she pleaded.

"Your father?" cried Mnesarchus, now repulsed to his core. This whole situation just kept getting worse for him and he sat down upon the bed opposite her, putting his head in his hands. He looked back up after a moment and sighed. "Fine, stay for how long it would have taken but please put your clothes back on," he offered. "I will lie for you, if you will lie for me," he finished and cringed. My father hated lying but given the situation it was a quite honourable option.

The woman redressed and sat upon the bed. "You know I could just use my mouth or hand if you find that less sinful," she reasoned.

"Oh please stop speaking!" begged my father.

They then sat awkwardly and silently for a while until the woman sighed and declared that a sufficient amount of time had been mimicked. "In fact given it was to be your first time it probably would have been even quicker," she said and laughed. "I have probably helped you appear more skilled than you are," she added as a final sting before walking out.

With the woman finally gone Mnesarchus undressed and climbed into his bed. He lay upon his stomach and turned his head so that he would be looking away from the door when Antonius entered the room. When Antonius did return he heard his uncle sniff as he walked towards his bed.

"All I smell is perfume! You must have been quite quick and unsatisfying," Antonius teased as he too undressed and the mattress creaked as he climbed onto his bed. "Well Mnesarchus do I not get a thank you?"

My father's blood was now boiling. He fought every instinct to jump from his bed and grab his uncle by the throat, shaking the man as he screamed the names "Brute" and "Pig" at him. Instead he swallowed hard and feigned a snore, hoping his uncle would believe him to be asleep which of course the old fool did.

"Ah, sleeping deeply after your first woman, that is thanks enough," Antonius chortled.

My father continued on working with Antonius and while nothing changed, Mnesarchus was at least relieved that things did not get worse. Antonius was a creature of habit so that it became quite easy for my father to fall into his own routine to deal with his uncle's vile behaviour. My father kept up his façade as well, convinced that no-one back in Tyre would believe him anyway. Mnesarchus never imagined that when his father asked as to his relationship with Antonius that Ruben was actually digging to see if any of the old traits of his brother still existed.

I would have imagined that as the years passed Antonius' character would have grown less jarring to my father as he became accustomed to his style but this was far from the truth. Each journey with his uncle only made Mnesarchus' hatred swell and just when he thought Antonius could not reach a new depth of depravity he indeed did and my father would once again wish someone else had been chosen for this "honour".

One day my father actually told me about Antonius, not so much to make me sorry for how he established himself but more as a cautionary tale. When he finished I asked him, "Why did you continue? Why did you not just return to the farm and your family?"

My father sighed, "Because I did not wish to upset my father and make him believe that he had chosen wrong for his son." Then he smirked. "Mind you if it had carried on much longer I do believe I would have returned to my goats…or ended it somehow."

That consideration went through my father's mind many times more than he would ever have admitted. It had been eight years of working with his uncle when he was finally sickened so much that his disdain could no longer be contained.

Mnesarchus had once more busied himself at a local taverna knowing his uncle was being entertained in their room. His eyes grew more tired by the moment and he finally made his way back to the inn, hoping he could climb into bed and sleep. He pushed his ear against the door and heard murmurs which although they meant that Antonius was busy it also let my father know that the act was well and truly completed as there was not a grunt or creak of the bed to be heard.

Mnesarchus heard footsteps approach the door and he jumped back a few steps. When it opened the young woman walked out and made her way to the stairs to leave. She held herself and my father saw that she trembled as she walked away. He also saw that her frame was slight with hardly a curve upon it—in fact if it hadn't been for her long hair and knowing his uncle better, my father might have thought she was a boy. It was then that Mnesarchus realised how young this girl was and he burst into the room to confront his uncle.

"You pig! You vile disgusting pig!" he screamed as eight years of anger and repulsion finally exploded.

Antonius was standing naked by a table, pouring himself some more wine. He swayed as he stood, clearly as drunk as ever. Antonius looked upon his nephew and just snorted.

"She was still a child!" my father continued screaming. "Your own daughters are older than her!"

Antonius sat hard upon a chair, took a swig of his wine and then smirked. "Well not all of us can be satisfied with making love to our hand," he said.

"You have a wife!" Mnesarchus screamed once more and Antonius now erupted into laughter.

"Oh my nephew, perhaps one day when you are married you will understand," Antonius said through his guffaws.

My father never would understand though and he most certainly could not as he stood there shaking with anger as his uncle just laughed. Mnesarchus went to his bed and threw himself upon it fully dressed knowing that it would now be some time before he would drift off to sleep after his outburst. He lay there and his heart finally began to slow. Then the silence in the room was broken by his uncle belching and Mnesarchus felt his heart begin to pound again.

As Mnesarchus fumed he prayed for the day when Antonius would die and he would no longer have to spend time with him. He thought of how much longer this could possibly be. When he realised that Antonius at forty-three had many more years to go he felt like punching the bed. That night he decided that he would just have to return to the farm and end this once and for all.

He didn't tell Antonius the next morning or the entire journey home. Each time that he thought that he might, something stopped him and Mnesarchus took this as a sign that perhaps he should speak with his father first. A part of him also knew that his father may indeed talk him out of it so that when he returned home and saw his father his tongue once again failed him. He went to bed that night still as Antonius' assistant.

Mnesarchus thought over and over as to how he would tell his father and he sighed knowing that he would have to lie. He could tell his father about the drinking and he might believe him but to speak to anyone about Antonius' whoring was another matter entirely. Mnesarchus was embarrassed that he had even been witness to such things. To tell his simple farmer of a father, here in his valley raising goats and seemingly oblivious to such things, made Mnesarchus feel sick. Besides, even though he never did quite like Antonius' wife he hated to spread her shame any further than needed. So he remained quiet and as each day passed that was another closer to his next trip with Antonius.

It was two days before they were supposed to leave and Mnesarchus' heart sank as he resigned himself to yet another journey with the old pig.

"*Just one more*," he thought to himself. "*Then I will tell Father.*"

Besides it was just a short journey down to Petra and back within a week. It had been barely an hour that my father had decided this when Antonius' donkey cart arrived at the farm with one of his servants upon it bearing a letter for Mnesarchus.

Antonius was ill. In fact far too ill to travel, the first time in his entire career. Still he did not cancel the trip. Instead he was asking Mnesarchus to journey and do business on his own. A smile spread across my father's face as he read the note. His own father approached him.

"I see there is some good news from Antonius?" Ruben asked.

"Wonderful news!" answered Mnesarchus and he laughed. "Antonius is ill."

Ruben frowned thinking he had heard wrong but Mnesarchus handed him the note and Ruben realised he had indeed heard his son correctly. He looked up and Mnesarchus was still smiling. "I know I can do this on my own, Father, and I know I will do it even better than Uncle does," Mnesarchus said.

"So be it," said Ruben plainly as he handed the note back. "I suggest though you remember some respect and not gloat to your uncle, or any others, until you have returned and proven this to be so. I might also suggest you visit your uncle to see as to his condition."

My father returned to Antonius' home with the servant just as his father suggested. His aunt greeted him at the door, clutching a handkerchief and dabbing at her eyes. As she lead Mnesarchus to Antonius' bedroom she spoke and her voice was broken as she fought tears.

"I have never seen him like this before," she whimpered.

When my father stood over Antonius as he lay within his bed all he could think was, "*I have seen him this way far too many times.*" For Antonius looked exactly as he always did when he had been drinking for an entire day; his face was red and swollen, his eyes glazed over and his skin was covered in a fine sweat. In fact for a moment Mnesarchus thought that Antonius was simply drunk and would have loved to turn to his aunt to tell her this. Then Antonius spoke and his voice was clear and steady, if somewhat slow, and my father realised he was not drunk at all.

"Ah Nephew, you have come to visit me," Antonius said as he tried to smile. "What a blessing that I have made you ready for such a time."

"Yes, the timing is indeed a blessing," said Mnesarchus as he laughed to himself, grateful that he could say this with no-one knowing the irony.

As Mnesarchus rode off to Petra two days later he could barely keep the smile off his face. When he reached the city limits of Tyre he stood up in the cart and screamed to the heavens then sat down to relish the silence of travelling alone.

Mnesarchus did indeed do even better than Antonius would have. His business style was more efficient as he kept small talk to a minimum and didn't enter into the bragging that his uncle performed with other traders. Not one of Antonius' clients or suppliers questioned that my father was alone and he even suspected that a few were quite relieved that this was the case. Just as my father knew he would, he returned to Tyre quicker and with a much fuller purse than ever before from trading in Petra. Not surprisingly so as he did not have to use extra time and money to drink and have sex.

Mnesarchus arrived at Antonius' home ready to gloat and was greeted as always by his aunt who now had dark circles under her eyes. "He is no better," she said plainly. "He has been sleeping most of the day and still does so now."

Mnesarchus was relieved as he had no real desire to see the man no matter how much he would have loved to see the look on his face when he told him the money he had brought home and the deals he had enacted. Instead he handed the purse over to Antonius' wife.

"I have taken my usual wage," Mnesarchus said as she took the purse from him and he saw that immediately her face changed as she felt the weight of it.

"You should take a bit more for the extra work," she replied, never taking her eyes off the purse as it sat in her hands.

"Not this time," Mnesarchus smiled, for he wanted to make sure that Antonius and his wife knew just how much money he had made.

When my father left, Antonius' wife walked to a table and spilled the contents of the purse upon it. Then she slowly counted each and every coin, organising them into piles to make it easy to recount which she did several times. She walked to the bedroom to check upon Antonius who had just woken and was shifting himself upon the pillows to sit up.

"Oh good, there you are. Fetch me some water," he said as he saw her in the doorway.

His wife walked towards the end of the bed and stood with her arms crossed. "Mnesarchus returned this afternoon from Petra," she said.

"What? That is two days early! The stupid boy must have done very badly indeed," he spat as he screwed his face up. It was bad enough he had missed out on his extra-curricular activities, now his assistant was probably ruining his business as well.

"He brought back twice the money you usually do from Petra, and in less time," she said curtly and raised her chin.

"Well, he must not have taken his wages," Antonius offered, quickly thinking up some excuse.

"He told me he had taken that," she answered sharply and began to tap her foot on the floor.

"Well…he must have just been lucky…oh…and he would have used a smaller room at the inn. That would have saved money too," Antonius' mind raced to think of things to satisfy his wife but she merely huffed and stormed from the room.

Antonius seethed with anger. "*That stupid boy, too foolish to even steal some of the money,*" he thought to himself.

Mnesarchus had just ruined Antonius' travels for evermore. Not that this mattered for Antonius would never travel again. What seemed to be a fever that would not leave was in fact the symptom of a venereal disease that he had picked up from one of his whores. It had begun to fester a month or two before Mnesarchus' trip to Petra. At first there was just a burning sensation whenever Antonius urinated but when they had arrived back to Tyre from the last trip, sores appeared upon his genitals that would not heal. The fever arrived soon after the sores and that was when he took to his bed. Antonius hid the sores from his wife knowing full well what had caused them and only his physician and the servant sent to bathe him knew the truth of his illness.

The fever levelled off with some tonics prescribed to Antonius but the sores would not abate. Antonius dragged himself from bed as the next trip planned was for Babylon, where his most favourite whores were.

Every step made his groin ache but despite this he was determined that he would travel. Antonius climbed aboard his cart one day to venture to the town centre sure that if he made himself active that would help the disease retreat. However each jolt of the carriage felt like a stab to his genitals so that he returned home in more pain than ever and that night the fever returned with a vengeance. The next morning he awoke and his pain was matched by his anger.

He called out to his wife, "Send word to Mnesarchus that he must travel alone tomorrow."

As Mnesarchus rode away once more with another huge grin on his face, Antonius watched him with a scowl. It had now been six weeks since he had touched a woman, the longest in all his time since Alexander had died. Here he was stuck in Tyre with a wife who did not excite him and who had moved to another bed lest she contract his fever. Even if she did show some interest in the sex that he wanted Antonius knew he could not touch her in his state. So one night he arranged with a trusted servant to sneak a local whore into his bedroom by the window.

The whore climbed through the window late one night when the servant knew all the family would be deep asleep. As she stood there in the lamplight Antonius grinned for the first time in weeks but then the smile was gone for his usual instant arousal was not making itself known. He drew back the sheets as the girl walked closer hoping it was just the sheet upon him that interfered but still nothing happened, not even when the girl slipped her dress from her shoulders and stood before him naked.

The whore sat on the edge of the bed and began to stroke his chest. Antonius looked down at himself and when he saw himself still limp he began to panic. The girl saw the look on his face and looked down also, recoiling as she saw the sores.

"I cannot service you Sir," she said bluntly and began to lift herself off the bed. She knew what those sores meant. She had heard enough talk amongst the other whores to know they could cost her weeks of illness if not worse.

Antonius grabbed at her wrist and pulled her arm roughly, "I have paid for your service and you shall supply it!"

"Sir, release my hand or I shall scream and wake your household," she said calmly knowing that she was under no threat from this sick man lying before her.

Antonius released his grip, throwing her hand back towards her, "Then perhaps you could just use this to pleasure me."

The whore cringed but it would at least mean that she would leave with some payment. So as Antonius lay back upon his pillows and closed his eyes, she reached down to his still flaccid member and wrapped her hand around it. Antonius sighed with relief but this was soon replaced with pain as the girl's hand dragged along his raw skin. Not surprisingly he still did not respond and after several minutes of suffering he realised that the physical rush he craved would not visit him. Antonius reached down and pulled the girl's hand away.

"You can go," he said flatly and closed his eyes, not even interested in watching the girl dress, and only opening them when he heard her slip back out the window. He looked once more down upon his body, pulled the sheet to cover it and then cried himself to sleep.

This time when my father returned from business Antonius was awake. His wife though told Mnesarchus otherwise so that she received the purse into her hands.

"I trust you have taken your wage?" she asked.

"Yes, I have Aunt as well as the commission Antonius and I agreed upon," he answered her smiling. "I also bought some new gems that were too much of a bargain to resist. I am sure we can triple their cost in Egypt."

His aunt smiled and nodded. "Now you must be tired. Go home and rest. Your family will be most pleased to see you," she said, anxious to have him gone so that she could count the money.

Once again she poured the coins upon her table and started to pull them into their piles. Once again Mnesarchus had returned home with more money than her husband ever had and this was after his increased wage and buying more stock. She walked into Antonius' room with her arms crossed and her blood boiling.

"Mnesarchus has returned," she said sharply as Antonius looked at her knowing her tone was far from pleased. She then added, "It seems he was once again lucky and found an even cheaper room."

Antonius festered within his home, growing weaker and bitterer as each week passed. Every time my father left for another trip this seemed to escalate as Antonius contemplated the freedom he had lost and also just how much his nephew continued to show him up. His wife now wise to his past deceptions, but mercifully not the details, treated him with contempt. Each time my father handed her the purse which grew heavier and heavier with each journey this hate for her husband grew even more.

It was not that she was not comfortable for indeed she and her daughters had all the luxuries they could dream of. It was in knowing there could have been more and that she had lived with a man who had lied to her for their entire marriage.

Antonius became like a stranger amongst his own family; treated with disdain by his wife and avoided by his daughters who could not bear the smell of his rotting body. It was a relief to everyone, including Antonius, when he finally took to his bed permanently and the physician told his wife to prepare for a funeral.

Antonius died just two months before my father turned twenty-five, almost ten years to the day that Mnesarchus began travelling with him. When news of Antonius' death reached the goat farm and then to my father he simply sighed and walked away from the rest of his family so that they could not see the smile upon his face. Eighteen months ago he had prayed for an end to his situation with Antonius and it had been delivered even more fortuitously than he had ever imagined.

Mnesarchus was not without remorse or gratitude towards Antonius though. While he had prayed that night in the inn that Antonius would die he had also hoped that a far less tragic solution would present itself. Further to this he also knew that regardless of his uncle's less admirable traits he had indeed taught him all that had made him the excellent trader that he was today. So on the day of the funeral as he joined the cortege to walk the body to the temple for its final prayers, Mnesarchus decided to mourn the teacher and not think of the scoundrel that he hated so much.

My father continued on with the business that was now his. Despite being entitled to all that he made he still visited Antonius' wife to give her a share. Each time she would cry as she took the small purse, "You are better to us than he ever was but you do not need to do this, Mnesarchus."

This was true as in the eighteen months that my father had run the business he had doubled her family's income and his aunt had been wise in saving, knowing in her heart that the business would soon be gone.

"You still have three daughters remaining who need dowries," he would answer and hand her the money.

"Perhaps you would consider one of your cousins for marriage?" she suggested one day. "You are more than of age to be married and start a family Mnesarchus. This could be your home then."

My father simply shook his head in response. No matter how customary it was to marry one's cousin, this was simply something he could never accept. He loved his cousins dearly but to take one as a wife would be like lying with his own sister.

At twenty-five though this was a conversation that Mnesarchus was having often; both with his father and his uncles, who also offered their daughters to the man who now would become the wealthiest in the family. He did think of marriage from time to time also but it never pulled at him the way that he saw it do to other men his age. Mnesarchus had the liberty of not needing sons to work a farm and while it would be nice to have an assistant for company and to teach his trade, he could just as well offer this to a nephew the same way that Antonius had done for him. In fact the longer Mnesarchus remained single and childless the more his brothers hoped this was exactly what he would do.

Another three years passed and not only did my father's business prosper but it also grew. Unhindered with the sea sickness that had limited Antonius and Alexander, my father now ventured west by boat to mainland Greece and Southern Italy. In fact this opened the whole of the Mediterranean to him for business and Egypt now was only a day's travel instead of the five it used to be by cart.

It was this new expanse of his trade that saw him land upon Samos. As a major trade hub of the region he would have been a fool not to have looked for prospects there. My father never realised just what an opportunity awaited him.

Mnesarchus was sitting at a taverna that faced out on to the town square of my mother's hometown. He sat and sipped upon his wine, relishing every mouthful as he soaked up the sunshine and enjoyed the breeze that carried from the shores nearby. Then he saw her. My mother walked across the square, her soft curls of hair framing her face upon which she wore the sweetest smile. Pythia looked across at my father and when he saw her eyes, deep and dark, yet bright he thought his heart would explode. Her smile widened and he saw her cheeks dimpled and then she turned her head away as she passed him by.

My father had seen many women in his life. From the whores who visited Antonius to the royal princesses of Babylon. He had seen women with skin like ebony and those with skin like cream, ones whose hair fell over their shoulders, red with henna and those who twisted it into ropes to pile on their head. They had been offered to him as wives and concubines and although some had intrigued him none had remained within his thoughts past the moment they had met. Today though as my mother passed him and walked away he threw his coin upon the table to pay for his wine, flung his satchel over his shoulder and followed her.

Mnesarchus laughed when he told me this story, "I still don't know what possessed me to follow her or what I thought would happen. All I knew was I wanted to watch her for as long as I could."

And watch her he did. As Mnesarchus walked behind her, at a respectable distance of course, he noticed every detail. He smiled as he watched her curls bounce around her hair combs with every step, the way her back sloped into her waist and then he sighed as he saw her hips sway under her gown. Even her tiny feet in their sandals enchanted him.

Mnesarchus continued on following Pythia as she made her way through the streets until finally she entered the door of her house. Then he stopped and sighed. This was the grandest home he had seen on Samos so far. He knew this home belonged to someone with wealth that not even Antonius without his philandering and drinking would have accumulated by his death. Here Mnesarchus stood, far from poor but a long way from the wealth he saw before him and he knew that what was inside would never be his.

Mnesarchus' shoulders slumped. "*Oh well, it was a pleasant walk at least,*" he thought and then he made his way back to the town square.

CHAPTER TWO

A heart can create some amazing synchronicities that the mind can never imagine. Without even knowing it my father set about a chain of events that he was not even aware of.

When Mnesarchus arrived back to the square he contemplated having another wine with the hope that perhaps his vision may appear again but decided he had lost enough time today on such things. Instead he made his way to the docks to see what trade he could muster as well as organise his passage back to Tyre for the next day.

From a distance he saw the captain of the ship that had carried him here and made his way to him to book his place. The captain though was talking to another man and together they were pointing at his ship's hull as they exchanged opinions. Mnesarchus stood back to wait patiently until they were finished but the captain saw him and called out.

"Ah, Master Gem Trader, you return to my boat," the captain shouted out to him. "See, it is a fine boat and people return to travel upon her," he said to the other man and laughed as he hit his shoulder. "This man also seeks my business but unlike you he wishes to take my money instead of give it to me," he said to Mnesarchus and then turned to the other man. "I do not care how fine your reputation is, this boat needs no work," he finished and laughed again.

Mnesarchus smiled, enjoying the banter which was common amongst any traders upon the wharves, as he too often softened potential deals in such a way.

"Ah, if only you would let me work your boat I will make it faster so that you will sail quicker and make more money," joked the boat builder. "Then you would not even feel the cost of my fees." They both laughed again. "Tonight come to my home, be my guest for dinner, and then you will understand," the boat builder offered.

The captain raised his eyebrows and turned his head to look at Mnesarchus. "Well I would be no business man at all to turn down free food would I?" he said making my father laugh.

"Fine and you, Gem Trader, shall join us also," said the boat builder to my father. "Bring your wares to do business."

The captain walked to my father as the boat builder made his way back along the dock and into the town. He grabbed Mnesarchus' shoulder.

"My dear friend, we have just received an invitation to the home of one of the wealthiest men upon Samos. I suggest we are both on our best behaviour else we may never land upon this island again." The captain didn't laugh as he said this and though he still smiled Mnesarchus knew that his words were not in jest.

That evening as the sun started to fade, a servant from the boat builder's home came to fetch the captain and my father. As they walked behind the servant they soon made their way through the square and were walking the very same streets that my father had following my mother that afternoon. Mnesarchus smiled as he remembered and then sighed at the memory of her. Then the unimaginable happened.

They were in front of the house that she had disappeared into and the servant turned and walked through the gateway that led to the door. Mnesarchus froze in his spot on the laneway and the captain realising that he had stopped walking turned to him.

"What is it?" he asked Mnesarchus.

"Is this the house?" my father asked while his eyes grew wide.

"Well I hope so or this servant is about to cause us trouble," the captain answered.

Mnesarchus took a deep breath and followed him inside. His heart was beating so strongly he almost felt like he could collapse but he gathered himself, angry that he was feeling like a young girl would. He stood within the vestibule of the house looking around as the servant left to call his master and let him know his guests had arrived.

"What is wrong with you?" the captain asked quietly. "You have turned red and are shaking."

"I have never been in a home like this," lied my father.

"Well pull yourself together. Remember we are here for business," the captain said and tried to smile.

The boat builder soon arrived to greet them with his wife upon his arm and Mnesarchus saw an older likeness of the girl he had followed that afternoon. Not that he looked at her for very long as there behind the husband and wife trailed their three daughters, including of course, my mother.

Mnesarchus took in such a sharp breath that the captain heard him and wanted to hit him. Then the captain looked at the girls and all became quite apparent. He tried not to laugh as my father's face turned an even darker red.

"Ah, welcome to my home. What a pleasure it is to have you both here," the host said loudly and gestured to his wife as he introduced her. He then beckoned his daughters to step forward and made their names known too.

"This is my eldest, Pythia," said my grandfather as he motioned towards my mother who looked to my father and smiled the same smile she had that afternoon.

"Oh, you are named for the oracle. It is no wonder you look like a goddess," said Mnesarchus.

His words should have stayed within his mind but somehow they left his lips and my mother looked to him as though entranced, and she suddenly recognised him from the taverna earlier that day. She dropped her head hoping to hide the heat that suddenly made her face feel on fire.

There was momentary silence and Pythia's father weighed up my father, all too aware of what intentions such words carried. Beside Mnesarchus the boat captain held his breath in disbelief that the simple gem trader who had been so quiet upon his boat should suddenly be so forward with a young woman and right in front of her father. The captain prepared for dinner to be cancelled and for the boat builder to show them both the door.

It was only the stifled giggles of Pythia's younger sisters that broke the awkwardness and my grandfather composed himself and continued with the introductions. He finished and pointed towards a doorway.

"Come, let us eat," he said and smiled.

Then he grabbed Pythia pulling her close to him, so that he would remain between her and my father as they made their way to the dining table.

Mnesarchus was horrified with himself. The second he spoke the words to my mother he wished he could have died. Finally he had met a woman to stir his heart and he had acted like Antonius; forward and with no class. The look upon my grandfather's face only made this more devastating. The one person he needed to impress to make any courtship possible had been mortified and within his own home. As they began to walk the captain turned to Mnesarchus and shook his head. My father then wished the earth would open up and swallow him.

Instead though, he made his way to the dining table with everyone else. He was seated beside the captain, my mother with her sisters sat upon the opposite side of the table while the master and mistress of the house took their expected places at each end. Mnesarchus was grateful that in the fussing of being designated seats and making themselves comfortable, somehow the discomfort from the scene in the vestibule was diluted. It was still there though and he didn't dare to look once more upon Pythia lest his stupid tongue would betray him again. Mnesarchus was even more grateful that my grandfather, with his own interest in re-establishing decorum and gaining new business, had begun fervent talk with the captain.

My mother though kept her eyes upon Mnesarchus, hoping to catch his attention once more. Even though she had barely given him a second thought after she walked by him that day she now recalled his face as he had looked back at her in the town square. His face was warm and kind, unlike many of the darker men who made their way to Samos. This in itself had made her smile back at him but tonight as he declared her a goddess before her whole family, young Pythia became intrigued. She watched his every move, from the way he held his spoon to how he turned his glass as he listened to conversation and her attentions were not missed by her father.

My grandfather was a shrewd man. His continued good fortune in business was proof enough of this but his wisdom was not limited to commerce. Mnesarchus had declared his intentions for Pythia quite clearly if clumsily and now as he caught his daughter watching the trader intently he knew that there was chemistry. A wealthy man cannot welcome any man to join his family nor let his daughter leave the family home with anyone wanting of honour or nobility. So my grandfather having struck a deal with the captain now turned his attentions to Mnesarchus.

Mnesarchus was asked as to how his trade had fared upon Samos and my grandfather nodded as Mnesarchus told of what he sold. The boat builder added up silently in his head just what money my father would have made in that short time. Then he asked as to my father's family history and Mnesarchus hesitated, knowing this was just the part of him that my grandfather would find issue with, but then Mnesarchus thought of his own father and spoke strongly.

"They are simple but hard working farmers. Their produce is well regarded and our men well respected in Tyre," he said and my grandfather noted the honour that Mnesarchus carried for his family and he smiled.

My grandfather asked my father as to how he became a gem trader and Mnesarchus shared the story of Alexander and Antonius. He then followed with his own story with Antonius—minus the drinking and whores of course. My grandfather smiled and nodded as my father continued on, telling of how he had expanded his routes and the new gems he now traded.

With dinner over Mnesarchus was asked to show some of his gems and my father smiled as Pythia and her sisters gasped and cooed as he opened the small silk sacks and brought the treasures out into the candle light.

"Daughters, choose a gem each and I will have a necklace made for you—that is if our young man will assure me a bargain," my grandfather said and smiled at Mnesarchus.

"But of course," answered Mnesarchus. "Especially after such hospitality."

Pythia's youngest sister reached over the table and grabbed at an emerald. "I have never seen such a green before," she said and my father delighted her in describing the mines in Macedonia where it had been found.

The second sister pointed to a sapphire, "These always remind me of the sea," she said and Mnesarchus then told her of the caves within the Babylonian forests.

"Men spend days beneath the ground to find these. They say their eyes soon stop working but their hands grow so sensitive that they can tell the difference between a rock and gem with no light at all," he said and placed the sapphire in the girl's hand.

Then came the moment Mnesarchus was fearing for now it was Pythia's turn to choose. He would have to gaze upon her face and he knew he might return to the buffoon who had begun the evening. He took a deep breath and looked up as she spoke.

"I want something from a place even more exciting," she said softly and smiling.

Mnesarchus remained composed and sure as he reached down to his satchel upon the floor and pulled out the last of the silk bags. "Then surely these are for you," he said and tipped a thousand tiny diamonds upon a piece of black silk.

They glimmered in the candle light and my father never took his eyes off my mother's face as she looked at them with her eyes wide and her mouth open.

"They are tiny, but rare and precious," he said to her. "These come from India, a land like nothing you or I know. The people are brown and speak a language beyond any way our tongues can work. They use elephants to drag the stones from the caves as they break them and each morning feed milk to a god with the head of an elephant to ask for protection."

Pythia's eyes grew wider as he told the story and she stared deep into his eyes as he spoke. Mnesarchus then picked up a ruby, "This ruby comes from beyond the south of Egypt. The people here are as black as ebony and their land holds all the gold that is yet to be uncovered. It takes them ten days to carry the gems and gold to the nearest river so they can then sail for another ten days into Egypt to trade."

Using the curve of the side of his hand Mnesarchus pulled the

35

diamonds into a neat oval and sat the ruby upon them so that the small white stones formed a border around the red gem. The beauty of the combination sparkled and the girls and their mother all gasped again and leant forward to look closer.

"This is the new fashion," Mnesarchus explained. "A simple stunning gem surrounded by a halo of diamonds." He looked at Pythia and smiled but she was looking at her father.

"Oh please Father, I must have them. Please say I can?" she pleaded.

"If Pythia gets diamonds for her gem then I want them too!" declared the youngest sister and immediately the second joined the petition.

"Alright, alright," cried my grandfather and held his hand up to silence them. "But I declare this has been a most expensive meal."

Indeed it had been more than he had imagined he would spend with Mnesarchus and he was yet to add something for his wife. However he had been just as intrigued by my father's storytelling as his women had been. Mnesarchus had continued to impress the man with his knowledge and manner as he showed his wares.

Mnesarchus made a handsome deal for my grandfather as this was a most substantial sale to have made upon the whim of a dinner invitation. Both men noted well the generosity of the other so that when the time came to say their farewells in the entrance of the home Mnesarchus' indiscretion here when he arrived was long forgotten.

My grandfather shook the captain's hand and laughed, "I thank the gods I made business with you that I may recoup my spending with Mnesarchus." He then turned to my father. He took Mnesarchus' hand in both of his own and while he still smiled his tone became quite steady as he spoke, "Mnesarchus, you are most welcome to return to my home without invitation."

Mnesarchus took a deep breath, placed his other hand over that of my grandfather's and nodded. "I would be honoured to return," he said softly.

The captain remained silent after this until he and my father had walked a distance from the home. He then burst out laughing and slapped Mnesarchus on the back, "You lucky bastard!" he yelled.

"Shhh!" hissed my father. "People will be sleeping." He gestured to the dark homes they walked past. His grin though was now from ear to ear and he joined the captain in chuckling.

"A day's trade in one hour *and* he all but gave you his blessing to wed his daughter," the captain continued as he laughed, "I must be given credit for my part in having you invited to his home. You must name a son for me!"

Both men continued to laugh as they walked. The captain, well lubricated with the fine wine that had been served, now danced around Mnesarchus and made his voice like that of the young sisters.

"Oh exotic traveller, tell me more about the mines your precious gems are from!" He dropped his voice back to normal. "I swear even I was so entertained you might have seduced me! The night is still young though. Would you care to tell me a story of a peridot to join me in bed?" he said jokingly and stroked Mnesarchus' arm.

My father laughed, "My travels may be lonely but old sea captains are far from my choice of bed partner."

"I am offended! Tomorrow I shall charge you double for your passage back to Tyre!" declared the captain and they both burst out laughing.

When Mnesarchus lay in bed that night he could not sleep. He kept seeing Pythia and the way she had looked upon him as he spoke. My father could not believe that something that he had thought impossible had actually happened. Not only had he spoken to this gorgeous creature and entered the home he never thought he would, but Mnesarchus now had also been given permission to follow his heart by the one man who could have denied it. It would be now a month before he returned to Samos. In those four weeks, hundreds of men would travel to Samos and they too could set eyes upon his beloved, perhaps even as they too sipped their wine in the town square. Worse yet they could be invited to dinner at her home and impress her father even more than he had.

Mnesarchus knew the boat he needed to sail upon would leave at noon. This gave him one last morning upon Samos to trade but Mnesarchus knew there were far more important things than gems to deal with tomorrow. There was only one matter that he would attend to the next day and that was ensuring that Pythia was his.

Mnesarchus awoke with the sun which was not so difficult. He had slept so lightly during the night that he greeted the first light with a smile knowing he could now make his way to the docks to find Pythia's father. He bathed and groomed himself as immaculately as he could. Mnesarchus even donned the new clothes he had bought upon mainland Greece that he had intended to save for his niece's wedding when he returned to Tyre. He made his way to the docks with a spring in his step but as soon as he saw my grandfather his stomach jumped and twisted with nerves. He stopped and caught his breath and then began to move once more before he knew his nervousness would stop him. As he got closer my grandfather saw him and recognising Mnesarchus he smiled and suddenly my father's fears were dissolved.

"Ah Mnesarchus, how nice to see you once more," he said and gave his hand.

"Good morning Sir," he said as he took the man's hand in his own. "I have come to thank you once more for your hospitality and business," he said just a little too quickly.

"I thank you also for appeasing and entertaining the women of my household," the boat builder laughed in return. "You will have made my life at home quite harmonious for some time."

Mnesarchus then stood silent, his next words catching in his throat. He had rehearsed his marriage proposal so many times as he lay in bed but now as he stood here before the man his words seemed stupid and ill prepared. My grandfather looked upon Mnesarchus and smiled as he saw the anxiety in the man before him.

"Perhaps we can go to my office and talk without so much noise around us," my grandfather offered knowing exactly the words that Mnesarchus wished to speak.

In the privacy of my grandfather's office away from the hustle and bustle of the docks my father once more found his voice.

"I wish to ask your permission to court your daughter Pythia with view for marriage should she find me a suitable husband," Mnesarchus said finding it difficult to look into the man's eyes as he spoke.

My grandfather hesitated a moment and this scared my father, making him believe that he would be refused. My grandfather was more than happy to consider Mnesarchus however there was one matter that concerned him.

"You will have my blessing to wed, Mnesarchus but there will be a condition," he said and crossed his arms. "You will make your marriage home here on Samos. I will gladly see my daughter leave her family home to begin life with her husband but I cannot bear to think of her leaving Samos. Besides it would kill her mother," he said plainly. He then waved his hand as he continued, "Oh I know once you are married she must follow wherever you choose and I will have no say. However what I can do is ensure that you never receive an inheritance!"

Mnesarchus nodded as he heard the words. "I can assure you Sir that I had no intention of taking your daughter from her family," he said sincerely for as he lay in bed the night before planning his life with Pythia, Mnesarchus only ever saw them upon Samos. "And I would never dishonour our agreement or my regard for you as a father by betraying this once I am her husband."

"Hmph!" grunted my grandfather and crossed his arms again, this time in triumph. He looked at Mnesarchus and smiled. Each time this young man spoke he just impressed him more and more. Even now as he had asserted his authority over him, the young man did not falter in his respect and demeanour. "I see you have been raised most nobly. I could not wish for a better man as a son," he said and smiled.

With their agreement sealed Mnesarchus asked one last question of the man, "Might I go visit with your daughter once more before I leave Samos?"

"But of course," he laughed in response.

So Mnesarchus with his satchel bouncing against his back as he walked, made his way once more from the docks, through the town square and then the weave of streets that led to Pythia's home. He stood and looked up at the house, smiled as wide as he could and then walked to the door. A maid on her way for water opened the door before he could even knock and as she put down her urn Mnesarchus asked that he might visit with Pythia.

The maid almost dropped the urn as she heard the words and realised who this man was. The sisters had not stopped speaking of him since dinner the night before and the talk had resumed as soon as they woke up. Over breakfast they had nagged their mother as to when they would visit the goldsmith who would set their gems so they could wear them soon.

Eventually their mother, Agathe, had screamed, "Stop! It is as though you girls have never had jewellery before."

They had finally managed to settle and be guided to do some reading or study when Mnesarchus arrived. The maid knew the house would once again return to turmoil when the man's presence would be discovered. Though there was one squeal when the maid announced his arrival they all managed to maintain some dignity while he was there.

Of course Pythia could not sit with my father alone, so as the maid walked to find my mother she made sure that Agathe was informed as well. In fact it was Pythia's mother who entered the room first to greet Mnesarchus and he blushed as he saw her stern face for once again he had been far too forward in just asking to see his beloved. Mnesarchus should have asked to see the mistress of the house first and her hard face made it quite clear that she was not impressed. Agathe had stopped Pythia in her tracks as she ran to their sitting room to see Mnesarchus.

"Go and pay some more attention to your hair and clothing,"

Agathe said sharply. "I will send for you when it is appropriate." Then, annoyed at my father's forwardness, Agathe made her way to greet him.

Mnesarchus in asking to visit Pythia, nor my grandfather in agreeing, had considered the fact that Agathe was uninformed of the men's meeting. Once more my father had to state his intentions and despite having the father's approval he was just as nervous as he spoke the words but then smiled as he added the part he now revelled in.

"I approached your husband this very morning at the shipyard. He has given me his blessing to speak with your daughter," he added and Agathe's face softened a little but her saw her jaw clench. "I realise that this visit must seem impetuous given you have not spoken with your husband. It is just that I leave Samos within hours and wanted to see her before I left. I beg your forgiveness Madam and assure you this will be the only lapse in respect that I will make with you."

Agathe nodded and raised her hand to signal for the maid waiting nearby to summon Pythia. "I accept your apology young man. Perhaps you could show how sincere you are by gifting me the gems to make earrings to match my new necklace? I don't suppose that is too much to ask of a future son?" she said as she smiled.

"But of course Madam. It would be my honour," answered Mnesarchus while inside his stomach uncurled with relief that he had won the woman over.

Pythia appeared at the door and my father jumped to his feet to greet her. "Good morning Pythia," he said so strongly you would never have known his nerves.

"Good morning Mnesarchus," she answered and her cheeks once again dimpled as she smiled.

Agathe now stood as well and looked from her daughter to my father. "I will leave you now and will sit within the room nearby," she said as much as a warning as it was an announcement of her departure.

Neither my mother nor father could have cared. They stood looking at one another barely hearing the woman's words and smiled even wider at each other once she was gone.

"Come let us sit," said my father and Pythia walked to the chair opposite him where she sat with her hands clasped together resting upon her knees just as she had been told to do when a suitor would visit. Her mind raced as to what else she was meant to do or say but she could not recall another thing so just looked at my father as she continued to smile.

Mnesarchus could have spent the entire day just gazing upon her but he knew the time his boat would leave was approaching so he began.

"Pythia, I have spoken to your father this very morning. He has

40

given his blessing that if you agree to it that we might court—as I wish to marry you," he happily informed her and then suddenly realised that perhaps he should indeed have spoken of some lesser things to begin with.

"Oh," was all that my mother could reply and then her face grew wide with a smile.

My father continued to talk but he would never remember what he said next. Neither would my mother as she was too thrilled to finally have a man not only brave enough to have asked for her hand, but who was also all that she had hoped for.

Finally the call of time made my father reluctantly bid his farewell and despite the fact that it would be weeks until they were together again neither Mnesarchus nor Pythia were sad to part. The rush of their love just would not allow such thoughts. Instead they both spoke of when Mnesarchus would return and the excitement to once again see each other.

"I will search and find you the most beautiful gem there is. Something you have never seen before," Mnesarchus promised Pythia as he kissed her hand one last time as her mother walked back into the room.

"As long as you don't forget my earrings!" said Agathe.

The next month was the longest that Mnesarchus had ever lived. He stopped through Tyre to attend his niece's wedding and announced his own impending marriage to the delight of all. As he sat and sipped his wine watching the dancing at the wedding he could not stop smiling as he pictured his own future celebration with Pythia. When the new husband and wife were farewelled so as to make way to their marriage bed, Mnesarchus caught his breath.

This part of his new life with Pythia he had not yet even considered. Suddenly he wished he had spoken with Antonius somewhat more about the subject or perhaps even succumbed to the advances of concubines as he travelled. Then he remembered the sanctity of marriage and Mnesarchus was glad that he had not fallen to such desires.

Still he worried that he would not know what to do, or that he might hurt Pythia who was most certainly a virgin as was he. As he walked with his family back to their home after the wedding he pulled Ruben away from the women and whispered in his ear, "Father, I must speak with you about my marriage."

Ruben nodded and even though his head was hazy from drinking he understood that his son was most serious. So when they arrived home Ruben sent his wife ahead to bed saying he needed to speak to their son.

"What is it? Surely you have not been asked for an offering for your bride? I didn't think they did that in Greece?" Ruben asked.

"No, no, Father. There are no concerns with money," Mnesarchus answered and then hesitated. He took a deep breath and then stammered, "I—I am concerned for my—duties…."

"Oh, you are worried about having sex?" said Ruben bluntly and Mnesarchus blushed like a girl. This only made Ruben in his drunken state burst out laughing, "In all your travels in all these years you have honestly never been with a woman?"

Mnesarchus dropped his head and shook it, "No, I was waiting for marriage as I believed I should."

Ruben stopped laughing and grunted, "Mmph! Good—as you should have. Your mother will be most happy. Thank heavens we got you out of here before you found the goats tempting. That's how Antonius had his first sample. I think that's why my father was happy to send him away lest he spoil all their milk," and then he started chuckling again.

When he eventually did stop laughing Ruben explained all the mechanics that Mnesarchus needed to know, but Mnesarchus was already well aware of these thanks to Antonius.

"Yes Father, but what if I hurt her?" Mnesarchus asked.

"Bah! That is most certain the first time. You cannot avoid it," Ruben answered. "But that is not your concern. If she has been raised correctly she will know to expect this and besides it is her duty whether it is painful or not," he continued bluntly and thrusting his hands about. "If she remains hesitant then you remind her that this is how she will have children. All women want children and we can remind them of this to gain our own pleasures."

Mnesarchus sighed as he listened. This wasn't quite the advice he had hoped for but then he had no other man that he could speak of such things with.

When he returned to Samos to see Pythia once again he could hardly look her in the eye at first after thinking of this act over and over as he travelled. Pythia in all her girlish excitement at having her beau once again before her did not notice Mnesarchus' hesitancy to touch her as he kissed her hand. Her gushing and giggling soon had my father smiling and he soon forgot any of his concerns at becoming a husband.

"Did you find me my gem?" Pythia asked bouncing in her seat as she clasped her hands together.

"But of course!" said Mnesarchus and as he opened his satchel

Pythia bounced even more and started squealing.

Mnesarchus reached into the satchel and took out a small roll of velvet tied with a ribbon. To Pythia he seemed to take forever to untie it and show her what was inside but when he finally did she gasped.

"I found it in Babylon," Mnesarchus said as Pythia reached over and lifted it off the velvet. "I don't suppose you have ever seen anything like it?"

She hadn't of course. It was a piece of pure garnet that looked as black as coal but as she lifted it up before her Pythia saw the flecks of deep red make themselves known as the light hit the gem's surface.

"It is like there are other gems trapped inside it," she said as she turned to smile at my father.

Mnesarchus nodded and smiled back as this was the very reason he had chosen it for her.

My parents married six months later within the grandest temple on Samos and the town square was the setting for the wedding feast. None of my father's family was there to see him married or share in the celebration but Mnesarchus did not care too much. The customs here would be so intimidating to them they would have been far from comfortable.

Now as he sat here surrounded by his Greek family as well as a myriad of his father-in-law's clients and business associates he looked across to the taverna chair that he had sat upon that day that Pythia walked before him. He turned to my mother and lifted her hand to his mouth to kiss it.

"My beloved, how I thank the gods each day for having you walk before me," he said softly so that she barely heard above the music and talking that filled the square.

Pythia smiled and kissed my father upon his lips in only the second kiss that they had ever shared, the first being at the completion of their wedding ceremony. Once again it was my father blushing as around them their wedding guests whooped and cheered at the display of affection.

"Bless the groom and his bride!" they shouted as was the tradition, though there were a few more bawdy comments amongst the more drunken male guests.

When the time came for my parents to bid everyone farewell my father could barely breathe. Mnesarchus suddenly wished that he had not consumed wine to quell his nerves as he felt everything swirl before him as he stood. It was Pythia with her steady head and hand that gripped my father's hand and all but led him to their new home.

My father really had nothing to worry about and he realised this the moment that he and Pythia were finally alone. Mnesarchus had barely closed the door of their bedroom and was turning to offer Pythia his understanding should she be hesitant to consummate the marriage, when she rushed to him and pressed her body against him. Grabbing at his head she pushed her lips against his and my father could do nothing but hold his new wife and lose himself in her kiss.

It was Pythia who was first upon the bed with her clothes removed and she watched my father begin to undress taking in every detail of his body as she relished the rush of excitement within her own. It was just as exciting as she had imagined and she thanked her friend for telling her it would be so.

As any young woman would, Pythia had rushed to tell her friends of her engagement and they squealed as she spoke of her beau. Only one of Pythia's friends was already married and it had been her home that she was walking from that day my father first saw her. When my mother told this friend the news she smiled slyly.

"How wonderful!" she said, honestly enthused for her friend, "Now you shall have shared with you the truth of what marriage entails." When Pythia quizzed her friend she merely giggled and replied, "Oh that is for your mother to tell."

When Pythia prodded her mother about what secrets marriage held she was told quite bluntly that "the husband pushes himself into his wife to plant his seed."

"Is that it?" Pythia responded, quite disappointed as she was already aware of such things.

My mother then made her way back to her friend to confront her. "I already knew!" Pythia said bemusedly.

"Oh really? Just what did your mother tell you?" her friend asked.

When Pythia repeated her one line of sex education her friend burst out laughing. "Well that is the plain version but now as you are to be married I suppose I could share with you some more details," she teased.

So Pythia in her innocence agreed to hear more and sat with her jaw open as she was told of the more sordid details of what sex could involve. She felt herself grow warm as she listened, even though she could not believe what she heard. As Pythia walked home she looked at men as she passed and pictured them being in bed with her. Then she would drop her head so no-one could see how red her face was.

44

That night as she lay in bed trying to sleep but with her mind racing, she imagined doing some of the things she had been told about with my father. As she did this she ran her hands over her body and felt her pulse begin to race just as her friend said it would. When she slid her fingers between her legs and felt the wetness she had been told about she gasped, then quickly pushed her face into her pillow as she giggled.

Now finally she was alone with my father and she could do this in reality. As she lay upon the bed grinning at him, my father began to fumble with his clothes, his nerves not letting him do the simplest of things. Then to make him even more jittery the now naked Pythia stood up from the bed and walked to him once more.

"Let me help you," she said softly and began to untie his clothes as my father stood in shock.

It was also Pythia that led my father to lie on the bed and Pythia who pulled him on top of her. Although she did gasp and clench her teeth in pain as he entered her, there were no tears and her cries were soon far from those of resistance. As my father soon lay upon his back catching his breath his wife rolled on her side to face him and declared, "That was fun!"

This routine played itself out each night with my mother usually being the one to begin proceedings. My father, though somewhat surprised but delighted with my mother's behaviour, was actually relieved when it came time for his first business trip. However the rest at night that he was looking forward to was outweighed by missing my mother and the loneliness of his travels now was even greater than before.

I guess I should be thankful for my mother's enthusiasm within the bedroom for helping bring my new life to be. With my father gone half the time it was the energetic resumption of their relations upon his return that saw me conceived early in the marriage.

Mnesarchus was returning from his third trip away expecting to find Pythia at the door to greet him as he called out to her. Instead the maid told him she was feeling poorly and was in the bedroom. Mnesarchus tried to hide his smile, sure that this was a ruse by his wife to coax him into some playful sex well before the sun was set. However instead of a naked, giggling wife he found Pythia fully clothed, her face pale and her body curled up as she lay on her side. She opened her eyes slightly and upon seeing Mnesarchus raised one hand with her palm facing him.

"Don't touch me!" she cried.

"What is it my love?" cried my father as he ran to the bedside and

45

dropped to his knees. He stroked my mother gently as he looked at her face closely as though it might reveal the source of her pain to him.

"I thought it was because I was missing you so much, yet you are here and I feel no better," she said and tears began to spill down her face.

Mnesarchus jumped to his feet and called out to the maid. "Have you sent for a physician?" he asked.

"Madam would not allow me to," the maid answered.

"Go now and don't ever be so foolish to listen to such words again when someone is ill," he snapped. "And on your return call upon her mother and tell her to come as well. Her daughter needs her!"

It was Agathe who arrived first, red in the face and puffing, having walked as fast as she could without running and losing her poise entirely. When she entered and saw the state Pythia was in she sighed deeply.

"What is it you are feeling Pythia?" Agathe asked, narrowing her eyes.

"I think I might be dying," my mother whimpered. "I cannot eat without it leaving me soon after and I cannot stand too long without feeling weak and dizzy."

Agathe sighed once more and looked to my father who was once again upon his knees by the bed stroking my mother's hair.

"And when was the last time you bled?" Agathe now asked.

Pythia screwed her nose up, "I cannot remember. It was some weeks before Mnesarchus left."

Agathe now smiled and stepped closer to the bed. "My dear child, it appears you are with child," she said trying not to laugh.

"A baby!" cried Pythia and sat up, suddenly forgetting her nausea and dizziness. "Mnesarchus, we are going to have a baby!"

My father had gathered this as Agathe spoke. Pythia didn't even realise that he had dropped his head onto the mattress and begun crying, equally from the pride at becoming a father and with relief that his wife was in fact not dying. He slowly lifted his head now and Pythia saw his eyes were red.

Behind him Agathe rolled her eyes and made her way to find the maid to get her to fetch the teas Pythia would need to settle her stomach and ease the dizziness. By the time the doctor did arrive he found Pythia sitting up in bed smiling while Mnesarchus rubbed her feet and Agathe gave more orders to the maid. All he could do was merely confirm what Agathe had deduced.

By the time the doctor left Pythia had well and truly forgotten her ailments. "What shall we call the baby?" she asked my father.

"I am not sure," he answered. Then his mind began to go through family names but he knew immediately that this child would need a Greek name befitting their birthplace and where they would grow up. "Perhaps they could be named after your parents depending on what it is."

Agathe was around the corner and as she heard this she smiled and nodded.

Over the next few months Agathe became somewhat of a permanent fixture at my parent's home. She would arrive in the late morning after attending to her own home and stay doting upon my mother until the sun began to fade. Agathe loved the walk to and from her daughter's home. In the first few days she beamed a smile as she told everyone that she passed that her daughter was with child and they in turn expressed their joy at her news.

As weeks passed she would then relay any recent developments such as how my mother's belly grew or what she was feeling. The women would share their own remedies or stories of their own births or those of their daughters. Agathe would always smile and thank them for their wisdom but then as she walked away she would huff.

"*Bah, I have bore three children!*" she would think. Agathe was not one to be told anything and so she would walk to my family's home and simply do as her own mother had done for her.

My father was a man more than happy to leave such female concerns to the gender he imagined knew of them best. Mnesarchus would merely watch, albeit sometimes bemusedly, and then step aside as Agathe stormed through the house checking that the maid and cook were performing their duties correctly. Mnesarchus was also truly grateful. He still had a business to run and to leave knowing that his wife and child were being watched over by the only person who could care for them as much as he was a relief beyond anything he could express.

When Mnesarchus returned from his next journey he walked into a clean tidy home filled with the scent of slow cooked lamb leg. As he always did he checked upon Pythia first, smothering her in kisses as he rubbed her belly and she giggled. He then made his way to find his mother-in-law.

Agathe was in the kitchen checking on the lamb and deciding on vegetables with the cook. She looked up as Mnesarchus stepped into the doorway. "Oh welcome home, Son. I am afraid your meal will be a bit longer so I hope you are not too hungry," she said.

"I can wait, Mother," he replied, "Please join me in the sitting room."

Mnesarchus stood aside and gestured for Agathe to walk ahead of him which she did somewhat curious as to why such an audience was being requested of her. She sat upon a lounge and for the first time in knowing her, Mnesarchus believed that she was nervous. Agathe cleared her throat and squared her shoulders and there returned the mother-in-law he knew.

"Mother, I wish to thank you for all your help in caring for my wife, my child and my home," Mnesarchus began.

"Nonsense," she replied sharply. "There is no need for such emotive speech. This is what a mother does."

"I know, I know," said Mnesarchus, "But I do believe you should be acknowledged."

With that he pulled from his pocket one of his customary silk rolls, untied it and lifted out of the material a perfect oval emerald set in exquisite Egyptian gold and hanging from a thick woven chain made of more of the same gold. Agathe's mouth dropped open. She was speechless and Mnesarchus had to take her hand to place the necklace within it. It was the largest gem she had ever held.

"Oh, I almost forgot," Mnesarchus said and he laughed as he reached back into his pocket to retrieve yet another silk roll. "You simply must have the matching earrings!"

Agathe wore her new jewellery home and of course everyone noticed. She may have been modest before her son-in-law but as the town saw her in her new adornments Agathe soon found the words to let everyone and anyone know that these riches were her reward for the duties she was performing.

Pythia revelled in her new-found status as expectant mother. She soaked up her mother's attentions and the gentility of my father when he spoke or touched her now. Not that my father was ever rough with Pythia or had ever treated her with anything less than complete adoration, but now his words and touch were as though she was the most delicate flower he had ever seen or held and this appealed to my mother so much that she decided she would be pregnant as often as she could manage it.

My father's adorations of my mother also fired the very impulses within her that would achieve just this state. Poor Mnesarchus could hardly believe that a woman in such condition would turn to him in bed and wish to have a man upon her while a child grew within her. However when he spoke of such hesitations to indulge in the act Pythia almost burst into tears.

"You don't think I am beautiful anymore!" she cried.

"No, no, my love! I just don't want to hurt you or the baby," he explained.

"You won't hurt us. I asked. I know it is alright," she said through her tears.

So Mnesarchus mostly from a desire to placate his wife as well as just a small desire to satisfy himself, physically raised himself carefully to lie over Pythia. He had assumed Pythia had asked the doctor who called upon her weekly to check the pregnancy. It was in fact the friend who had informed Pythia upon her engagement who now encouraged her to continue such things during her pregnancy.

"Why should we stop having fun just because someone grows inside us," the friend said and laughed, then dropped her voice. "Besides if we do not continue this for our husbands they may look elsewhere. My dear, you have a husband who travels as well. If I were you I would ensure that he does not seek to travel to another woman."

Pythia jumped at the thought of her husband being with someone else. Her heart knew that he never would but her friend had planted the seed of doubt within her mind. So when my father refused her with explanation of his concerns she also imagined him touching another woman with a flat belly.

When they finished making love that night she lay upon her back and once again her tears flowed. Mnesarchus heard her sniff and turned to her, lifting himself upon one elbow.

"What is it? Did I hurt you?" he asked, almost crying himself.

"No," she whimpered. "Mnesarchus, do you ever touch other women while you travel?" she asked.

"No! Never! I could not. I simply love you too much," he said emphatically. "Do you know how many women I saw before I found you? Yet the moment I laid my eyes on you I knew there was no other woman for me. Now you bear me a child and other women are not only insignificant but invisible to me. You have my heart, Pythia and you always will."

Pythia's tears stopped. "Really?" she asked.

"Yes, really," answered Mnesarchus and curled against Pythia who finally drifted to sleep with the widest grin possible.

While my mother had concerns for my father's fidelity Mnesarchus' only concerns involved my mother's health and the future of his child. He would watch my mother's belly expand picturing my body growing bigger and stronger. The happiest day of his life was when my mother grabbed his hand and placed it upon her belly so that he felt my foot pushing outwards and stretching into a new position. This confirmation as to my vitality though was not enough to truly satisfy the curiosity that seemed to plague him with endless questions and thoughts.

These thoughts began to permeate his dreams with images and scenarios alternating between joy and horror. After one of the nightmares where Mnesarchus saw me emerge from my mother's body deformed and howling like a jackal, he woke with dark circles beneath his eyes. He walked about our home with such a pained expression that day that Agathe would have had to be blind not to notice. She knew immediately what was happening to my father.

"You are heading into unknown waters my son," she said knowingly. "My own husband had such dreams when I was carrying Pythia. It is just your fears coming to the surface."

"Well they can return to where they came!" he answered.

"Perhaps you could seek an oracle to soothe your head," Agathe suggested. "They will know of the sex and the child's nature. That should help you prepare for being a father and to what this child will need."

This appealed to the businessman within Mnesarchus and he nodded. Yes, if only he knew some more of this child then he would be prepared and all these surplus thoughts could be left behind.

Agathe only mentioned Mnesarchus' intention to consult an oracle or seer to one person and over the next few days there was an endless stream of "gifted" people upon the doorstep offering their services. He turned most away knowing their methods to be questionable. Mnesarchus may have been open to finding out about me in less tangible ways but he did not see how reading animal entrails or incense smoke would inform him of his child. The few that he did allow in didn't satisfy what he wanted to hear either. One in fact only cemented his fears by screwing up her nose as she waved her hands before my mother's belly and announcing, "The child does not wish to communicate!"

It was then that Mnesarchus knew the answer was not upon Samos and he remembered the very oracles for which my mother was named. So with even more fear that such powerful channelers would give him news he didn't wish to hear, he made way to the Greek mainland under the premise of doing business. This was so that if he did hear such things that did not suit, then his family would never need to know.

Upon reaching the mainland he was greeted by his assistant, a young man called Leo who Mnesarchus was finding more dubious on each journey. Leo was often unmotivated and lacked energy or interest in learning the finer details of the gem trade yet he was always ready with the cart and knew his way. For now this was enough for Mnesarchus and besides he may now soon have sons to truly learn from him.

After the first morning of trade Mnesarchus asked Leo if he knew the way to Delphi. The young man turned and looked to Mnesarchus, screwing his nose up. "Why would you need to consult the oracle?" Leo asked truly puzzled.

"As my wife bears me a child and I wish to hear of its future," Mnesarchus said plainly not impressed by his assistant's forwardness in asking.

It was a four hour ride to Delphi which they made quite comfortably but not in enough time to attend that day's readings. As they pulled into the outskirts of Delphi they passed other pilgrims making their way home. Mnesarchus saw some were smiling while others hung their heads and yet others were in tears. Mnesarchus sighed as he was once more reminded that he might hear something he might not like.

At first light Mnesarchus made way to the site with Leo driving the cart. Leo, knowing that Mnesarchus would be some time, drove underneath a tree to claim what he knew would be one of the rare places of shade when the day wore on. He indeed made his own fortune that day for as Mnesarchus climbed the mountainside and stood at the top of the amphitheatre he saw that many others had arrived before him. Mnesarchus took a deep breath and found a place to sit and wait his turn for a private audience.

As each person stood and made their way to kneel before one of the women who allowed the gods to speak through them he listened intently at first, hearing tragedies and triumphs described. As the hours wore on though Mnesarchus grew weary and even started to doze. When his stomach began to rumble, he realised it was past noon and he was grateful that he had packed some food as the innkeeper had advised him to. He was also grateful he had done so for Leo who he imagined would be sleeping by now upon the cart and he was not wrong.

Finally it came his time to stand before the oracle and this, my dear readers, is where I truly join the story.

I had drifted towards your human realm from the outer realms where spirits play deciding whether they will join once more in this game of human or pass back to that place of pure energy from where they originally came. I had remained attached to my last life in Egypt and those I had loved there but now they had let go of me and I truly had let go of them. So I floated towards the earth looking for my next adventure and was drawn to Greece and the energies of Delphi.

I saw the deep immense energies of the archangels as they hovered over the oracles waiting for their turn to be heard through the women while the people in turn waited to hear what messages would be shared. It was something I had craved to see; this bridge between where I was and where I had left and I finally had found where it could occur. I went in close to see if I might partake of it and at this very moment my father was called forward to kneel before the young virgin who would deliver his message.

I saw the girl close her eyes and take in a deep breath and when she did the energies surrounding her came in so close that she suddenly seemed to blend with them. Then just as quickly they pulled back and I saw only one stayed close to her, swirling around and through her as her breath deepened and her face softened. Her body twitched but her arms remained relaxed by her side.

"What is it that you wish to know?" she asked, her eyes remaining closed, her expression serene.

"Most sacred oracle, speaker for the gods, I wish to know of the child that my wife bears for me," Mnesarchus trembled as he spoke but the father within me felt and knew the joy and excitement of a new child. I went in closer to share in this as much as possible.

I swept before all the others there and was so close to the girl that she turned her head directly to where I was. Even though her eyes were closed I knew that she saw me and I was intrigued to see her smile. She kept her head turned and Mnesarchus also looked to where her face seemed to be fixed.

"I see your son," she said smiling as though she wanted to say "*I see you!*" to me. I hung in place now utterly curious as to what she would say next.

"A son!" Mnesarchus beamed at the words.

"Yes a son," the oracle continued and I felt as though she asked me to come closer still, so I did. Her head slowly moved as though she was examining every part of me and then she continued. "He is a grand being, destined for amazing things," she smiled broadly now at me. "He is fit and strong with a mind to match, but it is his mind which will offer him grandeur in this life. Nurture this early and his name will be known by many."

"How should I nurture this?" my father's eyes were wide with awe but now also with a fear of undoing this amazing child who had not even been born yet.

"Egypt," was her answer.

"Egypt?" I cried out in unison with Mnesarchus.

"Yes, Egypt," she answered to us both. "The scholars of Egypt will teach him much."

The smile that the girl had carried with her words now suddenly faded and I saw her body start to tremble. Two other women rushed forward to grab her arms just as her knees bent and she began to fall.

"The oracle has no more words for you today Sir," said one plainly as they carried her away.

Mnesarchus stayed upon his knees for a moment and looked down in shock replaying what he had just heard. His mind raced over all that had been said and then he remembered the one word that made him smile.

"A son. I will have a son!" he repeated as he lifted himself to his feet and turned to leave.

Leo was lounging in the donkey cart chewing on a twig, his legs hanging over the side of the seat. He saw Mnesarchus making his way down the mountain sending small rocks ahead of him as he walked. The young man jumped up and stood as Mnesarchus walked towards him.

"Was it good news?" he called out to Mnesarchus.

"The best of news! I will have a son!" Mnesarchus answered.

"Surely we must stop at a taverna to celebrate then?" beamed the young man.

"Surely we must make haste to reach the shore lest I miss the last boat home," Mnesarchus said sharply as he lifted himself into the carriage. "One day you may understand that life is not about seizing every opportunity you can to drink! Now get these animals moving."

Somehow I was tied to Mnesarchus and I could not understand it. That woman had described me yet she had also described the child about to be born to this man. Perhaps she had confused the two and my having stepped in so close had interfered with what she should have heard from the angels. Then again perhaps she had said exactly what all three of us had chosen to be said. Either way I decided to follow Mnesarchus.

Mnesarchus bounced along in the cart beside the young man and I saw his mind now race as they made their way. They finally arrived at the dock and he jumped from the cart. Mnesarchus grabbed at his satchel and slung it over his shoulder. As he gathered another bag he spoke to Leo, "Tomorrow we rest, but the day after you will meet me at the usual dock. I will come on the first boat and we will make our way to the open sea docks and sail to Egypt."

The young man had groaned internally at the thought of meeting the boat that sailed at first light but upon hearing of Egypt he groaned outwardly, "Argh! Egypt! We will be gone for a week."

"We shall be gone for two weeks!" said Mnesarchus looking up. "We are long overdue a trip for trade and I now have other business there to see to. If this does not please you feel free to seek other employment," Mnesarchus finished and tilted his head as though waiting for a reply.

"Fine, I shall meet you at the usual dock," Leo moaned again.

Mnesarchus smiled and went to climb aboard the boat that would carry him to Samos. His smile would not leave his face and the boat owner looked at him as they bounced over the waves. "I see you have had a good day of trade," the boatman joked.

"The very best day has been given to me with even better to come," Mnesarchus joked back unwilling to tell this man his news lest the entire island would know within a day. The oracles were considered all knowing but they sometimes were wrong. Despite Mnesarchus' very heart believing she was correct he would not embarrass himself with the possibility of sharing a mistaken message.

Mnesarchus jumped from the boat calling out his farewell and walked quickly to his home that was nearby the dock. He smelt the lamb before he was even in the door. It was the same smell that greeted him whenever he was due home. A small comment made early in their marriage had led Pythia to believe that slowly stewed lamb leg was his favourite dish and she excitedly had the cook prepare it every time he was expected back from a trip. Within the few months of their marriage it had indeed became his favourite meal as that smell meant the rigours of the road and dealing with merchants was over.

Mnesarchus entered the small courtyard that was the front of their home and called out to his wife. Pythia appeared quickly, as though she had run and then stopped grabbing at a column to lean against while she held her rounded belly and caught her breath.

"I keep forgetting I cannot move so fast these days," she giggled.

Mnesarchus walked towards her, dropping his bags upon the floor as he made his way. He quickly pecked her upon the lips and then reached down to her belly pulling her dress tight around it. "Let me see how much he has grown," he said softly.

"He?" said Pythia as Mnesarchus looked back to his wife's eyes and she saw he had tears beginning in them.

"I saw the oracle today," he said never taking his hands from her belly. "We are having a son and he will be grand and magnificent!"

"Really—a son?" she gasped. "We thought that from the beginning didn't we?"

"Yes we did!" Mnesarchus answered and then took her face in his hands to kiss her.

I knew with every part of my being that this child was to be my new life. It was an instant understanding that was neither processed nor analysed. I knew these people would be my parents and it had been more than coincidence that I had appeared at Delphi when my father had. I could tell you that the archangels had led me there but they did not. It was all my doing.

As my parents kissed tenderly I swam forward and blended into the tiny body that lay within my mother's womb. The sense of constriction was immediately overwhelming. The rush of sensations as I once more had blood rushing within me, lungs expanding and the shots of electricity through my nerves were intense and exciting. My little form too adjusted to my energy as it felt the blend of having a spirit now begin a new journey within its frame. It all happened within the blink of an eye but was so potent that my mother jumped back from my father's kiss.

"He just moved," she said but she knew it was different from all the other times she had felt her baby stir and she stroked her belly trying to settle me as she feigned a smile.

"Are you alright?" asked my father.

"Yes," Pythia said and laughed. "He has just never moved so strongly before."

Now my father laughed, "Bigger *and* stronger! This is a most wonderful day."

CHAPTER THREE

From that day on my mother felt me differently inside her and she assumed it was just the knowing that I was male. Her belly now seemed to grow by the hour and her small frame began to struggle with the extra weight so that her pregnancy ended much as it had began with her spending most of her days upon a bed or lounge. Agathe's presence which had diminished as my mother had settled into pregnancy once more made itself known in our home.

It was Agathe that found Pythia upon her bed breathing heavily, having just felt a contraction. It was Agathe who screamed for the maid to fetch the midwife and it was Agathe who grabbed the other maid and told her to start heating water. She walked to the bed and rolled her daughter onto her back and then pushed her to sit up.

"You won't get the child out on your side," Agathe said purposefully as she pushed pillows behind Pythia. "Stay sitting up now no matter how bad the pain." Agathe pulled at Pythia's daughter's dress revealing her legs and everything to her waist. "Open your legs," she now said so sternly that despite Pythia's every instinct to keep them together and somehow keep the child within her to avoid what she knew was about to happen, she flung them apart. "Now keep your legs open so you are ready for the midwife." With this Agathe turned and made her way to the door.

"Where are you going? You can't leave me!" cried Pythia.

"I need to check on everything," Agathe snapped back. "You are far from the final moments when you need anyone."

Pythia though didn't feel this was at all true. She could feel my head pushing so hard down into her pelvis that she was sure I would find my way out soon. So much so in fact that she reached down and gently felt between her legs expecting to feel the top of my head. When she only felt her soft folds still in their usual place she felt some relief. Then she thought of my father.

"I want Mnesarchus!" Pythia yelled to the empty doorway hoping her mother would hear her.

Agathe was in the kitchen seeing that enough water was being boiled when she heard her daughter. She looked up realising that she had indeed forgotten about my father altogether. Not that getting Mnesarchus was a priority. Men were hardly required for childbirth and she had some time in which to send a maid to find him. Just as she decided this she heard Pythia cry out in pain as another contraction grabbed hold. Agathe stopped in her tracks. That was very soon for this stage of labour. She grabbed at the maid.

"Go find Mnesarchus," Agathe said and pushed her to the door.

It was indeed a small time between contractions for my mother was far from the early stages of labour. Pythia had been feeling pains for over ten hours now but they were just deep dull pains that came and went as did much of her discomfort these days. She would just shift and they would settle as they always did. When her mother had found her she had just suffered the worst pain yet and Pythia knew she was about to give birth. Now sitting up with gravity to help me make my way everything was intensified and the dull ache that had wrapped over her belly from her back had become that sharp slicing pain that she had been told about.

"I want Mnesarchus!" Pythia now screamed even louder as Agathe ran to the bedroom to find her daughter red in the face and sweating.

Mnesarchus was at the docks collecting a shipment from Babylon when he saw the maid walking fast towards him and he knew instantly my time had come. He quickly finished his payment and smiled at the boat captain, "My child is arriving!"

Mnesarchus walked into the house just as Pythia had another contraction and when he heard her scream his smile dropped as he ran to the bedroom. He stood in the doorway to see his wife at the end of the bed grabbing at her knees to sit forward while the midwife squatted before her. Agathe stood to one side, her eyes also focussed on the place I would emerge.

"Mnesarchus!" cried Pythia with relief as she saw her husband in the doorway and he ran to her. However just as he arrived by her side, Agathe stepped in his way.

"You should wait outside. This is no place for a man," Agathe said more strongly than she ever spoke.

"No place for a man! I am the father. I need to be here for my wife and child," he said stating his case.

Behind them Pythia screamed with the pain of another contraction and Mnesarchus moved Agathe aside to get to his wife. Agathe indignant at being treated this way inhaled and prepared for another attempt to remove my father from the room but when she saw the relief on her daughter's face, Agathe let her breath out and returned to the midwife's side.

"Surely it is almost time!," Agathe snapped at the midwife. If no-one else in the room would pay her heed then at least this woman had to.

"Yes Madam," she said as she once again felt between Pythia's legs. "I can feel the top of the head."

"You can feel him?" said Mnesarchus looking to the midwife.

"Keep your eyes to your wife's face, Son!" shouted Agathe.

"Bah! It was alright for me to be down there to put the child in but now that he leaves, it is forbidden to me," thought Mnesarchus and though he wished to speak the words out loud he held his tongue for the sake of Pythia.

Then my mother, holding my father's hand with my grandmother to watch over us all, began to push and I entered the world.

My first moments of this life were of shock. It was not mine but of those around me. Pythia became a mother, Mnesarchus became a father and Agathe became a grandmother. As the midwife caught me and lifted me up all three watched me as though they had never seen a baby before. I decided to break their trance by having my first scream and then the disbelief was replaced by laughter and crying.

"He's here, he's here!" cried out Pythia.

"He is indeed," answered Agathe.

My father though remained silent. The oracle had been right and now all he had been planning for this moment, should I be born male, could begin.

When the oracle spoke the name of Egypt to my father as the place that would support my nurturing he headed there the very first opportunity that he could.

"Egypt?" cried Pythia when Mnesarchus told her, "But Greece has the finest minds here. Why would we need foreigners to teach our son?"

"Well, my dear, you forget that his father is a foreigner!" replied Mnesarchus with a smile. "Besides, the scholars of Egypt are privy to the ancient mysteries. If we allow him to study there who knows what knowledge that will allow him to uncover."

Mnesarchus who had been packing his bag to leave for Egypt stopped as he said this. For as the very words left his lips he felt a chill run down his spine, the same sensation he had felt as he knelt and listened to the oracle. Mnesarchus knew that the words he just spoke had been affirmed by the gods. "Pythia, imagine that our son should be known for sharing his wisdom with Greece. Imagine that our son should be sought to be learnt from as the very teachers we will send him to."

This was too much for Pythia to comprehend right now but she nodded to her husband as she rubbed her stomach. "Yes, Mnesarchus," was all she could say.

When Mnesarchus landed in the city of Rhakotis it suddenly looked different despite him having been here dozens of times to trade. As he walked down the gangway of the boat, instead of searching amongst the men that filled the docks for possible deals to be made, Mnesarchus peered out to the city beyond. It was not that on every other occasion that he had been here he had not noticed the city for indeed he had walked its streets many times. Today though the city was different.

Mnesarchus looked to the palace that the Pharaoh stayed in when he attended business at the delta. He stared at the temples that soared above all else and then he too felt what Pythia had spoken. How could he trust his son to a land so different not only from where he would be born but so different even from where Mnesarchus himself had been born. Then he closed his eyes and remembered the way in which the oracle had spoken the name of Egypt to him. Mnesarchus opened his eyes and began to walk to the city.

Leo followed behind him, carrying bags over both shoulders and a canteen of water around his neck which swung as he tried to keep up with Mnesarchus. Mnesarchus ducked and weaved through the crowd picking up his pace every time there was room to do so. The boy did his best to get a move on but having risen before dawn, several hours earlier than he was used to or cared for, he was already fatigued.

"Mnesarchus, please slow down!" Leo finally called out. "What is the rush this journey? You are like a man possessed."

Mnesarchus stopped but he didn't turn to look at the boy until he finally caught up with him. "Sorry Leo," he said, still not looking at him. "It is just there is much I wish to achieve here." With that he walked on albeit more slowly.

It didn't take much for Mnesarchus to find where the scholars were within a temple school on the city outskirts. It was even easier to be granted an audience with them, but that is where the ease in establishing my future ended. The old men smiled as Mnesarchus walked towards them and took his seat before them.

"Welcome to you," said the eldest and clearly the most senior as he sat in the most central seat. "What might it be that you seek to speak with us about?"

Mnesarchus shifted as his throat tightened but he remembered the smile of the oracle as she spoke of his son and he looked up and into the eyes of the men before him. "I wish to secure a place for my son within your school that he might share your wisdom and in turn teach this wisdom to others."

The elders all nodded and then once again the leader spoke. "And how old is your son as we speak?" he asked.

"He is yet to be born," Mnesarchus said plainly.

The men once again looked amongst themselves but this time as they did their faces grew wide with smiles. The leader even put his hand to his face and rubbed at it as he softly laughed. "Do you not think perhaps you are somewhat ahead of things at this stage?" he asked. "Perhaps it is best that you allow him to actually exist and therefore are within the circumstances to organise such things?"

"But I have spoken with the Pythian oracle at Delphi. I was told my child would be male and he would achieve much grandness if he studied with you," Mnesarchus pleaded.

The old man shook his head, "Such fantasies are wonderful to soothe a mind in search of comfort and an ego seeking reassurance. However we are somewhat different to the oracles. We deal with reality. We deal with the tangible. I suggest you go home and when you can finally hold your son then you may think of approaching us again. But please do not journey here until he can read and write lest we have to turn you away again," he said and finished with a gentle knowing smile.

When Mnesarchus finally left, walking with the posture of a defeated man, the leader watched him and the old man sighed. "It is a shame that I will most likely be gone when that child does arrive to study," he said to the others. "Any child born to a father with that much dedication is sure to become a man who will choose to inspire others."

So as Mnesarchus looked down upon my little naked body with all my birth fluids still upon me, all he could picture was the man I would become.

The months it took for me to grow responsive were an eternity for my father. He would hold me as a newborn and speak to me, trying to catch my eyes with his in the few moments they would be open between my sleeping, but he knew my eyes could not focus properly. He would hand me back to Pythia and sigh, "I don't think he will ever grow."

"Mnesarchus, hush!" Pythia would say and she would pull me close to her as though she was trying to stop me from hearing. "He has already gone through three sizes of diapers since he was born. Why can't you just enjoy him being a baby?"

I was three months old when Mnesarchus finally headed off to his first trip since I was born. He had delayed his business for as long as he could to be with Pythia and I, but letters had started to arrive from his associates eager to recommence trading. So he left home now even more reluctantly than he ever did.

When he returned a month later my mother greeted him as she held me in her arms. Mnesarchus stopped in his tracks. Having finally been away for a significant amount of time he could now see just how much I was grown.

"Oh my," he said as Pythia placed me in his arms. "He is double the size."

Not only was I double the size but my eyes were now focussed and I took in my father's features as I listened to his familiar voice. Mnesarchus looked down upon me and smiled. "Ah my son, now you know me!" he said. Mnesarchus then began my education.

At four months of age my father would prop me up on pillows upon a couch. Then he would kneel before me and show me gems. He would wave them before me, catching my eye, then moving the gem and smiling as he saw my eyes follow the colour.

"Look Pythia!" he would call out if I gurgled or moved a hand as he did this. "Look how he responds already."

My mother would often be sitting nearby and she would smile politely to my father.

"Yes my darling, he is most clever," she would say.

When my father would finally leave me alone with my mother she would sit me upon her knees, holding me to face her. She would push her face close to mine, kissing me and smiling as I would gurgle and wave a hand to try and touch her.

"Ah my little one, it is a shame your father does not realise it is him that you respond to and not his silly stones," she would say softly.

Despite Pythia's knowing of this she never once stopped my father. Even though she did not understand Mnesarchus' impatience with my development she understood his dedication to my nurturing. This was something that she adored of him. So even when at six months my father sat me upon his knee at his desk, placed a quill in my hand and then guided me to write, Pythia said nothing as she stood in the doorway and watched. Afterwards he held the paper up for her to see.

"Look Pythia! His first writing," Mnesarchus said.

Pythia as always nodded and replied, "Yes my darling, he is most clever."

My father's impatience for me to grow was only ever matched by his dedication to my learning. When I could finally sit up he would surround me with objects to see which I would respond to. When I began to crawl he would place them further away to encourage my movement. Then he would place them onto chairs and low tables to push my abilities to stand myself up.

Even when my mother became pregnant again as I began to walk he did not abate.

"There is no need to seek the oracle for this child," he said to my mother quite plainly as he watched me stumble across the floor to grab at a small statue of Apollo. "Pythagoras will show all other children of ours the way."

My mother just nodded and rubbed her stomach protectively. In her heart she too knew that my training and education would indeed be passed on to any other children. Just as she learnt her way as a mother with me, so too was Mnesarchus finding his way as a father.

My brother, Eunomus arrived when I had truly found my feet and was beginning to discover the proper use of my tongue. I watched as my mother grimaced with the first pains of her labour and cried out to her maid. I stood with a toy horse in my hand as the maid rushed in and, realising what was happening, wrapped her arm around my mother's waist to lead her to the bedroom. As they walked away my mother crumpled again with another pain but as she straightened and continued to walk she turned her head and tried to smile at me.

"I am alright my son. I will be much better soon," she said as cheerfully as she could pretend.

I sat back down and returned to amusing myself as around me a full production began to play itself out. Agathe soon burst into the scene which did not surprise me so much as dramatic entrances were always her way. She was soon followed by the midwife who passed by me as though I was invisible. Then soon after my father rushed in and his normal greeting was almost non-existent. I put out my arms to him expecting to be gathered and spoken to as always. Instead he simply said "Hello Son" and quickly headed to the bedroom as all the others did.

This I did not like. It was bad enough to have my mother carried out of the room before me in distress but to now be seemingly dismissed by my father was truly wounding. It did not matter that the other maids checked upon me and offered me company; I sat and stared in the direction that my parents had disappeared and pouted. Then as I heard my mother begin to scream with the final pushes of her delivery my tears began. Who knew what horrors were occurring to her while I sat here forgotten.

When my father appeared before me with his face red and beads of sweat still hanging on his brow, I hardly wanted to look at him. He gathered me in his arms anyway and kissed me gently. I could feel him trembling as he spoke softly, "Come, I will take you to see your brother."

I pulled away, unsure of his words as he walked towards the bedroom door that hid all the day's events from me, unsure as to why I was now included and wondering what a brother was. Mnesarchus pushed open the door and the first thing I saw was the midwife gathering the afterbirth in cloths. This meant nothing to me and my eyes searched for my mother.

Pythia was sitting up in the bed, propped by pillows. At her breast was a tiny creature sucking and pulling at her nipple. My mother's face was also red and wet with sweat and despite having something attached to her she was smiling down upon it. My father carried me closer and as he leant in over the bed I saw the tiny face that was nuzzled into my mother.

"Pythagoras, this is your new brother. How wonderful that I now have two beautiful boys to be with me," my mother said to me beaming an even wider smile.

As I looked back down at this tiny person I realised he had been the source of my mother's screams, he was the reason my father had almost ignored me and now he would need my mother more than I did. I did the only thing I knew at the time to express my sheer distaste at his arrival. I hit him.

The arrival of Eunomus started a new phase of life for me. No longer being the sole attention of my mother and father initially seemed to be something of a loss for me but instead I suddenly gained a new freedom. Now walking solidly and with enough nous to plan and set goals for adventure I began creating my own days. This is not to say that the gentle hands of our maids or the strong and desperate calls of my mother were entirely absent from my escapades but the frequency in which I gained success grew.

I knew that the first whimpers of Eunomus would send at least one maid scurrying and luckily this was usually the maid who was also watching over me. She would look down at me, assess that I had enough toys to entertain me, that there was no imminent danger and then she would head to my parent's bedroom where his crib was. I would sit still and play my part as I knew was expected, listening for the usual conversation between the maid and my mother as Pythia arranged herself ready to feed the baby. This was my window of opportunity and I seized it at every chance.

In the beginning I would simply wander the rooms of our home, heading into the quarters that I didn't frequent and delighting as I frightened the cook or other maids as I silently appeared next to them. I would be ushered back to the salon where I was supposed to play and the maid who by that time had realised I was gone would grab my hand and scold me.

"Why can't you ever just stay put?" she would say exasperated and embarrassed that the simplest of her duties was once again undone by a child.

I never did understand the concerns. All I wanted to do was walk around as I saw all the adults around me do. They moved about without concerning others or being dragged by maids back to one room. So as soon as the opportunity once again presented itself I simply would make my way back through the house to see the places that were somehow deemed unsuitable for me. Then one day the grandest possibility was laid before me.

In the usual melee of the baby's cries for my mother's milk there was added the morning chores of water gathering and sweeping. It was the general flurry of early day activities to organise and settle the house before the heavy heat of midday set in. Eunomus began his wailing and my mother and maid began the steps of their routine within the dance of the rest of the home. As usual this signalled my cue to explore. This day however, as I walked towards the kitchens and maids' quarters a bright light caught my eye and I turned towards the foyer at the front of my home. Instead of where the door should have held solid and dense, there was a bright rectangle of sunlight shining itself upon the floor. The door moved slightly with a breeze but had no intention of closing itself and the maid who should have actually performed this duty was nowhere to be seen.

Every instinct within me now was at battle. Part of me wanted to run and head outside. This was my final frontier—to actually make my way outside on my own, without someone carrying me or grasping my hand as though trying to attach our skins together. I stepped into the brightness and felt the heat upon me and hesitated. If I did step outside I left the comfort of my home, the knowing that my mother or a maid was only a room or the hearing distance of a cry away.

The heat of the sun started to warm my skin and I squinted my eyes. "*I will come back*," I thought to myself and stepped across the doorway.

I was now in the front courtyard of our home. The furthest I had ever been on my own and I turned to see if anyone had realised where I was, half wishing that someone was in pursuit to end the debate within me. Then I turned and looked at the gate that led on to the laneway before us. I had seen this opened many times and even though I had to stretch my legs and arms to reach the latch, I could do so. My tiny hands grabbed the metal slip and pushed. As the latch released the gate swung outwards and I looked down at the line that was formed by the boundary of the gateway. One more step and I was gone but I still hesitated and looked back to the open front door of the home.

I heard some sounds from the nearby town centre. It was the bustle of markets and people making their way back and forth from them. My curiosity now outweighed my fears or reasoning that I should not leave and I stepped through the gateway and walked towards the noise. I could always come back.

I walked for some time past familiar buildings with the same cracks in the plaster they always had. I saw new flowers in some gardens but I kept walking and the sounds of people grew louder. People now started to pass by me and no-one seemed to notice or care that a child of barely two years of age walked amongst them alone. In truth they all assumed that a parent or caregiver was nearby and continued on with their business. This was even more the case as I got closer to the markets and the crowds grew.

I was still not scared as I walked into the crowds of people bargaining and assessing goods. I stopped and looked up at them all towering over me, their clothes flowing and brushing against me as they passed by. This amused me at first that I seemed to be invisible, that no-one grabbed me by the hand to drag me home but the novelty soon wore off. I suddenly did want attention and I decided that perhaps I would like to be home. However now as I looked to make my return I could not see which way I needed to go.

The crowd seemed to swell and all around me was swathe after swathe of clothing with hands clutching baskets to their side. I could not see beyond the wall of moving clothes and even though my heart began to step into anxiety I did not cry. I knew I would get home. How and when I would was what concerned me.

My heart began to twist again in my chest as I pictured my mother and wanted to be with her. It was then that I felt two hands slip under my arms and lift me up. I was suddenly above the crowd and now all I could see was an ocean of moving heads swimming between the market stalls. I was carried amongst them to the edge of the crowd and the hands now turned me around so that I could see the face that they belonged to.

"Where is your mother, little one?" said the face of a man not unlike my father.

I stopped as I realised this was nobody I knew and then listened to his words. I opened my lips saying in my own way that she was at home with the maids and Eunomus. He now carried the same expression as the maids did when I spoke to them and I knew my words were not enough for him so I pointed. I'm not at all sure where I pointed but it was enough for him to realise that she was not nearby and he turned his head where my finger indicated.

"The gods only know where you belong," he muttered and swung me up upon his shoulders. "At least this way anyone who owns you will see you. Hang on!"

Thankfully I knew his words and grabbed onto the cloths he had tied around his head. Knowing I was safe and on my way home I relaxed and enjoyed the fun of my ride. As my new friend walked through the market he called out, "Whose child is this? Does anyone know this child?" But mostly his cries were lost amongst the din of the bargaining and bragging. The few that did hear him did not know or recognise me and instead made jokes as to whether I had been purchased for a good price or what I might fetch if sold.

We had not continued on for too long when a flour merchant looked up at me and rubbed his chin. "That is Agathe's grandson. He belongs to her eldest daughter but none of her maids are due today," he said as he scanned the crowd to see if he could see anyone from our household.

"Well I don't think I can carry him until they do come," my rescuer responded. "Perhaps I could take him home."

The flour merchant gave the man directions to my home and soon we made our way out of the market crowd and into the quieter laneways that led to my home. As the crowd thinned he reached up and grabbed me again, swinging me down so that he held me under one arm, balanced upon his hip. He looked at my face and shook his head.

"You are not even worried!" he muttered as he kept walking.

In the meantime at my home a more frantic scene had erupted. My mother lost in the reverie of breastfeeding did not notice my absence but the maid who walked back into the salon to check upon me did. She called out to me and my mother looked up from Eunomus and smiled.

"Your brother is wandering the house again," she said softly as she turned her attentions back upon the baby.

However when she heard my name called out again and again her amusement soon vanished. She cradled Eunomus against her as he continued to feed and made her way to where the maid was calling. By this time several other maids were also rushing about the house, looking behind furniture and opening cupboards. My mother's fears now amplified and with a child suckling at her breast she too joined in calling out my name and walking about the house.

When Pythia arrived near the entrance of our home she found a maid standing still, her eyes wide with horror and a hand over her mouth.

"What is it?" Pythia cried as her eyes followed the maid's gaze.

Then she saw just what had made the maid freeze. The door stood open but even worse than that was the open gate beyond it.

"Don't just stand there! Go outside and find him!" Pythia screamed and the maid launched into action rushing outside bellowing my name for the entire neighbourhood to hear.

I was only a street away still being carried when the maid flew around a corner and almost straight into us. She gathered herself as she made her apologies to the man then her eyes grew wide once again as she realised just what he was carrying.

"Pythagoras! Thank the gods you are alright!" she cried and grabbed at her chest.

The man looked at me as I casually smiled at the maid. "So you have a name then," he laughed and held me out to the maid. She grabbed me and held me tight then started bouncing me as though I needed consoling. I nuzzled into her, glad to be in familiar arms once again.

"Sir, I thank you most sincerely," she said still breathless from her running and still rocking me. "I am sure my mistress would gladly offer you her personal thanks as well as some refreshment." She meant this more as her own show of gratitude for she knew that she would bear the brunt of the blame for my escape. To return home with the stranger would at least delay the confrontation and hopefully diffuse Pythia's anger at her negligence.

"That I would gladly receive," he answered and nodded his head. He did indeed desire a cool drink and some food but most of all he was curious to see the place that I had escaped from. He watched the nervous expression of the maid as they continued to walk back to my home and saw that her face stayed red.

"You know he didn't go so far. I only gathered him a few paces from where you found us," he lied with a smile.

The maid stopped and looked at the man. Then her face softened and she smiled also.

"Thank you," she replied, barely above a whisper and then continued on.

My mother having just put Eunomos down heard the gate closing and was at the door to greet us before anyone could summon her.

"Pythagoras!" she cried as she grabbed me from the maid and hugged me so tight I could barely breathe. "Don't you ever scare me like that again." Then with pure relief she burst into tears. As her tears wet my hair I knew I never would again. I now knew why I had hesitated at the door. It was not about breaking rules or putting myself in danger. It was about upsetting the order of what was and to make my mother cry was simply not worth it.

Her tears subsided and then she realised that another person stood with the maid. As he saw her eyes try to register his presence he spoke up as he bowed his head, "Good day Madam."

"This gentleman found the young master just a street away. I invited him to receive some drink and food," said the maid too quickly for Pythia's liking and received a harsh glance from her.

"But of course," Pythia said as she turned her gaze and tried to smile at the man. "I am eternally grateful, even if such a favour should never have been needed."

"It was no great deed," he answered softly and slightly bowed again. "In fact I feel honoured to have met a young boy with such character. He has the heart of an adventurer!"

"Yes indeed, spurred on by the ambitions that his father holds for him no doubt!" said Pythia and she tried to feign a slight laugh but her red eyes didn't make it seem much like a joke.

Eunomus now cried out once again from his crib. Having had his feed disturbed by my search, his belly now wanted to have the rest of its fill. Pythia handed me to the maid and turned to the man one last time, taking his hands in hers she lifted them to her mouth and kissed them.

"I thank you eternally for returning my son," she said. "Alas my next son calls out for his milk and I must go to him. My maids will see to it that you receive refreshments."

She let go of his hands and turned to leave the room.

"Come. Follow me," said the maid and led the way to the kitchen.

She sat me across the table from my rescuer and gathered some fruit and biscuits to place before us. Then she poured some wine for the man. We ate in silence though the man watched me with curiosity as I grabbed at grapes and popped them in my mouth. He sipped upon his wine and then asked the maid, "What trade does his father work in?"

"He is a gem trader," she answered plainly.

"He must do well" he answered as he gestured about the room, but meaning the entire home. Then he quickly put his hand down, realising the impetuousness of such a statement and within a home offering him hospitality.

"Yes, he does and mistress' family are also most generous to our household," she said wondering if she had spoken too much.

"Mmph…" responded the man as he watched me again. "So my young friend, what will you choose to do with such a life set out for you?" he asked me and leant into the table.

I merely laughed and ate another grape as I garbled a reply.

"I somehow imagine great things," he answered for himself and I nodded.

I did not know exactly what I was nodding at but I liked being spoken to like this—as my own father often spoke to me in such a manner also. It made me feel beyond the years that I was. It made me feel like I was the equal of the adults around me and that I was not merely the little child that I was expected to be at two years of age. At this time I still remembered too much from my past experiences to settle for that role but somehow I also instinctively knew that this would pass soon enough. Fortunately I remembered the special joys of childhood. I also recalled the burden of responsibility that came with increased age and that was something I was not in a hurry to return to just yet.

The man opposite me swallowed the last of his biscuit and threw back the last of his wine. "I imagine that is enough time and food to feel rewarded for your safe return," he joked as he stood up from the table. "I thank you for your hospitality," he said to the maid before leaving. He was almost to the door with the maid and me trailing him when he turned to me one last time.

"Good luck with your future adventures, little one," he said with one last laugh and then he was gone.

He made his way back through the laneways and into the bustle of the market and then out the opposite side to head towards the docks. He was almost there when he heard his name called out.

"Anaximander! Where have you been? We've almost missed our boat thanks to you!" the voice cried out.

"I had a most intriguing encounter," Anaximander said, smiling broadly and picking up his pace as he approached his friend.

"Really? Well it better be a good story to save you from a lecture from the Teacher when he sees you," his friend replied and waved him in the direction of the boat they were to catch.

"Oh it is. I met the most extraordinary child. I don't know what drew me to him—or him to me—but we were supposed to meet today. I just know it," said Anaximander as they walked quickly together along the pier. "Perhaps one day we will cross paths again."

CHAPTER FOUR

My sense of adventure did not diminish so much after that day but happily I soon had another way for it to be expressed. It was only another year later, when I was just over the age of three that my father decided to take me with him upon his smaller journeys. My mother's resistance to this was strong and vocal but she knew that there was no stopping Mnesarchus in his quest for my grandeur.

"Have I ever come to harm upon my travels my darling?" he asked of her as she cried through her protests. "I promise I will only take him upon my smaller trips for now. Besides he has never seen my family or birthplace—surely I have the right for my son to know these parts of my life."

It was only then that Pythia felt some comfort and she also recalled the words of the oracle. "I imagine if he is destined to be known by many then he must experience such things," she said resignedly.

"Yes my dear, and surely the gods will protect someone who they have declared to do great things," answered Mnesarchus with his ambitions for me now fired up again.

So my mother came to the docks with Eunomus upon her hip and tears pouring down her face. She waved goodbye to my father and I as the boat slid from the dock. I watched her for as long as I could, fascinated to see her and my brother growing smaller and smaller. Then realising that Samos too was growing smaller.

Suddenly I could see the entire shoreline and then within a short time more I could see the very limits of the island. I now realised that this place which had been my entire world was just a small piece of something much larger. Soon it was gone altogether and another world appeared across the waters.

This fascinated me, that one place could disappear and another appear just by moving the boat across water. I walked the deck with my father, stumbling as the boat hit waves and sometimes falling. This was much to the amusement of my father who would grab me and stand me up. I watched as the sailors and even my father walked with ease, adjusting to the rolls and dips of the boat as though they expected them. Yet here I was as though I had only just learnt to use my legs.

"You will get your sea legs too, Pythagoras!" Mnesarchus said as he gathered me up yet again. "It's just about getting used to it."

I did finally get my footing but it seemed I had only just done this when the sailors started to call out to each other as we were approaching a dock. Ropes were thrown, sails were rolled and then there was the bump and scrape as we made our way into our berth.

Back upon land, I now had to readjust once again. Only it was not just my legs that needed to reset themselves. I looked up at the sky and it looked the same but the sun felt different. The light it shone felt like it wanted to burn me and the breeze here was not as gentle as it was at home. Like Samos there were swarms of men upon the docks and though they looked like my father their faces were much harder and darker.

I grabbed at my father's clothes as hard as I could. I knew if I lost my way here I would never find my way home to my mother. Mnesarchus looked down and smiled at me.

"Ah, you know you are somewhere different don't you?" he said and lifted me into his arms. "Get accustomed to different faces and ways Pythagoras. You will be seeing so much in your life which is why I bring you here—so you will be used to many things by your manhood."

Mnesarchus carried me away from the boats as a young ship hand carried our few bags. As the crowds thinned my father's pace picked up and he called out a name and then spoke words I did not know. "Eli! Thank the gods to see you here," he said in his native tongue to his brother who sat upon a cart with two donkeys before it.

"What sort of brother does not come to gather his family after such a voyage," he answered and then looked at me. "My, my, look at your son. He has your blood no doubt Mnesarchus. Father will be most proud when he sees him."

My father hoisted me upon the seat beside Eli as he directed the ship hand to put the bags upon the cart. Mnesarchus then lifted himself up next to me and with both men talking in more words that I did not know we began to make our way.

I'm not sure when I fell asleep but it was well before we arrived at my grandfather's farm. Even the noise of the family greeting us upon our entrance or being lifted from the cart did not wake me. When I did stir I was in a simple bed stuffed with hay that smelt like the markets on the days they sold live animals. I looked around and the momentary panic of realising that I was somewhere unfamiliar was eased as I heard my father's voice from nearby, albeit once again speaking Phoenician. I looked under the bed for a pot, as I had more urgent matters to attend to than making my way to find my father just yet.

But there was no "under the bed" here as I realised that my mattress was in fact upon the floor. I looked around nervously and soon saw a pot in the corner of the room. It didn't look the one I had at home but it would do. I gathered my clothes up and aimed. As my urine hit the thin metal it sounded so loud, not like the heavy pot I was used to, and I jumped a little, splashing some over the side. I didn't care too much, as I was sure there would be a maid along soon to clean it just as there was if something like this happened at home. However no maid popped her head around the corner as they did within minutes of me waking in Samos, so I made my way towards the voices.

I didn't have too far to walk and now along with my father's voice I heard others all sounding the same but talking much louder. I made my way to a large open room. There was my father and Eli sitting upon huge pillows around a low table, joined now by a dozen other men all with faces that were a variance of my father's. Some were thinner, some rounder, some younger and there was one that was much, much older— that of my grandfather. They did not notice me until I was by my father's side and pressed myself against him, rubbing my eyes to get rid of the last of my sleep.

"Ah Pythagoras, you have woken and come to meet your family," Mnesarchus said in Greek so I understood him. He hugged me tight to him and kissed my forehead.

I looked up and saw my grandfather staring at me intently. When my eyes caught his, he smiled gently and looked up to my father.

"He is certainly of our blood, Son, but I can see the Greek in his eyes," Ruben said still smiling and even though I didn't know the words I knew he spoke of me.

"Yes Father, he holds some of his mother as well," my father replied and hugged me to him again.

Ruben nodded and held out some bread to me. "Here you must be hungry," he said and waved the bread as though that would help me understand what he said. There was no need, I understood perfectly and took the bread from his hand. Ruben grunted with satisfaction at having connected with me and then returned to the conversation around him.

We only stayed a week with my father's family and that included small day trips for my father to speak to local merchants and traders. However by the fourth day I could understand everything that was said. The simple words were the quickest to come to me so on the fifth day I sat at the dinner table, confidently pointed across to a dish and said "I want bread" in perfect Phoenician. The whole table went silent and looked to me. I dropped my hand thinking I had done something wrong but then just as quickly the men all erupted in cheers and laughter.

My father rubbed my hair and I don't believe he could have smiled more if he had tried to. "Well done, Pythagoras," he said as he passed the bread to me.

My father spent the rest of our time in Tyre speaking only Phoenician to me and I answered more than ably, rarely defaulting to Greek to fill in any gaps in my speech. Mnesarchus would just nod as I answered.

On our last day though as we prepared for our return to Samos he looked at me and in Greek asked "Do you remember your language from home?"

"Yes Father," I answered and then I tapped my head. "It is still here."

Mnesarchus laughed outright. "I should know better with you by now, Pythagoras. As I should have known you would teach yourself a new tongue."

I was so glad that our visit to Tyre was only short as was my father. As much as he enjoyed my company and showing me off to his family and others, it had not been so easy dealing with a small child on top of travelling and business. When I ran into our home calling out to my mother she came to greet me by hugging me tighter and crying even more than the day I had wandered away from home. As my father watched her crying with joy to have me back he knew that neither Pythia nor I were ready for me to travel as much as he thought. Well not just yet anyway.

When Pythia did finally settle and stop her crying she swept me up into her arms.

"Come, I will bathe you and while we wash you can tell me all about your adventure," she said and then she turned to Mnesarchus. "You could do with a bath as well, but I would like a kiss first."

This Mnesarchus duly did as always upon any return before he would have made way to bathe. This time though Pythia carrying me led the way. The maids had made the huge sunken bath ready and they now poured in some hot water. Mnesarchus sank into the water and leaned back relishing every sensation. On the other side I stood up on the stairs while my mother scooped water over me then washed me down with a cloth. All the while I spoke about the trip.

"Samos disappeared and then another even bigger place came before us... Their cheese tasted funny and so did their water...The bread was flat and grandfather used to eat it with everything even fruit and the fruit was not like ours... The bed was on the floor and it smelt like the markets… The sun made light that made my skin really hot…" and so I went on as my mother watched me smiling the whole time.

Mnesarchus sat quietly and did not say anything, even though he watched with amusement as I spoke about his homeland. Then just as it seemed I was finished he spoke in Phoenician to me, "Tell your mother of what else you learned."

Pythia looked over at Mnesarchus realising that he had spoken his native tongue and then looked back to me.

"He wants me to tell you that I can now speak Phoenician," I said plainly.

"Is that right?" she asked Mnesarchus.

Mnesarchus nodded and my mother looked to me and narrowed her eyes. "But it has only been a week. Most people need months to learn a language."

"Yes, well our son is not 'most people' my beloved," Mnesarchus said as he laughed. "Tell your mother in Phoenician about the boat ride home."

This I did only faltering every so often to find a word. When I finished Pythia turned to Mnesarchus and raised an eyebrow.

"He only said three words wrongly," he said smiling.

Pythia looked back to me and pushed my hair away from my brow. "Well my son, you certainly are most clever."

It was from that day onwards that Pythia began to take my father's training of me more seriously. Mnesarchus now chose to nurture my ability with languages and spoke Phoenician with me as often as Greek to ensure I did not lose my new knowledge. When he was away then Pythia would continue this, asking me to repeat sentences in this foreign language. Even though she could not correct me she knew I was retaining and reinforcing my ability.

A few months later when my father felt I had the full grasp of Phoenician and he could see that it didn't compromise my native tongue he began teaching me Aramaic. This was really just a derivative of Phoenician anyway so the skill was in being able to meld my tongue to the differences in tone and remembering the small nuances of different nouns. For a young mind still free to grow this was also not a huge challenge.

"I only wish I knew to speak Egyptian that I might teach this also," said Mnesarchus when I had mastered Aramaic.

Somehow I instinctively knew that this was not an issue and

decided even at that young age that I would learn this language also to make my father happy.

While Mnesarchus had focussed somewhat on my spoken language Pythia decided that it would also be of benefit to start my knowledge of written language. I was still a year or two off from what was formally considered the age to begin writing, but now like my father had from my birth, my mother didn't consider me to be part of such conventions.

One day while Mnesarchus was away on a business trip my mother put on one of her nicer gowns and dressed me and Eunomus just as respectably. Then with Eunomus upon the hip of a maid behind her, she took me by the hand and we walked to the huge temple on the outskirts of the city. The largest temple upon Samos was also the home of the wisest men of the island. Or so she thought.

For in Greece at this time there was a new division growing between religion and knowledge. The wise men of the temples were slowly being usurped by a new breed of sage that did not give the gods credit for all that surrounded us. Science and philosophy were making their mark upon society and now being regarded as powerful as anything taught at temples by the holy men.

So when my mother arrived at the temple with me by her side and began to spruik my talents in the hope I would be chosen as a student by these men, they did not rejoice as they would have done in the decades beforehand. Instead their blood now raced with fear that here was yet another "truth-seeker" who could undo their ways.

It was the eldest priest of the church whose face grew the darkest as my mother spoke. He eyed me as she talked and I felt his gaze burn me so much so that I had to look away. Each time that I did allow my eyes to go back to him I felt that heat again and turned away. My mother finished speaking and the elder leant forward towards me.

"What is your name?" he said in Aramaic and I answered my name.

"Where do you live?" he asked in Phoenician and I answered him in Greek which made him laugh at first. "Answer in Phoenician," he snapped and this I did.

Pythia could tell that such simple talk did not impress the old men at all. The elder's laughter was full of mocking and even when I did answer in Phoenician he still smiled broadly.

"Why don't you tell them about your trip to Tyre—in Phoenician?" she asked me softly.

The elder grunted as though he had already decided not to be impressed. I spoke anyway not wanting to disappoint my mother. The smile gradually fell from the elder's face and his eyes grew dark again.

"Very impressive Madam," he said with a drawl to Pythia. "But you could have been preparing him for this and I am just seeing a well rehearsed performance."

"Then Sir, you choose a topic," she said curtly resisting every indignation that made her want to say much more.

"Mmph…" grunted the elder. "Tell me of the history of Samos—in Aramaic."

"Sir, he is too young to know such things," protested Pythia.

"Well then, what do you know of young man," he said to me and laughed once more.

"I could tell you about the day I went to the markets on my own," I offered hardly looking up at the man.

"Fine," he said throwing his hand in the air, "Tell me of that day—in Aramaic!"

So this I did in such detail that now the priests smiled once again. This time however there was no mocking in their expressions. The elder's eyes remained dark though.

"Tell the story again in Phoenician," the elder snapped.

This I did and as is when retelling a story, enough was changed so that he knew that nothing that I spoke had been rehearsed. Now his heart raced as he listened to me. As I finished I saw him take a deep breath and he clenched his hands into fists and he turned to my mother.

"And just what do you hope to achieve by bringing him here when it seems you are doing quite well tutoring him?" he asked tersely.

"I wish that he might study here so as to learn the writing of each language. My husband travels so any tuition from him is sporadic and broken. If you were to take him as a student then it would be more consistent …and your knowledge would be wider," she added this at the end knowing she had to pander to their egos somewhat. She knew that Mnesarchus was as knowledgeable from his travels as any of the men before her.

The elder turned and went to sit down. He grunted as he straightened his clothes around him then squared his shoulders as he looked back up at my mother.

"If we accept him here as a student then he learns the way of the priesthood," he said bluntly. "We are not concerned with simply being a school for gifted children."

At this my mother froze. Mnesarchus and she had no dreams of me being a priest with its inevitable limitations. This would mean no studies outside of the lessons taught in temple, no travelling, and no children to carry on our family. She now realised just what a mistake she had made in bringing me to the temple.

Pythia lowered her eyes to try and hide her disappointment but it was too late as the priests had seen it.

"Go home now and remember your place in society. The gods set such order and in your heart you know it! Do not trouble us again to try and elevate your family beyond anything you are unless it is to serve the gods," said the eldest.

With this Pythia gently nodded her head to acknowledge the men but she could not bring herself to say any words. She took me by the hand and led me from the temple to make our way home.

It was with a tense silence that we walked home. I could feel my mother's disappointment which of course I believed was caused by me. I thought my behaviour had led to the priest's harsh words and now her sorrow. I looked up every few minutes but her face did not change and her eyes stayed dark. Finally I worked up the nerve to speak.

"Mama, I am sorry I did not do better," I said softly.

She stopped and looked to me, her face still hard. "No my darling, you did fine. It was I who made the error today. One day I may have to ask you to forgive me."

This puzzled me. What could she have done wrong? I certainly saw no mistake on her part. Pythia was my mother and as always she was perfect. What I did not know was that she now had to face my father and tell him of what she had done. The one time that she had stepped into the process of my education had caused me, and her family to be mocked— and by the local priesthood. This would make its way through the town she was sure. Pythia now felt that she had ruined anything for me that Mnesarchus had worked towards.

"*Perhaps we could move to the mainland and begin again there,*" she thought to herself as she walked.

Mnesarchus was indeed unimpressed when Pythia, full of shame, retold the story. His face turned red and Pythia thought she would now have to bear the brunt of his anger. It was not Pythia's actions that angered my father though; it was the attitude of the priests and he understood exactly what had happened.

"Narrow-minded fools!" he shouted. "They just fear losing their positions and power. One day they will cry with joy that he is a son of Samos and want to claim a part in his glory but it will be too late. Their actions today are a sad loss for this island. Pythia, you mark my words!"

Pythia nodded as he spoke, utterly relieved to be told that it was the priests who had done wrong.

So my parents continued on with my teaching. Eunomus was soon walking and talking and though he was actually just as intelligent he always paled beside me due to the sheer fact that I was ahead of him. My youngest brother, Tyrrhenus, joined us when I was almost five and our family was complete.

The few years I had ahead of my brothers soon became a luxury to me and somewhat of a curse to them. I was always so far in advance of them both that, even though they were just as likely to achieve the same as me, my parents, in particular my father, always seemed to focus upon my nurturing. Though they would never admit to it, they truly believed I was the family's blessing and that my brother's were lucky to have someone as special as me as their eldest sibling. So my parents continued with the belief that my natural abilities would serve to teach Eunomus and Tyrrhenus.

It was after Tyrrhenus was born that my father decided I was now old enough to travel more with him and my mother this time agreed. This travel they decided would spread my wings so to speak. It would enrich my abilities with language and I would cross paths with teachers from all over who might open up another talent yet to be discovered. It was also my father's opportunity to begin to make my name known.

"Every little seed, no matter how small, grows and bears some fruit to carry on," he once said to my mother.

This was (and is) indeed true. Every little action and experience leads to something whether it is perceived as good or bad. It simply moves us forward into our experience. A chance encounter can lead to something much more. The decision to stop and have a glass of wine can lead you to the love of your life. Mnesarchus understood this better than anyone. So even though my mother cried as much as she did the first time I left with my father, Mnesarchus did not let this affect him and what he knew needed to be done.

This time the boat did not travel south to Tyre. Instead we made the short journey across to the mainland that we could see from the eastern edge of Samos. We were soon upon the lands of Anatolia which you now know as Turkey. Then upon a hired cart we made our way inland to the region known as Persia.

I was delighted and more than able to practise my extra languages and became quite the entertainer for anyone who crossed our path. I knew when to be quiet too though as I grasped immediately the difference between my father making small talk and when he was

81

brokering a business deal. I did listen occasionally but when I felt him slip into his business mode of speaking I would let my attentions drift elsewhere. The talk of figures surprisingly did not interest me given the way that mathematics would eventually consume me. This was because I knew the discussion was not so much about numbers as it was a power play that eventuated in who would gain the most money from the interaction.

I worked out money quite quickly in my youth. Surrounded by wealth from birth I knew that I had all I needed or could want for, due to my family's wealth. I walked the markets and understood that the exchange of goods and service was all about money so that those trading could attain the goods and services they in turn required. It all seemed so circular and I realised it was just a cycle of exchange. Those pieces of silver and gold, and occasionally promissory notes were just symbols of this. As soon as someone handed another these tokens, as soon as someone offered the goods they had created, they simply entered into the cycle and process. In its simplest form it was pure and beautiful; a way to honour the inextricable links we make with one another to become part of a society. In its darkest form it becomes a play on power and control.

While I loved my father unconditionally I knew that he walked the fine line of this darkness in business. I also knew that he did this for his family more than his ego or pride. The element of survival was strong in his business practice. Still this did little to entice me to want to study this anymore than I needed to. So I would sit and let my attentions go to those things that did interest me.

I was fascinated at how the sun could change its ways after an hour or two of travelling. It was still the same sun I was sure, but that its heat or light could change intrigued me. Then there was the soil; dark and soft close to the waters then light and flowing freely through my fingers as we travelled to the arid plains.

I even loved the differences in the people. The way their skin changed colours as we travelled, the different clothes, even the way they walked differently. It all enthralled me. I could see the commonalities that all people possessed and how these differences were so superficial. So it surprised me to no end that someone would seem shocked when I would run up to them, intrigued by their clothes or mannerisms and speak their language hoping to find out more about them. It was as though some strange animal was about to attack them. They would cry, "Away, away!" as they waved their hands at me.

Mnesarchus would run and gather me in his arms as he offered an apology. Then he finally lectured me, "Son, you have to understand you are different here."

"But we are not so different and I can speak the same," I protested.

"Yes but they do not understand that. Most people have not travelled or done business as we have. Their lives are simple and anything that differs scares them," Mnesarchus offered knowing full well that it was an explanation that was not satisfying to either of us.

"Father, that is sad," was all I could respond with.

So I eventually settled with observing from a distance and perhaps this was better. Sometimes it helped me see even more and then I did not have to deal with their emotions which only ever confused things. So I would sit in a taverna as my father dealt with a local trader and watch as people passed by in the streets making up stories about them. I would see a woman leading two children while she balanced a basket on her head. I would decide that she was widowed and her children had to help her gather food from the hillside outside their village. I could entertain myself endlessly as I ate my biscuits or whatever local treat was placed before me.

The only times I grew frustrated sitting beside my father as he dealt with business was when he did so within a trader's home. This rarely offered me a window to view passersby, so I would have to entertain myself with soaking up the details of my surroundings. I would be fascinated by how they were decorated or what the home was constructed with.

One time in Persia I was so overwhelmed at the endless ornaments and embellished fabrics in the huge room around us that my head would not stop moving, much to Mnesarchus' embarrassment. As the trader's servant carried in a huge tray with tea and sweets, Mnesarchus took the break in conversation as an opportunity to quietly reprimand me.

"Pythagoras! Will you find some manners and be still!" he hissed.

"Oh Mnesarchus, your boy is more than well-behaved. I am impressed that only his neck moves. Any other child would have been running about the room touching everything they could reach by now," laughed the trader and then gestured to the servant. "Take the boy and entertain him."

So the tall, dark servant led me out of the room. I followed him down the corridor and was amazed at how he walked so softly that his sandals barely made a sound upon the stone floor. His arms were crossed behind his back so that his right wrist was encircled within his left hand. He looked forward and his chin was slightly raised as he floated along and I realised, even as young as I was, that his posture was part of his role.

Then just when I least expected it, without even slowing, he turned his head to look at me and I saw him allow a smile to cross his face. I felt him want to say something but he needn't have used any words. It was the most playful smile I had ever seen and one I had never seen upon an adult. I returned the smile and that was when he stopped and turned to me, his arms remaining behind his back and he bent slightly forward to meet my height.

"So young traveller, just how should I be entertaining you?" he said softly but never losing his smile.

"Might we go outdoors?" I asked back just as softly, understanding this was part of the game.

The servant straightened his back. "A wonderful idea!" he answered and smiled even broader. Then he turned and continued walking, turning eventually to face a large double doorway. He finally brought his hands out from behind his back and opened the doors, then stepped to the side and signalled for me to walk through. His hands returned behind his back the moment the gesture was completed.

I walked through the doors into a garden and was immediately taken by its beauty. Three walls surrounded the space, joining onto the house so that it was entirely enclosed. I could hear some noise from the city but it was not enough to spoil the privacy that this place owned. A fountain bubbling in the centre seemed to take over any sounds here. I took a few steps forward and then stopped, looking back at the servant, unsure of how free I was to explore.

"Keep going. You are quite safe," he said while he stood straight. "I will fetch you something to eat and drink. I will return soon. In the meantime play to your heart's content," he said and turned to walk back through the doors.

So I did just this and ventured all over. There were paths to lead you amongst the plants, statues stood as though watching over everything, and then I would find a seat to rest a moment.

I was grateful when I heard the servant call out to me as my stomach had begun to dance with hunger. I walked towards the doorway and saw he had been joined by two other servants who carried a small table and chair. They arranged the setting and the first servant placed a tray upon it.

"Sit," he said and pointed to the only chair.

So I did and upon the table before me he poured me some tea. As I sipped upon the hot drink he once again smiled at me as he uncovered a plate filled with fruit and bread. He lifted the plate to me and I took a piece of pear to have with my tea. Then I saw beside the plate a beautiful tin. It was octagonal with the most beautiful pattern upon its lid and sides. It even had some crystals to embellish the design. I could not take my eyes off it and the servant noticed.

"Once you are done with the fruit you can have some sweets," he said with a half smile.

"I am done with my fruit now," I said and smiled at him. I would have loved some more fruit but I was too intrigued as to what this tin held.

"Very well," he answered and bowed. He then pulled at the lid of the tin, setting it to the side. I leant forward, looked within and was sorely disappointed. All I could see was white powder. My disappointment must have been clearly upon my face because the servant chuckled.

"Oh there is much more than sugar dust in here," he assured me.

Then using a small pair of gold tongs he reached into the dust and pulled out a small cube of something that looked nothing more than a solid piece of sugar dust. He placed it upon my plate.

"Try it," he coaxed, "I promise you will like it."

So I lifted the cube, leaving a trail of white dust from the plate and up my chest towards my mouth. I could smell its intense sweetness before it even touched my lips and when this combined with the sensation it gave my mouth, I surrendered to the most delightful experience. My first mouthful melted upon my tongue, the sweetness seemed to now give way to my tongue being covered in a velvet jelly and then the sweetness was everywhere.

Now I had sweets before but this was like nothing I had ever tried. That day I revelled in the new sensation. It was beyond just trying a new food. It was opening a whole new experience with sensation. It was the gentle bubbling of the fountain, the dappled sunlight through the trees, the scent of the tea in its glass, the tickle of the sugar powder under my nose and that rich jelly coating my tongue. They all combined together in a moment I knew, even at that young age, could never be replicated.

"Would you like another?" asked the servant, once again grinning as he watched me.

All I could do was nod and another cube was placed upon my plate. Four more followed and then suddenly I was done. I finally reached that place where no matter how much I enjoyed the experience, my physical self could not continue. I was almost thankful that at that moment another servant appeared and announced that my father's business was completed and I should return to him. I almost sighed with relief and then took one last look at that tin filled with its treats. Then my reverie was called to an end as the servant stepped forward and grabbed my napkin.

"We can't have you return to your father covered in sugar," he laughed and began brushing at the dusting of sugar that was down the front of my clothes.

He gave my mouth one quick wipe which thankfully wasn't able to remove all the sweetness so that as I walked back to my father a quick lick of my lips helped me relive the taste of the sweet. I watched the servant as we walked back and noticed that as we approached the room where his master and my father waited, he slowed down a little, the smile that had been upon his face once again dissolved and he adjusted his hands so that they sat behind his back in the manner they should before his employer. This made me a little sad, but I knew such things well enough from my own home, so that when he opened the door and gestured for me to re-enter the room I too kept my smile hidden and simply nodded to him as a farewell and thank you. Then he was gone.

"Ah, did my servants treat you well?" asked the trader.

"Yes, they did," I answered. "I had the most delicious sweets," I added and then I could not contain my smile.

"Oh yes," beamed the trader. "That is my cook, the most talented woman in Persia. She could win a war with her sweets." With this he yelled out to his servant who appeared again miraculously at an instant. "Gather some sweets for our young friend to take home as a gift."

Mnesarchus politely protested but the trader quietened him with the wave of his hand. "After your generous deal it would be only fitting to offer you a small gift in return."

We were at the front doors of the trader's home making our final farewells when the servant appeared holding the beautiful octagonal tin in his hands. He handed it to the trader who then bent down to hand it to me.

"Enjoy young man. May you remember your visit to Persia with every taste!" he said and cupped my face in his hand.

I looked up and said a simple thank you. Over his shoulder I saw his servant steal me a smile which disappeared as quickly as it was offered.

I sat upon the cart as we made our way back west clutching the tin like it was a treasure I had searched my whole life for. At night when we stopped at an inn I would open the lid carefully so as not to lose one speck of that magic sugar dust. I would smell in its sweetness so deeply that sometimes I could feel the sugar tickling inside my nose. But not once did I have a piece. I wanted to wait until I returned home. I wanted to sit in my own garden with some tea or wine and relive that moment in Persia. Also too I wanted to share this with my mother and brothers.

We were on the final leg of journeying to the shore to catch the boat back to Samos. As per the rest of the trip the octagonal tin sat upon my lap and I nursed it with both hands. I slowly lifted the lid and stared into the white powder, then for the first time I dipped my fingers in and felt amongst the sugar. I could feel the cubes nestled in there and noted that the tin had been refilled. The pieces I had eaten replaced by the trader's staff so that I would have a full tin as a gift.

I looked at the amount and then thought of the people to share it with. I gently pushed the cubes into four groups; one for me, one for my mother, one for Eunomus and one for Mnesarchus. My youngest brother was of no concern as he was still only on milk. Then I thought of my grandparents and our maids. Surely they too would like some. So I divided the groups yet again. Looking down at dismay at how small an amount this was for each person, and especially myself, I pushed the cubes back into four groups and decided that my parents and brother were more than enough to share with.

"Pythagoras, if you keep playing with them they will drink that sugar and you will have nothing but one sticky mess!" Mnesarchus joked.

Despite his joking this horrified me to think of my precious sweets ruined. I had one last quick look at the four groups, pushed the sugar dust back around to cover them as best I could, and then quickly closed the lid. I did not open the tin again until I was safe within my home.

Back in my own garden with my mother and Eunomus sitting with me we each lifted the dust covered cubes to our mouths. I closed my eyes and tried to imagine that I was back in the garden at Persia but I knew instantly that it could never be the same. The smells and sounds of our garden were different. Here the air was damp and this in itself changed even the taste of the jelly as it hit my tongue.

I opened my eyes to see my mother's eyes squinting from the intense sweetness as she brushed the sugar from the front of her dress.

"Oh my," she said feigning a smile so as not to upset me. "And I thought our sweets were rich!"

Eunomus still worked upon his mouthful that was now like glue between his tongue and teeth.

"Do you like it?" I asked him.

I received a wide-eyed smile and a nod as an answer. What child could not delight in something so disgustingly sweet and messy.

"Thank you for sharing such a treat with us, Pythagoras," my mother said as she took a sip of some tea which I am now sure was to dilute the sweetness in her mouth.

I took another cube and put it in my mouth. I closed my eyes again for a moment and thought of the garden in Persia again just quickly. I saw it clearly and heard its sounds again. Then I opened my eyes and it was gone. I was home with my family.

What was here was real and happening. My past was gone. I carried something with me to remind me of what it was that I had done but here that thing was different; changed by the circumstance of its surrounds and even the people I shared the moment with.

I was too young to truly know just what all this meant but I would come to understand that each moment is its own creation. Each moment is unique. That although we have objects or remembrances that we carry with us from one moment to the next, each moment in itself is a completely new way for those things to be experienced.

A maid came in to clear our garden tea party. I watched as she closed the lid upon the tin of my Persian sweets and I wondered what they would taste like the next time I ate some.

The years between the ages of five and ten were all very similar. I studied more and travelled more. My parents grew increasingly protective of me and my talents but they balanced this with letting me have some independence and sense of being a child. It was something they inherently allowed of themselves but I also found ways to encourage this.

One day when I was eight I asked that I might explore some of the shoreline near our home. After the usual lecture on safety and to make my way home as soon as the sun began to lower itself, I set off with Eunomus by my side, a knapsack of food and a canteen for water.

"Where are we going?" Eunomus asked as we headed along the road that led out of the town.

"We are going to find somewhere new to experience," was my answer.

"Experience what?" he pushed.

"Well as it is new I do not know yet," I answered somewhat frustrated.

"But what if we get lost?" Eunomus now whimpered.

"We live on an island. How can we get lost when there is nowhere else to be but here! Now if that scares you too much perhaps you would like to go home and play baby games with Tyrrhenus" I yelled.

"No!" Eunomus screwed up his face as though he was trying not to cry. "I want to have an adventure with you."

"Fine! Then be brave and stop saying stupid things," I snapped.

We walked on quietly for a while as Eunomus was now too scared to say anything from fear that he would be returned home. I too was quiet as I scanned ahead looking for a place for us to explore.

We could soon hear the sound of waves upon rocks and this was my signal to now walk away from the edge of the roadside. I took Eunomus by the hand when needed to guide him down the rough incline that led down to the water. Sometimes I would even lift him over a rock or down a space that would have been too hard for his small legs.

Finally we sat upon a huge rock that was on the water's edge. It was a few feet from where the waves broke but occasionally a large wave would send a mist over us making Eunomus at first shriek but then giggle as the waves repeated. I took some bread and cheese out of the bag and handed it to Eunomus.

"We will sit for a while and watch the waves," I said and he nodded, happy to be resting and eating.

I sat and as I chewed, I counted. I counted how many waves it took in-between the ones that sent salty mist over us. I counted the space between each wave. I watched how they crashed upon the smaller rocks and dissolved. I saw how the water curled around the rocks and became part of the wave that was coming in. It soon became predictable and I grew bored.

"Let's find somewhere else," I announced and we made our way slowly back up the hill.

We walked further along the road until we came to a cliff top overlooking the ocean.

"Please don't make me climb down there," Eunomus begged as he peered down the huge drop.

"We don't need to," I answered and lay down at the edge looking over it.

Eunomus lay beside me and as I began to watch and count the waves he fell asleep. This I was grateful for. I knew that he would sleep for at least an hour having exhausted him with walking and climbing. Now I could study in absolute silence apart from the sounds of the ocean and the occasional cart that passed by.

I saw that the waves carried the same cycle of building up and then diminishing. I saw how the crashing upon the rocks here blunted the edges of the waves, shaping them into an arrow head and I saw how the rock that was hit by the peak of this arrow head was being worn away more rapidly than those either side of it. I looked further out into the ocean and watched how the belly of the sea rose so slightly. In fact from a distance it looked like it was just rising up and down. Yet this movement was travelling towards the shore where it would turn into the speeding and churning white water upon the rocks.

I watched mesmerised at how it all worked together and then I too fell asleep.

It was Eunomus who woke me, shaking my shoulder and calling my name.

"Pythagoras! Pythagoras! The sun is falling and we should get home," he cried.

I rolled onto my back and squinted into the sun as I stretched. The sun was barely beginning to set but we still had a long walk home. I sat up and had a drink of water as Eunomus relieved his bladder against a tree near by. This made my own bladder suddenly desire the same so I got to my feet and found my own tree.

As I let my body do its thing while still half asleep, I stared back out at the ocean and saw the same patterns of waves within the water. I let my robes fall back down against my legs and turned to see where Eunomus was. He was standing at the roadside clearly anxious to be going home.

"Let's go home little brother," I said and began to walk with Eunomus following close beside me.

"This was not the most exciting adventure, Pythagoras," he said bluntly. "All we did was walk and look at waves."

"Well I saw more than that, Eunomus," I said back just as bluntly. "Perhaps when you are older your eyes will let you see more."

Eunomus frowned and looked down at the road. He barely spoke again all the way home.

Mnesarchus was waiting when we returned. He gathered us in turn in his arms to hug us and ask about our day. As usual it was I who dominated the conversation describing what I had noticed about the waves and their patterns. Mnesarchus nodded as he listened with Eunomus in his lap.

"Very good Son," he finally said. "You observed today the very principles of the waves that sailors learn to move ships by." Then he turned Eunomus in his lap to face him. "And what of you second son, did you see such things also."

I didn't wait to hear my brother's reply and snorted as a response making Mnesarchus look at me wide-eyed.

"He is too young to see such things," I said with all the arrogance I could muster.

"And did it occur to you to share what you were observing?" Mnesarchus asked while raising his eyebrows.

I hung my head and muttered, "Well he fell asleep."

"And was he asleep the entire time. There were surely many opportunities to converse," Mnesarchus continued. "Pythagoras, knowledge is a wonderful asset but it is worth nothing if you do not share it. Remember that as you seek the knowledge of the elders who gather wisdom ahead of you. A clever man knows much, a wise man shares and serves all wisdom for the good of us all. Surely you choose wisdom?"

"Yes Father," I said softly, "I choose wisdom."

The situation with the priests upon Samos had not changed during the few years that had lapsed since my mother took me to see them. Philosophy was still making its presence known and as scientific knowledge grew, new schools began to emerge through the Middle East and down into Egypt. The temples that flourished were the ones to embrace the expanded thinking and new concepts.

This is not to say that the old style schools disappeared. They remained too but even more protected than before. By this I refer to the "true" old schools; the ones that taught the ancient wisdoms in their pure forms. These schools would never disappear. They just became harder to find.

Mnesarchus returned from one of his rare trips at this time with a smile upon his face that seemed wider than his skull. He had been into Babylonia and as always had explored whatever was happening within the schools there. It was at one such place that he got his grandest idea yet and couldn't wait to return home.

"We do not need the old temples to teach our sons," He said loudly to Pythia. "We will build our own."

So upon a nearby cliff top the trees were cleared and our very own temple was built.

When it was complete Mnesarchus had it dedicated to Apollo, in honour of the oracles who served under this god and who spoke of the life I would live. The dedication was performed by a young priest, called from the mainland as none of the local priests would be involved in what they saw as a sacrilegious indulgence. His hands shook as he performed the rites; a combination of his inexperience and the knowledge that the local priesthood had declared our temple a blight upon the gods.

Blight or not, our temple was beautiful and it served our family well. Mnesarchus invited scholars, philosophers and artists to visit with us and share their knowledge.

I would sit for hours thoroughly engaged with all that was shared while Eunomus and Tyrrhenus would fidget. Their lack of interest frustrated me to no end, but I tolerated it as long as they did not interfere with my learning.

I decided one thing as I watched them waste what was being offered. Wisdom may be a wonderful thing to share but it is lost upon those who have no true desire for it.

I thank my brothers for helping me decide that while a student should be selective of his teachers, a teacher should be even more selective of their students. I decided I would never waste anything I learnt or knew upon anyone who was not truly committed to learning.

If my father was disappointed in my younger brothers' disinterest in learning he certainly never showed it or spoke of it. He merely enforced the ideals that a certain level of education needed to be met by them and they, as all respectful children do, followed the ways set by their father. Mnesarchus knew how far he could push this and he did not fight it. Instead he just put his focus where he knew it would flourish; upon me.

Even though he did not travel so much with business these days he made excuses to travel with me by his side. Instead of spending days dealing with other traders or miners, he now travelled different ways to find the schools, monasteries and the occasional hermit, who all held the ancient wisdoms that he knew I would understand.

At eleven years of age I sat in a cave in a cliff face deep in Persia and was asked by a magus to look out upon the scene below me and tell him what it was that I saw. I looked out and described the village and the roads leading to it and the rise of the hills around it. The magus shook his head and said, "Look again."

I leaned forward as though I must have missed something. Then realised what I had missed. I described the colour of the soil, the curve of the few trees that dotted the landscape and the way the wind with the sand had curved the side of the hills.

The magus shook his head again but then he smiled, "Your mind is a wonderful thing young man and developing well. Do not forget the other parts of you though."

Mnesarchus sat and waited at the base of the cliff for me. As I wandered back down with my brow so creased you could have planted seeds in it, he jumped up.

"What happened?" he asked and now his brow looked like mine.

"Apparently there are parts of me that I am neglecting!" I declared.

"Ridiculous!" cried Mnesarchus. "You are healthy of body and sound of mind. What more could you need?"

This weighed upon me as I travelled home. What had the magus expected me to see? Did he expect me to have visions as the oracles did? And how would such visions serve me as I gained my wisdom and knowledge?

But also what were these parts of me that I was missing? I looked upon my body and saw how fit and strong it was and had always been. I looked out to the distance and then drew my hand close to my face focussing upon the lines on my fingertips. My vision was perfect. My ears and sense of touch were also as they should be. I closed my eyes and pictured my home. I recalled a lesson I had learnt a year ago. All these thoughts were uninterrupted and clear.

Then I felt a flash of something. It was quick but the sense of it lingered even as I opened my eyes. I looked back around me and then lifted my hand again. Everything looked the same but they felt different. I could not put words to it and this simultaneously scared and fascinated me. I sighed deeply and Mnesarchus sitting beside me on the cart turned to me.

"What is it?" he asked.

"I don't know," was all I could reply.

Back in the quiet of my own home I sat once more and I decided to repeat the things I had done that somehow summoned this "thing" I did not understand. I will admit I did it with that fear that the unknown strikes in all men. This thing could undo me or overtake me but my fear of it was matched by my determinedness to understand it and rule over it.

So once again I looked all about me then to the fine lines upon my hand. I touched the arm of the chair upon which I sat and the texture of the robes that wrapped around me. I listened for the sounds in the distance of the maids doing their duties in other parts of the house. Then

I closed my eyes and I heard the sound of my breath and felt my heart pumping inside my chest. That was when the "thing" came back.

This time it was not like a flash of lightning. This time it was like a warm wave washing over me. The sudden desire to escape it came but I heard myself say, *"no, let's explore this more,"* and I did. Everything outside of me was suddenly gone; there were no noises from my home. All I could hear was my heartbeat and my breath as it made its way in and out of my nose. As I surrendered to the "thing", these became stronger and louder until I felt the world had disappeared.

That was when I decided to open my eyes. When I did, I did not see the room as it was upon Samos. Instead I saw a room three times the size, made of sandstone and carved and painted with symbols. I looked down and saw my chest was bare and a skirt was wrapped around my waist. My skin was much darker and I felt a weight upon my head and shoulders.

I closed my eyes again, feeling my breath and heart quicken. I decided that I had played with the "thing" enough.

"No more!" I said aloud.

When I opened my eyes the room was as it had always been though my eyes took some time to adjust. I put my hand upon my chest and felt my heart was pounding. I needed some water but as I stood to make my way to the kitchen my legs swayed beneath me and I fell back into the chair. It was as though my body was not mine in that moment. I realised that this was the power of the "thing"; to separate me from my body as though it didn't need to work with me as a whole being.

I decided that I would not play with it again.

In the next few years as my father and I travelled I avoided the magi and the oracles. I had no interest in their investment in the "thing". Besides they truly did not know how to teach about it and the few I did ask would simply say such things as "You need to tell me about it!" or "That which cannot be seen needs to be felt and known, not talked about."

This I decided was a ridiculous way to speak of knowledge and did not serve my quest to gain wisdom. Instead I focussed upon the men who would teach me the patterns of numbers, the paths of the stars and intricacies of music. As soon as they would begin with talk of anything but what they could show me on a scroll or speak to my ears, Mnesarchus would politely end the interaction.

"I will never understand why they insist on diluting their

knowledge with these other vapid fancies that serve no-one but themselves," he muttered one day after a teacher began to speak of "listening to my inner guide".

Mnesarchus' direction to my learning would end a year later. In my fifteenth year our travels together were no more as my father grew feeble. Then one day I returned from a walk to the sound of wailing coming from my home. In our salon laid out upon a sofa was the body of my father. He was found by a maid slumped at his writing desk. It must have been sudden and though I looked upon his body, hardly registering that I would not hear his voice again, a part of me rejoiced that he had not suffered a long slow illness.

Now he was laid out in his finest robes, having been washed and dabbed with oils. Mnesarchus would lie here for two days while my mother and all our family would cry by his side. Now all the people he had travelled to see, all the people he had helped with their businesses and all the ones who had traded with him would travel to see him one last time. They would weep as they saw his body and offer a gentle kiss to my mother and a polite nod to me and my brothers.

I sat one evening after the mourners had left. Lamps had been lit by the maids and the waxy look upon Mnesarchus' face was now exaggerated. I had noticed that as the few days had passed his face had changed even more. The initial sunken look had then been replaced by puffiness and then the sagging around his eyes seemed to return even more pronounced this day.

As I looked upon his body I then looked over at the maid who walked around his body dabbing his feet and hands with a swab of cotton dipped in rose oil. I saw her face was warm and pink and the way her muscles moved beneath her skin as she stepped around the couch helping to hide the smell of the now rotting body.

I looked back upon Mnesarchus, his body so still and pale. I suddenly did not even see him as a body but as an object. I turned my eyes once more to the maid and wondered what her body would look like dead but I could not picture it. She touched my father one last time with the swab, nodded her head and then left the room. My mother in the chair in which she had sat for the last two days, had closed her eyes as she dozed now, tired from all the visitors.

I stepped towards Mnesarchus quietly and gently I pushed upon his right eyelid with one finger to open his eye. Then I slowly opened the other eye so that he looked up at the ceiling. I leaned over his face to look into his eyes but it was as though I was invisible and he was seeing straight through me. It was then that I felt it again, that "thing" made itself known and I heard it say "*look left.*"

I turned my eyes to the left and for the slightest moment imaginable I saw Mnesarchus in the corner of the room. Then he disappeared. I quickly looked back down upon my father's face and closed his eyes. I could not get back to my seat quick enough.

Mnesarchus' funeral rites were performed at the beloved temple he had built for me and my brothers. I stood and listened to the chants of the priests and breathed in the smoke of the incense. I knew this temple would never be the same now that funeral rites for anyone had been held here. It was as though the priests that day implanted into the temple some weird sort of memory of Mnesarchus that would never be erased.

I looked to my mother standing beside me, now so small and frail and wondered how long it would be until death made her but a memory and the priests embedded that into the temple. Then someday it would be my turn.

At this thought I froze. This was something I was yet to truly consider. What would that be like? How would it happen and what age would I be?

I looked to my father's body, wrapped in linens as it lay upon the altar. My father had lived a grand and noble life. He had excelled in his profession. He had been a loving husband and a nurturing father. There was nothing of Msenarchus' life that anyone could have criticised or besmirched. I hoped that in his last moments, as he felt his life leave his body, that he had somehow been given a moment in which he could have seen this of himself.

Mnesarchus' life had been so full with his own pursuits and yet he still had made time to guide me towards the destiny that the oracle had spoken of. As I thought of this I had tears fill my eyes. I decided then and there that my life would be as well regarded as my father's. I promised him and myself that I would fulfil my destiny and I too would face my last moments without regret or remorse for anything that my life had encountered.

The next few years I did not travel. I was now the eldest male in the family and as such I played a new role as the patriarch despite my youth. I consulted with my mother about household matters and finances.

I oversaw the education of my younger brothers who continued to be a source of frustration although lessening with time.

I never though neglected my ambitions and continued to study and practice my languages and writing. The contacts my father made for me were still being honoured and men continued to travel to our temple to share what they knew though something now began to change. Once the lesson was finished the teacher would turn to me and ask me of things I had seen in my travels with my father.

Some days I would share even more than they would. Soon my role as student within our temple was over and men from all over Greece were making their way to Samos to learn from me. You could call it my first school but I never saw it that way. Too young to feel as though I had gathered the wisdom of men twice and thrice my age, I shared what I had learnt so far, simply and with no airs as to what I had achieved so far. This in itself garnered me more praise than I could have imagined. The unassuming way that I shared was seen to be a reflection of my innate wisdom.

As you can imagine my father had always been quite forthcoming in sharing what he had been told by the oracle at Delphi. This may have closed one door in Egypt but it had opened many others. However much it had been disregarded by the elders in Egypt the story had spread as far as we had travelled. Many men arrived in Samos to share their teachings expecting to be in the presence of a godly being. So my even temperament and grace in sharing just fed this part of my public image.

As time passed the stories grew and so too did the regard and respect held for me by the men of knowledge that were in Greece and beyond. Samos too was now known as a place that held the keys of wisdom as much as the men in their caves in Persia and down to Phoenicia did.

Samos though changed as time went on. The gentle nature of its past was now moving into a new era. The banter amongst the men on the docks was now replaced with a heaviness that I was glad my grandfather was no longer alive to see. I would stand there and watch the dark faces of the men as they threw their ropes and hauled cargo. I remembered my grandfather as he walked here laughing with ship captains and something inside my heart twisted.

In that instant I felt how a place can evolve and change as much as a man himself can. But this was much more than that. For a man to bring about change there is inner dialogue, there is searching and learning. A man changes through his consciousness as he experiences the situations that occur in his life. For a place such as Samos to change then these changes of individual men combine, and that to me seemed so much more than what one man changes within himself. For when these experiences combine to effect change on a social scale they then also impact the experience of the individual.

Now I know that is quite a circular philosophy and the core of this is that change always begins within the singular being. Standing here now on the dock watching these sullen men I now understood how powerful my teaching could be if I combined with others. I now understood that pursuing knowledge for myself would then impact much more than my own experience. Ironically the man I had to thank for this was also the man I most despised at this time in my life; Polycrates.

Polycrates was what is known as a tyrant. Now I need you to let go of the way you use the word tyrant in your day, but not entirely. Polycrates had seen fit to take power of Samos by force in a way I both admired and was revolted by. It was during a festival to celebrate the Goddess Hera. The main cities were abuzz with festivities both day and night for three days. This translated into most of our men, including any soldiers, being constantly drunk and our island offering the most perfect opportunity to be overthrown.

Polycrates sent men ahead posing as travelling merchants much like Mnesarchus travelled. They watched and waited until they knew the time was right and then one went to the very cliff upon which I had lay watching waves. There he lit a torch so that the ships waiting off shore would know that the time had come to land and begin the siege. It was brutal and unrelenting but resolved relatively quickly. Samos now had begun its new era.

My mother changed immensely alongside Samos. Having lost her parents and her soulmate, she now aged watching her beloved island home lose its innocence. Pythia lost some of her uncles during the initial siege as the boat builders were seen as a threat. Those of the family that did remain were subdued by now only being allowed to build and maintain Polycrates ever growing armada of battleships. This scenario unfortunately included my younger brothers who had become involved in the family business when our studies truly lost all interest for them.

So beloved Pythia, who had enjoyed a life full of lightness and harmony, now watched as her family fell under the rule of the tyrant.

"So much has changed Pythagoras," she said to me full of sorrow one day. "If only all changes were for the better. But that is for the gods to decide. I truly wonder though why the gods chose such a man for Samos."

I could not answer her for I did not understand this either. Part of me suspected that the gods had no part in this. It made no sense for one man to be favoured so greatly that he should affect the lives of so many in such a negative way. Even when Polycrates built his infamous aqueduct and the island somehow seemed to progress in civil developments, the manner in which he began his reign shadowed over anything that seemed positive for us as a society.

Then Polycrates declared just how serious he was about his power. Secure in his place and certain that the Samians were no longer willing to challenge him, he then dealt with the only threats he felt he had; the two brothers who had been by his side to make the coup a success. One he publicly executed, declaring him to be a traitor. Polycrates held up letters, all forged of course, that stated plans for his brother to overthrow him.

I watched from within the crowd at the town square, horrified and fascinated at the same time. Before the gathered crowd Polycrates called his brother the lowest names imaginable while all the brother could do was kneel and tremble upon the wooden floor of the dais beside him. The brother was bound so that his hands were behind his back. His face was dark blue with bruises and there were welts across his shoulders, arms and back from whips and straps. Occasionally he would look out to the crowd and you could barely see his eyes through his swollen skin. His mouth was gagged and this told me that his last chance to speak his truth was robbed of him. His eyes though said much more. Within them all I saw was his desire for this to end.

Polycrates ended the scene with his usual style. He read out his brother's confession and held it up for all to see. He then grabbed his brother's hair, pulling his head backwards and exposing his throat. Polycrates nodded to the soldier standing on the other side and with one quick move the soldier sliced across the brother's throat. Polycrates smiled as he let go of his brother's hair and let the body collapse before him. His brother's life slowly ebbed away as his blood pooled around him.

I was appalled. That power could so consume a man to kill was horrific to me, even within the act of war. To so coldly kill a man before others to make a point for your own power and to induce fear in those that remained sickened me. To do it to a member of your family did more than horrify me; it astounded me.

There was not one part of Polycrates that stopped to consider his innate bond to this other man. They surely must have played together as children, eaten meals together with their parents, and shared their joys and their sorrows. All that clearly meant nothing to Polycrates. All there was for him was power and control. It even superseded money for there were many families upon Samos such as my own that held more wealth than him, they just did not have the contacts or the gall to pursue force in the way he did.

This total disconnect from the links that had shaped his life was what made me despise this man so much. I am sure his own father had nurtured him as had mine and this is how he repaid the man; by slaughtering his child. This disconnect from all that was holy and from love now washed over Samos. Polycrates had not only shown us that he was formidable, he had also shown us that family and its laws did not matter.

I began to sense that my studies would not expand anymore within this new Samos and I knew I should leave but my mother held me here. Men still came to share and learn despite the interrogations on their arrival and being followed by a soldier as they made their way to my temple. Often the soldiers would sit and wait, lingering within the temple as we spoke to make sure that we were indeed "studying". This was a futile exercise on Polycrates' part for most of the time we may as well have been speaking a foreign language for all of what the soldiers would understand of our concepts and ideas. As long as they did not hear any military terms then they could report back that all was well at my temple.

I did begin to suspect that many did not listen and one day decided to test this by slipping from speaking Greek to Aramaic with one man. When my friend jumped slightly at my impetuosity I replied in Aramaic, "He is not even listening and I am proving that right now."

Which I did indeed prove because the soldier did not say a word and continued on scratching at his stubble.

This monitoring became so boring for some soldiers that sometimes I would be speaking with someone only to be distracted by their snores echoing through the temple. One day the snores grew so loud that we could not help but burst out laughing which in turn then woke the soldier.

"Ah, my tyrant may choose men for their bodies but definitely not their minds," I said in Phoenician.

It was then that my visitor leant forward and also speaking in Phoenician he said quietly, "Pythagoras, surely this is not the manner in which the gods said you would learn or teach. You should have young men watching over you with interest and a hunger for knowledge, not wielding spears and shields."

I nodded my head. "Yes," I said, "It is time to leave."

My dedication to my studies was the one shining light in my

mother's life now, so as hard as it was to tell her I was leaving, and as hard as it was for her to hear it, we both knew this was for the best.

"This is just what your father would have chosen for you also," she said through her tears.

# CHAPTER FIVE

I left Samos at night and yes, you might say deceitfully, but this was not through fear. I did this for the freedom of travelling without being followed. I did not underestimate Polycrates as I was sure that if he had decided to pursue one of Samos' greatest minds then he would have. As I suspected though when nothing happened within the weeks after I left, he had soon lost interest in me and my family who remained.

I made my way to Miletus, a city upon the coast of Anatolia, not so far from Samos, where I knew a teacher called Thales lived and worked. One of his students had been one of the men who had come to my temple at Samos. As soon as he mentioned the man's name I knew he would be one who I would visit. In fact he had been a teacher my father had sought out years ago as we travelled together, but as we got close to Miletus, Mnesarchus began to hear stories that made him doubt the quality of Thales' mind. My initial impression of Thales was that my father was more astute and intuitive than I had given him credit for.

When I landed upon Miletus it was still night so I sought a room. As the innkeeper showed me where I would sleep he asked as to my business in Miletus. This was a common question of any innkeeper of the time. It made conversation and it also let the man know of what clientele he was dealing with. As soon as I mentioned Thales' name his eyes grew wide and I saw him try to pull back from smiling.

"Oh yes, many seek Master Thales," he said and now he couldn't help but smile. "He is a most interesting man."

Too tired and relieved to finally be within paces of a bed I could not be bothered to ask that he expand upon just how and why Thales was interesting. Besides I am sure many people upon Samos found me "interesting" also. Not understanding someone can do that. Finally alone and drifting off to sleep I thought about how much I had learnt so far and how much more I wanted to learn. I pictured myself returning to Samos, the most learned man I could be and transforming my home back to the free and joyful place it had once been.

I thought of my mother and prayed to Apollo that she be protected no matter what would become of me and my brothers. Then I fell asleep.

I sometimes looked back to that night and wonder what I would have thought if my future had been shown to me. Would I have chosen not to see Thales the next day? Where would I have gone next then? How would that have changed what was to eventually shape history for so many?

All those questions though would always be redundant because the next morning I awoke and made my way to Thales. It was the true beginning of my manhood that day and it would be thirty-six years before I ever set foot upon Samos again.

I made my way to Thales' home with a spring in my step. Already I felt expanded being away from Polycrates and the Samos of his rule. The sky felt bigger here and I remembered travelling with my father and how amazing that was. For a moment I even thought I felt him by my side and turned my head as though I might see him.

Eventually I asked for directions as I felt I was walking much farther than I should have. When I mentioned Thales' name to anyone I spoke with they gave me the same amused look that the innkeeper had and then they would point along the road.

"Keep going," most would say as they looked me up and down. "You will eventually get to him. You travellers all seem to find him."

They were right. Suddenly I was along a piece of road that seemed miles from anyone or anything but I kept going. Then sure enough I found a tall wooden gateway and just knew this was the place.

The house was modest but far from small and outside I could see sheets of canvas tied amongst trees to form small tents. These were the student accommodations that I had been told about. I wondered how living "rough" affected their learning but once I met Thales I realised these small private retreats were more luxurious than you could imagine.

I approached the front door of the house and as it was wide open I stepped though and called out a hello to announce myself. There was no reply but from the sandals and slippers gathered in the entrance way I knew there was someone about. I began to slip my own sandals off and noticed a sign upon the wall.

"Leave your shoes and stupidity here."

It was in Aramaic, then repeated in Greek and Phoenician. It was Thales' own Rosetta Stone and within those few words one could know much about the man.

Now with bare feet and hoping my stupidity was not just left at the doorway but in Samos, I stepped further in. I soon heard a voice and made my way to where it was coming from. The voice became louder as I walked and it was very clear that someone was being berated.

"How dare you say that to me!" the voice bellowed.

I turned a corner and there stood a middle aged man. He held a much younger man by the robes over one of his shoulders and he was hitting the young man about the head with his other hand.

"Why do you waste my time, and yours, by speaking such stupid things," he yelled and on each second word he struck the young man again making sure the blow as he said the word "stupid" was the hardest.

I was dumbfounded at this display, wondering what on earth the young man had done to incite this. So I am sure that as the old man turned to see me finally, my jaw was hanging wide open.

"Yes!" he said loudly to me while he still clutched the young man by the shoulder.

"I have come to see Thales," I said as composed as I could.

"I am Thales. Who are you?" he asked.

"I am Pythagoras of Samos," I said and feigned a smile.

"Pythagoras! I have been waiting for you!" he said and he smiled so broadly and warmly I could almost have forgotten that he still clutched the young man with the red face before him.

He turned to the young man and pushed him away. "Go!" he shouted at him and the young man left as quickly as he could.

"Hah…He has learnt much today!" Thales said and grinned.

"Is that the manner in which you always teach?" I asked hesitantly.

"Oh no! Only when a student decides they will forget their knowledge and speak rubbish. Can you believe that he actually asked me if there was a possibility that the world was flat! I mean I spend all this time with them sharing knowledge that has been known for thousands of years and then they say stupid things like that to me," Thales explained and then he laughed. "I doubt he will dare to say such things again."

He gestured towards a doorway and began walking so I followed close behind and as we strode he continued talking.

"So Pythagoras of Samos you finally make it to me!" he said loudly and grunted.

"You said you were expecting me yet I sent no word?" I enquired.

"Mmph…and there in that sentence you have shown me how much you have to learn!" he snorted and then we were outside.

Another young man sat upon some grass below a huge tree. He leaned back upon his hands and was looking up amongst its branches. Thales approached him from behind and kicked one of his hands out from under him. The youth composed himself and jumped to his feet.

"Yes, Master Thales," the youth said.

"What has the tree taught you?" Thales asked as he crossed his arms.

I saw the young man begin to tremble as he answered. "I have noted that the trunk separates into four main branch ways. These in turn have four main inferior branches which also separate into four. This continues on to the leaves," he said and he bent down to pick up a small twig with four leaves upon it showing it to Thales.

Thales stared in silence at the boy for such a length of time until there was discomfort between all three of us.

"It has been three hours since I left you here. What else do you have to tell me?" Thales said sternly.

The youth stammered, "Ah—well…" He looked up and pointed, "It sheds certain branches to make way for new ones." He continued to look up as though this might delay any criticism.

Thales once again stared hard at the youth then he too looked up and walked close to the tree. He then circled the tree as though examining every branch until he returned to his original position. Then without so much as looking at either me or the youth he walked around the tree again. He arrived back to the place before us and paused then circled the tree one last time. I sighed deeply and suddenly wondered what had possessed me to listen to the man who had told me I should come here. Then finally Thales spoke to the young man.

"Well done," he said plainly. "Some students take days to see what you have in just hours. Go rest and eat, tomorrow you may attend your first geometry class."

"Thank you, Master Thales, thank you," he said and walked off.

Thales turned to me, "I heard that sigh Pythagoras. You are wondering what sitting before a tree for three hours can teach you. I'll tell you what it just taught him; that young man now can see the details of every plant he walks past. Do you think he will take even the simplest weed for granted now? No, he won't—because now he will stop and know the geometry and harmony of every part of nature."

I thought about my afternoon watching waves make their way to the shore of Samos and I nodded.

"Yes, nod Pythagoras! I know you know the truth of this. Every mind that seeks knowledge reaches this point at some time. Knowledge is not always about what you can cram into here," he said and tapped at his forehead, "It is also about what you are willing to see." And he pointed to his eyes as I continued to nod.

Thanks to my preceding reputation I was not made to endure the tree staring initiation and was allowed to attend classes immediately. This caused some jealousy with other students but once they had heard me ask a few questions or indeed answer Thales correctly more than once, this dissipated. Then I found myself surrounded by other students during my breaks asking me of what else I knew. I looked up one day as I had a crowd around me to see Thales watching me from a distance. He did not smile or frown. It was his usual "poker face" that he used to neither coddle nor distract us. Nevertheless I decided to approach him about it.

I spoke as openly as I could. I asked if he felt I was interfering with his teachings or if he saw this as disrespectful.

"I find it neither Pythagoras," he said and slightly smiled. "All I see is someone inspiring and stimulating my own students to expand their own knowledge. This is never a bad thing within a school. But what I see more than this is someone who is now beyond what I have to share. I will never expel you but I most certainly must encourage you to move on for your own benefit and all that you will discover about yourself."

Despite this encouragement I was still at Thales' school a month later. We never repeated the discussion again but I sensed an agitation with me, within Thales, that grew. He was harder on me as I drew up my geometry, he snarled questions to me as we looked at the stars during astronomy and then one day he finally hit me. This was the first blow I received in all my months here after watching him do this to others numerous times. My beating though was without the usual provocation such as a "stupid" question or an ill-timed opinion. My blow to the ears was due to my procrastination and it arrived upon my head unexpectedly.

I was sitting out in the sunshine quite ironically looking at the trees and the natural patterns of geometry within them. I barely heard Thales approach when I felt the sting of his hand to my left ear. Thales may have been a small man and a scholar but his force was as good as any farmer or athlete. My ear was so stunned with pain that I actually could not hear his first barrage of words as I gathered myself.

"Why are you still here?" he shouted again and this time I heard.

"I am not ready to leave," was the pathetic answer I gave and then I cowered as he leant forward to hit me again. He held his hand back though and just shouted.

"Not ready! Not ready! More like you have chosen stupidity to rule you other than that which you know to be true," he yelled even louder and behind him I could see a few other students peering around corners to see who the latest victim was of a Thales attack. "Get up!" he yelled, "and I will show you what being stupid will stop you from!"

I got up as quickly as I could and followed after Thales who was walking towards the huge wall that separated the school area from the rest of his property. In the centre of the wall was a huge double wooden doorway. He slid back the bar which held this closed and then struggled to open one side of the wooden door. I rushed forward to help him and we barely opened it enough to squeeze between when he said abruptly, "Enough!" and then he slid his way through and I made my way also.

Once past the doors I saw Thales walking further, his fists swinging by his side so that I knew his temper was still flaring. I hurried my steps to catch up and just as I did he stopped and pointed to some machinery that was before us. There were a dozen of them; huge stone bases with a stone wheel sitting on top, wooden cranks and a spout carved into one side of the base.

Thales turned to me and sneered, "Do you know what these are?"

"They are olive presses, Master Thales," I answered calmly.

"Oh so you are not so stupid! You do know that at least," he snarled.

Of course he knew that I would know what they were. Any Greek over the age of five knew what an olive press was. This was just his chance to dig at me a bit more.

"Now you are wondering why I would beat you and drag you to some olive presses. Even more so you are wondering why a sage would have so many olive presses?" he posed.

I shrugged my shoulders. I had no idea what he was talking about. In fact all I thought at this moment was that his mind had completely collapsed and, as is the way of the sane, I indulged what I perceived to be his insanity.

"I have these presses because someone told me that I was incapable of something. He told me that all that there was to me was learning and teaching. He said to me that I would never be able to run a business or know how to provide goods that contributed to a community. He said all I had was this…" and he pointed to his head. "So I decided to show him just how I could use it. That week I was in the market buying food with my servants. I was gathering the usual side glances from the peasants who did not understand what I do with my teaching when I overheard a conversation between some farmers. They were talking about the lack of rain and how it would affect their crops. I felt sorry for a moment but then as I was walking back to my home I passed an olive grove and saw the trees were full of fruit. I also saw the trees were full of life and I quickly calculated the weather patterns that Miletus had been experiencing. I knew there was nothing to worry about in the long term."

Thales continued on, "So I decided to show my town of Miletus just how clever I could be. I waited till the current olives had been picked and pressed. Yes, there was a slow down in the new ones coming and this was when I began my plan. I got some new students to go to each farm and offer to buy the olive presses. Now the stupid farmers had all bought into the talk of "bad" seasons and had grown other crops now or taken on more livestock to produce alternate goods so they happily sold their presses. Some were even pleased to see them gone. It was one less concern for their farms and provided ready money in their purses. Also they knew that when their olives did finally come they could simply borrow their neighbour's presses. Hah!" he exclaimed and then continued.

"None of them would admit to the other that they had sold their presses. Their pride would not allow them to speak of it and confess such. So finally the time did come that they had olives that needed pressing. Not only that but within six months they had all harvested as many olives as any season. Then the fun began!"

At this Thales began to laugh so much that he had wrapped his arms around his belly and doubled over. He straightened up and tried to speak but he couldn't as his laughter took over again. I even joined in as it was that exuberant. Then finally he stood up and wiped at his eyes as he went on.

"Each farmer went to the other—'*Can I borrow your press? Oh, I have no press anymore; I was hoping to use yours!*'—Can you imagine it!" Thales said and collapsed into laughter again. "So I sent a student around to all the farms to let them know that now as well as providing a school of mathematics, astronomy and thought, I was also providing a service to press olives."

Thales' laughter was suddenly gone and he now looked me in the eyes with a cold, hard stare.

"They still don't understand me, Pythagoras, but they will never call me stupid," he said and smiled slightly. "I made enough money in that season to fund my school and its students for twenty years. Then I sold the presses back to the farmers, for a profit of course, and made enough money for another ten years. The money though is not the point I am making to you today, Pythagoras. What I hope you will understand for yourself is that comfort is not enough reason to stay here and avoid what else is in store for you. I could have stayed here teaching and never tried anything more but I did—and I believe I taught myself and others much in that act." He sighed and went on, "Please choose to move on because your heart knows it is the best for you and not to prove yourself to me or anyone else.

I knew exactly what he meant by the word comfort. I was in

a stable and nurturing environment. Even the students who were hit by Thales knew it was through his dedication to teaching them. I had learned to love my canvas tent under the trees. It was my private haven—I heard all around me and felt the intricacies of nature (albeit sometimes harshly). Thales recognized what had been brewing in me. I knew it was time to move on and yet each time I did those voices inside would start their own dialogue;

"*If I have no money then how will I eat? Where will I stay?*"

I decided to confess this to Thales.

"Money, food and lodgings? These are your reasons to delay your adventure?" He exclaimed.

Now I smiled and laughed. Having now heard it spoken out loud, and in Thales inimitable way, I could feel just how stupid it was. Then Thales gave me a reminder that I will always treasure.

"You came here with barely anything but most importantly the faith that you would be received. I am not the only one ready and waiting to teach you, Pythagoras. It is time to find the others," he said solemnly.

We began to walk back to the gates when I stopped and looked back at the presses.

"You said you sold the presses back to the farmers. Why then do you still have these?" I asked.

Thales turned and smiled. "They belong to the man who told me I was good for nothing but teaching. He has never been able to afford to buy them back from me."

With that he chuckled all the way back to the house.

I packed my satchel the next morning and filled my canteen at the well. It was time to move on. I went looking for Thales and found him standing by the front door of the house.

"I was going to give you a few minutes more, and then I was coming to give you either another beating or lecture. I had not quite decided which yet," he said with a smile then stepped forward with his arms out to embrace me. "I feel like I am sending off a son to begin his own life for that is what you have become to me. There are few students I can say that of."

I received his embrace and returned it. For a moment I almost felt like Mnesarchus was the one holding me and I saw this as showing me Thales' words were true.

"Where shall you go now?" he asked and crossed his arms.

I knew to choose my words carefully as this was not a question to make small talk.

"I shall head south and seek the mystery schools through Phoenicia and make my way to Babylonia," I said hesitantly.

Thales shook his head. "These lands hold much for you but I suggest you make your way further south to Egypt. This is where I trained and this is where all the knowledge begins from. Head to Phoenicia and Babylonia by all means and you will just get the same wisdom but diluted with local traditions. I studied in Egypt and it is the priests there that hold the keys to all things. Just use your judgement as to which schools are authentic and which ones are simply to pacify the Pharaoh. The priests are very clever at protecting their learning."

So I finally left Thales' school but I did not head directly to Egypt as he suggested. In fact I did not even leave Miletus. Instead I made my way to another school in the city that was run by one of the only other students of Thales that he had referred to as a son; Anaximander.

Now Anaximander's school was in no way competition to Thales' school. It was Thales himself who set up this other school to expand his own work. There was also another reason and this was because Thales knew he needed to train someone to take over once he was gone. I sometimes wondered if I had shown up before Anaximander if he might have chosen me to start this other school. I even wondered why he did not ask me to set up a Thales school in Greece. I later understood why; it was because he wanted the Miletian schools to be known as their own phenomenon in the evolution of thought that was taking place. This was exactly what happened. Somehow too I believe he knew that I would outgrow these schools.

Anaximander received those students whose time with Thales was judged as solid and complete. These were the students who simply wanted a retreat to review what they had learned and make it more concrete in their minds and memory. Some students arrived from other schools throughout Persia and other places. They were only received should they have some new knowledge or thoughts to share. You could call it the first "think tank".

Days here were not spent in regimented classes as with Thales. Everyone was free to do as they pleased and the openness and serenity of this was palpable from the front gate. When I arrived I found men sitting in the gardens reading scrolls and quietly talking with each other. A youth came from the house with a small bell and rang it gently three times. The sound was so soft that it almost floated off into the breeze before you heard it. The men looked up and smiled at the youth who returned indoors. Some men stayed where they were while others stood up and made their way inside.

I approached one who stayed sitting on a bench under a tree reading.

"Hello, might you tell me where I could find Anaximander?" I asked quietly. I almost felt like I was breaking some untold rule by speaking.

He looked up and smiled. "He will be inside about to start a discussion group so it will be some time before you can speak with him. Feel free to go inside and join them though," he said and looked back down at his scroll.

I made my way to the door that all the men had entered and could hear the low rumble of talking inside. The door led me straight into a large room empty but for a circle of chairs and a large slate upon one wall. The men who had come inside were now all seated and talking quietly amongst themselves. I walked a little closer and they all stopped and looked up, making me freeze in my tracks.

"Welcome, welcome," one said and beckoned me with his hand. "Sit wherever is free."

I nodded and made my way to a chair to sit down. I slipped my satchel under the chair and sat back curious to see what was about to take place. Just as I did this an older man walked in, made his way to the slate, and with chalk divided the board into four. He then wrote a name in Greek at the top of each segment.

"Today I would like to talk more about the elements," he said as he wrote the last word and then turned to face the men. He was about to continue speaking when he noticed me, the obvious new face in the group.

"Welcome! Might we know your name and where you have come from?" he asked.

"I am Pythagoras of Samos, and I have just spent five months at Master Thales' school," I said plainly, hoping this was enough to warrant me being here.

'Ah, you are Pythagoras," he replied as he smiled. "Master Thales told me to expect you." With that he turned and began to write upon the slate.

"*Damn Thales!*" I thought. "*Always one step ahead of me!*"

On the outside though I smiled and my smile grew even more as the discussion began. There was hearty debate and well expressed theories on all matters to do with the elements. Were they opposite? Were they the source of all things physical? How do they transform matter? Do they transform each other?

I sat quietly in the beginning relishing the depth of conversation which reflected the vast diversity of the knowledge and background that all these men had gathered. I also noted that Anaximander joined in as though he was a student himself, never once correcting anyone and when he did challenge someone it was with genuine intrigue as to how they would support their words.

I smiled and sat back in my chair. This was what I was looking for. Almost immediately though I felt something very familiar—it was that sense of comfort which had held me with Thales. I knew immediately that I needed to move on quickly. Although these men were talented I would not learn anything new here which supported my truth or the teachings I would one day share. As wonderful an insight as it was to give myself it was also like a slap from Thales because once again it brought up the question; *"Where do I go now?"*

Now the answer should have been simple; Egypt. Still something pulled me to head to Phoenicia. I missed much of the final strains of the discussion group as I was lost within my own thoughts of moving on. Suddenly they were all rising from their chairs and heading back outdoors or to other rooms. All except Anaximander who remained in his chair and smiled at me. I began to rise as well when he put up his hand motioning for me to stay so I stopped and remained in my seat. When all the men were gone he spoke.

"Did you enjoy the conversation?" he asked and slid forward a bit in his chair so that he now leaned back, his hands resting on his stomach.

"Very much so," I replied.

"I did notice you drifted off towards the end though. I find that a bit surprising given your reputation as an astute student," he said and laughed. "Care to tell me where your mind went?"

Anaximander knew already, he just needed me to say it out loud for us both. So when I told him that I knew I needed to move on and that his school was not for me at this time he simply nodded. Then he leaned forward so that his elbows rested on his knees and his hands were gripped together. He looked to me and smiled again.

"You don't remember me do you?" he asked and raised one eyebrow.

I scoured through my mind for some memory of this man. I looked over his face trying to recall it in some other scenario but just couldn't. I furrowed my brow and shook my head.

"I am so sorry but I cannot recall anything," I said quite

embarrassed.

"Well I guess that is not so surprising," he laughed, "You were quite young. Do you remember being lost in the markets of Samos?"

With that one sentence a rush of memories came flooding back. The feeling as I walked out the gate of my home all alone. The overwhelming sense of the crowd in the markets and then the relief as this man had lifted me from the ground and began to take me home. Now I too smiled and nodded my head.

"I knew we would meet again one day," Anaximander said gently. "I am just relieved that you know where you are and where you are going this time!"

"Well I know I should be going to Egypt but I also think I should be going to Phoenicia. So I am not so sure I have any greater sense of direction than I did the last time we met," I said and feigned a smile.

Anaximander did not return my smile. I saw him take a deep breath and then he said, "Any man who does not know where he is going is a liar. No man takes a step without some sense of where he wishes to be. It just takes being honest with yourself."

I nodded and sighed. Now I knew I would be going to Phoenicia.

Here I feel I must share with you just what I had learned from my time with Thales. I realise this is jumping back a bit but this will help you understand how I approached the next few months of my life as I made my way down to Egypt.

The Miletian schools under Thales and Anaximander were well ahead of their time in many ways and yet they taught all the ancient knowledge with the purity with which it should be shared. Thales did not lie or exaggerate when he said that many of the schools throughout Persia, Phoenicia and Babylonia had diluted these teachings with local customs or the idiosyncrasies of those who taught. Now while this may seem somewhat close-minded and detrimental to the evolution of the teachings it was quite the opposite.

When I speak of this as detrimental I am referring to the "classical" teachings of astronomy and geometry. These teachings held constant values and patterns which did not change. They were as defined as the sun rising and setting each day was. However there was another element of teaching that was rising forth at these schools. This element was that of thought and it was within this era of the Miletian schools and thence my own school that the first records of philosophy are found.

This "new" practice of philosophy was exciting for all of

us involved with it. It was also frightening to those who could not understand this new style of teaching or thinking. This was the dawn of an age where men could expand how they perceived the world around them and how they interacted with it. No longer bound by the limits or unpredictability of a group of gods who dealt out punishment or random acts of nature, we could now see the order of things around us.

This order started with astronomy and geometry, but the philosophers took this further by applying these sciences to nature, music and human physicality. When I left Samos to further my knowledge I stepped into this world. Each day that I opened myself to exploring and expanding my understanding of the world through philosophy, the more I understood that there was much more than what we could see, hear or touch.

The most profound way in which I was shown this was at Thales' school. Thales loved to cram our days with geometry and mathematics and then at night we were dragged out of our tents for astronomy classes.

"Drawings and diagrams can only teach you so much," he said. "You need to stand outside under the stars to truly know and respect them."

So for a student of Thales this meant your days began at sunrise to assist in the chores and tasks which supported the school such as gathering fruits and vegetables or doing maintenance upon the buildings. By mid-morning classes began and continued until dinner was had in the evening. There was time for some rest and exercise and then when it was dark you were summoned to the open area outside to commence astronomy until at least two hours past midnight. If the sky was cloudy then you were expected to read until the same time. This gave you barely four hours sleep.

When I first arrived I was amused at the discipline and even found it somewhat exciting to have my days so full with learning. Then came the day when like many others I would be in class and find my head rolling forward and my eyes straining to keep open. Those who could not keep awake were deemed weak and lacking dedication. Not surprisingly they were soon sent on their way.

Thales though knew that it was all about the patterns that your body had grown accustomed to. Just as your mind could learn new knowledge or develop its own thoughts, then so too could your body learn new patterns and behave in the way that you desired. He never said this to us outright, it was something that he expected us to understand inherently as we stepped into the process of adjusting our activity and sleep. One aspect of this teaching that he did state explicitly was that of our diet.

"Learn to eat efficiently and your body will function efficiently," was how he expressed it.

Eating efficiently involved choosing foods that were as pure as possible, as light as possible and that could be prepared with as little "interference" as possible. Not surprisingly this meant our diet at Thales' school was predominantly fruits, vegetables, legumes and grains. Cakes, sweets and (hardest of all) meats were no longer part of my menu. I groaned silently as I was told this at my first meal.

Here I was in the lands of my favourite sweet and I could not indulge in it. This I knew I could deal with but the meat was a whole other issue. Meat was a staple of all my meals from childhood. Fancy telling a Greek they could no longer eat lamb or goat. It was the one thing I challenged Thales upon and he quickly showed me the proof of his theory.

"But surely Master Thales we need the nutrition of meat to sustain us?" I asked remembering all the times I was told by my mother to finish my meat above all else at our dinner table.

"Mmph," he grunted. "So you doubt me? Follow me!"

I was led out to the garden where Thales' dog was sleeping in the shade of a tree. He pointed at the dog.

"See my dog sleeping," he said and kept walking.

We rounded the corner of the house and there was Thales' cat also asleep and curled under a bush to avoid the heat. Thales pointed to the cat.

"See the cat sleeping too," he said and kept walking.

We continued on until we came to a place clear of the garden around the house so that we looked out upon the nearby farms. Cows, sheep and goats were all wandering about the fields as they grazed. Thales pointed now to these animals.

"They wake with the sun and continue through the day until it sets. They may rest a while but they do not sleep. Their food is minimal and yet efficient. They require little care and yet yield much for their owners. Look how gentle they are. They do not need to attack other animals for the land gives them their food," Thales said as he looked out at the farms.

We walked back past the cat and Thales smiled sideways at me and then we were back before the dog.

"Meat slows the body. It makes it heavy and all your processes are then involved in its digestion and elimination. When your body is so focussed upon one thing then so too your mind and its thoughts follow. Eat lightly and of those things that support your body but do not consume its processes and you free your mind. Your body will soon learn this new way and you will thank me at every meal," he stated and then walked off.

So I did indeed follow Thales' diet regime and surprised myself at how my body responded. My body grew thinner but not weaker and my sleep adjusted just fine within weeks. But then came the day that the smell of roasted lamb somehow made it through the air to meet my nose as I wandered outdoors. In an instant I was back upon Samos and at my family table. I could see the huge platter of lamb and the dishes of heavy vegetables set beside it. I groaned in a mix of ecstasy to remember such times and also with longing to be living them once more.

I looked around and saw that it was time for our rest which meant that I was not needed or expected anywhere. I went to my tent and gathered my purse which held the little money I felt to carry from Samos with me then walked to the entrance of the school. Once I stepped through the gateway I stopped and looked back. I had a sudden remembrance of doing this once before and I felt that young boy wanting to break the rules but also hoping he would be stopped.

"Oh for goodness sake! I am not a child anymore" I muttered to myself and headed into town.

I went straight into the first taverna I could find and ordered some lamb and the heaviest vegetables they had. Of course this would not be complete without some wine. As the waiter brought me my dish he raised his eyebrow.

"Aren't you one of Thales' students?" he asked knowing full well we did not eat meat.

"Of course not! I would not be here eating meat if I was!" I lied.

"Oh that's what you all say," he laughed as he turned to walk away.

I didn't care who he thought I was. I pulled the plate close to me and just sat for a minute taking in its odours. I leant in as close as I could and breathed the meal in. That alone made me almost giddy with delight to be doing this. Then suddenly a wave of sadness arrived as I remembered my mother and my family.

"They would be eating this very same thing at this time," I thought to myself and so to honour them and to imagine that I was joining them I raised my glass and called out, "To family!"

All around me men lifted their glasses and joined my salute. I took one swig of wine and began to eat. Then all else was a blur.

I have some remembrance of stumbling back to the school and seeing the other students gathering for astronomy as the stars were beginning to appear. So I swaggered to join them also, remaining as far back from Thales as I could lest he smell my meal and the wine upon me.

I looked up at the stars that he was pointing to but my vision was too blurred and now my neck started to ache with fatigue. Then before I could stop it a huge belch erupted from me. The entire class including Thales turned to look at me. Thales returned to his diagrams and then pointed back at the skies, continuing on as though nothing had happened. I knew that Thales knew exactly what I had done.

I could not wait to get to my bed. It was as though Thales dragged the class on just to spite me. He didn't though and the class ran to normal time. The next morning the sun rose and I did not even notice it, even though its warmth made me kick my blanket aside. What did wake me was the sound of the tent canvas being swept aside. I looked up to see one of my fellow students holding it open as he looked upon me.

"Get up! Get up! Thales is looking for you!" he said frantically but as quietly as he could. He then dropped the canvas and ran.

I was out of my tent before I was even dressed properly and finished adjusting my clothes as I walked as fast as I could to the gardens. I ran to the furthest section where the beans grew up high in their trellises. Crouching down I began to pick what beans were ready.

"Pythagoras!"

It was Thales yelling out across the gardens. He did not do it formally but each morning he made sure that we were all pulling our weight with the chores.

I stood straight so that I could just peer over the beans.

"Yes Master Thales! I am here. Did you not hear me when you called through here last time?" I responded but cringed inside to be lying to my teacher like this.

Thales screwed up his face and grunted. "There you are. Carry on," he said.

I watched him walk away and around me the glare of my fellow students burnt upon me.

"No-one else would get away with that," one muttered.

I ignored him and went back to the beans.

I may have missed being punished by Thales but I could not escape the lesson my body chose to teach me. All morning all I wanted to do was head back to bed. My still bloated belly made it uncomfortable to bend as I picked beans and the constant pull of lethargy did indeed consume my mind. I thought I would be grateful when classes finally began and I could sit inside without the sun seeming to add to my desire to sleep. Once indoors and seated it was all worse. My eyes ached with wanting to close and my neck felt as though it could not control my head position.

The tiredness was one thing. My bowels in the meantime were re-adjusting to dealing with the huge amount of meat I had taken in. I could literally feel its movement through me and how slow it was. My stomach growled as it pushed the meat through and this distracted not only me but the students that were close by.

"When it finally gets out of me then this will be over," I thought.

So I visited the pits as often as I could but nothing would clear. I would squat for as long as I could, while others came and went, but for me—nothing. I then began to fear that it would never leave. It seemed my body had so forgotten what to do with meat that it would remain within me forever, almost to haunt me for my lack of discipline. Now this consumed my mind and I knew I must find some way to deal with it.

I daren't go to Thales as he would call me out as to why this had occurred. So I went to our cook. Alessandra was a beautiful woman, a distant cousin of Thales who was raised in Miletus and loved to cook. She did so for the school in return for her own sons being taught there in the hope they too would become grand scholars. One did, while the other two returned to the farming of Miletus that was far more comfortable for them. Alessandra, now a widow, was happy to continue on here at the school though, helping to nurture more men as they found their way.

When I walked into the kitchen she was stirring a huge pot of soup and humming to herself. She reached to her left, picked up a small handful of salt and added it to the pot. Her right hand never stopped stirring and she never stopped humming. I almost felt like I was intruding upon a ritual and decided I might leave when another twisting sensation in my bowel made me call out her name.

"Oh, hello young man. How might I help you? Has the fruit bowl in the study emptied again?" she asked as she smiled at me.

"No, there is still plenty of fruit," I answered and then stated the real cause of my visit.

Alessandra listened politely and as I finished she smiled.

"You aren't the first pupil to come to me seeking a laxative and I imagine you won't be the last. Does Thales know about this?" she asked.

I shook my head and my face turned red. "Please do not tell him!" I begged. "I think he already knows but if he learns that I have suffered like this I could not bear to have his gloating on top of it."

Alessandra nodded and smiled again. "As I promised all others so too I promise you I will not speak of this. Thales may be my cousin but you students are like my children. Tonight after your meal, make sure you are one of those who helps to clear and wash the dishes. I will have a bowl of greens waiting for you here," she pointed to a place upon one of her benches. "Eat them and drink all the juices with it as well. By morning everything will be back to normal."

After I left Alessandra went out to a place beyond the gardens which was not cultivated but where wild herbs and greens grew. It may not have been as organised as our food garden but she knew it bore just as much. Here she gathered a few leaves of this and a few of that until she held in her hand a powerful bouquet.

When I walked into the kitchen with a pile of plates that night I saw the bowl immediately. So too did some of the others who were doing kitchen duties.

"Ha! Looks like someone's bowels are in need of a fix. It's Alessandra's remedy," one of them laughed.

I didn't care who of them now knew and who they might tell. I grabbed the bowl and tipped it back into my mouth, slurping up the juices and washing down the first pieces of the greens. Then when it was drained I grabbed at the wilted pieces and pushed them in my mouth. The other students watched me with astonishment and then one started laughing.

"Please don't visit the pits before me tomorrow. You're likely to fill them after eating that much!" he chuckled.

I leaned back against the bench and sighed as I reached down to my belly and rubbed it.

"*Please, please, please work!*" I begged my own body.

It heard me loud and clear. The next morning I did not need the sunlight to wake me. My bowels let me know I would not sleep anymore. I raced from my tent without even dressing and thanked the heavens that the usual pilgrimage to the pits had not begun yet. I sank down over them and then thanked the heavens again that I was alone because of all the noises and the smell my body was unleashing. It felt so good and it did indeed feel like I might fill the pits.

I finally stood up and stretched my arms over my head, then patted my stomach and thanked it for finally returning to this much more balanced state. I began to make my way to the kitchen to thank Alessandra when I remembered I was naked. So instead I headed back to my tent to dress and continue with life as it should be. My normal diet now would never include meat again.

The efficiency that I had trained my body with served me well as I began to travel. In fact it would continually reveal to me the benefits of what it had been taught. The foods that I needed to fuel its activity were easy to find and of reasonable cost. If need be I could even forage amongst the roadside for something to sustain me til I found a more substantial meal. As was the way of the time many people were happy to give a traveller something little to eat. Sometimes this was purely an expression of hospitality and at other times they would offer it to me in exchange for an errand or other favour.

The little sleep I needed, along with the fact that it was not the heaviest of sleep required, meant that I could rest anywhere. I did not have to have a soft bed or stay at a fancy inn. I could sit at the base of a tree and doze for four hours and be ready to move on at sunrise. Not that I would ever turn down the offer of a room. I may have released my attachment to such comforts but it was always nice to indulge in them occasionally.

Fortunately such measures as sleeping by roadsides were few and far between. I rarely journeyed more than two weeks by foot in all my thirty-six years of travelling. As Thales had reminded me, it was often as though people were waiting to receive me or offer me some time upon a cart. The less I even paid attention to such matters the more readily such help and support seemed to appear.

The coins that I had within my purse since leaving Thales school were still there and it never even crossed my mind to use them once. This fascinated me so much that I even considered giving them all to the next beggar that crossed my path. The following day such a possibility presented itself to me.

A man, twisted with old age, wearing only a simple cloth about his loins and leaning upon a staff stood ahead of me at the entrance to a village I arrived at. As I neared him he pushed out his free hand towards me.

"Please! Anything!" he cried out.

I tried to smile at him as I extended both my empty hands before me.

"Like you I have nothing!" I said.

"What—not even a scrap of bread? Not even a biscuit? You must. You look well fed," he insisted.

I shook my head and moved on past him. Then I stopped and turned back. I opened my mouth to say something but the words were gone. So I turned and kept walking. My words would have been lost upon the man anyway.

I wanted to ask him why he thought he needed to beg. How did he end up in such a way with barely enough cloth to cover himself? Where was his family? Did he have no friends to help him?

In an instant I felt to just let the questions go. I immediately saw the contrast between his life and mine. I understood the freedom I had created for myself by allowing such human needs to somehow be just small things within my life. My life now was about much grander things than the triviality of gaining some food. In the pursuit of grander things I knew such small things would come to me.

Was it the gods who shone upon me, supporting me in this quest? Most likely so.

I looked back upon the man. He had few years left even if he did find all the food he needed. Perhaps the energies of creation did not choose to support those that were not contributing to the greater good. Perhaps the energies of creation supported those who it knew were assisting with the progress of mankind.

As I walked into the village this realisation burnt into my consciousness. I now knew why I had chosen the father I did. He nurtured me to begin upon this path that I now knew was bigger than I had imagined. In pursuing such knowledge and wisdom for myself I was doing so for mankind and it must be in an even bigger way than even Thales had offered to tell me. He knew I needed to realise this for myself.

I looked back at the beggar one last time. I could go and tell him that life could be easier but would he even understand? Perhaps he enjoyed his simple life. Possibly there was some enjoyment in speaking with every person who entered the village. He was free of home and land to maintain. He was free of the politics of family and the duty of taxes.

There was always some beauty in any life no matter how it was chosen to be lived— I was glad though I had chosen the path that I had.

 # CHAPTER SIX

I was finally close to Tyre; my father's homeland within Phoenicia. I was making my way by foot through what felt like quite harsh land. Here the ground was dry and dusty with barely any vegetation. I was almost to the end of the water in my canteen and looked ahead hoping that the nearest well would not be so far away.

Despite not knowing when my next fill would come I stopped to swig at my water. I was just lowering my head from taking a drink when something flashed in the corner of my eye. I turned my head to the left and looked at a cliff face that ran down the side of a mountain nearby. I was about to turn away and continue walking when I saw the flash again.

It was quick but this time it was as though it pulsed. Then it was gone. The sun was quite bright upon my eyes as I tried to see what it could possibly be from. Then it flashed again and this time pulsed four times in a steady rhythm. I smiled and realised someone was playing with me. Then with less of a delay it flashed again, this time with five pulses. I began to walk towards it.

As I walked the series of pulses grew more frequent and on each occasion the number of flashes increased. By the time I reached the side of the mountain, almost fifteen minutes later, it was like a steady stream of light was being sent out. I stopped at the base of the mountain, now no longer able to see it. I was just wondering how I would now find the source of the flashes when a man appeared from around an outcrop of rocks and stood before me. I almost jumped out of my skin.

"Well done! Now follow me," he said dryly and began to walk.

"Um—well —it might be nice to know who you are and where we are going." I replied cynically.

"I am one of the ones who decided to see if you were going to come and join us, and now I am taking you to meet the others," he said just as dryly as before and then he turned to keep walking.

"*Well that makes sense,*" I thought and followed him.

We climbed up the side of the mountain through a trail that seemed well used and yet you would not know it unless you were directly upon it. Looking ahead you could not tell where it led, and behind you it seemed to disappear. It was as though only the places beneath your feet existed. I looked off the track down the mountain to see how far we had come and lost my footing, sending stones scattering as I caught myself just in time.

"Watch my feet and yours will follow," said my guide with a sigh.

Thankfully the climb was not so much further. We were now upon what appeared to be a level platform that led into an opening within the mountainside. My guide walked in, disappearing within the cavity. I followed once more and was soon inside a big cave. There was no light and I stopped, almost scared of what I had allowed myself to get distracted from my journey by.

"Wait!" I heard his voice say in the same tone as he spoke everything else.

So I stood still and slowly my eyes adjusted. I could not see everything clearly but I could start to distinguish shapes and forms so that I realised I was in an even larger space than I first imagined. Then I noticed a small pinpoint of light to the back of the cave.

"Ah—a torch!" I thought with relief.

But when I saw that it did not flicker I knew it was not a torch at all.

"You can see the light?" asked the voice of my guide from somewhere nearby.

"Yes," I replied.

"Walk towards it. Do not worry about your feet or your head. The way is well clear. Just make your way to the light," he said.

So I did just that. The floor was indeed even and clear and I could feel the space was open all around me as the guide had said. The source of the light became bigger as I walked and made the space around me more visible. Then I was before what seemed like a small doorway. I lowered my head and stepped through it. I was now in another huge cave but unlike the other it was open and exposed to the side of the mountain. Light filled every corner of this space and within it stood five men all with their arms crossed. They looked at me intently and then one stepped forward.

"Hello," I said but none of them answered. The one who stepped forward now circled me looking up and down my body. It reminded me of Thales walking around the tree at his school. After two circles he stopped before me.

"Why did you see the signal?" he asked.

"Umm," I was wondering what he could possibly mean by that when I remembered the way I had been addressed by the guide on asking him a question. "Because I was looking at this place when the signal was sent."

The man shook his head. "No, that is not the right answer. There has been a mistake. You need to leave," he said.

The men behind him made some gasps and this man who seemed

to be the leader held up his hand to silence them. "We cannot just take in anyone!" he said sternly to them.

"But he followed the signal—that must mean something," one of the men said.

The leader looked back at me. "Why are you travelling this road at this time?"

"I am a man seeking knowledge. I have studied with Thales and Anaximander in Miletus. I now seek the schools of Phoenicia before I make way to the schools of Egypt," I said as simply as I could.

"See, it is not random! He is the one for today," said the other man again.

The leader looked me up and down again and took in a deep breath.

"What sort of knowledge do you seek? Astronomy? Music? Nature?" he asked of me.

"I seek all disciplines as I know they are all connected. You cannot know one without knowing the others," I said and lifted my chin proudly.

The men all gasped and the leader's eyes grew wide and then he smiled.

"So you knew what we were doing then when we flashed that silver piece at you?" he beamed.

"Why yes!" I responded telling the biggest lie of my life. I had no idea who these men were or what they were doing up here in the side of a mountain. I had just seen a flashing light and followed it out of pure curiosity. The fact that the details of why I journeyed somehow fit into their agenda now amused me to no end. I was now absolutely curious as to what would happen next.

I had heard of such schools that you would know as mystery schools. They were renowned for such eccentricities as hiding in obscure places so that only the "chosen few" would find them. They pushed the boundaries of what was considered traditional teachings yet claimed to hold the secrets of the ancient mysteries that came from before recorded time.

"Lunatics and pompous apes," Thales had declared them all to be. "Hide yourself in caves and dungeons sharing weird ideas that no-one is then allowed to pass along to anyone. How does that serve humanity?"

Now here I was standing within one and I could have burst with laughter at having found it despite having had no interest in doing so.

The leader turned to the men and nodded.

"We will start then," he said and lowered himself to sit upon the stone floor cross-legged so that he faced out to the sunlight. The other men joined him forming a semicircle with a space of several feet between each man. I followed their lead and sat at the edge of the formation. I finally took a look out at the view and smiled. It was such a beautiful place from up here. It still looked harsh but there was a stillness that made it majestic. Yes, if I was going to hide a school this would certainly be the place to do it. Then my thoughts were ended by a low hum coming from the leader.

It was a deep full sound, almost just like a pure vibration. Then it grew louder and the men on either side of him started to hum also making the sound even larger. I watched them as they did this. Their eyes were closed and their bodies stayed still. For a second I could almost see their bodies vibrating. Then the last two men joined in and the sound now echoed around the cave making it more than triple in volume. Each man joined into the perfect pitch, all sounding exactly the same. Now they opened their mouths and held them half open making the sound lift from a hum to a solid tone. It felt like the whole cave was vibrating.

I realised now that I must join in too. I closed my eyes and felt the sound vibrate through me. I too started to hum and once I had held this constant I opened my mouth also. I instantly faltered as I realised my tone did not match the others and I felt the man beside me slip in his sound too as though I had pulled him out of the group vibration. I heard something within the sound. I thought it was the leader's voice but it was so blended with the tone it couldn't be.

It said "Hold with the sound" and so I did. It was as though the others tuned me. Soon I matched their frequency perfectly. Now all six of us were in perfect vibration with one another and the cave echoed it back upon us. I wondered for a moment how far this sound could be heard and I immediately dropped out of the group dynamic and had to connect with the sound again.

This continued for almost an hour. My mouth grew dry and my throat grew sore. I had to stop. I slowly opened my eyes and saw the men still as they had been before I joined in. There was one difference though. Each one was floating a clear two to three inches off the floor.

I blinked thinking it was simply my eyes tricking me from being closed and in such a different state for so long. But this was no mistake of my eyes. I saw their clothes hang down and even move with a breeze that made its way in. Then one by one each man slowed their toning and I saw them gently settle back upon the floor. They went quiet and then slowly opened their eyes.

The leader looked to me and shook his head.

"No, this school is not for you," he said and I knew it also.

There were many things I wished to learn and share with others.

How to live in a cave and float off the floor was not among them. Thales was right; I too could not see how this would serve humanity.

Back upon the road to Tyre I reflected upon my short visit to the mystery school in the mountain and laughed out loud. Then I suddenly stopped. I looked down at my canteen, now almost empty. I looked around me for the telltale signs of a well or even a river, but there were none. I realised these men were far from any water source and then I looked around the landscape as well. I saw no animals being kept or any source of edible vegetation. They were a distance from any village to purchase such things and yet I had seen no sign of a food storage area.

"Perhaps they float their food in?" I thought and chuckled to myself.

I knew though this was not the case. Just as I had tuned my body to need less I knew these men had done so that their bodies needed of nothing. For a second I almost regretted that I had been rejected as a student. Then my stomach growled and I thought of how nice it felt with a good bowl of beans within it. I smiled once more and picked up my pace to get to Tyre.

I had been to Tyre many times as a child and as a youth with my father. It was the first foreign place he had taken me to but to visit his family it had not felt so strange. Now returning as a man it felt different.

The huge goat farm still existed on the outskirts but was now more like a commune being run by several generations. Few of my uncles remained and those that did were now frail and simple of mind. One did remember me but then would call me by my father's name as his memory slipped from present to past within a breath.

My cousins received me with the hospitality expected but I could feel their discomfort in not knowing of what to speak with me about. The talk was very small and awkward and they would soon find an excuse to be off attending to the animals or some chore. I appreciated their attempts to connect with me and I truly enjoyed spending time with them. They were a great reminder of how simple and fulfilling life could be. But once again I was reminded that the path my life had chosen began with the opportunities afforded to me by my father.

If he had not left here, he would not have met my mother and I would never have been born. This visit renewed my love and respect for my parents in a whole new way.

I made my thankyous and excuses after barely a week with them. I had travelled out from the farm to visit with scholars in Tyre but it was truly too far to do on a regular basis by foot or the hope of a cart ride. So I decided to find lodging closer to town. When I told this to one of my cousins he laughed out loud.

"Ah, we should have thought of that sooner! Our cousins, the daughters of Antonius live within the township. Surely they owe you lodging," he declared.

Now the full story of Antonius and his mentoring of my father was only known to me. Mercifully it had only been told to Antonius' daughters in parts. Everyone, apart from Mnesarchus, knew the sanitised and socially acceptable version. Antonius' wife had figured it out but kept it to herself so that her shame was buried with her body.

When I arrived at the house of Antonius' youngest daughter I looked upon the grandeur and smiled because I knew my father had helped create this for her. In a way he too had created it to aid my journey which made me appreciate and admire it even more.

"Oh look at you! It is like your father has arrived back from one of his journeys," she beamed as she approached to kiss and hug me.

I was spoiled beyond my dreams here. I was given the grandest bedroom and the most splendid meals. On the first night when I baulked at the meat offered to me my cousin screwed her face up with concern but nodded as I explained myself and my diet to her.

"I would not question you, Pythagoras. I know your father raised you to be as wise a man as he," she said. "Now let me tell you some stories of your father…"

So each night she would tell me some story of my father's time within her home as he worked with her father. She would laugh as she remembered Mnesarchus rolling his eyes at another of Antonius' commentaries on society. Then one day she told me about how after Antonius' death he would still come to their home with a purse after each journey to give money to her mother. Tears poured down her face as she spoke.

"If it was not for your father I might not have this home. I am so glad I could return to him my gratitude through you," she said softly as she turned her glass in her hand before her. "We miss him so much."

"I do too," I replied. Then, for the first time since his death, tears also filled my eyes to think of him.

The schools of Phoenicia were an interesting time for me. I now see them as preparation for Egypt in more ways than one. I know now that it was an important place for me to walk upon. These were the lands that I had ruled over during my time as Pharaoh Thutmose. Once I rode upon these lands in a gold chariot striking fear through the native people. Now I walked upon them with the hope I might be offered a ride upon a donkey cart.

These lands did not offer me any memories that I could clearly see from another incarnation of my existence. However they did offer me times when I would feel something beyond the moment in which I was standing.

The relics of Egyptian rule here were growing fewer by the day. Most had been destroyed as soon as the lands were reclaimed by the local tribes and then the empires that soon made their way west. To remove the temples especially was seen as a great exorcism of the blight of Egyptian rule. Clear out the religion of your oppressor and then the largest sense of being ruled over was also eliminated.

In some regions though the structures were kept and remodelled. The cost of demolishing and rebuilding was simply prohibitive. Much like Thutmose did in erasing Hatshepsut from the walls of his beloved Karnak, so too did some of the Phoenicians, Babylonians and Persians see this as a way to clear these temples and make them their own.

One day I walked through a temple that had been redone with only a minimal of skill and aesthetics. The gods painted on the walls had been scraped away. Hieroglyphs carved into walls were filed off but done so roughly you could still make them out. I walked amongst the columns and walls looking at the defilement. I was thinking how funny it seemed that by scraping at some rocks this somehow made the wrongs of the people who built this go away.

Then I observed a place of some erased hieroglyphs. I traced the outlines that remained beneath the hack marks of the chisels. As I ran my finger along the wall I saw the outline of a cartouche still intact but the markings inside were entirely removed. I knew what a cartouche shape signified. It once held the name of a pharaoh and this one was now completely gone. It struck me how easy it could be to have your name wiped clean. Even carved in stone your posterity was not assured.

I wondered if my name would ever be recorded or remembered—even if it was, for how long? I dropped my hand down to my side and looked around the temple. I realised there were no guarantees for anything you wrote lasting and yet somehow knowledge seemed to live on. It did not matter who documented it or who discovered it, wisdom just needed to be taught and that was enough for it to survive once the teacher was gone.

I leaned back against a column and took a deep breath. I decided that records were not important. What was important was to speak and share whatever I learnt and whatever I discovered. This became one of the core principles of how I would eventually run my school.

I travelled to the eastern edge of Tyre and it was in this region that I spent some time at the schools run by the descendants of Moschus. Moschus was known as a "physiologist" in that he studied the ways of the body. Moschus taught biology in the most holistic of ways. He taught how the emotions were linked to certain organs, how the intellect could be shaped by knowing your body thoroughly, and how the elements of nature worked with or against the body. Most importantly he taught his students to respect their own bodies as the physical embodiment of their spiritual experience. Moschus was ahead of his time and yet this was one of the most ancient of all the mysteries.

The teachers who ran his schools now were at least three generations after Moschus' life and they were just as passionate as when the material was first taught. Their teachings spread into the local area so that many people practised their methods or followed their disciplines— such were the long reaching effects of what Moschus taught.

When I arrived at the first of the schools I was greeted by the teachers with warm embraces. They clapped their hands as they circled me and sang me a song in Babylonian that made me smile. It was an ancient song of welcome and my heart swelled with joy as they sang. When they finished I clapped and bowed with thanks for their greeting. I would never receive a reception like this again.

It was almost midday and I was grabbed by the elbow and led to have lunch with them. We sat upon huge pillows around a low table as platters of food were put before us. Then the questions began.

"Where have you been so far? What disciplines have you learned? How long have you been travelling? Is Thales as—umm—interesting as he is described?"

Some meat was offered to me and I waved it away as I said no. This stopped the talk altogether. Then a fresh barrage of questions began.

"You do not eat meat? How does your body feel without it?"

I relayed all that Thales had taught me and indeed how more efficient I felt my body and my mind were for it.

"So you feel your thoughts are clearer?" one asked as he pulled at his beard.

"Yes," I answered emphatically. "And my bowels as well."

They all laughed at this and I relayed my story of the time when I snuck from Thales school to the taverna to eat lamb and what ensued. This had them howling in laughter.

They gathered themselves and another asked, "What about sex? Is that different? Do you think it has affected your seed production at all?"

Now anywhere else this may seem a highly personal question but in a Moschus school this was asked with the full intent of learning and pure curiosity. This I knew as I sat there but suddenly I was not Pythagoras the scholar and seeker of wisdom. I was now Pythagoras the young, sexually inexperienced man. I stammered a bit and felt my cheeks turn red.

"Umm—I have not experienced sex yet so I cannot compare," I said avoiding eye contact with anyone.

"Well even in pleasuring yourself have you not noticed some difference?" he pushed on oblivious to my discomfort.

Now I felt my face get even hotter. Even in my times and within such a school to speak of such things was quite awkward. It showed me how at ease these men were to discuss bodily functions to gain knowledge. It was no wonder my constipation story amused them so much.

I opened my mouth to reply but I couldn't find the words immediately. The truth was I rarely pleasured myself so that any changes in this too were not noticeable to me. So I merely shook my head and finally said, "No. There is no great change there."

Then we all went back to eating as though we had discussed the most mundane and ordinary of subjects.

My time at the Moschus school helped show me just how balanced Thales was. Yes, there were some wonderful classes where we philosophised on how emotions worked within the physical and how certain organs responded to certain stimuli. Then I attended the classes to deal with physical sensations.

Moschus had taught that experience is the best method to learn. When I was told this in theory I agreed wholeheartedly. That was until I realised just what this entailed in order to fully understand the physical.

For example to learn about pain you had to experience it. So I was cut, pierced and burnt. I was whipped with cords and straps of various widths and lengths. This was all to gain knowledge of the different types of pain. Thankfully experiencing a broken bone was voluntary so

I passed on learning about that. Mind you those that had partaken in this told me it was one of the most amazing things they had ever done. I told them I honoured their choice to do so and would rely upon their wisdom gained with additional respect.

One day there was a commotion at the gates as a cart arrived to the school. It was driven by one of the senior teachers and he was hitting the donkeys to go as fast as they could. All the teachers ran out to greet him and he could hardly speak as he seemed so excited.

"Its fresh but only just," he said breathlessly. "It was found this morning but it is possibly already a night old."

"Fine, fine," said another of the senior teachers. "Let's get it to the table as quick as we can."

Six of the teachers then went to the back of the cart to where a large object was. It was covered in canvas with ropes holding the heavy cloth around it. It took all six men to lift it awkwardly and then when they were balanced they carried it inside.

"What is it?" I whispered to another student beside me.

He did not have time to answer though as one of the teachers faced us all and shouted out, "We have been gifted a fresh body to study with. Make your way to the surgery room immediately if you would like to take part."

With that he began to run to catch up with the men carrying the body as the students all whooped with joy and followed him. My curiosity carried me along also.

This was indeed a huge event for the school. All cultures of our time had strict burial rituals to assist the soul and ensure its passage into the afterlife. No family would offer the body of loved one for dissection lest it hinder that person's journey. Even to use the body and then have the rites performed was seen as desecration. So the school relied upon other sources—tribal fighting and its subsequent casualties that were unclaimed or could not be returned home before they rotted. There was also the occasional death of a vagrant that no-one knew or wanted to spend the money on. The ways were limited but they still could occur. Our generous subject was indeed one of the latter.

"It is actually very socially sound to have them come to us," explained one of the teachers. "They may not receive traditional rites but their body teaches so much that is much more useful than simply leaving it to the vultures and scavengers."

As I watched the dissection that day I noted how respectful the teachers were of the body as well. They sliced it delicately, as much to make sure they did not cut into anything that they needed to show us. Each organ was lifted out like it was a newborn baby being lifted from the womb, cradled in the teacher's hands, and then gently placed upon another table so that we could all file past later and inspect them closely.

I stood at the back upon a chair so that I might look over the students standing in front of me. Several of us did this and we were offered a wonderful view into the abdomen as the teacher pointed to each organ and had us note its placement before he meticulously nipped at the mesentery anchoring it. It was as much a ritual as a class that day and the body received as much honour as any elaborate funeral.

After the organs were extracted another teacher stepped in and began to remove the skin so that we could now see the muscles and how they were placed. This fascinated me even more than the way the organs arranged themselves. Here were these straps of tissue binding across the bones and joints. They did everything from lifting your hand through to making you smile and they worked seamlessly with each other.

I stopped and looked at my own hand, then back to the stripped hands on the table before me. That day I gained a new-found appreciation for my body and all that it did for me. It was like renewing the vows I had subconsciously made with Thales to honour my body. I took a deep breath.

"This is how I wish my own body to be used when I die," I decided.

After my time at the Moschus school I once again contemplated my passage to Egypt. However I knew that the time for me to be there was not quite yet upon me. I started to head back north and as I did so I continually debated with myself as to why I was not only avoiding Egypt but also taking myself even further away from it.

I was once again north of Tyre and had experienced even more of the schools of Phoenicia. It was also at these schools that I finally understood why I had not been to Egypt yet. As I became more known in the region and proved that I was genuinely here to gain knowledge I found that many of the teachers became more open with me. This willingness to share kept me here longer.

It was at the final school that one night over dinner with the help of some wine one of my teachers gave me the answer I had been looking for.

"You do know that all we teach started in Egypt? We are nothing but the remnants of what the Amun priests brought here under Pharaoh Thutmose," he slurred and the other teachers nearby gasped. "Oh hush! I am not telling him anything he will not find out when he finally gets there," he continued. "There was nothing here but superstition and fear until the Egyptians claimed this land. It has all expanded since then and, even though they decimated some of our traditions, I am grateful that they did."

At this one of the other teachers threw a chunk of bread at his head as he called the teacher a traitor. The teacher who spoke picked it up and threw it back.

"Make your way to Egypt and when you do ask all the questions you can to show them that your hunger for knowledge and wisdom is without respite. This is what they want in a student and this is what they will look for before they share with you the depth of the mysteries that they hold. The mysteries come from a place before even Egypt and yet no-one can tell you about that place. It is like it disappeared." He paused and tapped upon his head. "Yet somehow we all connect back to it through here. That is the final mystery that we need to understand."

"You're a fool!" yelled another teacher and threw a fig at him.

This time he picked up the fig and bit it.

"I love figs!" he declared and his eyes began to droop as the wine truly took a hold of him. "Pythagoras, ask the questions and keep the chain going. You owe it to all before you and all that will follow."

With that he slumped upon the floor beside the low table and began snoring.

"I wish you would take him to Egypt with you!" groaned another teacher.

Then we all left the snoring teacher upon the floor and made way to our beds.

After that night I now felt clear about making my way to Egypt. I was grateful I had spent the time I had in Phoenicia and even if I was just going to relearn all of this when I made my way to the southern land I knew I would be prepared. I would arrive as a willing and able student ready to expand. I puffed my chest out at this thought. I would become a teacher in no time at all.

It was after this last school that I decided to make my way to the coast and find a boat on its way to Rhakotis. Every boat heading south went to this port and it would be easy to find one. I was just to the south of the Mount Carmel ridge so I knew to just follow this to the west and I would be at the sea in less than a day.

As I wandered along I stopped and realised that I had walked for some time without passing anybody and this made me curious. The roads along here were always busy with carts moving goods or travellers and yet today there was not one. I stopped and listened to see if perhaps I could hear any sort of noise; a cart approaching, a river, or even a nearby town. But there was nothing.

I looked up at the mountains nearby. They looked amazing at the best of times but today they were majestic. I thought of all the legends that these mountains lay claim to; from the stories of the Egyptian army's passage through them on the way to Megiddo and the stories of Elijah. It was as though they invited you to play amongst the cracks and crevices. It was as though they ached to be filled with stories.

I smiled as I imagined how many schools may be hidden within its depths along with rogues and hermits all trying to escape society. It was as I was doing this that I saw a flash come from halfway up the side of one peak. I laughed out loud, telling myself that my imagination was simply playing with me to satisfy my ponderings but then the flash appeared again—and again. I paused and for a moment I was tempted to make the journey to see just what I was being invited too.

I knew it would be a sanctuary for at least one night and then perhaps tomorrow the road would have more carts upon it to make up for the time I had lost in stopping. I also had enough food in my satchel and water in my canteen for a few days so even if they were non-eaters I could sustain myself. I might even learn their ways and make my food last longer or even redundant.

I took a deep breath and looked along the road and then back to the mountain. For a moment I heard her call me.

"*Come to me,*" she seemed to whisper and I knew that it was not my imagination.

The flash pulsed again but I did not walk towards it. I walked towards another peak of the ridge and spent the next three hours finding my own cave.

I found a lovely small hollow not too far up from ground level. It had barely any sun and the stone floor was cool to sit upon. My satchel and canteen were beside me on the floor as I settled into a cross-legged position and looked out upon the plains below. Once I was comfortable I looked to the stone walls around me.

"Now what?" I asked the mountain out loud.

"*Be quiet and still,*" was the answer I heard but it was not the female voice of the mountain I had heard outside. This time it was decidedly male and felt like my own.

So I sat and was quiet and still. When I finally moved it was two weeks later.

CHAPTER SEVEN

My hermitage did much to prepare me for Egypt. When I finally stood and walked to the edge of the cave and felt the sun upon me I knew that I was now ready for anything. All that I had experienced of the schools in Phoenicia now felt like they had been a part of me forever. I felt aged and yet renewed. It was like I had completed an entire life and yet had all the energy to now start another. My mind was clear and strong as I stepped out and began to climb back down the mountain.

I was at the coast in what felt like less than an hour yet it had been much more. No cart passed me by to offer a ride and the thought never even occurred to me that one should. I just kept placing one foot before the other and when I saw the first glimpse of the blue of the sea I stopped and breathed in the whispers of salt air then picked up my pace.

I was nowhere near a port or dock and yet there at the water's edge I saw a large sailboat pushed up on the sands of a beach. I had intended to follow the shoreline until I found some sort of marina but the timing and placement of a boat here seemed more than coincidence. As I walked towards the boat I saw a man lying at the edge of the beach under a tree. His arm was over his eyes as though blocking out the sun and as I got closer I heard him snore and realised he was sleeping. I looked at the boat and saw another man walking upon the deck arranging some sacks. Then a third man walked from the trees nearby carrying a sack full of something over his shoulder.

"You know a little help wouldn't go astray!" he yelled out to the man on the boat.

"Well, you wake him if you dare," was his curt response.

I walked down the sand only a few paces behind the one carrying the sack and he felt my presence immediately even if he mistook who I was.

"Nice of you to break your slumber and join us," he snarled over his shoulder.

"Oh, I am not your shipmate," I said trying not to laugh.

At this he stopped and dropped the sack at his feet.

"Who are you? What are you doing here?" he asked quickly and I saw some red in his face. The second man jumped down from the boat and was beside him in an instant.

"I am a traveller and I am wondering if you might be on your way to Egypt," I asked knowing somehow to keep this simple. "I have money. I will pay you," I added and pulled my purse from within my clothes and showed them a coin.

The second man's eyes lit up.

"But of course we can take you to Egypt," he said and grabbed the coin from my hand. "We leave as soon as we load the boat. The quicker we load, the sooner we leave," he finished by nodding his head to the place between the trees where the other man had emerged from.

"Fine. As you can imagine I am quite tired after walking from the mountain ridge. I will join your other friend in resting before we leave," I replied and made my way to the shade of a tree away from where the remaining sacks were and a distance from the snorer. I was tired but not terribly much so. The sailors' attempt to have me help them was worth the disregard I gave it. I was paying them more than their due fare and the fact that they were loading their boat away from a recognised port made it fairly clear that their cargo was illegal, stolen or both. Taking passage upon their boat was enough support for whatever they were doing.

As I walked away to my tree the first man turned to the one who agreed to take me as a passenger.

"What are you thinking?" he hissed. "He will give us away for sure!"

"Hush! When we get to Egypt we will sell him on as a slave. Look at his physique. We will get good money for him and this coin will seem like nothing," he laughed as he tossed it up and caught it. "You need to think a bit more creatively. Besides did you not hear that he just walked from the mountain ridge? Who does that alone? He has been there praying or studying some weird school. What threat is someone like that?"

His shipmate nodded. "Let us hope you are right or else you know what will happen to all of us."

The boat was finished loading in well under an hour. One of the men called out to me. Then he walked to their colleague still sound asleep under his tree and kicked him in the side.

"Wake up," he yelled and walked to the boat.

The sleeping man sat up and rubbed his eyes.

"Ah, now I am ready for a full nights sailing," he said and stood up. Then he noticed me walking towards the boat.

"Who is this?" he yelled to his shipmates.

One replied in a very strange dialect that I could not understand and the sleeper doubled over with laughter.

"Oh my! Welcome to our boat," he said and bowed to me as he continued laughing.

I paused for a minute as he did this. I was clearly being mocked and suddenly I thought of Thales and his olive presses. I smiled and continued on to the boat.

The boat had been pushed into the water lest it be too heavy to launch once fully loaded and so we all walked into the sea up to our thighs to get in. Two men lifted me while the third pulled at my arms. Then in turn I helped pull the other two aboard. Once we were all on deck the one who had taken my coin began to give orders to the others. He was clearly the captain or person in charge so I approached him.

"Where shall I sit to be out of your way?" I asked plainly.

He looked around the deck as he scratched his arm. "There," he pointed to a bench near the front of the boat. "You will be out of the way there."

I went and sat upon my bench looking out to the open ocean and imagined Egypt somewhere upon her. As the sailors yelled their calls to coordinate the lifting of the sails I felt the boat begin to move out beyond the waves. I felt no desire to look back upon the land I was leaving.

The gentle rolling of the ship as it made its way to the open water began to lull me into a state of half-sleep. It was in this gentle state that I had spent my time within my cave. It was both seductive and addictive. I had cherished it while I was alone and imagined I would need to find another such refuge to connect with it again. Yet here in the open, with the unsteady sea below and men yelling out directions and rude jokes, I felt it wash over me once more.

The more I surrendered to it the more the sounds and sensations around me seemed to fade or simply not seem so abrasive. The men's voices softened, the sea did not move so much and the sun was gentle and caressing. I closed my eyes and breathed in deep and felt the gentleness of all around me seem to swell. Each breath took me deeper back to the sensation of the quiet and solitude.

I opened my eyes and realised that one of the men was beside me. He was holding out a piece of meat on some bread for me. I smiled and waved it away as I shook my head. He shrugged and with his other hand offered me some wine. Now I smiled as I said "No." He once again shrugged, muttered something and returned to his shipmates.

"He wouldn't take it," he said to the captain.

"Well he mustn't be hungry. He most likely has something stashed in his satchel for when he does," the captain replied but he sensed something was not right.

This feeling grew as night began to fall and I had not moved from my place upon the bench. I had taken a few light sips from my canteen but none of them had seen me do so. So when I once again refused the offering of meat, bread and wine the captain began to watch me intently. When the time came for him to retire for the night he approached me.

"You are welcome to a bunk below to sleep should you care to join us," he offered.

"Thank you, but I am just fine up here," I answered and smiled.

He tried to remain calm but I saw his brow furrow slightly as he walked away.

"Keep an eye on him," he said to the sailor who would stay on deck through the night.

"Why certainly, because as you know I do not have enough to occupy me," the sailor answered sarcastically.

"Perhaps you too would like to be sold into slavery. I wouldn't get much for you but at least I would not have to hear that smart mouth again!" the captain snapped and climbed below deck to sleep.

The sailor watched me as he went about the deck and laughed at his captain's paranoia. He eventually made his way beside me and stood arms crossed and swaying with the boat.

"A beautiful clear night. You chose well to sail at this time to Egypt. The sea can be most unfavourable on this route," He said attempting some small talk.

"Yes, my father told me that also. He went to Egypt many times," I answered.

The sailor looked at me quite surprised that I had engaged in talk so easily. He had been told by the other two that I had emerged from Mount Carmel and imagined I would have nothing to say beyond one word answers. We continued on with our conversation which I quite enjoyed. We shared our family and travel histories even making each other laugh as we did so. This warmed the sailor to me even more.

"Look—you haven't had anything to eat or drink since you came on board. Surely you must be hungry by now? Let me get you something," he offered.

I raised my hand. "I am fine. I have had some water and my body needs little for sustenance. Besides what you have to offer me I do not eat. We are only another day away. I will eat my fill when we get to Egypt. I hear the dates there are exceptional," I said.

"Indeed they are," the sailor answered and smiled. Then just as suddenly he stopped smiling as he remembered the captain's plans for me when they arrived. "What do you have planned for yourself when you get to Egypt?" he asked.

I then told of how I would find the schools that would show me where all knowledge stemmed from. Then suddenly I was pouring out my plans for my entire life; how I wanted to fulfil my father's vision for me but even more importantly how I wished to serve humanity by ensuring wisdom and knowledge would continue to be taught and to expand what was already known. I have no idea why I said all this but I am glad I did.

The sailor looked at me when I finished and didn't say a word. I thought it was because he didn't understand anything I had just explained to him. Why would a simple sailor appreciate that? But he identified with it more than I could have imagined. Here before me stood a man who himself had such plans but somehow had lost his way off the path that he had hoped for. He looked down at his feet for a moment then looked back to me.

"I hope the gods grant you all that you wish to achieve and I will be amongst the first to give them thanks when you do," he said softly and then he turned to continue his work.

The sailor was checking upon the ropes that tied the sails in place. He was thinking of how he was now part of disrupting my plans and he frowned. Then he remembered the paranoia and fear of his captain as he had asked that I be watched during the night. At this he smiled and almost began to laugh. In that moment the sailor whose own mind was not going to accomplish noble things decided to help someone whose mind would.

When the captain came above deck at first light, before even assessing the weather, he looked to see was where I was. When he found me still in the same place and with the same posture he called out to the sailor who had done night duty.

"What did he do during the night?" the captain asked.

"He did what you see him doing now," the sailor answered.

"What? Surely he moved? Surely he lay down to sleep?" the captain said and the panic in his voice made it hard for the sailor not to laugh out loud.

The sailor kept his voice steady though. "No, he stayed awake and sitting all night," he answered and shook his head. "It was amazing to watch."

Now this was a blatant lie as I had slept for several hours albeit sitting up but the captain was not going to doubt the sailor. His face began to turn red and the sailor seeing that he had fallen for his report continued on.

"I offered him food but he said that he didn't need it. Can you believe that? Makes you wonder just what he was doing in the mountains. I did talk to him for sometime. He has visions just like the great prophets and he foresaw the calm seas at this time so knew it would be safe to sail to Egypt to continue his work." The sailor stopped at this, afraid to spin too much of a story but he had achieved what he set out to do. Besides he was tired now and just wanted to head to his bunk and sleep.

Now the captain was truly scared of me. He approached me some time later with some food and wine to test me.

"You must eat!" he snapped as he shoved the food at me.

"I do not need to," I replied simply and looked back at the ocean.

He walked away breathing heavily and kept his distance for the rest of the day. As the sun set the night sailor came on deck and began his duties. The captain grabbed him by the arm and dragged him to the back of the boat as far away from me as possible.

"Will you be alright alone with this man?" the captain whispered.

"Why? What happened today?" the sailor asked.

"Nothing. He did nothing once again. It is not normal. There must be something working within him that is supernatural," the captain hissed.

"Oh," replied the sailor and feigned concern. "If I do feel threatened then I will surely call out for your help. Please do not sleep so deeply tonight!"

The captain called to the other sailor and together they retired to their bunks. This left me once again alone with the night sailor. He walked to the front of the boat and stood beside me which made me jump just a little with surprise.

"I am sorry—it is just that your colleagues kept their distance all day," I said as I laughed.

"They are confused by your behaviour," he replied and then he laughed too. "They think you have special powers that you may use on them if they come too close."

At this we laughed together and the sailor went about his duties.

The next morning the captain and other sailor had dark circles under their eyes. The night sailor saw this and knew they had slept poorly.

"How was your night?" the captain asked and the night sailor began to speak of the weather and wave heights. "No—not that! What did *he* do?" the captain spat.

"The same as he did since he came aboard," said the sailor plainly and looked pensively towards me. "I hope he does not suddenly perish or weaken from no food. You will never get a good price at the slave markets for him then."

"I have forgotten the slave markets. What if he casts a spell on me if I do? I just cannot risk that!" the captain said as he narrowed his eyes.

"A wise idea. Last night a huge wave was approaching. He saw me panic and raised his hand. The wave flattened immediately," the sailor said. "I thought it was my eyes playing tricks but I am sure now that it wasn't."

The captain almost retched at hearing this. "Thank the gods we will be in Egypt soon!" he muttered.

So I spent another day in my "solitude" while the captain and his daytime sailor went about their duties as far away from me as possible. It was late afternoon when the coast of Egypt made herself known and I sighed with relief. There were other ships making their way in the waters and the men on my boat dropped their sail to slow our passage down.

"If we try and make our way amongst these larger vessels we will get crushed," he offered as he stood upon the prow but I knew it was because he had stolen from several of these ships and wanted to avoid being seen. "We will go to a smaller port west of Rhakotis," he announced eyeing me cautiously to see my reaction.

I merely sighed and shrugged my shoulders. "You are the captain," I said simply and closed my eyes.

Two hours later we were docked upon a port that you would miss if you did not know it existed. It was barely a port at all. There was a rudimentary pier that even our medium sized boat threatened to crush as it berthed. There were a few men about but it was nothing like the mayhem that we would have encountered at Rhakotis. Several of the men recognised the boat and walked along the pier to meet the captain. My night companion having heard the calls from the pier and the sounds of the ropes being thrown to tie the boat awoke and joined us in the sunlight.

"So you are now in Egypt!" he said to me and smiled slyly.

"Yes, I am," I replied as I stood and began to have a stretch. "It has been a long journey."

I do not think there are many more moments in my life that I felt such joy as I did to finally arrive in Egypt. As I stepped off the pier and upon the sands I could not help but raise my hands in the air almost like I was saluting and congratulating myself for finally making it here. I would have loved to have screamed out, "Father, I am here at last!" as well but I refrained. I dropped my hands by my side and turned to thank the captain and his men.

The captain was already busy in negotiations for his cargo but as I turned I caught his eye and he made his excuses and headed towards me.

"Do not go yet! Wait here!" he said nervously. He turned and yelled out to his two sailors. They ran to join him and together they made way to the small market stalls nearby. All three returned soon enough, their arms full of fresh fruit. As I stood upon the beach with the water lapping nearby they piled the fruit at my feet. As the captain stood up, he put his hands together and bowed repeatedly.

"Thank you, thank you," he said barely able to look me in the eye. "I wish you the best of fortune upon your journey." With that he walked quickly back to his ship to resume his trading, followed by the day sailor.

My night companion held back for a moment. I looked at him and shook my head. I did not know whether to laugh or not.

"Enjoy your dates," he said and smiled. "Enjoy Egypt." He leant down, took a date, popped it in his mouth and so too returned to the ship.

I sat down before my "offering" and looked at the delicious fruit before me. I ate as much as my stomach could bear after so long with hardly anything. Then I filled my satchel with the remains and began to walk to my new education.

It took probably an hour more than it should have to reach the main ports of the delta. I could not help but stop every now and then to soak up my new surrounds. It was not so different to where I had been and it took me some time to truly sense the distinction. I soon realised the difference about this land was not the trees, the smells or the temperature. Egypt's difference was its age.

The lands I had walked upon to get here had their lengthy history but I felt immediately that it was not of the same depth that was here. Everywhere you walked there were some symbols or suggestions of this. If it was not a temple, then it was a mastaba or tomb. The uniform manner in which all of these were constructed only made this sense stronger.

In the lands of Phoenicia, Babylonia and Persia, and even Greece and Anatolia, each era or empire that dominated soon saw their idiosyncrasies and arts take over. It was like each ruler wiped the slate clean and began new. Even though some styles and nuances persisted it was nothing like the flow with which the Egyptians carried on traditions and also that they did so with the utmost respect for their forebears. It was as though preserving their ways somehow set up a never ending cycle of reverence for tradition that could not be broken.

It also served the egos of the Pharaohs well. Maintaining the legends of those before made sure they were part of an elite group. It also gave them something to measure against so that they could surpass it.

A grand temple such as the one that Thutmose built at Karnak not only assured the favour of Amun but also set a benchmark for civic work and artistic merit which is still revered in your modern time.

This continuity of tradition also made me acutely aware of just why Thales and indeed the oracle knew I should be here. This place felt like the source of all civilisations. I truly believe that the Egyptians knew this when they began the custom of working with stone for it ensured the immortality of their society. It was not just ego and a taste for grandeur which drove them to do this. It was also a sense of duty to carry on and add to what had been the seeds of their existence.

The permanence was just a reflection of the eternal and limitless knowledge that these people possessed. I know they dressed it up with images of gods and the endless rituals they designed for them but the essence of what they were doing was much more. As time moved on and their society flowed with the natural processes of progress and reinvention, the knowledge fell upon the shoulders of those who could best serve it. That was the priesthood and they took this responsibility most seriously.

As with all human endeavours though, politics, emotions and egos came into play. Funnily enough this actually benefited the priesthood. There were those happy to play out the machination of a Pharaoh and his court. There were those happy to serve the commoners and their beliefs. Thankfully there were those who were more than happy to avoid the trappings of the more glamorous roles and to remain loyal to the ancient mysteries. It would be my goal to seek this latter sect of priests out and study with them.

The ancient port that I have referred to as Rhakotis would later become known as Alexandria. That would be another few hundred years later when the great Alexander came to Egypt. It was at this place that I would start my studies in Egypt.

I stood amongst its bustle, once again feeling like the young child in the market at Samos. I suddenly sensed Anaximander by my side as though he was ready to guide me. Then I remembered his words.

"No man puts one foot before the other without knowing where he is going."

I nodded to myself and silently thanked him. I was a man now and it was my choice of where to go and how to get there. I had no parent to consult with. No teacher to seek advice from. This was all my doing and would always be my own. My task now was to find the temples where the original mysteries were taught.

This didn't prove too hard a task. All I had to do was find one of the major temples and begin asking questions. The temples around the delta were mostly for the commoners. The priests and priestesses here practiced the day-to-day rituals to protect and guide the traders and farmers who lived in the vicinity. The school that my father had come to in the months before I was born was on the outskirts of the delta trade region. This was not so surprising as these schools needed quiet and seclusion as had all the schools I attended so far.

When I arrived at the school I stood before the stone building and looked at the huge wooden doors that formed the entrance. Suddenly I was taken aback. This wasn't quite what I had expected. Temple schools were usually open and you could wander in yet here they had almost set up a fortress with these huge doors.

I walked to the side of the building and saw only solid walls. The back and other side were the same making it clear that the doors at the front were the only way in. There were smaller buildings around the main building but with just a quick look I recognized that they were just sleeping quarters. I braced myself and walked up the stairs to the wooden doors.

I knocked my fist upon one of the doors and as soon as I heard the dull thud I realised that they were much thicker than normal doors and there was no way the noise would be heard unless someone was standing directly behind it. I took a step back and yelled at the doors.

"Greetings!" I shouted as loud as I could and waited—and waited—and waited.

"I seek the teachers of this school that I may join you!" I now yelled and waited—and waited but still no response.

"*There must be no-one inside,*" I thought to myself. "*I'll just wait til someone appears.*"

I sat down upon the topmost step for some time. So long so that I had to shift as the sun moved to find more shade. My stomach began to grumble so I pulled out some of the fruit in my bag. I was about to put a date into my mouth when I stopped and studied it for a moment.

"How long did you wait to get ripe to then just have me stuff you in a bag and then eat you?" I asked it and laughed.

Time wore on and I eventually lay down upon the stone floor

before the doors and rested. When I say I rested I simply took some strain off my back while I recounted some teachings. There is no better way to spend some quiet time than to revisit some knowledge you have attained already. It cements it in your mind and invites it to expand. Refreshing your stories of learning is the best way to build upon what you have.

I was doing this for so long that the sun finally set. I sat up as the red hues made their way up the stairs to my feet. I was fascinated at how the colours played upon the carvings and the paintings on the front of the temple. Then I saw a sliver of light from beneath the doors of the temple. I knew someone was inside as that flame could not have burnt all day on its own.

I jumped to my feet and walked up to the doors.

"Greetings!" I yelled out again. This time I did not wait as long until I sat down again. They would have to come out eventually and I had the time and patience that was needed to be here when they did. Even if I eventually chose to sleep it would not be so deep that they could sneak past me.

It grew far darker. I pulled another piece of fruit from my bag. This time I chose a plum. It was already very soft; a combination of faster ripening in the heat and of being squashed in my satchel.

"You are on the verge of spoiling. Fortunately I am not about to turn as you are," I said to it and laughed.

I was just contemplating lying down to take my sleep when I heard some sounds from behind the doors. It was the scrape of the beam holding the doors closed being moved. I jumped to my feet in anticipation of the doors finally opening and when they did move my heart jumped with joy.

As they parted I tried to get a peek inside but being just lit by lamps there was not much that I could see. I stayed calm and when the doors were open wide enough two men walked out with their heads down.

"Hello," I called out to them but they did not respond and kept walking. Then another two followed and another set of two men. A silent procession now made its way from the temple and all I could do was stand back and watch. They made their way down the stairs and into the nearby quarters.

As the last of the men left the bottom stair I sighed and wondered what I should do now. Just as I resigned myself to spending the remainder of the night upon the portico in the hope of getting some attention in the morning a deep voice came from within the temple.

"Enter!" it boomed and I turned to make my way through the doors.

Once inside my eyes adjusted. There were the usual columns forming an aisle that led to a raised platform. There was no altar there though. Instead there were four chairs and upon them sat men who were clearly the elders of the temple. As I got close to the dais another younger man walked quickly from amongst the columns and placed a chair at the base of the stairs before them. He gestured to the seat indicating I should sit down, which I did, and waited for the men to begin speaking.

This took some time and I silently noted that if I was going to learn anything at this school it would most certainly be patience. The elders measured me for some time and the second from the left spoke.

"Who are you? Why are you here?" he asked.

"I am Pythagoras of Samos," I said confidently and paused hoping that my name had somehow made its way here. The blank looks upon their faces told me this was otherwise and I continued. "I come to seek the ancient mysteries that I may expand my knowledge and become a teacher to others."

This was also met with no reaction. Then the elder second from the right spoke.

"Why should we teach you here at our school?" he asked with no emotion.

This I knew was my opportunity to share with them all that I had done. I told them everything from the story of the oracle and my early start with languages through to my recent time in Phoenicia. I spoke loud and strong. I waved my hands to emphasise points while they sat still and quiet. I knew they listened though as not once did their eyes move from me. Then I was finished and once again all was silent.

"Come back in the morning," the first elder said. "We will inform you of our decision then."

I was stunned at this. After all I had shared and they still had to discuss me! I swallowed my pride and remembered that these men must be respected. They held the keys to my next phase and I would bend to meet them if I must. I knew not to cause waves at this stage lest I affect my admittance to any other schools.

"Might I have a bed to sleep for the night?" I asked.

"Certainly," I heard from amongst the columns and the man who had carried my chair appeared again from the shadows. "Follow me."

I stood and bowed to the elders. "I will see you in the morning," I said and bowed one more time before following the man.

He walked me back to the front doors and down the stairs.

"How long have you been here?" I asked him but I gained no

response. He just kept walking and led me to one of the small buildings. He pushed open a door and handed me the lamp he had been carrying.

"There should be an empty bed in here. Just make sure it is actually empty before you lie down. Do not speak with anyone. Be back at the doors at sunrise," he said brusquely and walked off in the moonlight.

I stepped slowly into the room with just the glow of the lamp before me. I heard the gentle sounds of deep sleep from several places within the room so I made my way towards a place where it felt quiet. I was before a bed now and slowly moved the lamp along its length. There was no gathering of the blankets or any other indication that there was a body within it. I set the lamp upon the floor and undressed.

Once in the bed I put out the lamp and enjoyed the gentle wash of the moonlight through the window and the cracks around the door. I was asleep in no time and thankfully so, as this allowed me to wake as the light began to change. The window of my room faced the dawn so the pinks of the pre-dawn woke me. I sat up, stretched, and then dressed. I was determined to be there upon those steps before the elders to show them my dedication.

I found the well nearby and splashed some water upon my face in the hope it would wash anyway the last traces of sleep. This it did and I felt awake and clear. I looked around for the telltale signs of where their lavatories were but my bowels could forsake that routine this morning to not risk me being late.

I bounded up the stairs and saw the doors were already open—and there upon the chairs at the opposite end were the elders.

"Approach!" one called out and I walked slowly to stand before them. The chair that had been placed for me was no longer in position and no-one appeared to get another for me. I would receive their verdict standing and this in itself was not a good omen.

Once again I was made to wait for some time as they stared at me with blank expressions. I wondered if perhaps they were waiting for me to speak but I instantly dismissed this. The schools just didn't work like that. Not one that I had been to would allow an applicant to address the elders without some sort of instruction or invitation. Part of me was amused but another part of me started to simmer with anger. My patience which I had always deemed endless had now reached a limit.

I took a breath though and let my shoulders relax. This was not missed by the elders and the one second from the left leaned forward to speak.

"We have deliberated and consulted with each other. It is the decision of the council that you will not be admitted to this school," he said plainly and rested back into his chair.

It took me several seconds to realise what I had just heard. It was in fact my first rejection or hurdle in any of my studies so far. The registration of this saw my feigned smile slip off my face as it in turn went red.

"WHY?" I bellowed at them and before I knew it my hands were curled into fists by my side.

Once again I was subjected to silence, though I did see a slight shift in one of the elder's body. This made me somewhat happy that my anger had caused some discomfort but I had completely lost any enjoyment in their methods. The elder second from the right now spoke without moving anything but his mouth.

"We need you to be different," he said calmly but with such strength that I could not doubt the conviction with which he spoke.

"Different? After all I told you! All I have done has led me to your school and you say I need to be different. Dear Sirs, in making this decision you negate all I have achieved," I said loudly.

"No, we do not," the elder replied. "Any negation of your achievements is purely of your own accord."

"Urgh," I muttered and threw my hands in the air. "Fine! Then tell me what do I need to learn to be accepted?" I asked.

As frustrating as this was and as offensive as I had deemed this to be I still needed to know what it was they were looking for.

"It is not something you need to learn. It is about what you need to remember," the same elder said.

Now my anger found a whole new level. I felt like my brain was going to explode out of my skull.

"*They are just playing with me!*" I thought and decided I needed to calm down or the game would just continue.

Once again I stood before them silent and somewhat calm. I relaxed my hands by my side, dropped my eyes to the floor and waited to be addressed. Once again they made me wait for what felt like longer than necessary.

"Pythagoras, do you wish to know how to revive these memories?" the same elder spoke once again.

I looked up slowly. "But of course," I lied. I had no true interest in these silly intangible methods, however I was curious.

The elder shifted in his seat and actually smiled. "Good. What is needed from you is that you will seclude yourself for forty days and nights. During this time you will fast and breathe."

"Breathe?" I asked incredulously.

"Yes, that is what I said," he replied.

I recalled my time in the cave upon Mount Carmel. I had already done such a thing and told them yet they seemed to think this did not matter. Then I wondered if they recalled this fact at all.

"Sir, may I remind you that I have done such a time already," I spoke as calmly as I could.

The elder shook his head. "That was merely a rest and you certainly did not do the breathing that we ascribe to."

I fought every instinct to once again groan outwardly and instead just sighed.

"My dear teachers. I must remind you that I do not come here seeking discipline. I am here to seek knowledge," I emphasised.

"My dear Pythagoras. I must remind you we are not interested in knowledge at all, we are interested in actual experience. No knowledge is true knowledge unless it is lived and experienced," was the composed response I received.

The first elder who spoke now leaned forward again. "Pythagoras, it is time for you to go. Should you wish to partake in the required forty day exercise then we will happily reconsider your admittance." He leant back and once again all four elders' faces went cold.

I looked at them bewildered that my first school application in Egypt had gone so badly. I also knew I would be wasting my time and words to attempt any further discussion.

It was a very long walk back to the temple doors and down the stairs. I was only a short distance away from the building when my temper flared again.

"*What if the other schools hear about this and I suffer more rejections?*" I thought.

At this my temper raged. If this were to happen then it would prove the oracle wrong and this I could not believe especially when so far all had confirmed it. Then I thought of my father and all he had done to ensure my success. I bent over and picked up a stone. Turning back to face the temple I flung it as hard as I could. The stone hit the top step and I saw it bounce across the portico and through the open doors.

"This day marks your loss and not mine!" I yelled and I was sure my words echoed into the temple.

As the stone scuttled through the doorway sending its tiny echoes towards the elders, they sighed and looked to one another.

"That was harder than I thought it would be," said the one who had addressed me the most. "I didn't expect that anger at all."

The one second from the left turned to him and shook his head. "So much passion and dedication. Perhaps we were wrong to dismiss him so quickly?"

The man who sat at the very left leant forward and looked at his three colleagues. "We did exactly as we knew we should. We were told what to do when the time arrived and we did it. His reaction is his responsibility and his to own."

"Yes, but perhaps we could have designed it a different way. An order from twenty years ago surely could be modified to suit the present day application of it?" the man next to him argued.

"Really? And I suppose you believe that the ancient mysteries should be adjusted to suit the times as well? Perhaps you should go and practice in the mainstream temples of the Pharaoh so you can adjust your teachings to every whim of the man?" he asked with his eyebrow raised.

"Yes, yes, I see your point," the elder conceded and sank back in his chair. "Do you think he will be back? I know anger can be transmuted into creativity but he just didn't seem open to that."

"He may not return to us but he will find his way into some school," the first elder predicted.

"Should we inform the other schools," asked the second elder.

"No!" the other three cried in unison.

"His path is his own. His failings here should not be based on by others to make suppositions," said the first elder. "Our duty has been done. There is no more we need to do."

The elders of this school had indeed been expecting me. This was the exact school at which Mnesarchus had arrived in the hope of enrolling me before I was even born. Though none of the elders from that time were still alive their records of that meeting had survived.

When Mnesarchus had left the school that day to make his way back to Samos he was broken-hearted at how closed the elders had been with him. The elders of that time while impressed with Mnesarchus' dedication and ambition for me were nonetheless concerned. They knew instantly that I would make a worthwhile student but they had some misgivings.

"When do you suppose the child may be brought here?" one asked afterwards.

"I imagine as soon as he can read and write just as we suggested," answered another.

"No," said a third elder. "He will not return that soon. This child will be a man before he walks through the doorway again." He furrowed his brow as he spoke.

"What concerns you about this," asked the first man.

"What concerns me is that he will arrive here full of preconceptions and expectations. He will have been doused with every bit of knowledge his father can access. Some will be worthy and much will be futile," he spoke strongly and then pointed his finger to the space before them. "He will stand there and speak of all he has done with great triumph as though that alone will make him worthy of admittance but it will not. That child will come here with great knowledge of everything but himself."

"What student does know himself before he arrives here?" argued the fourth elder.

"Our students arrive here knowing nothing. They do not know themselves but they also know no geometry, astronomy or anything else we teach. They are blank slates to write new stories upon. That child will arrive with his slate so full you won't be able to see between the markings. He will have to undo everything to be of any good here or to find any good with us," he spoke emphatically and the other elders nodded.

"What if he arrives after our passage from this life?" the second elder put to the men.

"I will write a recommendation to those who will come after. It will be their choice as to how it is followed," the third elder said.

So it was that a scroll was written outlining how I should be admitted to the school if at all. Now the elder who wrote it did not know my name but my circumstances were such that my reputation and background were as telling as my name. Whispers of my attendance at the schools in Phoenicia and Miletus had made their way south and into Egypt, so that weeks before I had even landed upon the shore the schools had been expecting me. All they had to do was look out for a self-assured Greek and in Egypt such men were rare.

That day as I walked towards the school I had noticed young boys playing alongside the road. They put their hands out asking for money and I shook my head, answering in my rough Egyptian.

"Where are you from?" one asked as he smiled never putting his hand down and walking beside me.

"I am from Samos," I answered.

"Samos?" he said and screwed his face up. "Where is that?"

"It is part of Greece and a long way from here," I laughed.

With that he smiled again, suddenly lost interest in begging and finally stopped following me. Or so I thought. What he did was run back along the road to a track which led to the right and circled around me. He was ahead of me and out of eyesight in no time and then continued to run as fast as his legs could carry him. The boy ran into the school grounds, up the stairs of the main temple and pounded on the door.

The man who had given me my chair and led me to my bed the night before opened a small section of the huge door and looked out.

"What is it?" he hissed. "You have broken the entire group's meditation."

"The Greek is on his way here!" yelled the boy breathlessly.

"What! Are you sure?" said the man.

"Yes, yes, I asked him. He looks Greek and I asked him. He said he was from Samos," the boy finished and held out his hand.

"You will get no money until he appears on our doorstep and we see that he is indeed the man," snapped the assistant and then he slammed the opening shut.

The assistant then hurried back to where the four elders were waiting to hear what the commotion had been about.

"The Greek is here in Egypt and on his way to the school," he said as breathlessly as the boy had.

The elders looked to each other and the eldest nodded.

"We are ready," he said plainly and then turned to the group of men sitting before them on the temple floor. "When he arrives we do not make a sound. Let us see how he chooses to approach us and how determined he is."

So when I arrived and knocked upon the doors the entire school had already made their pact. As I called out they sat in silence as though they heard nothing. Except the elders who looked once again at each other.

One elder turned to the assistant. "See what he looks like and how his demeanour appears," he instructed.

So the assistant walked silently to the front doors and peered at me through the gap between the doors. I had taken my seat by now so had my back to him but he saw enough. I was indeed Greek and as robust as I was rumoured to be. He relayed this to the elders.

"Watch him and tell us all that he does," they instructed and so this is what he did.

When I pulled out my date and spoke to it this was relayed to the elders. They raised their eyebrows as they heard this.

"This is the infamous Greek we have heard about? A man who speaks to fruit?" one muttered and then their vigil continued.

154

As the night grew and the students within the temple contemplated sleep, as I did outside upon the portico, the elders looked amongst the students and knew they could not hold out any longer.

"We shall let the students make to their beds and we shall grant this man his audience," one proposed and they all agreed.

"And we shall remain firm upon following the suggestions of our predecessors?" another put forward and the other three nodded.

So the assistant was told to walk amongst the men and let them know they would soon be in their beds. They were to form a procession and no-one was to speak. Their exit from temple was never this formal but they all knew that making it look like a ritual would make it difficult for me to approach them individually.

As the last of the students made their way down the stairs the elders all took deep long breaths to ready themselves to meet me. Then the eldest on the very left called out that single word that began it all, "Enter!"

When that night meeting had ended they knew just how right the elder who had sat before Mnesarchus twenty years earlier had been.

CHAPTER EIGHT

I walked away from the school and the further I got the more my anger subsided. However if I recalled the words and demeanour of the elders it came back upon me instantly. I had never felt like this in my life. Not even the disgust and frustration with Polycrates had made me feel so agitated. I was not enjoying it and knew that I would have to gather myself before I approached anyone else.

I found a tree with some shade to sit beneath. Resting my head back upon the trunk I closed my eyes and went over the meeting again. They were the same things I had said to any school that had asked me when I arrived and I was perplexed as to why these same words had failed me this time. All I could do was shake my head as I replayed it again and again.

Then I began to dissect the bigger picture. I was in a different land so to change my ways was the only solution that seemed to make sense of this. I looked down at my clothes. I was still wearing Greek dress. My hand reached up to my face and I scratched my beard then realised this was another thing. No Egyptian man had more than a small goatee upon their chin, if one at all, and these were the high ranking men. My full head of hair was another issue altogether. So I decided that to become part of the Egyptian schools I would at least start by looking Egyptian.

It was not too hard to find someone to trade my clothes with. The ample cloths of my Greek garb could be recycled in a number of ways. I felt naked to be standing in a knee length kilt, my chest bare and only a tunic and shawl to throw over the top should it get cold or the sun too harsh. However, I also finally felt some relief from the heat that was more searing here than anywhere in Phoenicia. Next was to find someone to shave me or at least get hold of a razor.

This too was not so difficult. I found an elderly man who not only traded me a razor in return for some chores that he could no longer do but he was also willing and greatly amused to actually shave me.

"Getting rid of all this hair is tricky to do on your own," he laughed. "And you may slip and cut yourself the first time. I would hate for you to see blood and faint. Then you may lose the nerve to finish. What a sight that would be! A half-shaven Greek!" He laughed so much at the thought of this that he doubled over and only stopped when he started to cough. I smiled as I remembered Thales' laughter by the olive presses.

The old man shaved me so slowly that I almost fell asleep. He was meticulous and so gentle with the razor that if it were not for the locks of hair falling around me I might have thought he was doing nothing but pretending. As the pile of hair grew upon the floor I felt something more than just a simple superficial change. I now began to get a sense of what the elders meant when they said I needed to be different.

If you change a man's appearance you change the way he interacts with others. Egyptians knew this too well. The clothes you could afford (or actually were allowed to wear) declared your status much more than any other country I had travelled. They were acutely aware of hygiene and shaving body hair as well as that upon your head was a huge part of this. To play the part like this would show that I not only accepted their ways but I was willing to live them. This surely would show any other school how committed I was.

Commitment though was the least of any schools' worries when admitting a student. Even the grandest of mystery schools had students leave when the material became too intimidating. Elders knew that the most passionate of students could change from one day to the next. Having students disappear overnight was of no concern and much preferable to the expulsion of a student whose commitment had long faded but who stayed out of lack of courage to leave.

So I foolishly moved on to the next school believing that somehow my new look would convince them of the commitment I thought they were looking for.

When I arrived at the next school my appearance did not conceal the fact that I was Greek. They too had been expecting me but gratefully had not heard of what had happened at the initial school. I will always be grateful for the discretion that first group of elders had.

This school like the last one was centred on a temple building that served as a classroom. As I approached it I saw that the doors were open. This I decided was a good omen. As I got closer I could see men inside talking. They were standing about in small groups and it seemed very casual. Yet another good omen I thought.

I walked up and stood in the doorway, looking amongst the men to catch one's eye as well as assessing just who may be a teacher or elder.

"Welcome," said the voice of a man who appeared suddenly beside me making me jump. He walked so close to me that I had to take a step backwards but this only prompted him to step towards me again so I simply leaned back as I spoke.

"Good day. I have come to seek admittance to your school," I stated.

Now he finally stepped back and I could relax my posture

somewhat as he looked me up and down.

"You are not Egyptian. Why do you dress and shave so?" he asked.

"As I saw it fitting to do as the country I am living in," I said simply and somewhat hesitantly as I did not want to offend or limit my possibilities so soon on such a trivial issue.

"Fine," he said as he nodded. "Follow me."

We walked into the temple and I saw that it had no altar space or dais upon which elders or teachers sat. It was just one flat space with the obligatory rows of columns along the sides. I looked up and saw that the inner row of columns raised the middle section of the roof creating a space for light to come in. This it did lighting the room and sending lines of shadows across the floor. I saw the columns were only painted and not carved. There were images of Isis with her wings outspread upon each column and this intrigued me. For a temple which would supposedly only teach men, this went against all traditions I had been told of. I would discover this was just one of several myths that would be undone during my time in Egypt.

As we arrived at the back of the temple's main space I saw that there were two doorways; one to the left corner and one to the right corner. They were slightly obscured by the two rows of columns down each side of the temple. Upon each door was a huge painting of Isis, standing with her ankh in one hand.

I was led to the left door and this made me wonder what was behind the one to the right. The room I was led into was lit the same as the main hall, with columns lifting the centre of the square roof. There were a line of chairs along each wall; each chair was beautifully carved and gold leafed to perfection. I suspected that this was a place that the Pharaoh frequented when I saw the opulence but there was no chair here which seemed grander than the rest. All were equally magnificent. Once again Isis was present. She sat across the top of each chair, her wings fanning out to reach the limits of each chair's back.

"Sit and I will gather the others," I was told and the man disappeared back through the door we came in.

I stood for a moment and looked at the chairs.

"*Which one?*" I thought and stared at each in turn as though they might give me a clue but they were all identical. "*Well then I guess it does not matter,*" I laughed to myself but immediately I felt concern.

What if this was a test? What if which chair I chose revealed something about me that would affect my admission? And what if they all arrived and I was standing here unable to make a choice about which chair to sit in? I quickly walked to the chair that faced the doorway and sat upon it.

"*Hah! Ready, waiting and facing you with confidence!*" I thought and smirked.

Indeed this did seem to please them as they walked through the door. The first priest smiled wide at me giving me yet another good omen to add to my list.

There were once again four elders but there was one difference. Two of them were women.

One man and one woman walked to each side of the room and sat together so that each couple faced each other. There I was along the wall between them. I could hardly hold back my smile at how perfectly I had seated myself.

Then one woman leant forward and smiled warmly at me. "Tell us about your life so far. Feel free to give as much detail as possible," she said and rested back in her chair.

So I told my story from beginning to now. I economised the details but it still took me an hour and a half. As I spoke they occasionally smiled at my recollections and every now and then I would see one turn to the other and then look across to their colleagues. This made my confidence swell. When I finished I looked at each one in turn.

The first woman leant forward again. "Let us contemplate for a moment," she said softly.

With that they all closed their eyes and were silent. I looked among them amused. I would have thought they would leave the room for this but they did not need to. I saw expressions skip across their faces as though they were considering something they heard or were offering an opinion. Sometimes one would even make a slight gesture with their hand.

Once again my initial amusement was lost. I felt I was being played with again but I decided to remain calm. It would be much harder to yell at a woman if I was rejected and that I just did not feel like doing.

Finally they opened their eyes and looked at me. The first woman leant forward again and smiled, making me smile in anticipation. My smile was soon gone though.

"Pythagoras, I am afraid you are not for our school at this time," she said softly and kept smiling.

"Fine," I said curtly and clenched my jaw. "Might I ask when the right time might occur?" If they were going to reject me then I wanted to know exactly why. If nothing else it might prepare me for the next school.

The female elder nodded and sat back. "Well I am happy that you would ask. Many who are not accepted do not ask and that shows little interest in their betterment," she said and looked at the others. "We cannot accept you, for despite all the wisdom you have thus far gathered there are fundamental insights you have missed."

"What insights?" I asked.

This made all four of the elders smile and they even softly laughed.

"That is not anything that we can tell you," she replied.

My lips may not have expressed my anger but the redness that now crept upon my face and the pounding in my chest certainly did. Just as the elders had spoken with each other silently they heard my truth in that moment.

"Pythagoras," one of the males now addressed me. "This is not a measure of your talents or experience. It is merely guidance for you to truly grow as a student and to become the sage and teacher that you are capable of. Do you not think that in your search this direction is exactly what you are truly looking for?"

"I do not imagine being played with as such. I get told there are things I need to know and yet I am not told them," I snapped.

"Because there are some things that cannot be told and cannot be heard from another person," was the response from the second woman.

"Are you interested in being able to hear such things?" asked the second man.

This stopped me in my tracks. I thought about that time I was quiet and saw myself sitting in Egypt and how that had scared me. Then in a flash I realised that vision I had was in fact the scene I was now part of. I drew in a deep breath.

"What did you just realise Pythagoras," the first woman said and leant forward. Her eyes grew wide and she smiled broadly.

"I predicted this occasion many years ago," I said.

She shook her head. "No, you did not predict it. You came here and felt it," she said.

This made no sense to me and I now shook my head.

"Do not shake your head as though you do not understand. This is something you have been scratching at and yet each time you gain some access you cover it over," she said excitedly. "In your story you told us this many times, even if you do not realise it or are not prepared to admit to it. If you are willing to explore this then we will take you on."

I sighed and took in a deep breath.

"Yes," I said as though defeated. "I will explore this."

"Very well then," she said as she nodded. Then she raised her hand and the man who had shown me to the room walked back in and to her side. "Take Pythagoras to one of the hermitages and let him get comfortable." Then she turned back to me. "You will undergo forty days of fasting and inner exploration. We will join you periodically to guide you as well as monitor you. You will not speak to anyone unless addressed to do so. You will not leave the confines of the hermitage before the end of the forty days when we inform you that this passage of time has ended. If you complete this time to our satisfaction then you will continue on with us. If you do not then we will ask you to leave. There will be no explanation as to why we choose not to admit you. That will be for your own discovery. If you have no questions or hesitations as to doing this, then we can continue."

I knew that if I asked a stupid question now or expressed any doubts then I would be asked to leave immediately. I nodded my head and resigned myself to the exercise that I had been asked to do at the first school. I wondered if this was coincidence or simply the standard ritual to gain admittance. Surely they did not put everyone through this but then I truly wondered how many students arrived here ready for the teachings. If I wasn't then who could be?

After my nod indicating my acceptance of their terms was acknowledged by the elders all stood in unison and I stood as well. The first woman gestured with her hand towards the door.

"Go with Ahk-min. One of us will join you shortly to officially begin your time," she said.

I walked out, bowing my head in thanks as I walked between the four elders. Ahk-min looked straight ahead as he led me to the door that had been to the right corner of the temple.

"*Ah now I will find out what is behind here,*" I thought.

Ahk-min opened the door and all I saw after an initial vestibule area was a long corridor with doors leading off to the right. We walked along and all the doors were closed. I could hear nothing from behind any of them. Then we were in front of one of the doors that was open.

I looked in to see a small room barely measuring eight feet square. There was no furniture except for a large flat pillow on the ground. I could see immediately that its stuffing had been flattened a long time ago and that it would provide little comfort. A large window on the wall opposite the door allowed fresh air and light to fill the room. It was small but far from stuffy thanks to this opening as well as the high roof. The only other things notable were a jug with a glass in one corner while in the other was a bucket.

"*One corner for 'in', the other for 'out',*" I laughed to myself.

"Make yourself comfortable as you desire without lying down,"

Ahk-min said. "An elder will join you shortly."

Then he was gone, closing the door behind him. I looked about me and pondered the pillow. Sighing I lowered myself to sit cross-legged upon it while facing the door and realised I had been right in predicting its lack of comfort. At least it kept me from the dust upon the floor.

It was not much later that the door opened again and the first woman elder walked in. There was no greeting or small talk as she began.

"I will instruct you in some observational breathing," she said simply and softly. She did not sit but remained standing as she continued. "Close your eyes and feel your breath. Feel it move into you. Note how it feels in your nose. Observe how it moves through you. Then feel its passage back out of you."

Then she said nothing. I felt my breath moving in and out. While I felt how calming this was I also kept thinking how useless this was. However if this was as hard as it would get then I could sacrifice forty days for the greater outcome. I kept observing my breath, waiting for some more detailed instruction. The woman was so still and quiet that at one point I thought she must have left and opened my eyes slightly. When I saw her still there I closed them again and kept on with the exercise. It was an hour later that her soft voice spoke again.

"Wonderful, Pythagoras. Continue on. One of us shall return when you are ready," she said and I heard the door close softly.

I opened my eyes for a moment, stretched my arms above my head and then my legs out straight before me. It was barely two hours and I knew that if I let any restlessness settle in then I would not be able to return my focus upon the exercise. I recrossed my legs, settled my arms upon them and went back to my breathing.

Surprisingly I was able to get through the next few hours with little need to distract myself. I would have a stretch every now and then but it was so momentary that it hardly broke the rhythm of my breath. The only noticeable external distraction was when the sun finally set and the temperature dropped. I was reaching for my satchel to take out my tunic to put on when the door opened just enough for a hand to come through and place a blanket upon the floor.

I murmured a thank you then grimaced as I remembered the "no talking" rule. Hopefully they had not heard me. I grabbed the blanket and put it beside me knowing that as night wore on I would need it.

I kept up with my breathing for several more hours but now as it grew late my mind decided to come and play. I began to wonder how forty days of this would affect me. I questioned why I had felt motivated to say yes to this exercise. Was it going to be worth it? What would Thales be thinking?

Damn Thales! He would have known about this and he didn't warn me. Then it struck me. If Thales knew not to tell me then even just the discovery of this for myself must have some significance. Nonetheless I was still somewhat agitated that he had not given me some hint of the different methods used here.

When my mind would not settle I decided that I may as well sleep and start afresh in the morning. I folded my decrepit pillow in half to give my head some respite from the hard floor and lay on my back pulling the blanket over me.

I looked out the window and could see the moon with a scattering of stars around her. This reminded me of another time but I could not remember when exactly. It made my heart jump a little but I was too tired to try and understand why. I was soon asleep.

The next morning I woke with the sunrise. I lay upon my back for a while looking out the window at the pinks and blues of the sky folding into each other. There is nothing quite like an Egyptian sunrise and it is no wonder they believed that Isis herself was a part of them.

Then I decidedly felt the need to use the bucket. When I was finished I strained my ears to find if I could hear anyone nearby waking to begin their day but I could not. I sat back down upon the pillow and began with my breathing exercise yet again. However the smell from my bucket became quite strong in the small room. So much so that despite my best attempts to ignore it I simply could not. I kept stopping at the slightest noise hoping it was a servant coming to collect the bucket. When at least an hour had passed and my stomach started to join in with its own repulsion at the smell I got up and stood near the window.

"I'll just breathe in the fresh air," I thought and continued on standing up.

The smell though was still there and now on top of this I had the distractions of the scenery outside. They had been clever enough to not face the window towards any common area that would let me see people moving about but being within such a bare room made even a falling leaf seem highly fascinating. Then another thought struck me and I jumped back from the window.

"What if they are watching me through the window," I thought.

I had no doubt they had many ways to monitor me and this also explained why I would have such a huge window within the hermitage.

Fresh air and light was the least of their concerns for me. The purpose of this window was to have me on display!

I looked at the bucket again and sighed. Then I made a decision that I did not care about the consequence. I opened the door just the width of the bucket and slid it out, closing the door immediately. The bucket would be close enough to let them know that I had not wandered, or so I hoped.

When I finally heard some footsteps outside my room followed by my door opening and a clean empty bucket being slid inside, I knew that what I had done was acceptable. Now I could relax and settle back into my breathing for the day.

This first full day went by smoothly as did the second. I had my moments of distraction with thoughts and memories coming in but this did not discourage me. I knew this was perfectly natural for any man, especially for me as this had been the manner of my life so far. Thinking was as natural and important to me as breathing, so when I began to ponder such things as something I had observed at the Moschus school, I did not so much see it as something that was interfering with my exercise but more as something my mind had decided needed contemplation at that time. As the days passed though, this became more difficult.

I had been left alone for five days before I received my second guidance visit. The first woman came again and stood before me. I looked up at her hoping she would ask me questions so that I might be able to speak and this she thankfully did.

"How are you feeling?" she asked me.

"I am feeling fine," was all I could answer.

"What distractions have you experienced?" she then asked.

I noted that she asked me as though she totally expected me to have had them.

"I have been distracted by changes in temperature and the smell of my bucket when it was full," I answered being completely honest.

This answer made the woman smile. "Wonderful," she said softly and then asked "What else?"

Not "Is there anything else?" so once again she was expecting my reply.

"I have had a few memories from my studies come forward," I said.

"And how do you deal with these memories when they present?" she asked and it seemed to be with a genuine curiosity rather than to test me.

"I allow them some time. I imagine they would not occur unless they are due their place in my exercise," I said looking her in the eye to measure her response.

She closed her eyes and I saw her take a deep breath. She kept them closed as she began to speak again.

"Close your eyes, Pythagoras and we shall breathe together again," she said and I heard her take another deep breath as I closed my eyes. Then she continued, "Feel your breath again as you have. Feel the sensations as it makes its way inside you and then out again. Now feel your chest expand as fully as it can. Do not force it. Just let your lungs and your ribs open as much as they can."

I did this expecting to feel my shoulders rise but they did not. Instead I felt my diaphragm push down into my belly as though my breath wanted to escape through my bowels instead of return through my throat. It suddenly faltered and sputtered out of me instead of its usual smooth flow.

"What happened?" I heard and I opened my eyes to see her watching me as I steadied myself.

"I—I am not sure—my breath just seemed to want to go down further than my lungs," I stammered still confused by what had happened.

The woman smiled. "Wonderful," she said and I wanted to scream it back at her as a question. I am still surprised that I remembered the no talking rule at that point.

"I did not think you would be ready so soon for the next stage but you surprise me, Pythagoras. This is a good lesson for both of us to remain alert to the unexpected," she said as smiled. "Now close your eyes again and we will continue…"

Then her voice softened. She told me to breathe again, to be aware of the sensations, to feel it move down as it had done before. Her voice suddenly sounded different as she invited me on to the next stage.

"Now feel your breath all the way down into your belly. Let it fill you so that you feel yourself expand. Do not mind the little jolts and shudders as your muscles adjust. Keep coming back to the rhythm. This is your natural state," she explained.

She stood beside me and we breathed together for two hours. My rhythm would falter and her soft voice would come in and I would be back to it in a breath or two. I would want to sleep but her voice would wake me just enough to keep going. Then I heard the door close as she left. Part of me wanted to slide to the floor and sleep but this felt so delicious I decided to carry on some more. This I did until the sunset and I decided to have some water. I breathed in this way until just before midnight and when I felt my head snap forward upon my neck I knew it was time to sleep.

As I began to doze I reflected on the peace and serenity in which I had spent the day. There were thirty-four days left of this and I imagined each day this sensation would grow. I would carry it with me as I continued on with my studies. It would make my reputation even more astounding. The rest of my hermitage would be marvellous I decided.

The next morning when I awoke that resolution was long forgotten.

When I awoke my head was pounding and this set the scene for the whole day. I rubbed at my head as though that would help but it did not. I relieved myself into my bucket then drank as much water as I could bear. This lifted some of the pain but not all of it. I decided to get back to my breathing to see what that would do.

I sat down upon my pillow but could not get comfortable. It now seemed thinner than ever and this agitated me even more. Nonetheless I began to do my breathing. I calmed somewhat but then my headache decided to come back with a vengeance and now my neck began to ache. I pulled my focus back to my breathing but now all the water I had drunk seemed to have made its way through me and my fresh bucket was yet to be placed. The longer I sat the more my full bladder seemed to press down in me and my breathing into my belly only made this more noticeable. When my bladder would somehow settle then my head would step in with a sudden new wave of pain. My breathing was now completely lost as my mind decided to join in the chorus.

"This is ridiculous," I muttered out loud and even the sound of my voice annoyed me as it sounded so piercing today.

I stood up and paced the room as I rubbed at my neck. I would stop by the door and listen for the sound of the fresh bucket being delivered and then when my bladder could wait no longer I flung open the door and added to the bucket I had left in the corridor.

I slammed the door closed and leant against it sighing out loud with relief. Even my head felt a little better for this. I stretched my arms above my head and sat back down again confident I had dismissed my distractions.

However now that my physical distractions were lessened my mind truly kicked in. I asked myself why after all the disciplines learnt of my body that such truly small things should cause me so much distress today. I knew why immediately; because there was little else to focus upon! I almost laughed out loud at this revelation and then feeling triumphant I settled again into feeling the breath moving through me.

Barely ten minutes passed and then I suddenly began to think of my family in Samos. First a huge sense of concern for them came to me and then guilt at leaving them overwhelmed me and I felt tears in my eyes. I shook my head, telling myself this was foolish. They were all adults and had blessed my leaving Samos. I began to breathe again.

However every few minutes another wave of thoughts would come in that disturbed me. I saw myself opening my dead father's eyes out of curiosity, rousing on Eunomus as we walked the island, the night I went and ate lamb when I was at Thales school. Regret after regret came in which in itself agitated me as regret was something I had never truly felt about anything I had done. It was so strong that my head pounded again and even worse than before. I was glad that my stomach and bowels were empty from my fasting as the sensations moving through me in waves were enough to make me vomit or empty my bowels from the sheer tumult of emotions.

I tried to breathe again but could not find that sensation of expansion I had the day before. Standing up I walked to the window and took in the fresh air there as I braced myself upon the window frame. I looked back at the doorway and all I saw was a wooden barrier to what I had come to Egypt to achieve. This made me cross the room and before I knew it I was standing with the door open. I looked to the blank wall across the corridor.

Then I remembered standing at the gate of Thales' school as I prepared for my exit to the taverna. I recalled my adventure as a young child leaving my home unescorted. I thought about what each experience had shown me. I then also remembered the time sitting at home in Samos when I had seen the very room where I decided to take part in this hermitage and then Anaximander's words rang in my ears.

"No man takes a step unless he knows where he is going...."

There was a flicker of something inside me. Do not ask me to explain it because I cannot. It was a deep part of my intuition and something more. It helped me remember why I had said yes to this. I closed the door and went back to my pillow.

This did not end my agitation though. I struggled for another two hours to get back to the state I had attained the day before. I did but then it did not last for more than two minutes and this in itself became another source of frustration. I sat myself in different places around the room; leaning against each wall in turn, then facing each wall. It was around midday when I decided I could not struggle with this anymore. I lay down, closed my eyes and surrendered to the one thing that went against all my teachings thus far; I slept through the day.

When the woman left my room the day before she went back to the meeting room where I had sat with them. The other three were there and every chair was filled with another senior student or a teacher. The woman went to the one last chair left empty for her. When she was seated she smiled.

"Thank you for waiting for me," she said as she looked around the room.

"How goes our new man?" asked a teacher.

"He does well," she answered. "Today we moved on to the third lesson within an hour of him having heard the second."

At this the room was filled with murmurs as they all turned to each other. One of the male elders leaned forward and shook his head.

"No, no, no! You have made a mistake!" he said emphatically. "Speed up his lessons and you will speed up the inevitable issues that this stage brings up."

"And what is the harm in that?" she said clearly not impressed at having her decision criticised like this.

"Because to not ease him through this will make the inevitable thoughts to leave and end his retreat even stronger. You know what the mind will do to stop this!" he shook his finger at her as he spoke.

The woman's face turned red and she clenched her jaw. "And you know that if he truly wishes to experience all that this has to offer then he will be strong enough to see through that!"

"We shall see!" he snapped back at her.

"Yes we shall!" she retorted. "Now can we continue on with the meeting as planned…"

I woke up in the late afternoon when the heat from the day hung hard and steady in Egypt before the evening breezes found their way to dissolve it. I sat up and dragged myself to a wall and leant upon it. I felt sluggish and heavy as though the sleep would not let go. I slid back down upon the floor to return to my slumber but of course sleep would not return. My body did not need it and even the desire to escape from the whirlwind my mind was still playing with could not pull me there.

"*If only I had some meat and alcohol!*" I thought and then I laughed out loud. For if I was partaking of lamb and wine I would not even be here. In fact I would never have left Samos.

169

This got me to thinking about how my life may have turned out. I thought about what I would be doing now if I had decided not to leave. I might have continued on teaching at my temple but at some point Polycrates would have clamped down on me even more. I probably would have ended up as a boat builder like my brothers, cousins and uncles were all were doing.

My days would be full of physical work. I would be as brown as I could be from being in the sun. At evening I would arrive to my home and by now I would have a wife and possibly some children. We would sit around a huge meal of lamb or pheasant followed by fruit and sweets. My sleep would be on a huge soft bed with the warmth of my wife beside me.

I looked around my room; instead I had chosen this! I stood and walked to the window, leaning out so my face could feel the breeze that had finally arrived. I thought about my father and what he had envisioned for me. I thought about the beggar at the village outskirts. I thought about the body of the man we dissected at the Moschus school.

Turning back to face inside the room I sat upon my pillow and breathed.

The woman did not return for five days. The only interaction I had was the hand that put the fresh bucket and jug of water into my room each day and the occasional bird that arrived upon the windowsill to observe me.

"I have even less than you!" I said to one as it sat and stared at me.

My physical distractions grew less as did the tumult that my mind had conjured by my seventh day. Not that they had disappeared but when they did come to play I knew now that it was simply because I was creating a diversion from my greater purpose. So when they did arrive I would acknowledge them, simply return to my breathing and they would abate.

Now I know I make that sound so simple and in truth, for the most part, it was. However our mind is far cleverer than we give it credit. I had spent most of my life developing mine so it was far more inventive than most. I could be deep within my breath and I would suddenly get a flash of a memory so strongly that for a moment I would think I was back there and my present was part of a dream. It was so vivid that it would take me some time to restore myself but I always did.

This, I decided, was what I was being taught by doing this; the ability to come back to my calm and continue on as I wanted to, no matter the setting or circumstance.

I felt triumphant when I came to this realisation and I hoped that as part of my next visit I would be asked a question through which I could share this in an answer.

It was day ten when the woman returned to see me. She arrived just after the fresh bucket and jug was placed. She slid them aside with her foot as she entered. Closing the door she placed one hand in the other and rested them on her belly. She tilted her head as she looked me up and down with a measured stare.

"How are you feeling?" she asked simply.

"I am feeling well and confident that I am proceeding as you desire," I answered and then wished I had used that opportunity to share my recent insight.

"Good," she answered then looked me up and down again. "Have you any desire to leave?"

"No, I do not," I answered.

"Good," she replied again. "Now we will continue."

I shifted myself to get comfortable as I knew I may not be moving for quite some time. I did not wait for her instruction to start breathing but immediately went into the rhythm that I had found over the past ten days.

"Good," I heard her say softly and I could not help but smile.

As I breathed deeper and deeper reaching that delicious space where I felt my physical being expand beyond its skin I waited for her to speak again. She said nothing though for what felt like over thirty minutes and my mind started up.

"*She has left the room. She is just playing with me. I have fallen asleep and cannot hear her. Maybe I should open my eyes to check what is happening?*"

All these things raced through my mind then I heard her but it was not her voice through my ears. It started as a sensation within my chest and rose up to my forehead. Then the words suddenly formed.

"Breathe, breathe, breathe. Breathe deep into your belly. Feel your energy shift," it said as clear as if the woman had spoken the words to me by her mouth.

But I was not convinced that this was happening. My breathing faltered and the sensation was gone. Then her physical voice spoke to me.

"What you felt was true Pythagoras. This is not magic. This is why you are here," she said.

"*This is why I am here?*" I thought and went into confusion.

"Yes, I know it does not seem what you are looking for but this is the key to the ancient mysteries," she said as though I had spoken out loud.

My eyes flew open and my breathing jumped to stay within my chest. I looked at her and she stayed calm and smiled.

"Please do not tell me you are so surprised that it should come to this," she said.

I shook my head. "No, I am not surprised," I lied and closed my eyes.

Eventually my breathing slowed again and went back into the peaceful state. I heard her voice again calling me to breathe. Then she said more but this time I could not pull it into words. It was just the sensation. I was deep in this state when I heard the door open and close, yet I could still feel the sensation of her "speaking" with me.

I might not have understood what was happening but my resignation to be here and complete this retreat now collapsed into surrender. It is no use to just lick something if you want to taste it, you need to bite into it and swallow. Each breath I took now was another swallow of what I was being invited to taste.

When the woman walked back into the main temple space she couldn't help but smile broadly at all who passed her. She made her way outside and then to the elders' quarters. She was looking for the man who had confronted her on the issue of her accelerating my tutelage and she found him at his desk writing.

"Yes," he said without even looking up.

"Our Greek is still here," she said and had to try not to laugh as she said it. "And today he achieved ka'an-trut."

"That is not so unheard of at ten days," he spat, still looking down at his scroll.

"No, that is true—but he did and we both know that if that is reached then he has accomplished the intention of the retreat," she stated.

Now the man looked up and narrowed his eyes as he looked at her. "I do hope that you are not proposing that his retreat be ended prematurely?"

"Well…" she began but he spoke over her.

"Because that will NEVER be considered while I am an elder at this school. He will complete the retreat as per the rules set out by the generations before us. As have all before him including you and I, and as will all students to come," he shouted.

The woman sighed and shrugged her shoulders. "I just thought if we made an exception for him we could truly test the prophecy that was told of him at Delphi," she proposed.

"Those prophecies are not part of our teachings and you know it. Do you want to create stories for our students as the High Priests of Karnak do for the Pharaohs? This is not our way at these schools and we cannot dilute the teachings of eternity for the games of prophecies. Besides can you truly warrant setting him above other students? That is against our very fundamental teachings no matter the talents they display."

The man, standing now, walked towards the woman and took her by the shoulders. His voice softened as he gently squeezed her. "You have done amazingly with him as you do with all your students. That is why you were made a teacher and an elder. Do not become attached to his energy with the belief that you will make more of him than that which he chooses for himself. Ego did not get you this far, but it will certainly undo you now if you let it."

With that he leant forward and gently kissed her on the forehead. The woman smiled back at the man.

"Thank you," she said softly as she reached up to take one of his hands in hers and kiss it. "You have reminded me of why I am a teacher and why I chose to marry you."

Another ten days passed as I continued on with my breathing. As before, some days were easier than others and some days were truly trying. The surrender that I had chosen on the last visit of my teacher was sometimes my comfort and at other times it was my enemy. I talked with the part of me that had surrendered. I thanked it and questioned it. It was both loved and hated, sometimes this was simultaneous.

The times I loved it was when I was truly deeply in the space of peace. My body would seem to disappear along with the room and anything else of material presence around me. It was just my breath that was present. My mind would not come in with its games. There was no regret or expectation. There was just my breath.

I would get the sensation within my chest as I had when my teacher spoke to me, but sometimes it would feel different. It would feel like Thales or some other teacher, perhaps even my father. I did not try to push the sensations. I just let them come to me. Each time I knew I was delving deeper into the energy that was this retreat and that I was getting closer to the mysteries that the school would show me.

Then there would come the days that my mind could not be silenced. They were growing fewer which I feel made them all the more disruptive and seemingly unproductive. I would feel angry with myself and then the school. It could become so intense that even the hand reaching through the door with my bucket and jug of water could incite a peak in my rage.

I soon found there was little to do when this set in but rest and sleep. Yes, it was escape but I knew to push through this did not ease the energies and only made my breathing work more disjointed.

I stood at the window one day looking out and my heart ached for it to be over. I was halfway but I may as well have been at the beginning. I was a prisoner of my own accord yet this irony did nothing to shift my yearning. Closing my eyes I took a deep breath and when I opened them the Egyptian scenery was gone. I was looking out to another strange land. Even my sense of smell connected with it.

There was water before me, like a huge river and across on the opposite bank I saw a beautiful building of white marble. It was like nothing I had ever seen. Its dome in the centre was like magic compared to anything built in any land I had known. I knew this place was not only far from here but not of this time.

I closed my eyes again and when I opened them it was gone and Egypt was returned. This I knew was enough for today. I lay down and slept through to the next morning.

It was five days later, the twenty-fifth day of my retreat when the door opened and the woman stepped through again. There were no questions today. She stood before me, her hands slipped within each other over her belly and she closed her eyes. I knew that what was required was to simply close mine also and go into my breath.

Once again I heard her voice from within me. It was beyond words even more this time and as my mind strained to translate the sensation I felt my breath shudder and I knew to stop trying to reduce this. I simply let the surrender that I had chosen explore this.

We worked together for almost an hour like this and then I heard the door open and close but I did not sense the woman leave and neither did I hear anyone enter. The momentary need to register this though was gone quickly and I continued on with my teacher for several more hours, delighting that she had remained with me this long today.

The cool of evening was upon me when I heard her tell me that it was time to rest. I opened my eyes and there was no-one before me. For a moment I thought I must have been hallucinating and shook my head, then rubbed at my eyes. She still didn't appear before me.

Then I reached another point of surrender. It was time to acknowledge that my eyes and physical senses were not the limits of my experience.

Now this is a pretty huge realisation to come to and that night I did not do so much of my breathing. Instead I lay flat on the floor and as I looked out the window to the stars and the moon, I contemplated the place that my physical senses played within this world.

I truly thought that I had explored this fully at the Moschus school but I saw now where I had missed one final connection to understanding it. It is one thing to know the intricacies of the body, to know how the body is designed and how it functions. Thales had also shown me this with teaching my body some discipline and I also believed initially that this was the core of the design of this retreat.

It is an immense wisdom to understand your body but until you can understand its connection to your greater self then it is nothing but a shell. Until you can see how it connects with the parts of you that are beyond the physical then it cannot serve you or your journey. When you understand that what you experience physically is not the limit of experience then you open up the possibilities for so much more.

I looked out to the stars and smiled. I would never touch a star and never know what heat it held. All I knew was that the same stars sat in the same places night upon night. I trusted my eyes with this information as had others for millennia before me, so much so that they created documents for others and I trusted what their eyes had recorded to learn from.

I could smell something nearby and trust my nose that the source of the odour would exist nearby also. I didn't need to be told by any teacher that having a bone broken would be painful. These were all things that had been ingrained in me from childhood. It was, and is, something innate as well as learnt.

When I was with Thales and began to reset some of my physical practices I had began to feel into this. I saw that what I believed to be my mind, was in fact the ruler of experience and not my physical self. I learnt that the part of my mind I viewed as my will would shape how my body became part of my existence. At the Moschus school I learnt the intricacies of my body and developed a new respect for it as a mechanical and chemical machine.

Now here in Egypt though I had discovered yet another aspect of my body. I now knew how much it did for me regardless and despite my mind or my will. These simple processes such as smell, sight and hearing worked for me continually, measuring my connection to everything around me. I trusted them implicitly, never questioning what they showed me or what they led me to believe.

This day had shaken up all this. I could now go beyond the limits of the simple connection to what was immediately around me. These senses could be opened up even more. I could hear beyond my ears capabilities and see beyond what was before me. If I delved into this even deeper what more would I sense? What more would I learn?

As I lay upon the stone floor which was cooling rapidly beneath me I smiled as I thought about this. I thanked myself for doing the retreat and fell asleep. I imagined it would be a gentle night of rest after such an immense day and I was right. Night moved quickly and without the disturbance of dreams.

I woke at first light as I always did. The first pangs of my stomach that always greeted me on sitting up were quelled with a sip of water. There was no rumble of my bowel which was long empty and every day now the bucket only received the equivalent of what little I took in. I was glad for the minimal disruptions of my bodily functions so that I could go deeply into the senses I wished to explore.

Today I was glad for the day to arrive and I went into my breath with pure excitement for what it would show me today.

It began immediately. I listened for what I could hear within the room, which was nothing but the sound of my breath softly escaping my nostrils. I pushed it further and heard the sounds of birds scratching outside my window and even further in the distance I could hear the yells of a farmer to his oxen. A smile spread across my face as I then heard so much in-between. I could hear a soft breeze now work its way into my room and the rustle of some trees as well. Then I pulled my hearing in tight and listened for my heartbeat which faintly beat its rhythm within me.

It was only after doing this for about an hour, almost like I was playing, that I pushed this further. I called out silently to my teacher, telling her I was ready to learn more. I listened but heard nothing and my mind could not help but step in but I steadied it instantly and listened again. That was when I heard her.

"Wonderful my dear student. You are doing well," I heard her say as though she whispered beside me. "Keep going and explore what you desire. Do not question what you experience. Just feel it, observe it, be with it." With that her voice was gone and I continued on my own.

I knew though that I was not alone. For if I could summon her like this then she too would be connecting with me even if I was not aware of it. This was comforting in a way for I knew that if I was to get lost in this energy I would be pulled back. Or would I?

At this thought a momentary panic set in and I opened my eyes. This felt just like when I had played with such things on my travels with Mnesarchus and then on my own at Samos. My mind this time was the one to allay my emotions. It was as though I was played a quick movie showing me all that I had learnt so far, how I had trusted and been trusted. I knew in that moment that I was safe for there was no-one or nothing else within my breath than me.

I closed my eyes once again and dived into myself.

Out in her private rooms my teacher smiled and turned to her husband.

"The Greek communicated with me of his own accord," she said smugly.

Her husband snorted at this. "I suppose you think that is another confirmation of the oracle's prophecy?" he said rhetorically.

"Well it is not every student that can do this during the retreat," she stated.

"And it is not every student who arrives here thinking they are owed a placement within our school!" he said and then he shook his finger at her. "You are still enamoured by this man and I do not understand why. You have never done this before and I fear it is somehow going to be your undoing as an elder here. Be thankful that I have more loyalty to you as a husband than as a teacher to my school but, my love, do not press my loyalties any further. I do not think they can stretch anymore."

The woman could say nothing to this. She knew she had pushed the boundaries far enough with this. She also knew that I was worth it. It wasn't anything she could explain but she felt it the minute she set eyes upon me. She knew I would accept the retreat and in fact when all four elders had closed their eyes to "discuss" me on that first day she was the only one who said yes immediately. Her husband was swayed with how immediate her senses had decided this and the remaining two were gently coaxed along as well. This was why she had been so invested in me doing well and why she loved to share my success so far.

All along, this sense that I would discover the mysteries quicker than most, bubbled inside her. She pushed me not so much to prove her point but in the hope that it would inspire me to explore myself and it had worked.

The other elders would never understand. Not even her husband. As she watched him walk from the room following their discussion she knew that she could not report anything about my development other than what was expected from now on. Beyond that, she decided, would be for me to share when I was ready.

She closed her eyes once more and felt into my energy. Her smile was enough to send me some warmth so that I knew she stood beside me.

CHAPTER NINE

When I was satisfied with having expanded upon my hearing I now decided to explore this with my vision. I opened my eyes and while I felt this might work I knew instantly it would not today. My momentary adventures into this previously would be different from how I would expand this now. I closed my eyes again and invited my vision to play things out for me as though I was dreaming.

At first there was nothing but swirls of colour; like stained clouds ebbing and pulsing. Then they cleared and I viewed the same scene I had seen upon Samos. I was within the room where the elders had received me but it was not the time when I arrived here. I looked down and saw I was covered in gold dust and wore a kilt of fine white cotton edged in gold ribbons around my waist covering down to my knees. In my hands were the gold flail and crook of a Pharaoh. I looked up and around the room and as I gazed at each person they dropped their eyes and bowed their heads. Then four priests walked in and dropped to their knees, prostrating themselves before me.

When they stood again the eldest declared, "Pharaoh Thutmose, you honour us with this visit."

I began to laugh in my present moment as I watched this, amused at the ritual being offered to this man whose eyes I seemed to have borrowed. I wondered if they could hear me if I projected my voice through this man before them so I tried.

"The honour is mine," I began. "Tell me of your current students," I added.

The elder straightened himself and began to describe the calibre and knowledge of those studying at the temple. Some were attuned to healing, others to astronomy and some to religious ritual. I noted that not once were the studies of the mysteries referred to openly, though I sensed the allusion to them.

When the elder was finished I heard Thutmose himself speak to the elder. "I will take the astronomer and physician with me to the palace. There are no others of whom I feel are suitable," he said decisively as the elder bowed.

The scene dissolved and the swirls of colour were back before me.

"Did I just make that up?" I thought.

Instantly I heard a response.

"Imagination is just another level of reality."

It was not the woman's voice but it was not a man's either. The answer was cryptic enough to distract me for a moment but it essentially was encouragement without giving away too much. I pulled my breath deep into me and asked for another vision.

This time I was high upon a camel. I looked around me and there were twenty other camels with riders travelling along with mine. My clothes were layered upon me and while I knew that they were of nobility I knew that they were not royalty.

Night was falling and the first stars were appearing. Suddenly one of the camels nearby picked up its pace and its rider pulled her beside me.

"Look Balthasar! It is even brighter tonight and appearing earlier. It is getting closer. Like it is telling us that we are closer," he said and then looked around the rest of the caravan. "Melchior! Can you see it?" he shouted as he pointed up to the sky.

"Yes! Yes!" Melchior shouted back."We should stop and take some more measurements!"

The man beside me smirked. "Melchior! Always with his measurements!" he laughed as he rode away from me.

As I watched this scene play out I felt a twinge in my heart. It was as though I had been in this precise moment once before. I did not know if what I was watching was the past or present. Somehow this now moment of observing these men was like living this hour over again. This was something I had never experienced before and it was enough to dissolve the scene and make me open my eyes.

I grabbed my jug of water and took the largest swig I could, then I poured the rest over my head not caring what spilt upon the floor. Leaning upon the windowsill I drew in some fresh air and looked out. I decided I had done enough for now and lay down to sleep in the hope this would rest my mind and senses completely.

Sleep though did not rest my mind. As my body gained some respite my mind and emotions kept churning through my dreams. Within minutes of falling into deep sleep I was once again upon the camel travelling with the other men. Though now we were stopped and the one called Melchior had out a strange instrument that he held to the sky as he called out numbers to a scribe beside him. Realising he was an astronomer I went closer to him to see if I could learn something new from what he was doing. I too looked up at the sky and the star that these men were all excited about. I knew that I did not know this star from my studies and this intrigued me.

As I looked upon the man his image shifted. I saw his face change and then his clothing so that he looked like someone else entirely yet I felt his essence remain the same. Then I realised the entire scene had changed. We were surrounded by buildings that were like nothing I had seen before. Lanterns were perched at the top of poles and though they emitted light I could see no flame. This was another land altogether.

Then the scene shifted again and again. I saw lands that were familiar and those that were beyond my imagination. I was within cities so crowded that I felt like I would suffocate and then I would be standing upon a huge open plain surrounded by a small flock of sheep.

I was relieved when my body decided to awake and that all that was around me was four walls and the ceiling. The simplicity of my surrounds helped to calm the sense of exhaustion that was upon me from what I had experienced in my dreams. I stood and went to my window to look at the night sky. I scanned the stars to see if I could see the star in my vision and then my dream.

As I did this I heard a voice. *"Not yet, not yet...."*

It soothed me and yet it piqued my curiosity.

"When?" I wondered to myself and immediately I heard my own answer.

It was many years to come and there was much to experience in-between. In that instant I knew the vision was of another time I would walk the earth and there had been times before this. It made sense— perfect sense. For how else could the knowledge of man grow unless those of us who gathered it continued on beyond the mere limits of our human life?

If we could feel beyond our senses then we could learn beyond our living mind. If we could bring things inwards in this way then it was possible to send information outwards as well. I then imagined the men in my dream measuring their star. If I could learn from them in my dream state then could they learn from me here in my time? I decided that this was so. This opened up the possibilities for teaching beyond anything I could have planned.

I lay back upon the floor and smiled. Within minutes I was yawning and began to drift to sleep again. I planned to explore more about travelling through time in my sleep and see who else I could visit to learn from. This I did quite productively and when I woke in the morning I remembered not one thing!

Even my revelation of communicating across time was but a mere sensation. It was now just that intangible feeling when you awaken that you have experienced something, yet you cannot form it into any shape, as though your mind had swallowed it all.

I sat up, rubbed at my face and tried to pull back all that happened from the night and then the day before but it was gone. It was as though someone had wiped a slate clean of its writing but left behind a thin film of dust spread over it. This could not affect the new day upon me though I decided. I sat up and once again began my breathing.

The next week went by quickly and for this I was thankful. My days were so full of expansion and my nights so busy exploring my dreams that time seemed to speed up. I lost track of my days here in the room and almost forgot about my teacher. Well to say "forgot" is the wrong word. I grew less expectant of her is more correct. She had still not re-appeared but this was of no concern as I would connect with her within my breathing. I knew she monitored me and that all must be going well as I was sure she would come if I truly needed some more specific tutoring.

I was truly comfortable with my progress and my existence. Food was merely a memory and sleep was not an escape from the drudgery of the day. The drop in human interaction to the mere glimpse of a hand passing in my bucket and jug was no longer a source of irritation. In fact it was now just an ordinary part of my routine. I had just washed my face and was sitting up for the day when the door opened a second time. I knew at once my teacher was about to arrive and was nearly disappointed to be disturbed.

It was indeed my teacher but leading the way was her husband. Though he tried to smile at me the way his wife did, I could tell it was strained and that he was not here with the intent to teach me as did his wife. He stood to one side and the woman stepped to stand beside him.

"It has been fifteen days since we have spoken, Pythagoras. I suggest you take a sip of water and warm your throat before we converse," she said.

Even though she spoke softly, her voice sounded hard and loud from all my time spent alone in the quiet. I took my sip and then wondered how indeed I should ready my voice.

"Just tone softly," she said as though she heard my thoughts.

So I began with a soft hum and then as my mouth, tongue and throat vibrated I opened my mouth and let the noise echo inside my cheeks, gradually getting louder. I looked at the woman and she nodded, letting me know that was enough.

"Good," she said. "You are keeping up your health."

How she could tell this from the noise from my throat amazed me, which it really shouldn't have considering what else I had experienced with her. I saw the man take a deep breath and within it I could feel his impatience and frustration with me. I turned my head sharply towards him and narrowed my eyes. I must have looked quite formidable as he jumped and stepped backwards. The woman lifted her hand and I was not sure if the gesture was for me or the male elder. She looked from me to her husband and laughed softly.

"You two truly underestimate each other," she said smiling.

"Can we just get on with it," muttered the man. "I have other students to attend to."

"Indeed," she answered. "Pythagoras, you have only five days left. How do you feel as the end draws near?"

"I feel I have gathered enough knowledge to practice this work beyond my retreat. I feel as though I could continue here like this forever and yet I am excited to move beyond this as well," I answered, my voice catching several times as my throat worked again.

"Good," she nodded as she spoke. "All else goes well thus far. You simply need to continue on as you have been doing. We will come for you in five days."

With that they both turned and left me alone.

Ah solitude! How I loved it so much now and though part of me wanted to spend the rest of my life like this another part of me rose up with the desire to now teach this to others. Only five more days and then my journey as a teacher would truly begin.

Funnily enough the next five days went slowly. It was possibly a combination of my desire to savour every last moment as well as feeling as though I needed to make every second count. I slept very little, trying to consciously explore what I could. Even when I slept this continued but once again when I woke I would not remember a thing. There were a few times that I would have a clear recollection for a brief moment but, as my memory clamoured to hold on, it would slip away regardless. I was confident though that somewhere within me it was stored.

When the final day came I woke with the sunrise and stood to look out the window. I took a deep breath and looked around the room taking in its details. I knew every last crack on the stone, every last curve of the grain in each plank of wood that made up the door and ceiling. I looked once more outside. It was now time for me to know all there was of the world outside. I was ready for this and knew it with every fibre within me.

I had imagined there would be some hesitation to leave here when my time was done. However now as that moment approached I suddenly was aware of the dank air, the lack of comfort and for the first time in weeks my stomach squeezed inside me. Now every second that passed felt like an hour until the door opened and my teacher walked in.

"Well done," she said and she walked towards me with her arms out gathering me into an embrace.

It felt so nice to be held that she actually had to push me back off her to end my hold.

"I apologise for my emotions getting the better of me," she said and I saw that she was blushing. "I cannot do such things in front of the others or they will think me weak and soft. Let us leave such things here before we return to the main temple."

I nodded, understanding completely. I too felt myself blush at having fallen into the embrace so fully. The woman led me out and we were once more in the hallway. My feet enjoyed the sensation of moving more than five paces in a row and my shoulders ached to stretch some more. The woman turned to me and smiled.

"We have a bath and a massage waiting for you," she said warmly. "But before this you need some tea to warm and stretch your stomach to ready it for food."

As she spoke we entered the main temple which was full of men conversing as they did the day I arrived. When they saw me standing behind the woman they all stopped and looked at me. I saw the woman nod and instantaneously they broke into applause. Tears filled my eyes as I bowed to acknowledge their recognition of what I had accomplished.

"Come," the woman said abruptly. "You must not get lost in your adulation."

Nodding my head, for I knew she was right, we continued on and out the front doors of the temple and headed to a smaller building to the left.

"I cannot come in. This is the male bath house. When you are done go to that building there," she pointed to another smaller building to the right of the temple. With nothing more to add she walked away and left me to the pleasures of the bath house.

As she had said, the first thing I was offered was some herbal tea. I was seated just within the doorway and a servant came with a tray immediately. A lesser teacher stood by to watch over me the whole time.

"Well at least you do not smell as bad as most by this day," he sneered as I drank.

I could not imagine smelling any worse than I did. I had bathed but only minimally with a corner of my clothing and what water my jug held. They had even thrown me some fresh clothes every ten days, but given how Egyptians were about personal hygiene my state was nothing less than disgusting no matter how noble an endeavour I had just completed.

I had probably drunk at least a litre of tea and my stomach could have beared no more. Thankfully the priest also decided this was enough.

"Let's make way to the bath. The waters would be losing their warmth by now," he said and gestured to a doorway.

As I walked through the door the smells of the oils hit my nose. I still had the strong scents of the tea upon my palette but now the essence of rose and lotus swirled around me. I sighed out loud as I saw the huge sunken bath before me and began to tear at my clothes. Two servants waiting in this room stepped forward and pulled my hands away.

"Sir, it is our job," one said and they proceeded to undress me.

Oh, to step into that warm, scented water and feel the oils on its surface start to coat my body. It was like that time as a child letting that sweet dissolve in my mouth. One hundred words came to mind and not one of them was good enough to speak of what it felt like. I sank down into the warm water and leaned back against the edge of the bath smiling.

It would have been wonderful to just lie here like this for forty days but just as quickly the servants too were in the bath beside me, each lifting an arm and scrubbing me vigorously. They gestured for me to sit on the edge of the bath and then did the same for my legs and then my back, chest and stomach. I was wide awake by the time they finished.

"Time for your massage," said the priest.

As I stood from the bath a servant wrapped a small cloth around my waist and then gestured for me to follow him. We walked into another room with a low long table. In the corner, incense was burning.

"Lie face down," the priest instructed and so I did.

Then once again the four hands of the servants were upon me, pushing and pulling at my muscles and joints. When they were finished I felt renewed and now the tea had settled in my stomach. I heard its first growl in weeks and the servants laughed.

"That's how we know your body has truly been woken up," one said and they both laughed again.

I was scraped down so that my skin turned red and then more oil was rubbed into my skin. Then I was slapped on my buttocks and told to stand up. As I did I swayed from side to side, almost losing my balance and bringing about another round of laughter from the men.

"Oh you need some food," cried one of the servants as they began to dress me.

Clothed again I made my way, more sure-footedly now, to the building the priestess had directed me to. I could smell the food before I was even in the door but to see it was even more enticing. It looked magnificent and for a moment I could have just thrown myself upon the table and grabbed at everything at once. Then another sensation came over me; I did not think I could eat a thing! My stomach that had been so long empty now spoke to me as though it had its own voice.

"Are you sure you need food? We have survived for so long without it," I heard it say.

Then it spoke in its more familiar way with a deep roar and it twisted within me.

"I hear the tea working within you and it seems the bathing and massage have done their job as well. You look much more presentable and alert now." It was the priestess standing across the room who I had barely noticed as I contemplated the food. Flanking her were the other three elders.

"Come," she gestured to the table. "We will sit and eat with you."

All in our places I finally began to help myself to fruits first.

"You do not wish to have your meat first?" said the husband.

I shook my head. "No, I have not partaken of flesh in some years and I do not wish to begin again." Then I told them of the story of how Thales explained the beauty of this to me. The man grunted and the second man leaned forward and now spoke.

"What do you feel you have learnt from your retreat?" he asked.

I took my time to chew and swallow what was in my mouth knowing very well that what I had to say next may be some of the most important words I ever spoke.

"I have learnt there are parts of me that are much deeper than any man can understand. I also know there is no way to these parts though my mind. It is through the breath that I was able to access them," I said as I turned to look each one of them in the eye. All but the husband nodded as I spoke and my teacher smiled.

"That's all very well," said the husband abruptly. "But how do you see this as being of any benefit to your life. It is one thing to know. It is another to live it."

I did not hesitate this time to speak.

"This knowledge that I have now opened will allow me to connect with the wisdom of the ages in much more ways than the average student. I know now that when I leave here I can communicate with my dear teacher within a single breath," I said this as I nodded towards the woman. "I know too that I can communicate across time as well as distance and this excites me even more. It is this beautiful knowing that I am not set by the limits of my mind and body that make me determined more than ever to teach and bring new wisdom to our times. And in doing so who knows who will connect with me across time and space to continue this on. I rejoice that our wisdom will never be lost and will grow with each person who connects with it."

I stopped and lifted my hand as though trying to pull at some more words but there was nothing left I could share within my speech. My teacher smiled so widely now I saw her teeth and she looked at her husband who kept his gaze fixed on me.

"You have done well, my Greek. But do not rest upon your achievements. The greatest folly of any teacher is to believe they are no longer a student!" he said coldly.

I do believe they were amongst the wisest words ever spoken to me.

I spent one further month at this school but as grateful as I was for what I had been taught there I had another place that I needed to be. I also knew I would always be welcome to return another time now that I had completed my initiation. So four weeks later my satchel was over my shoulder and I was making my way back to the first school that had rejected me.

As I walked I looked about me with fresh eyes. This sense of things having changed was not entirely new. I had felt this after my time in the schools in Phoenicia and Babylonia. It was quite incredible to have a physical sense that your new-found wisdom or knowledge had transformed you in a way that affected your very interaction with the world around you. After my time in solitude and having gone to the very depths of my breathing and having all this expanded, the sensation of my growth was greater than ever. In fact the first few moments beyond the confines of the school were almost overwhelming.

I saw people in a whole new way. Someone could pass me and before I would have noticed that they may not be smiling but now I sensed if there was anger or grief behind their frown. As you can imagine, walking through a crowd of people became like a flood of awareness that was both disturbing and enlightening.

At one point I had to stop. The wash of emotions from the people around me was too much and my head actually began to ache. I took a deep breath and asked myself for an insight to deal with this. My answer came in an instant.

"Do not take what is not yours!"

Within another breath I shook loose what I had been picking up and continued on, feeling just what was within me and leaving the emotions of those around me to the person that owned them.

When I approached the first school I had no secret escort to meet and measure me. There were no spies expecting me this time and even so they would have had a hard time identifying me as "the Greek" as I looked every part of the Egyptian initiate now.

As I arrived at the school I laughed as I saw the doors to the main temple wide open. I made my way up the stairs with a jump in each step, smiling as broadly as I could. When I reached the top of the last one the assistant appeared from nowhere and stood before me blocking my way to the door.

"Who are you and what brings you here?" was his polite but direct address to me.

"I am Pythagoras of Samos and I arrive here to once again seek admission to your school," I said loudly and without trying to hide my smile.

The assistant gasped and took a step back as he looked me up and down.

"No! It is not you!" he said. "Pythagoras has been here and it was not you."

"Yes, it is me and I have much changed," I said with a laugh.

"Wait here!" he snapped and turned to run inside.

I stepped back and leant against a pillar of the portico. I considered taking a seat upon the top step but I knew somehow that I would not be made to wait so long this time. As I predicted the assistant was back within minutes. His face was red and he stammered as he spoke this time.

"The elders are gathering. I—you—follow me. Don't speak to anyone. Oh—um—just follow me," he sputtered without any of the decorum he had shown previously.

I walked behind him and saw that this time they did not clear the temple of any students. Instead they were left to watch me as I made my way. Each one stared at me intently and this just amused me more.

"Ah, so they intend my rejection to be more public this time if needed," I thought and tried not to laugh.

Well, they could make a spectacle of me if they so chose. At the least it would just add to my already growing legend.

As I continued to walk I saw the elders taking their places in the usual positions upon their chairs. This time though they looked far from the stiff and strong men who had addressed me before. I saw them shift in their seats as I got closer and I saw the once stern faces now had the odd red flush upon a cheek. Here before me were four wise men, ill prepared and not knowing what was about to be put before them.

I reached my place, bowed to them and stood straight, looking them in the eye and waiting for them to begin. I may have had them on the back foot, so to speak, but I would still be respectful to their ways.

"Greetings to you, Pythagoras," said the eldest sitting second from the left. "What brings you to our school on this day?"

He launched in with no small talk or any great sense of familiarity. Not that I was expecting such.

"I have come to you this day to ask that I may join you to study the teachings of your school," I said simply and bowed as I finished.

As I straightened up I saw all four take a deep breath and shift once more in their chairs. The same man spoke again now.

"And why should we believe you to be more worthy now than the last time you stood before us?" he asked as he lifted his chin.

"Because I am not the same man who stood before you previously. I have taken the time you suggested to breathe and fast. I stand before you a changed man for now I know the truth of what you offered me in suggesting this. I now know the difference between knowing and feeling," I said strongly looking each one in the eye by turn.

They all shifted in their chairs once more and looked at each other. I saw one raise his eyebrows as they exchanged glances. Finally the eldest addressed me for the second time.

"Fine. You will sleep here again tonight as we deliberate. Present yourself here in the morning for our decision," he said bluntly and then stood to leave, prompting the others to also rise and follow him without one giving me so much as a sideways glance.

Once within their private rooms they collapsed into chairs and did not speak for a moment as they gathered their thoughts. The eldest one's face turned deep red from frustration when another jumped from his seat and began to pace the room.

"We were not prepared for this. The past elders did not leave any suggestions should this arise," he said as he threw his hands before him, stating just what the other three were also thinking.

The eldest began to shake his head. "How can we even trust that he did the retreat?"

"Oh, Paxus! You could see it in his eyes that he did! Can you deny it?" shouted another.

The eldest shook his head, "No I cannot deny it. His eyes are the clearest I have seen since the elders who chose me to attend this very school." He dropped his head and lifted his hands to rub at his temples. "The real question is—are we obliged to enrol him?"

"No! No! No! The real question is whether he is adequate to become our student. Retreat completed or not, wise or not, studious or not—is he acceptable to study here?" cried the one pacing.

"I think you are all missing the point!" shouted the fourth man. "This is not about obligation or acceptability. We are running a school and we have guidelines to conform to. If he fits those then he attends. Why are you all making this so complicated?"

The one pacing raced to this man's side and leant in close to his face. "Because he made it complicated!" he shouted, spitting fine drops as he did. "Before he was born he challenged our structure by having his father come here. He arrives with attitude the first time and then returns as though to mock us. No student has done this and if we send him away no further students shall. We teach the wisdom of the ages and how we do that is not to be challenged or changed!"

The man sitting remained calm and looked the standing man in the eye.

"And do you not suppose that such challenges are what is needed for wisdom to evolve?" he said softly. "I say he attends. I say that this kind of change in energy is what we have been looking for."

"And when he fails and our school is in disarray, full of mediocre students who arrive and are accepted because they are 'different' what shall you say then of the 'change'?" the standing elder mocked.

"I won't need to say anything for that will not occur," he replied smugly. "Instead, when our school is remembered through the ages for this man having attended, it will be because we helped him find his truth."

"I agree," said the eldest with an air of submission and relief.

"As do I," sighed the fourth.

The standing man straightened and looked at each one. "Your decision was made before you even returned to this room, wasn't it?" he asked.

The other three men nodded.

"So be it," he replied and stormed out of the room.

Back in the main temple everyone could hear the yelling even though we could not make out the words that were spoken. I took a deep breath as this was happening and when it was over quite quickly I knew that I was accepted. Those around me though did not feel this.

As I turned to leave I saw the smirks upon some of the students and they whispered to each other. I was almost out the door when one spoke loudly behind me. "Congratulations! You are the only man stupid enough to return and be rejected twice."

I spun around to see if I could catch the face behind the voice but they cleverly all acted as though none had spoken. I smiled in response and then kept on walking.

Once outside I found a bench under a tree and sat. I looked about the school and saw some men walking between the buildings quietly.

"Why did I feel the need to come back here?" I asked myself.

I closed my eyes and took a deep breath and surrendered to the rhythm of my lungs. Ah, that sweet space that I knew so well now. What a haven it was and how thankful I was to have found it. I heard my answer within and it was not what I expected.

"Because you need to know what you missed," it said to me softly and I nodded more to acknowledge it than to agree.

Opening my eyes I saw a man approaching me. He was not an elder or an assistant. It was clear from his dress that he was a student and not much older than I was. My hand gripped the edge of the bench, bracing myself for some more torment. Instead the smile I saw on his face was far from mocking and he held out his hand in greeting.

"Welcome to you, Pythagoras. I am Tiberius," he said as his hand tightened around mine. He let it go and nodded his head to the right. "Come. I will introduce you to some more students."

He walked away at such a pace that I had to run a few steps to catch up with him.

"You are not Egyptian," I more stated than actually asked.

"No, I am not," he said smiling as though this was something he was proud of. "I am from Babylonia and the students you are about to meet are the rest of the non-Egyptians." He laughed after he said this.

"Why do you laugh?" I asked genuinely intrigued.

Tiberius just shook his head. "Do not worry," he said, but it was because he was so amused at how I had the nerve to show myself for a second chance at admission.

He led me past the buildings I thought were the entire school, past the barracks in which I slept the first time and towards another set of small buildings. I could smell the spices of Persia and Babylonia as

I approached and as we got closer still I heard the strings and flutes of these lands as well. Tiberius led me into a huge room and I saw that two men played the music and the smells were from platters of food in the centre of the room on the floor. Around the edges men lounged; eating, talking and some even sleeping.

"Welcome to the foreign students' quarters," Tiberius said as he gripped my shoulders.

"Why are you in separate quarters?" I asked.

He shrugged his shoulders. "It is just easier this way," he offered but I could not help but frown.

No other school I had been to housed its foreigners apart from its locals. I had even delighted in having women at the last school. No separation should interfere with the act of learning; not age, sex, culture or wealth. No barriers should be set up to wisdom. It was the great leveller, the one thing which bound us. Wisdom was that which was universal. It was like the sun; every man knew of it, experienced it and could not be denied it. It ran through each of us waiting to blossom and unfold.

I sat hesitantly with some of the men and picked at the food. My hesitancy came from not wanting to contribute to the division anymore. I wanted to ask them why they felt the need to be separate and did they not realise that it just fed into this separation between themselves and the locals.

As I ate more food I now joined in some banter and even began to sway to the music I knew so well from my travels. Then it struck me and I looked up once again at the men here; bloated from their food and singing their native songs. It is one thing for men to leave behind their homes to improve themselves, but yet another for them to truly leave behind the comforts and security of how they had lived their lives.

I understood completely. I knew how much my heart had ached for some lamb and Samosian wine when I studied with Thales as it would remind me of home. Once again I smiled as I thought of the crazy old man for I realised the depths of what he had taught me. Releasing our habits no matter how much they seemed to have nurtured us allows us great freedom. It is all too soon in life that we allow these customs to shape us, but to let them go allows much liberty in our further growth.

Finishing up with one last mouthful of food I stood, gave my thanks and made to leave.

"Pythagoras, we have not shown you where your bed shall be," said Tiberius.

"There is no need. I shall sleep in the same bed as I did

previously," I said and bowed my thanks.

As I walked back to the barracks in which I had slept on my first visit it became quite clear to me that what I had just observed was all that I really needed to learn at this school. When I stood before the elders the next morning and was offered a position to study here I had to say "yes" though. To say "no" would have shown me as someone who returned just to mock them, confirming one of their theories of me.

So I attended and was most diligent. I mixed and spoke with all students regardless of their country of origin. This made me a figure of intrigue to everyone. I had challenged the usual way in which to seek admission and now I was going against the social structure as well. I was watched carefully by the elders and I am sure the lesser teachers reported back to them often.

I played out this game for six months. It was far longer than I had intended and far longer than I needed. I learnt nothing new here. There was the daily time spent breathing. Each morning we recorded our dreams and interpreted them which I found to be quite fatuous though I came to enjoy it. We went over astronomy, sacred geometry and anatomy; all the disciplines that I had studied thus far but with nothing truly new. Indeed there was a regional flavour to what they taught and the elders insisted upon including the local mythology within these. The latter was all part of appearing acceptable to the outside.

However each time I watched a teacher speak, his words seemed to be lacking something. It was as though he knew there was more to say to us but he could not share it. It irritated me beyond belief! I wondered if I were to graduate into more senior classes if they would then utter those additional words that they were holding back. So I snuck into such a class one day, unwilling to wait the years that it took to be considered worthy to do this.

I was spotted within ten minutes but this was enough time for me to see that things in these classes were no different. This made my irritation and curiosity grow even more. As I was pushed through the door of the senior class back outside the head assistant walked towards me shaking his head.

"Follow me. The elders wish to see you," he muttered with frustration.

"How did they know that I was in there?" I asked.

The assistant sighed and slumped his shoulders. "They know everything that occurs here. Test them! Ask them to tell you how many times you urinated yesterday," he smirked.

I was not dragged into the main temple but to their private room, the one in which they had decided my fate twice. They sat casually, some leaning on the arm rest to one side. As I walked in they barely changed their posture.

"Pythagoras, you do understand that we have rules and structure in place for a reason?" one asked before I was entirely within the room.

I nodded as the next one began. "So you understand that when we say you need to be here for a certain amount of time before attending certain classes that too is for a reason?" he asked.

I nodded my head again and opened my mouth to speak but yet another began before I could get a word out.

"You are also aware that if you choose to break such rules or act against our directives then we are entitled to expel you?" he said.

I nodded yet again and didn't waste my time trying to speak as he leaned forward to begin again.

"But before we decide whether we shall do this we would like to hear why you chose to attend this class of your own accord?" he asked and sat back in his chair.

I breathed deep knowing that once again what words I chose would affect my immediate future. In that instant I considered lying. I thought I would make up some lie about being curious or so hungry for knowledge that I could not help myself. Just as quickly I decided to be honest and the words were out before I knew it.

"My dear elders, I did this because I feel that your teachers are holding back the truth of the wisdoms your school acts to offer. I imagined that perhaps this was different in the more senior classes but it is not. If you choose to expel me then you may indeed be doing me a favour. As in the past I will respect and honour your decision. I imagine I will see you in the morning for your judgement," I spoke firmly and with resolve knowing that even if they allowed me to stay on I would leave tomorrow.

I was dismissed even more coldly than they had at any other meeting and I hardly cared. These men to me now were not teachers; they were actors playing a part. There is a huge difference. To stand before others and repeat information does not make you a teacher. A true teacher shares their connection with the material. They inspire the student to want to dive into the information being shared so they in turn can discover their own connection.

This was the beauty of studying with the female teacher during my retreat. She had not just spouted how I should do it; she guided me, allowing me my own insights. This allowed me more expansion in those forty days than the six months I had wasted here and what for? I had shown myself nothing truly new in the teachings. All I had shown myself was that my journey should not be hindered by doing what would make me look respectful or what I thought was expected of me in order to fit in.

The anger that bubbled up in me was now boiling over as I walked outside. The assistant approached me again with his face furrowed and I clenched my fists prepared to argue in whatever way felt right in the moment. He moved quickly and as he got closer he did not slow.

Instead he hissed at me through clenched teeth as he passed. "Follow me and do not dawdle!"

We kept moving at a fast pace between the buildings and then beyond them into the scrubland behind the school. Few students took notice of us as we passed so I knew that the gossip of what I had done had not spread yet.

When we were clear of everyone and everything he finally stopped and looked at me. "You need to leave here!" he said strongly.

"Oh, I know that!" I spat back.

"You don't understand Pythagoras. What you did today—and I do not speak of sneaking into that class, I mean what you had the audacity to say to the elders…." He stopped and put a hand to his forehead and then I saw him smile. He shook his head and tried not to laugh. "Truly that was inspired. Inspired but stupid—well possibly not so stupid given what I am about to tell you."

It seems this assistant was not all that he seemed and what he spoke of next, unfortunately, confirmed my theories. This man was, in simple terms, a spy of sorts. Sent here by the temples that taught the mysteries in depth, he was in fact here to make sure that this school was indeed what I had gathered it to be; a college of measured wisdom, doling out only the barest of knowledge to satisfy those that came here. The assistant kept an eye out for those that were deemed worthy to be told of the "true" schools.

"But why put them through the forty days of fasting and breathing?" I asked.

"Well that helps sort out the dedicated from the egotistical. It also helps sort the sheep from the crocodiles," he laughed outright now. "Those who complete it successfully would usually move on within weeks but the sheep who play along with what they think is expected of them remain longer. Until today I had you pegged for a sheep."

I nodded my head. "Yes, I allowed appearance to lead me for these past months."

"Well, are you truly ready to shed your wool?" he asked.

195

"Of course. I will leave tomorrow regardless of the decision," I said.

"Why tomorrow? Why not now?" he asked as he raised an eyebrow.

"Because I should wait til the elders are ready to speak with me," I answered.

"Sheep!" he yelled.

"What!"

"You heard me. That is what a sheep would do. If you know what you want to do then you do it," he crossed his arms and tilted his head at me. "You're very good at putting things off for silly reasons aren't you?"

I nodded my head and sighed.

"Shall I go to the elders now and say you need to see them immediately?" he asked with a smirk.

I nodded again and returned a smile as the assistant walked back to the school.

My resignation was quick and simple. I was not so brazen as I had been in calling them out but my tenacity was just as evident. The looks upon the faces of the elders was sheer relief.

"Go immediately and do not speak with any others," was all that was said spoken to me. I think it was the eldest but it was as though all four voices merged into one.

"I will escort him and make sure this is so," said the assistant with his usual decorum.

I gave him a quick glance and could not help but smile at how easily he slipped back into this act before the elders. It reminded me of the servant in Persia. We walked silently to my bunk and I gathered my satchel. Then he led me to the well to fill my canteen and to the kitchens for some basic food to carry.

As we reached the gate the assistant dropped his act with a deep sigh.

"Good luck Pythagoras. Where do you suppose you will go now?" he asked.

"I will head back to the school where I held my retreat. I feel I dismissed my teachers there too soon," I said with a shrug.

"No, that is not where you will go," he said and pulled a scroll from within the folds of his sleeve. "This is where you shall go. Do not unfold it until you are far from here and if you tell anyone I gave it to you I shall deny it. Take this also," he handed me a small stone amulet.

It was shaped like a cartouche. On one side was carved the ankh and on the other were three hieroglyphs. I recognised one symbol; the centre one which spoke of being a god. The other two would have usually indicated the qualities of the god being spoken of but I did not recognise them even though one looked like the symbol for gold which did not relate to any god I had heard of.

"Go back to the main ports at the delta. Find a cargo boat bound for Nubia. Its captain is called Fazi. Show him the amulet and he will give you passage to your next school. Don't ask where. He will know where to drop you. Then you follow the map. When you get to the school show them the amulet and they will know I sent you. Guard it as though it is made of gold," he said as he pressed it into my palm.

"What does it say in the glyphs?" I asked.

He burst our laughing. "That is what you are going to learn now! Farewell Pythagoras, I trust we will never meet again," he said as he walked off laughing even louder.

CHAPTER TEN

I walked along the roads which would take me back to the marinas of the delta region. It was not so long since I started that an ox cart came up behind me.

"Care to rest your legs traveller?" called out the man driving it.

He was one of the most robust men I had ever met. In fact for a moment I was quite dazed at his size and the definition of his muscles that were gleaming with sweat.

"That would be most appreciated," I said finally finding my voice. "I do hope you are heading towards the docks or else you may make my walk longer."

The man chuckled, "Well this is your lucky day! I am heading there to have my produce shipped to the Pharaoh. He favours my gourds above all others," He finished by turning and slapping one that sat on the top of the pile that filled his cart.

It was perfectly timed and perfectly created. As we rode we swapped stories of our past and I don't think I have laughed so much since…well, I cannot remember any time I had laughed like this. It was quite refreshing to be with someone who lived life simply and without the constant analysis that a scholar felt compelled to be part of.

As we compared stories our differences made for interesting questions. I would be asked if I craved for a home that was mine alone each night while I wondered if he had experienced anything but farming. We asked each other out of pure curiosity and our answers were met with a nod in acknowledgement.

"Mmmm…I see," he would say when I explained my drive to travel as far as I could to learn all I could.

"Tell me though, is the sun so different in all these places?" he asked.

"Well yes, its temperature and light can feel very different," I replied.

"But it still rises in the east and sets in the west, does it not?"

"Well, yes it does," I answered.

"And men; do they still have the same structure and function?"

"Well, yes," I laughed. "And they are as crude and rough."

"Mmmm…I see," he finished quietly.

I did not push upon him what I had seen; how the intricacies of men changed from region to region. This was for each man to learn by his own will and adventure. Here sat a man content with his life and content with all that life had to show him. There is nothing wrong with that at all when it is what has been chosen.

We arrived amongst the bustle of the marina five hours later and my driver directed his cart towards a huge ship at one of the docks. He yelled something out to the crew in a rough dialect. They all cheered and waved to him and then ran to the cart rolling barrels before them to load the gourds into.

My driver approached one man who was obviously the captain and grabbed his arm pulling him towards himself in a playful embrace. They both laughed and spoke in a dialect that I could barely understand. There was one word I heard though—"Fazi"

I waited until they finished their banter and my driver walked back to check on the unloading of his cart. Then I approached the captain.

"Is your name Fazi?" I asked the captain.

"Yes it is," he answered as he measured me, glancing up and down.

"I believe you may provide me with passage south on the Nile," I said hesitantly, not sure how this was supposed to be played out.

He crossed his arms and puffed his chest up, "Why would I give you passage on my boat?" he asked defiantly.

I said nothing. All I did was pull the amulet from my satchel and show it to him. His chest deflated and his arms dropped.

"Certainly," he said as he looked past me and then to each side. "Now put that away before anyone sees it! We leave this evening when the sun cools so do not stray far as I do not set a time for this. I decide in the moment. If you are here, you board. If not, well then you try your luck with someone else. If anyone asks why you are onboard then it is because you have business in Thebes and I am doing you a favour as our families know each other. They should not ask anyway. Understand?"

I nodded and smiled. "Thank you," I said softly and put the amulet back in my satchel. I thought for a moment to ask him if he knew what the glyphs said but knew immediately not to. That could wait. For now all I should be concerned with was getting to the next school.

Fearing I would indeed miss my ride I did not wander from Fazi's boat. Looking at all the boats, some of which I realised would be making their way to Greece, made me think of my family. I decided I should send a letter home to my mother, just to let her know that all was well. Little did I realise that rumours of me had spread through the Middle East and across the sea to her ears. She knew I was well and doing as I planned, not that she doubted it for a moment anyway.

Not knowing this though I still found a ship headed for Samos and slipped one of my remaining coins into the hand of a man I decided was trustworthy. It was a simple message that I sent to my mother;

"All is well and going as planned."

It would comfort her immensely. It would also make its way back to Polycrates. He now knew I was in Egypt and as I travelled and studied in this land he used my presence as a political ploy with the Pharaoh, gaining favour and, without my being aware, a diplomat of sorts. As long as it didn't affect my studies I would not have cared anyway. Just over twenty years later when Cambyses, the ruler of Persia and Polycrates' ally, decided to invade Egypt this made me a liability. But until that time I would drink up all the knowledge that Egypt had to offer.

I saw Fazi standing upon the bow of his ship. He had climbed right up upon the edge of the railing and was looking south down the Nile. Then he turned and looked north. Without gauging where his feet would land he jumped down onto the deck, turned to his crew and put one hand on either side of his mouth.

"Prepare to sail!" he yelled and instantly the already busy crew stopped what they were doing and began the tasks needed to get the boat moving. I ran up the gangplank along with the last few men on the ground.

Fazi saw me and smiled. "Welcome aboard. Somehow I knew you would not miss this launch."

"Where can I sit so to be out of your way?" I asked.

Fazi burst out laughing and then leant in close to me.

"You may be getting free passage but do not think I will let you sit idle! You will work your way to your destination as every man aboard my ship does. Now go help pull the anchors," he said and then walked off shouting commands as he made his way along the length of the deck.

I stood shocked for a moment. Indeed I had been aboard enough boats since my childhood to know what occurred when a boat sailed but how to be a part of these machinations left me stunned. I looked to my left and then my right, deciding to join some men then changing my mind. I would head towards one group pulling ropes and as soon as I arrived they would finish and move on so quickly that I felt stupid to ask what was needed next.

Finally I saw one young man struggling to pull up a rope so I walked to him. He grunted as he yanked at it, but then smiled at me as I grabbed upon the rope with him. The rope slid easily over the railing and onto the deck. I have no idea what it was for but I was helping and that was all that mattered.

Finally we were out of the docks and slipping along the Nile. I had never sailed upon a river before so this was entirely new. Instead of the boat rolling as it hit the open ocean, Fazi's boat settled after the initial manoeuvres out of the docks and now glided. In fact the only disturbance to the water was that which we created.

I was given more menial jobs which made sense and in fact it was a relief to not have too much responsibility. We were into our second day of sailing when I began to wonder just when I would reach my destination. I had taken a glimpse at my map and it only showed from the shore I would be dropped at. My curiosity kept niggling me so I decided to risk asking Fazi just when we would reach my dock. He saw me approach and pre-empted my question with a new order.

"Grab a bucket and head below. We have a leak and there is water to bail. You are on this duty for the next three hours," he said with a grin.

"*Well then,*" I thought, "*I will not be disembarking any time soon!*"

I grabbed a huge bucket and joined a line of five other men. We made a chain and so only had to move five or six paces at a time to pass the bucket from one man to the other. However we also took turns in our positions so that each man had his fair share of time climbing stairs or standing with his feet in water within the hull.

Soon enough it was my turn in the water. This was not so bad as it was barely to the ankles. We were clearing it fast enough so that it would not gather any real depth. As I scooped the bucket I watched where the water seeped or sprayed in through the planks of wood and saw it was just in places where the rubber and oils used to seal the wood had grown thin.

"Surely Fazi carries the materials on board to repair such things?" I said to the next man as we stood waiting for an emptied bucket to make its way back to us.

He and the next man burst out laughing. "Oh you truly do not know Fazi!" he said still laughing.

"If ever there was a man who knew how to stretch a coin it is Fazi," added the next man.

"*How ridiculous,*" I thought. To save money by risking your ship and the cargo not to mention the men on board seemed the most illogical thing to me.

I looked about after I scooped the next bucket and had passed it on. Our light was from a lamp and I considered using the oil from this but knew it would not work. Then I saw what I wanted. In a shallow dish were the dregs from the last candle that had burnt within it. I used my thumbnail to lift the solid wax from the curves of the holder and rubbed it in my fingers til it softened. When it was soft enough I pressed it into the closest leak, one that was a fine spray at my eye level. I worked the wax across the join that was weakened, pushing and rubbing till it was seamless and the water flow had stopped.

"Hah!" I cried out, quite satisfied with what I had done.

"Wonderful," said the man next to me sarcastically. "Now can you keep on with what we are supposed to do." He shoved a bucket at me like an exclamation mark.

"If we repair all these like I just did then we won't need to do this stupid bailing," I said. "You can continue with the bucket while I get more candles."

"What makes you think that will hold?" he asked.

"Well look at it. It is doing quite well," I said and leant in close to check on it.

Just as I did this the wax gave way. The water it had held back had built enough pressure to pop it out. So not only did the wax fly forward but it was followed by a less then gentle spray of water which I now wore on my face. Behind me I heard the raucous laughter of all the other men.

"I take it you will not be needing any other candles?" one said and I felt the bucket pressed back into my hand.

"No, I won't," I said and joined them in laughing.

I also decided that in no way should I mention that I was in fact an eighth generation male from the most powerful shipbuilding family in Greece. Somewhere I could feel my male ascendants cringing.

It was the following morning that Fazi approached me for what I assumed would be my duties for the day.

"Get ready to disembark," he said with a smile.

I nodded and looked about, but my excitement to be finally on foot to my school was soon flattened. There was no town where we were approaching. I could not even see a road or signs of a farm. There were just the usual palms and grasses along the banks and beyond these was flat barren land. Nothing was there. Nothing.

"Fazi, are you sure this is where I get off?" I said quietly.

Fazi burst out laughing. "Yes, yes, yes! I am most sure!" he said emphatically and called out for the small boat hanging from the side to be lowered.

Two men went ahead of me down onto the smaller boat and then I followed, being lowered by rope as they had. They rowed me to the eastern shore, allowing the ship to stay a safe distance from running aground in the heavy mud.

I jumped from the boat onto the soft bank, my feet sinking instantly into the mud. I looked down and sighed at my less than graceful start to this leg of my adventure.

"Good luck!" cried out one of the men in the boat and I heard the other snicker as they pushed the boat back into the deeper water with the oars.

My feet came free from the mud with belching sounds as the muck released them, albeit with a lovely thick coating. I went to a part of the bank where some grasses provided a firmer ground and washed my feet as well as I could then slipped my sandals off to rinse both them and my feet once more.

I sat upon the grass to take a look at my map as well as use the opportunity for my feet to dry. I unrolled the scroll and once more took in its details to hopefully find something nearby to help me get my bearings. There was a symbol drawn on the scroll that looked like a mountain but I could see no rise anywhere, not even a large rock that might match. There were roads marked but without some sense of scale they could be a day's walk away. I threw the map on the ground as I shouted out in frustration.

Damn Fazi! I was sure he had dropped me at the wrong place but then knowing how such things worked now it was as likely to be the perfect place.

As with all of Egypt, things do not happen so far from the river. No-one survived more than an hour's walk from this lifeline. I had been told this over and over. In fact as we had sailed the occurrence of buildings, temples and farms had been constant. To be left here in what appeared the middle of nowhere was merely a test of my common sense I decided. So I got to my feet, gathered my scroll and began to walk south alongside the river.

I had only walked five minutes when I saw something to my left. It was a small temple that appeared as though out of nowhere. There was a small rise in the land between the river and the temple, so gradual and subtle that it could not be noticed. It was enough to block the site of the temple unless you were in the exact right place. I laughed softly as I congratulated myself for trusting my own directions and made way to the temple.

As I got closer though, my initial joy at finding it sank. This was far too small to be a school as well as a temple. There was only one building and it was definitely not large enough to be of any consequence even as a religious establishment. It was most likely one of the dozens of temples built by Pharaohs more as somewhere to offer temporary shelter if they were travelling by land. I decided to approach anyway and see if perhaps they could help me with the map.

The temple was edged on all four sides by stairs that lifted it up and off the sand in the way all temples were designed. Upon the top step I saw there was a man sitting. When he saw me walking towards the temple he stood and dusted his hands off on his skirt. Then he waved to me. This stopped me in my tracks for a moment but I returned the gesture with gratitude to at least being made to feel welcome.

"*No more games please!*" I thought to myself as I kept walking. I could not bear anymore cryptic interviews or initiations. I just wanted to learn.

"Good day," yelled out the man who I now could see was dressed as a priest. "Welcome to our temple. May the mighty Amun be praised for your safe arrival!" He said as he lifted his hands to the air and then lowered them. "Come inside and have some respite from the sun." He walked towards the huge doors of the temple, beckoning me with a wave of his hand.

I was impressed to be invited inside without having to explain who I was. Inside the usual cool air of a stone room invited a deep breath from me. It was indeed a relief to be out of the harsh Egyptian sun.

As I looked around I became even more convinced that this was just what I had imagined it to be; a resting place. The temple was ostensibly just a square box. There was minimal decoration and nowhere near the amount of carvings that were in most temples. I could not even pick out one god that the temple seemed dedicated to.

There was the usual altar with dishes of incense smouldering upon it but it was placed further forward than usual. It was also upon the same level as the rest of the floor, missing the usual dais that raised it. I was about to ask for what purpose or order the temple served but the priest began to speak.

"It is such a joy to have someone come to our humble little temple," he said grinning.

"*Our? Just where are the others?*" I thought and wondered if perhaps the priest had been alone for too long.

"Oh, you are wondering where the others are," he said and laughed. "They are out gathering supplies which can take some time due to our location. To be honest, even though I do miss them, I relish the time and space to myself. You can imagine it gets crowded with five of us in here."

I saw there were two doors behind the altar, one to each side and smiled. This was a hint that this may be a school as this was something that had been the same in them all. Although at this school they would likely lead to nothing bigger than a large storage room. Nonetheless this fired my belief that this was indeed a school and I was being measured each moment as much as I had been upon my arrival at any other school. I decided to save some time and effort and end this part of the process.

I reached into my satchel and drew out the amulet. Without saying a word I held it before me on my open palm. The priest stopped and stared at it, then his grin widened even more.

"Thank you for not waiting for me to ask," he said and started to laugh. "Some men have let me babble for hours until I was forced to do so," he stopped to sigh. "And some, well they leave before I can find an opportunity to ask or they can find the courage to show me. This is a wonderful start for you."

He walked to the back of the altar and pulled aside the huge rug that lay there. This exposed a wooden panel that sat flush with the stone floor. The priest then took a small flat stick from below the altar and pushed it under one edge of the panel lifting it enough so that he could now grip it with his hand. He looked up at me.

"Could you help?"

I grabbed the edge to the side of where the priest was gripping and together we lifted it free of where it laid and slid it over onto the solid stone floor. Where the panel had been was now an opening and as I looked in I could see some light. There was a ladder and the priest signalled for me to climb down below. I slung my satchel around to my back and knelt down so that my hands could help me find my way onto the first rung.

It was barely fifteen rungs but this was deep enough and I could feel the air cooling even more as I descended. I saw that the wall behind the ladder was solid rock and wondered how long they had taken to carve this space out. When I finally stepped off the final rung and turned around I gasped out aloud. The space before me was enormous, even bigger than the temple above and even more bare. In fact the only thing of note was a row of lamps which were hung halfway up the walls along each side, providing the light that I first saw.

"This must have taken years to dig out!" I exclaimed and ran my hands down the wall.

"Quite possibly," muttered the priest as he climbed down the last few rungs. "No-one knows for sure as it has been here since before any records that have survived. Now, head down that way. Wait in the next area and someone will come for you." He pointed to one corner of the space and as my eyes adjusted I could see this was another opening and a faint light came through it.

"Won't you be coming with me?" I asked.

"Oh, no. I have to go and cover the entrance in case someone else arrives," he said and began to climb.

I found it hard to imagine that someone else would arrive so soon but this only demonstrated how protective they were of the school. This bode well, I hoped, for what lay in store for me and I now walked towards the other doorway as I heard the priest dragging the panel back into place.

This entry led to another huge space not quite the size of the first but what it lacked in size it made up for in its decoration. At first glance anyone who may have found their way here would imagine it was the tomb of a noble. The paintings were rich and detailed. I saw images of Isis, Horus, Anubis and Osiris. Amongst them were hieroglyphs telling the story of the holy family as you might find in any regular tomb.

Then one detail caught my eye. It was a cartouche and within it were the same three symbols on my amulet. Two doorways led off from the wall opposite to where I had emerged. I was glad I had been told to wait and did not have to choose which door to progress through.

I heard some steps approaching but I could not tell which direction they were coming from. Then at each of the doorways a priest appeared so simultaneously that I did not know where to look first. Each one bowed their head to me inturn and I responded likewise.

"Welcome," said the one on the left. "What is your name?"

"I am Pythagoras of Samos," I answered.

"Come Pythagoras, come. We have much to do and should begin straight away," he said and beckoned me with his hand, while the other priest smiled and returned to where he came from.

I followed the priest into his doorway where he waited for me smiling.

"Oh it is so good to have someone new. We just sent off the last student and it's always so quiet and staid until someone else comes along. When Habin sent word of having sent you we were so excited. It's been a while since he saw fit to send a foreigner to us so that made it even more interesting," he spoke as we walked along a corridor.

The paintings here were just as elaborate as the last space, once again mimicking a tomb in its layout and appearance. They looked perfect, as though freshly painted but I knew this was otherwise.

The corridor soon opened out into another space as large as the first one and almost as plain. There were markings on the walls to the left and right of the doorway but they were simple, without colour and the illustrations were something else entirely. In fact there were hardly any drawings. Along each wall just above head height was a series of diagrams; just simple shapes drawn two dimensionally and then below them a list in cuneiform, the alternative to hieroglyphs.

The wall opposite the doorway was lined with shelves filled with boxes. Though the boxes were all made of the same material and in the same style they were various sizes. In the middle of the room was a table surrounded by chairs.

"Sit wherever you feel you would like to. There is no wrong or right place. This room is your private school for now," he said, chuckling as he walked to the shelves and took down a box.

He carried it to the table and placed it before me then walked back to get another. I soon had a row of five boxes in front of me. The priest took a seat so that he sat to the side of me at the table and when he was settled he placed his hands within each other and smiled at me.

"I think it would be wonderful if we breathed together for a few moments so we can truly connect and set the energy for what we are about to do," he said softly.

I nodded in agreement. It would be wonderful indeed to settle my breath and relax as I knew this would help me take in what I was about to hear.

So we breathed quietly for a few minutes. Oh, how I cherished diving into that space now. I felt how old the temple and these caves were. I felt the men who had carved the rocks out and those who had painted it. I felt the line of teachers and students who had been here before me. Within these men I connected to the ancient wisdom that they carried and shared. It was like each one of them was whispering something to me.

Then I felt the men who were here now; the anticipation as I had approached and their curiosity as to what I would be like, followed by the relief when I arrived before them.

It was when I stepped into the energies of the present moment that I suddenly became aware of the boxes before me. Even though my eyes were closed I could sense them moving but as I tuned in closer it was not the boxes that were moving but what lay within them.

I breathed more and focussed on one; it was vibrating. The second felt like a glow. Each one had its own quality and now I was almost desperate to find out what was inside them. It was then that the priest spoke again.

"Mmmm. You have been taught well," he said with his ever present smile.

He then stood and opened each box, watching my reaction as each lid was swung back on its hinges. I leant forward and saw that within each was a crystal sitting atop a small velvet pillow. Each one was a different colour and a different shape. It was like looking at five different flowers; each one unique but all as beautiful as the other.

He carefully lifted each pillow with its crystal out and sat it before the box that housed it. Then he sat again and I saw his smile straighten a little and his voice now was more serious.

"Before you are the remnants of a time and place that are long gone but that we still have much connection with. It was at this place that the ancient wisdoms were expanded beyond anything that we can comprehend today. It was this expansion that was also this civilisation's downfall. The crystals you see here," he pointed to those before me and then swept his hand towards the shelves and the multitude of boxes still sitting there, "are what were saved when this place destructed. They were taken underground in places much like this one to protect them and the knowledge and power they held.

The people survived and continued on despite their minimal numbers. When they eventually made their way above ground they created Egypt and her religion to carry on some of the knowledge. However it was agreed that the truth would remain hidden. It would be held for those who sought it with integrity and intent for the knowledge to remain pure. They had seen how the wisdom could be corrupted and what it had led to. That could never happen again.

The truth would be passed on to those who would carry it with balance. They would be chosen and if they did not keep with the integrity and intent to protect the wisdom then they would be stopped before the destruction and corruption occurred again.

Do you understand?"

As he finished there was no trace of a smile left on his face. I still felt his warmth but I knew he had not only just shared with me the history of all the schools I had attended but he was also asking me to take a vow.

I nodded.

"I understand completely and I promise to serve this wisdom with all the purity and integrity I can," I answered softly because I did and I would.

"Wonderful. Let us begin then," he said and the smile returned.

I took a deep breath as we began and I felt something within me shift. It was the full understanding of all I had experienced so far. Part of me wished that I had been given this history lesson earlier. I would probably not have been so petulant or cynical as I had been when the other schools had played their little games with me but then perhaps I may not have appreciated the magnitude of what I was just told. Nor would I have understood the depth of what was to come.

The entire experience in just getting to this school was part of what I needed to appreciate in order to fully integrate what would be shared with me now. From the toning and levitating to the dissection and the breathing; it all led up to this precise moment. What I was about to be shown would expand my world in ways I could never have imagined and it ignited my passion to teach and learn more than anything else ever would.

My teacher stood and went to one of the boxes upon the shelves. He took from it a length of wire and when he sat back down he reached before him and took the first crystal. It was long in shape compared to the others, its surface was smooth and its edges met at sharp angles forming distinct surfaces that ran its length. Each end tapered into a point as though it had been chiselled and looked as though it could pierce something if you forced it. The teacher handled it as though it was the most fragile thing on the planet.

He took the wire and gently wound it around the crystal in a spiral, taking great care that each turn of the wire had some space between it. When he finished he lay it down upon the pillow and smoothed out the ends of the wire so they lay pointing out from the crystal. He looked up at me and grinned.

"This is Pyhirric quartz crystal," he said then turned in his chair and pointed to the wall to the left.

There on the wall was a drawing of the crystal. I saw its name below it in the Egyptian cuneiform and I realised the list below was the qualities or powers it held. I saw the word "fire" and "current" and I looked back at my teacher with my eyebrows raised. He laughed out loud.

"Yes, yes, yes," he said, "It is quite a test of the mind and its memory isn't it? Now watch…."

With that he picked up the two ends of the wire that trailed from the crystal and slowly brought them together. He did it so slowly that it felt like he was teasing but when I saw what would happen I knew why.

As the two ends came closer I saw his hands begin to shake and I saw the ends of the wire emit a slight glow. Then suddenly an arc of miniature lightning flashed between the ends of the wire. My teacher's hands flew apart as I jumped in my chair.

He laughed so much that he had tears in his eyes.

"Oh, I love to start with that one! It always gets the same response. Pardon me for indulging my amusement with you so," he said as he wiped his eyes.

"What was that?" I gasped.

"This crystal was one of the last things to be explored by these people. They were using it as a power source of some kind. It could generate light and even power machinery. They were working on making this available to the common people when the destruction began," he said matter-of-factly as he began to unwind the wire.

Then my questions came thick and fast; "Why weren't the priests developing this for the commoners now? Why hadn't they shared it with the Pharaoh for use in his empire? How did they harness this lightning? Did the crystal ever lose the inherent power it held? How did it carry through the wire? How did such a small thing emit such force?"

The priest held up his hand. "Slow down!" he said. "That is why this remains hidden. Look at how your mind races with questions and creates scenarios for it. Immediately you want to take its power and use it for things that are not necessary, that do not serve wisdom or the evolvement of civilisation. Lighting a home and building empires does not serve mankind. Understanding how power flows is the key and that is what this crystal serves to teach us right now.

Commoners are not ready for such things. They still believe that gods shape their world. The Pharaohs know that if they place power in a crystal then all it takes to usurp their power is for the crystal to be stolen. The kings that do know of its existence are happy for it to remain hidden. It scares them more than it excites them for the fear of what it will oblige them to take part in. Sometimes it is far more comfortable to remain small than become big!" He laughed at this last point. "Sorry I was just thinking of the priests who were offered the opportunity to learn here and who remained in their temples burning incense. We all choose how much we are prepared to experience and it all fits perfectly together. Now shall we move on to the next one?"

I nodded once more.

He picked up the next crystal. It was more rounded but nowhere near a sphere. It was more like a group of crystals all joined together into one form, each one pushing out of the shape to form its own curve. As he handed it to me it seemed to change colour. At first it looked mostly green but then the lamplight caught flecks of yellow and orange. I lifted it close to my face and could see even smaller crystals caught within it that were almost clear in colour, like glass.

"This is called Amunite," he said and pointed to the wall to the right this time.

I scanned down the list and saw the words "expansion" and "dimensional travel". This time I screwed up my face as I turned back.

"This helps you open your human limitations," he said but I did not see his lips move and I understood completely. Then once again with not a sound I heard him say "Nod your head if you can hear me" and so I did.

"Marvellous," he said out loud. "This crystal usually helps me measure where my students are at. It looks like you will not need to be here for so long."

With that he moved on to the other crystals. Some held the qualities of physical healing, others gave off sounds that became music within me. Each one was unique and focussed on spaces within me that I knew were deep and just beginning to open.

When he had shared with me ten of the crystals I saw the teacher hide a yawn behind his hand.

"I do believe that is enough for today and I must admit my stomach begins its evening chant to be filled," he said and chuckled. "Come, let us join the others."

As intrigued as I was and wanting to see more, my stomach too was calling out for food so I was quite happy to follow him. We walked back to the room where he had greeted me and made our way through the other doorway into a replica of the first corridor. This led into another space at which four priests were gathered around a table set with a very simple meal that they had already begun.

"You must be an adept student to have occupied Rakeen so long," one said and gestured to a chair as an invitation for me to join them.

"Yes he is," answered Rakeen as he began to reach for the food before his behind had even landed on the seat.

I looked before me and was relieved there was no meat, saving me from yet another explanation of being vegetarian. Instead I saw dry flat bread, some hard cheese and dried dates. The only thing fresh were some lotus pods that were being split to eat the soft seeds inside.

"As you can see we must make do with what we can store and gather close by for most of the time," said another priest. "Other schools bring us fresh food when their schedule allows but as I am sure you know our bodies can make do with much less than our minds think they can."

"This I know well," I answered remembering my forty days of breathing.

To be honest the meal we had was more than substantial anyway. Each item was heavy and filling so that only a little was needed to satisfy my stomach. I could imagine how exciting it would be to have a visit with the arrival of fresh fruit though.

After our meal I helped gather our plates and glasses. There was a small room off the dining room where a spring bubbled up from one corner within an enclosure and then fell away into a drain on one side.

"This is our only water source. Use it to bathe and clean but be mindful that nothing goes into the source," one priest said as he showed me and then pointed to a stack of buckets nearby. "When you want to bathe, fill a bucket and then go next door."

Adjacent was a small room barely six feet square. Towards the back was a large hole in the floor.

"Wash close to the hole so the water runs in. Any waste can go in there too—just wash it down with some water," he said plainly.

I looked at the hole not realising I was looking at possibly the oldest indoor toilet in the world. I did wonder how deep it was and where it went to but I doubt even the current priests knew. The lack of an unpleasant odour in the immediate area indicated that it worked and that was all that mattered.

We returned to the dining room and I was led through another doorway opposite of where I had walked in with Rakeen. This led into another corridor and I could see a row of doorways along the right side reminding me of the temple wing where I completed my retreat, though it was minus the wooden doors to close the spaces off.

I was taken to the third opening and the priest gestured inside.

"This will be your private space during your internship. Use it for sleep and meditation," then he chuckled, "or for whenever you need to get away from the rest of us. Believe me, within these caves that will be often!"

With that he left for his own space and I went into mine. There was a simple bed in one corner and in the other a low desk which I assumed would be for writing or studying. I went and lay upon the bed, surprised at how comfortable it was. Sleep came within minutes but it was not quite the rest I had hoped for.

My dreams came fast and thick throughout the night. The scenes changed but one element remained constant throughout; the crystals. It began with me digging in mines and finding coloured threads of these rocks within the soil. Then I was in a laboratory studying them.

The scene would shift again and I was sitting in a circle telling young children about them. Then the most disturbing scene of all came to me.

I saw myself in a great room much like the classroom here in the caves. Its walls were lined with shelving and I could see them filled with boxes just like those that held the crystals here. There were five other people with me; two men and three women, and they were pulling down the boxes.

"We cannot take them with their boxes!" one of the men yelled. "Take them out, stuff what you can in your clothing. The less it looks like we are carrying anything then the safer they will be!"

Ten more people rushed into the room and began to help grab the crystals, then another ten. Within minutes the room was a mess of open boxes strewn across the shelves, tables and the floor. Some of the people were now crying and others wore faces of pure anger.

Then the sounds of drums made their way to us. It was like the pounding of a heart and we all froze.

"They are here," said the man once again but this time he did not yell. The words were spoken with a soft resignation. "Make way to the exit behind the altar as quietly but as quickly as you can. We should still have time to get to the caves. If anyone falls behind do not stop for them. Keep moving for the sake of what we know to be true."

With that we all began to run. I felt myself being swept along and even though I did not know where we were going it all felt familiar. We passed great rooms decorated with such beauty that I could only imagine the wealth held here. As we ran the drums sounded louder and louder within the building and then we heard the crashing of walls falling down. This made us run even faster.

Then we were in the final room. I saw the altar and the first to arrive were already disappearing behind it. When I got there I saw a huge hole and those just before me were jumping into it so I followed.

I landed hard on the dirt floor below and scrambled up as I felt others land right behind me.

"Keep moving! Keep moving!" I heard the male leader yelling now as we found our feet once more.

If anyone was hurt they did not show it as they kept running into the dark corridor before us. A glow ahead was all that showed us the way. Behind me now the drums were louder than ever and I heard the undeniable sound of a person screaming, then another.

"Drop the rocks!" screamed a voice behind me.

Just as I heard this I was pushed forward into those that had been ahead of me. Several others shoved themselves onto me and I realised the running had stopped and we were all still.

I turned and saw four of the men were holding ropes that hung from the ceiling. They all pulled at them and within seconds a huge wall of immense rocks fell, blocking the tunnel. Dust flew around us while the sound of coughing and the rocks settling wiped out the sound of the drums for a moment—then we heard them again, but this time they slowed and then stopped.

We stood where we were and looked about us. The male leader held up his hand to tell us to remain silent. When a few minutes passed he looked around at the group and began to count us.

"Two. We lost two," he said. "Lets keep moving."

We walked on covered in dust and the only sounds now were the scraping of feet, the odd cough and some quiet sobs.

Soon the tunnel opened again and we stepped into an enormous natural cave lined with the hugest crystals I had ever seen. They seemed to respond to us because at first what seemed a slight glow from them amplified as more people walked into the space.

"I suggest you all find your own area and do some breathing. Settle your bodies and minds, and readjust your feeling space," the same male said to us all. "When we are rested I will ask for volunteers to walk the caves and see if any others have made their way below ground."

This was where my dream ended. I sat up in my bed breathing heavily and for a moment wondered where I was. Of course I remembered in seconds but I had no window with moonlight or breaking dawn to let me know what time it was. The flicker of some lamplight from out in the corridor was the only light I could see.

Then the outline of one of the priests appeared in the door.

"Oh good, you're awake. I truly thought we would have to rouse you. It is time for the dawn ritual so make your way above ground when you are ready," he said.

As I got up I heard the murmurs of the priests talking and walked to the bathing room to find two of them urinating together into the hole. I decided to wait until they were finished and leant against the wall in the corridor, closing my eyes to get a few more seconds of sleep.

"I see you had a busy night."

I barely needed to open my eyes to know it was Rakeen. I could even see his eyes before I lifted my eyelids and nodded as I did so.

"We will talk about your dreams in class," he said and walked away.

CHAPTER ELEVEN

It was wonderful to go above ground and somewhat of a relief to know they did this each day. The morning ritual was as much from necessity as it was of tradition. No matter how cool the air below was, it did not circulate and this would become an issue to any human no matter their level of ability to self heal. It served to not only give us some fresh air, but the two hours that the hatch remained opened created a current within the caves that in a sense flushed out the stale air. All thanks to the waste hole and wherever it led to!

Coming out to the dawn also gave us some much needed natural light. It allowed us to sit and receive it gradually, with our eyes adjusting easily and not with the shock of stepping out of lamplight into the glare of the Egyptian sun. We would sit upon the stairs and look out over the hills to the east where it would rise, enjoying the swirls of colours in the sky. I loved also to watch the shadows of the hills grow and change as daylight came.

On the first day as we all took our places upon the top step of the side facing east I suddenly looked around me at the priests all sitting casually. Some leaned back upon their hands with their legs stretched out, others sat forward holding their knees. I saw some let out a yawn while others would talk quietly to the one beside them. I smiled at how relaxed it all was.

"You do not say prayers?" I said to Rakeen on that first morning.

He laughed so much he almost fell on his side and then he yelled this out to the others who also broke out in laughter.

"By the time you leave here you will answer that yourself," he said as he wiped his eyes and regained his composure. He then pointed to the sky, "Now let us enjoy the show the sun will give us today."

When we went down below that morning the change in the air was palpable. It was still cool but the scents of the priests and even the food was no longer there. The best way to explain it to you was that the air felt cleaned and this seemed to set the energy for the day; like everything had been refreshed and ready for a new start. The beauty of the sunrise entertained and recharged us all.

Rakeen took me back to the classroom while the others went off to do their own private studies. There were rooms beyond the sleeping quarters where I was told records were kept but I would not see these and I did not feel the need to ask that I should. Somehow I knew that what I would be shown here, as was customary for a visiting student, would be enough for what I needed in my journey.

When we sat down Rakeen folded his arms and leant back in his chair.

"So what do you think you were shown in your dreams?" he asked.

"I believe I was shown the history of the crystals," I answered beaming, quite proud that I found something meaningful in what I was shown.

"Is that all?" he asked now.

I stopped, unable to say anything more because I could not pick out what else was of importance from what I had seen. Rakeen looked me deep in the eyes and I knew he was speaking with me but I could not make the words form. I took a deep breath and then I knew what he was hoping I would have discovered.

"I saw my part in this?" I said and screwed up my brow for though I had some perception of past lives I still didn't understand them completely.

"I see this is something for you to work on," he said and smiled.

"So I gather you will not be explaining this to me?" I asked rhetorically.

Rakeen gave his trademark chuckle. "Ahhh, no I won't. We have other things to do right now," he answered and got up from his chair to collect some of the boxes from the shelves.

The morning of day two of my crystal studies were very much like the first. I would be shown a crystal and then told of its qualities. We would play (for want of a better word) with it for a while before moving on to the next. If its qualities were not upon the wall then Rakeen would go to a huge book to show me what was written there.

It was the first book I had ever seen. Until now all records were held in scrolls but this was flattened pieces of papyrus, bound along one edge. It was quite fascinating but fragile.

We continued on until our midday meal and when we were finished eating I stood up as Rakeen did, expecting to head back to the classroom with him, but he shook his head.

"No, I won't be joining you," he said and saw that I looked around at the others wondering who would be my teacher now. "No-one will replace me either. You will go back to the room alone and teach yourself for the remainder of the day. Revisit crystals I have shown you or find some new ones. Read about them or just hold them. It is your choice. There is no wrong or right way to do it. You will find clean papyrus and inks to encourage you to make notes but even this is not important. Just explore."

He finished and walked off towards the private rooms. I reached down and started to help clear the table.

"Go and study," said one of the priests taking the plate from my hand.

And so I did.

As I walked towards the room I couldn't help but smile at the freedom I was being offered to study these precious specimens on my own. I felt privileged and honoured to be allowed this after only one day. However as I stepped through the door and looked at the wall of boxes this all slipped away. Instead I was overwhelmed at what little I knew of them and the fear I would not utilise my time profitably.

I walked to the shelves and gently brushed one box with my finger. A small charge vibrated up my finger into my hand and I saw the hairs on my forearm stand up. This made me chuckle much like Rakeen would and when I realised this I laughed even more. Taking that box from the shelf with my hands buzzing from its vibrations I went to the table to begin.

That day I decided to only look at boxes that Rakeen had not shown me yet. It seemed more fortuitous to discover new ones then review ones that I already knew; especially given the ability I had to store information within me. I am not sure if this was a talent that was with me from birth or one that I had developed but it served me and I appreciated it more than you can imagine. So as I opened a new box I would scan the walls and then the books for information regarding that crystal's quality.

I used this method of study until Rakeen appeared in the doorway. He nodded and smiled, "Have you had fun?"

"Yes," I said.

"Good. Come and eat," he answered then turned and walked away.

That simple conversation marked the end of my studies for that day. I had imagined I would be quizzed over dinner but I was not. In fact the meal was silent but for the noises of eating and the occasional request for something that could not be reached. I had thought to ask questions but the downward looks of all the priests including Rakeen made it clear this was not the time.

We silently cleared and washed afterwards then we all retired to our private rooms. It was obvious that I was expected to know the routine by now and fall into line with what was happening. Once in my bed though I could not sleep. I stared above me watching the eternal flicker of lamplight throwing its lines on the stone hoping it would in some way lull me to sleep but it did not.

Sitting up I looked at my desk and saw that some writing materials had been placed there. I had hardly noticed them as I came in; such is the way of living in half shadow combined with having a mind full from a day's study. I had nothing to write though and lay down once more but sleep would not come.

It was then I decided to go to the classroom. I had not been told I could not go there during the night. In fact there had been no rules given to me at all about the room or its contents. I grabbed one of the lamps in my room and stepped into the corridor, looking each way. The only indication of anyone else being nearby was the mix of snores echoing through the dormitory.

There was no-one within the dining area either and no-one within the vestibule. The air now was rank at this time of night, saved only by the extra dip in temperature that night brought.

Once in the classroom I lit the lamps there from my own and topped up their oil setting them all upon the table to give me the best light possible. Then I made way to the shelves and began.

I am not sure how much time passed before I fell asleep at the table but I woke suddenly and grabbed at my ear. The pain I felt there was stinging and hot. I looked up and Rakeen was standing over me holding one of the lamps. I realised he had held it right against my ear, burning me to wake me up.

"This is why we do not study at night," he said plainly and there was not a hint of a smile or intended humour. "Imagine if you had knocked the lamp onto the book as you slept? And I would like you to tell me what the last thing you learnt was?"

I was sitting up straight now and looked before me. There was a crystal there but I had no memory of even taking its box from the shelf. The book was open but I had no recollection of anything upon the pages that the book was open to. I sat dumbfounded and just shook my head; as much to answer Rakeen as with disgust at myself.

"As I imagined. You cannot take in this knowledge during this phase of your daily biology. Your body needs to rest so that your thoughts will integrate with your feeling state. Now I know this will go against much of what you have been taught elsewhere but I am sure you have realised that this is not your usual school. Now come, let us go back to our beds," he finished and gestured for me to rise and leave.

As we walked back to our rooms something struck me.

"How did you know I was in there?" I said to Rakeen's back.

He stopped and turned around. "Because we are not just teachers and priests. We are the custodians of the crystals. It is our job to not only protect their wisdom but to protect their existence. That vow sets up a powerful link within our senses. If I was in the deepest sleep and a mouse entered that room I would know it."

Rakeen was serious as he spoke but more than anything I felt his pride. He turned and kept walking. I then heard the softest laugh from him and in a voice barely above a whisper he turned to me again. "Once there was a mouse in there and you should have seen the panic." He waved his hands around as though to show me the confusion. "Once we found it and settled down we realised the gift it had been. We knew then to be calm even when we feared the worse … oh and that we needed to fine tune our senses. An inconsequential rodent does not wake me these days though a full-grown Greek does!" He dissolved into another quiet laugh as we walked on.

The next morning we all sat upon the portico and watched the sunrise in silence. It was one of the most beautiful moments I ever experienced and I thought how lucky these men were to have created such a life for themselves. I wondered if they might consider me to remain here as a teacher and custodian. What a truly noble life that would be. Then as though I had spoken the words out loud Rakeen turned to me.

"I hope your enjoyment of your time here does not affect your passion to continue on when you are complete," he said and within those words I knew that staying was not an option.

I merely shook my head to answer and he said "Good" as he looked back to the sky.

Rakeen took me to the classroom when we returned below ground. We both sat down and he leaned back in his chair, took a deep breath and smiled.

"So tell me what you learnt yesterday," he said.

So I did, with as much detail as possible, as he nodded.

"Which crystals do you feel you want to explore more?" he asked when I finished.

I stopped for a moment and looked at the boxes upon the shelves. To choose those that I felt an affinity with didn't quite match what I thought my studies would entail. At this stage I was simply hungry to learn as much about as many of them as possible. Having had this asked of me though I did stop to consider what Rakeen wanted to know.

"Don't think about it too much," he said as he watched me. "Just feel into the ones that you were the most comfortable with."

Then I knew immediately.

"It would be the ones such as the Amunite that seems to open up my communications," I said confidently.

"Mmph...." Rakeen nodded. "Then for the remainder of the day you will explore those crystals."

With that he stood to leave.

"Ahh, Teacher! Is that all the instruction you will give me today?" I asked somewhat confused.

"Well, yes," he said grinning. "I know you are thinking I am not much of teacher after all but you will thank me and understand soon enough." And then he was gone.

I grabbed the five boxes holding the crystals that I had spoken of and then sat with them before me. The Amunite was the first one that I took from the box. I took the deepest breath I could before lifting it off its cushion and was hit with a wave of dizziness. I dropped it back down on its holder.

"*Well, what was that?*" I thought.

I decided not to worry so much and moved on to the next. Before I did though I sat still and breathed to settle my head and my thoughts. When I reached into the next box I knew why the Amunite had stopped me. I now held in my hand a smooth flattened oval of pale purple.

I had liked this crystal the moment I had opened its box yesterday. This in itself had amused me; that I would have some superficial emotional response to an object. When I had held it then I had felt warmth which seemed to belie its appearance. Today when I held it that warmth seemed to pulse and my palm tingled beneath it. It was like my connection with it was growing. If I did not know myself better I would even have said that the crystal had chosen me.

I looked down on it and for a moment I felt I knew why Rakeen smiled so much. To play with these treasures each day and have these experiences must be a constant source of delight. I was sure that in whatever amount of years he had been with them that they still surprised him regularly. The heavens knew you would need something like that to keep you from insanity in these caves.

The pulsing of the crystal stopped and the warmth now dissipated. I quickly put the crystal down fearing I had somehow drained it of its charge or power, especially as my hand was still warm.

I quickly turned to the wall where its drawing and list of qualities were painted hoping I would find some explanation. I scanned down—warmth, heat, transduction, and so on. To me none of what I read made sense of what had just happened. In the meantime the warmth in my palm was spreading up my arm.

I forced myself to breathe hoping this would give me some insight and calm the spread of the heat. This just made the warmth spread even quicker and now my heart began to race. Jumping from my chair I ran to find Rakeen.

Rakeen was sitting in his private room, calmly reading over a scroll. I had yelled out to him the whole way but as I stood in the doorway, holding my left arm with my right hand as though I was injured, he barely looked up.

"Ah I see you started with the Perondite," he said not even looking up. "A great choice! In fact the wisest you could have made." Now he looked up. "It has given you an infusion. I suggest you go to your room and lie down for a while as it integrates."

He turned back to his scroll but I just stood there.

"What is it my Greek?" he said not looking up.

"I have no idea what you mean by an infusion," I said becoming frustrated.

"Yes I know. How wonderful that you don't. This can all be a big surprise and isn't that a fun way to learn," he chuckled.

"No! It is not!" I shouted back.

Rakeen took a deep breath, rolled up his scroll, stood up and walked towards me.

"Pythagoras," he started and put a hand on my left shoulder. "All will be clear when the infusion is complete. Go and rest. You just need to trust me—and yourself—for the time being."

Then with his hand still on my shoulder he turned me and pushed me out of his room.

His final words did comfort me but I still did not enjoy not knowing what it was that I was supposedly going through. This was something that would remain an issue with me my whole life. I needed to know *everything!* And I needed to know it *now!*

Thankfully I learnt to balance this (precariously) with some patience. It was this patience I now tapped into as I lay down to complete this mystical infusion.

I thought I would just lie there awake but I was asleep within minutes. I did not even need to do some breathing to settle and the spin of my thoughts did not delay this either. The sleep was incredibly deep. So deep in fact that if I did dream at all they were so buried that I had no recollection of them as I opened my eyes.

When I did awaken I listened for any telltale signs of what time it might be. The echoes of snoring and the dankness of the air told me that it was well into the night. I was not so surprised at this and if it had not been for my stomach and bladder I imagined I would have made it through to the dawn.

I visited the toilet first and then made way to the dining room. There upon the table was a plate of food that had been left for me and I sat down to devour it. It was then I noticed that beside the plate was a note.

"You have slept well. We checked on you hourly and the infusion is deep within you now. Return to your bed when you have filled your stomach. Do not even think about going to the classroom."

I laughed at the last part. They all knew me by now as this was indeed my intention. However as the food settled into my stomach, my eyes became heavy again. It was as though I almost did not make it to my bed that sleep was upon me so fast once again.

When I woke this time I had the faces of all six priests looking down upon me.

"How do you feel?" Rakeen asked and scanned my body as he waited for an answer.

Having only just woken I wasn't so sure but I took a breath and knew.

"I am feeling fine," I answered.

"Good. Let us all make way to the dawn," he said and began to walk.

As the visiting student I was usually the last in the procession to climb above ground but today one of the younger priests hung to the back and waved his hand before him indicating that I should walk ahead. Puzzled by this I simply nodded and did so but as we walked I had the distinct impression that he was watching every slightest move or gesture I made.

When we climbed out of the hatch there was also a change to the usual routine. The priests would normally have made their way outside but today they all stopped and watched as I climbed from the hole and remained in place until the last priest was with us.

"Pythagoras, today you will lead the way outside," Rakeen said and nodded.

"What?" I said, truly not sure if I had heard correctly.

"Lead the way," he said once more and waved his hand just as the priest below had.

This time though the gesture sparked something and I jumped back a little.

"What is it Pythagoras?" he asked and his eyes grew wide. I looked at the other priests and they too were watching me intently. I knew this was a test of some kind and as usual this got my back up.

I looked from one face to the next hoping to gather some clue as to what was going on but could feel nothing. Even going into my breath gained nothing for me. I nodded.

"As you wish," I replied, bowed my head and walked towards the huge double doors at the front of the temple.

I slid across the wooden bar that was its lock and grabbed at the handle of the left door swinging it open. The first pale wash of the dawn crept in as I now also swung the right door open. I turned and looked back at the priests. They were all still in their same places but now facing me. No-one said a word, so I continued on and walked outside to the east portico to get ready for the sun.

As I took my place upon the top stair the others followed closely behind and seemed to glide into their places. There was no small talk this morning and no smiles, not even from Rakeen. Even though I was with this group who I thought I knew, I felt completely alone.

I looked down at my left hand, the hand that had held the crystal, looking for some change from what had happened yesterday but it looked the same. I could not feel the warmth anymore, not even when I really dived into my senses.

The first pinks of the dawn were now above us. I loved how each morning it was different. Some days the pinks would have streaks of orange or great holes that let the blue through. Today it was as though someone had taken a great paintbrush and wiped from left to right creating a soft continuous wash of pink.

It glowed and the more I stared into it the stronger the glow seemed. I waited for it to change but it didn't. The pink just hung there without a noticeable change to it as though time had stopped. If there is one part of the day that lets you know that time is moving it is the dawn, but today she was breaking her rules.

I looked about at the other priests. Usually a significant pattern or burst of colour elicited some sort of discussion but today they were silent and still. Eerily still in fact. So much so that for a moment I truly believed that time had stopped.

"*That is ridiculous,*" I thought and within a second of that thought I felt a breeze upon my face and saw it move the sleeve of one of the priests. I looked back to the sky and the pink had finally shifted, allowing in the usual oranges and yellows as the sun came closer to the horizon.

Now I was convinced that time seemed to be moving I decided that everything was just moving slower. The dawn seemed to be taking longer than usual with the sun making a gradual and graceful entry rather than with the burst of energy that it usually did.

I looked about at the other men and they remained as still as before. Part of me wanted to scream something, anything, to break the spell we all seemed under but I knew this would serve no purpose. Taking a deep breath I looked back to the sky and soaked up her colour show. It was then I felt it.

I cannot tell you what it was that I felt because that would make it seem simple. This sensation was far from simple. I realised the change that had occurred in my sleep. The outside had not changed at all. All that had changed was within me. I realised this was the beauty of my teachers silence. They simply wanted me to discover this for myself. I closed my eyes to shut off the outside entirely and breathed.

In this space now I felt even more than I had in my retreat and fast. This was something beyond seeing visions, hearing the thoughts of another or to even feel the vibration of a crystal.

I could hear myself.

I could hear myself in a way I had never before and it felt wonderful.

Now all that was left to know was how to use this newly discovered part of myself.

We all sat silently for some time more even after the sun had risen clear of the horizon. Rakeen, usually the first to stand and make a comment that would get the rest of us moving remained in place. I looked to him but he kept his stare ahead of him and so did the others. Then I realised that if I had led them outside then it was I who would lead them back inside.

I stood and stretched my shoulders as I wondered what I should say. Then I smiled and said the words with no planning or thought.

"What another beautiful start to the day. Let us return to our studies," I said just as I imagined Rakeen would with a gentle laugh.

The other priests including Rakeen looked at me, nodded and smiled. Then they too all stood up and followed me back into the temple.

Rakeen was the one behind me as we climbed back down the ladder into the vestibule. I nodded my head to him and walked towards the corridor that led to the classroom. From behind me he called out, "I will join you shortly."

I knew he needed to speak to the others before we continued and I kept my pace but when I thought I was within the shadows of the passage I stopped, hoping to hear what would be said. It was a simple conversation and though it did not reveal too much to me I was still glad that I heard it.

When the last priest had stepped off the ladder I heard Rakeen talking in his serious mode.

"I am sure you all agree that the infusion was successful but I need to hear it from you all before I tell him the truth of the mysteries," he said and I raised my eyebrows.

I heard the muffled "yes" spoken by each priest in turn as their answer.

"Good. Then I will be with him for the remainder of the day. Perhaps you would be so kind to bring the midday meal to us but we shall join you in the evening before we rest."

With that I knew not to listen anymore and walked quickly to the classroom so he would find me seated at the table as though I had begun without him. I should have known better than to try to fool Rakeen.

"Nice act my Greek! We all saw your shadow upon the floor and I can hear your heartbeat from here. Do not try to make any sort of profession from deception," he said and burst into laughter. "Now you can put the book away as what I have to share with you is in no book and never will be."

What my teacher shared with me next was something I had sensed but had not been able to put into words. I will be very honest and say that I am even hesitant to share this with you now as it is such a deep truth that unless one is ready to hear it with such intense honesty with themselves then it will sound like a fanciful and elaborate story. But then if you have found your way to my story and read on to this part then there must be something within you that already knows this or is ready to hear it.

Rakeen looked down before he began and I knew this was his way to call in all the wisdom he had gathered so that he would share with me as purely as he possibly could. When he looked up I could see his eyes had a sparkle that made them appear even more bright than usual. Then he shot me that smile and began.

"The crystal you chose to hold that began this was your start to true awakening. Within it was the vibration to open up the knowledge that you hold and that has been with you since the dawn of existence. The ones that came before us in Egypt knew this and it was those that came before them that charged the original crystals to seed other crystals that would carry the infusion for whoever should find it."

A thousand questions flew through my mind but I did not dare to interrupt Rakeen as this lesson and information flowed from him.

"When the time of change came to the civilisation who first charged the crystals they knew this knowledge may be lost. Well, I should say that they knew it would never be truly lost but that man would forget. It would be buried within new directions of experience and this was not a good thing. So they gathered crystal seeds and they pushed—well pushed is not the right word but it is the best one to give you … they pushed certain knowledge within the crystal seeds and then planted them in caves and other places within the earth where they would be found when the people were ready for them.

Some crystals were kept in places like this, others remained hidden for millennia. The elders who began this knew the earth would hold and protect them until the men who could do this would find them.

The ones we have here are part of the very original library that was created. So you could say they are even more special but they aren't. The powers and knowledge within each crystal does not dilute or fade as they reproduce and grow. In fact some say it even expands.

As you can imagine there have been those who would want to destroy such libraries or to gather all the crystals so that the knowledge and power was theirs only. I know you dreamt of this one night, did you not?"

I nodded and Rakeen nodded back.

"You also saw what was done to make sure this did not happen. This school is part of that original cave network where those priests hid and these crystals are the very ones you saw carried by them. So you see why they are so protected. But I have digressed and it was the Perondite that we needed to speak of first!"

He went to the wall and took this crystal's box from the shelves and put it on the table before me.

"It called you. I know it did because it calls everyone—eventually. That is why we leave you to study alone. You need to find it in your own time and yes, most find it by the time that you did, and very few take more than a week. Although there was this one lad who took a month…." Rakeen shook his head. "We were almost tempted to just tell him—almost!"

He chuckled and opened the box, lifting the crystal out and placing it in my left hand. I expected the same warmth again but I did not feel it in my hand. This time I felt it within my belly.

"You can feel the warmth within you now can't you? Good! Perondite is what we call the master key for more than one reason. Once you have let this key turn in you then all the others will be able to work within you in a whole new way."

Rakeen could see my mind racing and I was finding it harder by the moment to hold back my questions.

"Patience my Greek! We are getting there," he laughed. "This urge of yours to know everything immediately is your blessing and curse. Now where were we…? Ah, the Perondite; this crystal was chosen to hold the core information. This core information allows all other knowledge to flow. Now before I actually tell you I would like for you to now speak. See your time comes when it is due. Now you tell me what you felt this morning as we watched the dawn," he finished and finally took a seat opposite me, placing his hands upon the table and leaning forward, eager to hear me.

I looked down at the Perondite and thought back to this morning, not even sure how I could put it into words.

"It was so strange. You all acted differently and then it was as though time stopped. Nothing seemed the same and yet to look around it was the same. Then I realised nothing had changed. It was just me. It was like that place inside of me that I feel when I breathe had expanded. No, no—that is not right either. It was like I could hear it in a new way—and yet that somehow doesn't seem to express it either. I feel the only way I can describe it is that somehow I know myself even more intimately," I stopped but I knew even that was inadequate in letting Rakeen know what I felt.

He leant back in his chair and that smile grew wider as he nodded, "Yes, it is hard to put into words isn't it. That is why it is hard to teach and hard to explain and that is why the crystals do their work so well. It is purely felt from them and your connection with them is as unique as the person you are. No two students ever learn here the same way. It has been one of the most difficult things for my mind to get around but once it did I saw the true beauty of this.

We have digressed once more haven't we? That is also the way of this teaching but fortunately, I usually remember to bring us back to our focus.

Now this part of you that you have touched, well firstly, once it has been awoken and remembered then the connection stays open."

I nodded with relief as he continued.

"It is the part of us that all men know but push to the depths of themselves. It is the part of us that we are taught every day does not deserve to exist. For some of us it bubbles to the surface and we allow it be there. From the stories you have told of your childhood we know that you actually had this part of you nurtured but you have never really allowed it to fully be expressed."

When he said this last part I had flashes to all those times that I felt that "thing" and pushed it away. Was this what he was talking of?

"Yes, that is exactly what I am speaking of," Rakeen said and nodded, even though I had not said a word. "It is the part of you that defies all laws of nature. It is the part of you that has no limits or boundaries. Yesterday you gave this part of you permission to now come forward and be part of your experience without the past fears that suppressed it."

Rakeen paused for a moment and he watched me, knowing my mind was racing. "Your next question to me will be—so how does this serve me? Is that right?"

I nodded for that was indeed true.

"Well it does not serve you. Nor do you serve it. Now this defies all that is believed to be true. For you this is especially so as you are a man gathering knowledge and skills to serve your quest for wisdom. This will indeed support your quest but it will not give you the intense enlightenment that you imagine it will.

Because Pythagoras, all that you need to know is within you already. The quest is in remembering it!"

With that he relaxed in his chair as though he was done. I looked at him for a moment wondering if he was going to start again but realised he wasn't going to. This made me angry.

"Is that it? Is that all you are going to share about the Perondite?" I asked and I am afraid rather tersely.

"Well yes, for now," he answered. "You really have issue with letting something sink in and integrate. You are always on the move in here." He tapped at his forehead. "That is fine but with this sort of teaching you need to slow that down. We will move ahead shortly. For now I would like to do some breathing with you as you hold the Perondite."

I nodded reluctantly and pulled my left hand with the Perondite towards me and rested it upon the palm of my right hand. Closing my eyes I went into the rhythm I knew so well. I felt that place within me that I was now connected with more intimately than ever before. My mind wanted to scan my body for sensations but the words of Rakeen echoed in my ears and I dived into my breath so that these urges were silenced.

Ah, that delicious space that I now knew was just me, all me, only me. Nothing from outside, no words of teachers, no expectations or rules. Just this pure energy within me. Then I heard something. It was a voice I knew but could not recognise. It called out to me softly, full of love and nurturing.

I heard the words; "*YOU ARE GOD*"

I wanted to laugh and cry out, "Who? Me?" but just as quickly as I thought this it was gone and I felt the energy of the words again.

"*YOU ARE GOD*"

I could have stayed with those words in that moment forever.

Across from me I heard Rakeen take in a deep breath and he said barely above a whisper, "Now it is time to continue."

I opened my eyes and nodded. Now I understood what I had opened up. Now I knew the connection I had needed. I looked down at the crystal in my hand and wanted to kiss it for helping me awaken to this truth.

But I knew it was not the crystal's doing. It was because I had been ready to hear it.

That moment when you know you are a creator is life changing. You are no longer a puppet of circumstance. You are no longer a victim of fate. It is you and you alone who creates your experience.

I would sit often and contemplate this. Where I once thanked my father for creating my path I now knew that he was a support I had called in to help me shape my life. My brothers were evidence of this. We were all given the same opportunities but our choices and aspirations had created far different experiences.

When I reopened this knowledge within me all else shifted about me as well. I no longer saw these schools as bastions of wisdom that I had to penetrate to be made privy to that which I did not know yet. Now they were merely opportunities to awaken some more. To stand before any man, whether he be a beggar or a high priest, and know that within the depths of that person was the same wisdom made me look at everyone in a new way.

Yes, there were times that I would have loved to yell this at someone but then I would remember the beauty of having found this out for myself. It was then I would smile and nod, murmur a "yes" to whatever they were postulating or pontificating. Sometimes it was just fun to watch someone wallow in their pre-awakening state. Especially so when I finally had my own school because then when they had awakened I could show them through their own words just how much they had expanded. Mind you not one of my teachers ever did this to me.

Certainly Rakeen never would and that day with him in the classroom showing me how much I had shifted was the whole point of this day.

"Let us now revisit some of the first crystals," he said and took the Amunite from the shelf.

He said nothing more as he placed it in my hands and sat back to breathe. I closed my eyes too and pulled in a deep breath. What happened next astounded me.

I felt a swirl of voices and my mind tried to filter them, to sort them so I could hear who they were. I left my mind to this and breathed some more. Then one by one each voice seemed to step forward and make itself known.

I heard the voice that I had used when I yelled at the elders of the first school. I heard the voice I used when I spoke to Eunomus as we walked the cliff tops of Samos. I heard my voice speak Phoenician with my father's family in Tyre. Each one was a part of me that had been and that I thought was gone.

It was amusing at first but then it became overwhelming. I felt myself say to them that their time was done. I didn't need them anymore. One stepped forward and spoke very clearly, "You are never done with us. We are still you."

I opened my eyes and Rakeen was watching me intently.

"I take it you heard something quite different this time," he said plainly.

I shook my head, "I don't understand."

"No you don't yet and this is one of the hardest things to know about yourself. So many parts of the one; past, present and future. All you need to know is that they are all you," he said and came to take the crystal from my hand.

I curled my fingers over it and pulled it close to me. "We aren't done with this yet," I said but he grabbed my hand and opened it.

"For today we are," he replied as he slipped the crystal from my hand. He kept his eyes upon mine as he placed the Amunite back in its box. "That has really shaken you hasn't it?"

I nodded my head in response.

"Well unfurl your brow and let it go. We have other things to move on to for now," he laughed.

I felt my face relax as he walked back to me with another of the crystals we had already studied with. He smirked at me as he placed it in my hand.

"Let's see what this agitates in you," he said and raised an eyebrow.

For this was what the whole day was like. Each crystal we reviewed was an irritant, showing me something new and yet something I could not understand—the one constant being that of Rakeen smiling and refusing to explain anything more to me.

Our lunch was brought to us as previously arranged. Even though my stomach growled loud enough to echo in the stone room, Rakeen left our meal to sit for an hour before he stopped and let me eat.

"We needed to get through a certain amount before our rest," he said and I didn't even bother to ask why as I knew it would just be met with a laugh and a tease from him.

My stomach once filled with food seemed to dull my irritation for a while. However when it reached the late afternoon I was once again hungry, even more irritable and now tired. Even the way Rakeen opened a crystal box increased my frustration with him.

"Here," he placed the Pyhirric quartz in my hand. "Breathe and tell me what you feel."

It had been the same with each crystal so that by this stage I felt like I was responding like a trained animal. I breathed but all I could feel was my need to eat and lie down.

"Focus!" Rakeen for the first time actually raised his voice and this did nothing to bring me back to the task.

Instead I went into my thoughts on how stupid this whole day had been and why did I choose this man to teach me.

"Focus!"

Rakeen now yelled at me and indeed I did now focus. I stood from my chair and flung the crystal across the room.

"There's your damned focus!" I yelled at him and stormed from the room.

"We are not done yet!" he yelled at my back.

I turned sharply. "Well if I am God then I can make my own choice and I am choosing this day to be over!" I swung back around and made my way into the corridor expecting to be followed or at least have something else yelled at me but there was nothing.

As I walked into the dining room area one of the other priests set a full plate down at an empty chair. He nodded to the dish letting me know it was mine. It appeared our shouting had made its way through the underground and he was expecting me.

I sat down roughly and began to eat, not looking at anyone else as we all ate in silence. Rakeen came in soon after and took a seat as far away from me as he could. A plate was set before him and I heard him murmur his thanks. There was no talk amongst the men, not that I could have heard much over my heart pounding in my chest and the throbbing in my temples. I had not felt such intense anger since being refused at that first school.

I quickly finished my meal and took my plate to wash it. I was blocked from the sink by a priest who offered me a slight but uncomfortable smile.

"Let me do that for you," he said gently and took the plate from me.

In no mood to argue I passed the plate over and made way to my room. Thankfully sleep came quickly but it was far from restful as a flood of dreams came in. Each one was more bizarre and twisted than the other.

Nothing within them made sense. I saw places I did not know, faces that were not familiar and scenarios that were truly unfeasible. They all had one thing in common; I walked through them as though I was only watching. At no point in time did I interact with anything or anyone. It was like I was invisible and floating through every scene.

I woke suddenly and sat up in my bed. The air about me was cool and fresh. There was even a slight draught and this I knew meant that I was missing the dawn ritual.

My clothes were flung on me as quickly as I could and I walked quickly to the ladder to climb up but as I reached it I saw the first pair of feet making their way down.

"Why did you not wake me?" I said to the feet not even waiting for the face of their owner to appear.

"Because Rakeen said not to," came the reply as he continued to descend. His face now below the opening he looked at me as he came down the final rungs. "You really take a while to understand things don't you?"

"Hush, Abbass!"

It was Rakeen. He had been waiting to climb down the ladder when he had heard me and the reply I was given. I stepped towards the ladder and looked up.

"Why did you hush him? Why can't someone else share with me?" I shouted up at him.

Another priest began his descent back into the caves and Rakeen crouched down and shouted back his response over him as he came down the ladder.

"Because, my son, you have a hard enough time taking in what I am sharing with you, let alone adding anyone else's insights," he said.

"I am not your son. I am here as your equal!" I said back indignantly.

This set off a round of guffaws from all the priests and my face turned red. Rakeen began to make his way down the ladder now. He stayed silent until he stepped off the last rung.

"Really? You are my equal? Well then, let us make way to the classroom and today you shall be the teacher!" he spat at me.

I stopped for a moment as something inside me twisted and my face turned an even deeper shade of red. I looked down and then back at Rakeen and took a deep breath.

"I am sorry. I forgot my place. Forgive me my disrespect," I said softly.

The other priests had all but left the vestibule at this time but the two that remained stopped in their places, looked at each other and then to Rakeen. Rakeen looked to them also then back to me. His face was entirely serious and I saw his shoulders raise and then lower with his breath before he spoke.

"I accept your apology," he said and then smiled. "But I am disappointed that you gave in so quickly. Let us go to the classroom and discuss this more."

He gestured to the corridor leading to the classroom and as I began to walk away I saw one of the other priests, his eyes wide as though shocked, open his mouth to ask Rakeen something. I did not see what Rakeen did but I am sure he held his hand up to silence the priest and then followed me.

I took my usual place at the table and then Rakeen sat before me and scratched his head.

"Pythagoras, I have studied with three hundred priests and taught over six hundred students. Each man has his own ways but none has challenged me the way you do," he began. "I have had that confrontation with many men but none—NONE—have quashed their temper as quickly or been as humble as you were then. In fact that is usually when I get hit!"

Once again his laugh filled the room and I too smiled. The heaviness now somewhat lifted, he went on. "I knew your sleep last night would be rich with other lessons. That is why we left you. In fact you were talking in your sleep as we passed your door. Now perhaps you would like to share with me what you showed to yourself last night," he finished and leant back in his chair, folding his arms around himself.

I described my dream as accurately as I could. Even the things I could not understand or the images that were of things I had never seen. Rakeen nodded patiently as I spoke but as I said one sentence his eyes lit up and he smiled.

I said to him, "It was as though I was floating through it all, just watching, never being a part of it."

Through his smile he asked me to go on. "Go into this more," he coaxed.

"I could see everything but there was a distance between me and what was happening, as though it was merely a performance staged to entertain me," I continued.

"Can you influence a performance you have paid to attend?" he asked.

"No," I answered immediately.

Rakeen nodded. "So how do you get to shape what occurs before you?"

This stopped me. I knew Rakeen was trying to show me something but I was not sure where he was going. I looked down.

"Stop thinking so much and feel what it was like to be just the observer," he said.

This I did and I remembered feeling that I did not know what would happen next and the frustration this brought up.

"Now feel what it would be like to go there again and be directing all that is going on."

This I did and the sense of purpose and control was wonderful.

"Now do you see how your dream has shown you something of yourself?" he asked.

I looked up and smiled, "Yes, it is showing me I need more control!" I answered emphatically.

Rakeen took a deep breath and as he let it out he laughed. "You are always one step to the left," he said as he chuckled and gently shook his head. "No Pythagoras, you were showing yourself the difference between living your life as an observer and living your life as a participant."

Now this to me still related to control and so I did not quite understand this straight away and Rakeen knew it.

"Participation is different than control. One is about being present, the other is about force. Not that force is always inappropriate—but this too can separate you from being present. For now let us just say that you need to be more of a participant in your life," he finished and stood up, making his way to the wall of boxes.

"No!" I stood up quickly sending my chair flying backwards. "I am sick of these beginnings and no endings with you. You give me these insights with no completion and then carry on as though you have said nothing. I have begun a hundred lessons with you and finished none."

Rakeen turned to me and I could see he wanted to smile but he didn't. "It is you that does not complete the lesson. Not me!" He lifted his chin and for a moment I wondered if he was offering it to me to be punched. "I cannot give you any more than I have while you continue to live your life as an observer. The completion you seek will come when you become the participant."

He walked back from the wall and pushed his chair under the table.

"Our lessons for today are complete," he said and I noted the irony in his selection of words. "Straighten your chair and then how you spend the day is your choice."

With that he left the room and soon after so did I.

I was only a few paces behind Rakeen and so I dropped back a bit to avoid catching up with him. I watched as he walked and saw that he had his usual swagger and even if he knew I was immediately behind him he acted as though he did not sense me. He continued on through the dining area and into the hallway of the dormitory. I stopped at the entrance to my room at the same time that he walked into his own.

"Pah! He is probably thankful for a day off!" I grunted under my breath and went into my room. I walked to my bed and considered a pleasant day of sleep to escape the nebulous situation with my studies but I knew instantly it would probably only add to it.

Instead I sat at my desk and drummed my fingers upon its surface. The prospect of writing pulled at me but I had barely unfurled some parchment to write upon when I knew that beginning that would be futile.

I looked out to the corridor and the flickering lights thrown by the lamps which lined it. It is hard to say whether I had the idea before I stood or if it struck me as I stepped into the passage. Usually I would have instantly turned left, back towards the bathing room, dining area and then further to the vestibule. Today though my neck turned my head to the right and then my body followed.

The first step felt really weird but then I made another and another. I walked past another doorway to a room and glanced quickly inside. There sat a priest reading diligently. He paid no attention to me whether he sensed my presence or not. I continued on.

Another door and another was passed. I no longer cared if I was noticed or not, even when I passed Rakeen's doorway. I simply kept walking and soon was at the last of the lit lamps upon the wall.

I had often imagined at this point I would be met with a solid wall; the implication that more would lie beyond the light being yet another tease to frustrate me—but as I stepped past the lamp I knew this was not so. Reaching back I took the lamp from the wall and held it before me. Each step I took now showed me there was more space before me and so I kept walking.

The hallway continued on for quite some time. The rhythm of doorways to my right also repeated for a substantial distance and then I only had solid wall on either side of me. Finally I had walked far enough from the dormitory that the light was no more. There was dark behind me and darkness before me. The circle of light around me from my lamp was the sum of my surroundings.

Paying no heed to the amount of oil I had left in the lamp I kept going. "*Surely there would be other lamps soon,*" I thought and just as this crossed my mind I felt the space around me open up. Finally I had reached the end of the corridor and into another space much like the vestibule at the entrance of the underground school. I walked around the edge of the space, lifting my lamp to scan the walls which were completely blank. There was no sign of glyphs or pictures but I was not looking for these. Instead I kept scanning for what I needed and there it was—the first of a line of lamps and as expected they were full of oil.

I lit the first one and swapped it for my near empty one, leaving it lit as well for some extra, albeit temporary light. Walking towards the centre of the room I then slowly turned around and saw what I knew would be there. Two of the walls showed huge black rectangles; doorways to the next part of the underground!

Having no idea what might lie ahead I simply chose to walk through the left one first. I felt for another lamp upon the wall and soon found it, lighting it more as a marker for my return, and walked on. This hallway was drawn upon and I noted it was almost identical to the passage that led to my classroom so it was no surprise that I was soon within an identical classroom. It was so similar in fact that for a moment I believed I had managed a full circle of some sort and simply landed back where I had started.

Everything was the same. Even the arrangement of the crystal boxes upon the shelves. I opened one and saw it held a precious stone. This was another complete library, probably a spare. My mind raced as to why it was sitting here in the dark and why it was not being used to teach. I looked around a little more and decided to leave. If they could sense me in the other library then they would probably sense me here too. Today I would rather explore without interruptions.

Back in the vestibule I made way to the second door way and lit its first lamp. This doorway too replicated the passage to the dining area and I was completely prepared to find another room like it with a corridor and dormitory leading from it and then another repetition of rooms. This is not what I found at all.

The space opened up again but the minute I stepped into it I felt it was different. The smell of wood and oils hung in the air. I knew that combination of smells well. The oils were to preserve wood. My grandfather had shown me this as a child as he built and repaired boats. It was a smell that you could not forget. Upon this was another layer and that smell I knew too. It was the decay of wood that was inevitable no matter how well you protected it. This I had smelt as a child too, of boats that were at the end of their lifespan, beyond repair and ready to retire.

I wiped my hand upon the wall looking for a lamp but instead felt shelving. I swung the lamp towards the wall and saw the shelves clearly now. At first I would have imagined that this was simply more sets of crystal libraries. The boxes looked similar but as I moved the lamp closer I could see they weren't. They seemed smaller and my nose had been correct; they were all in various states of decay. I daren't touch any lest even the gentlest touch would prove the box's final challenge to hold its form.

Some of the boxes had been reinforced with metal straps around them and within this cage the wood was starting to buckle and collapse. Through some gaps I could see the silk lining and this too, now exposed, was becoming thin. I could hardly begin to imagine how old they were to be so decrepit despite the attempts to preserve them.

Walking along the shelves it seemed they went on forever then finally I reached a corner and yet another wall lined with the same shelving filled with more of these miniature chests. I lifted my lamp upwards to see just how high the shelves might go and all I could see was that it was way above my head. The single lamp could not reveal the roof and I imagined that it was much higher than the other rooms I had been in.

Now as I made my way along the shelves looking at one box falling apart after another I saw something other than their size which made them differ from the teaching library. Each box had a small plaque attached to its front. It was made of metal and upon it was engraved a word. Some words I did not recognise as they were written in different languages and scripts, but every now and then there was one I could read and they all had something in common—they were a person's name.

They were written in Greek, Aramaic, and any other script that was used in the ancient world. I suspect there were also many in languages that were yet to be, as well as those that were long lost. This amused and intrigued me to no end and I continued on reading out of pure curiosity as to whose names were upon them. I half expected to see Thales name or even the teachers from the schools I had been to but none showed themselves.

I was almost to the end of the fourth wall, about to reach the doorway to make my way out when I saw that one group of boxes' plaques were all in Greek. I slowed down and saw names that would remain in history forever though I did not know them at the time. Then there it was at the very end. Almost like I was meant to see it last of all. It was sitting apart from the others as though it was making sure it would not be missed.

It was the box with my name upon the plaque.

It was engraved in perfect Greek of the time and not in the Egyptian derivative that I would have imagined. Its wood was as decayed as any of the others and one of the pieces was even crumbling. I reached out to it but pulled my hand back immediately.

What if it wasn't mine but another Pythagoras? I knew instantly that this could not be true. Then I wondered what would happen if I touched it without permission?

"*It's mine!*" was all I could hear.

I picked it up as gently as I could; cradling it into my left arm as though it was a newborn. Then after one last look around I made my way back into the vestibule and back to the dormitory. I kept my left arm in a soft curve and even walked slower but despite my extreme care I felt parts of the small box crumble so that as I made my way into the final corridor of the dormitory I was nursing a bundle of disintegrating wood rather than a box.

I saw the line of lamps that I had left to begin this little adventure and within the glow I saw the outline of Rakeen. His silhouette showed me no signs of his demeanour so I braced myself for whatever he would say. As I stepped into the light and saw his face he simply sighed, looked down into my arm and said, "Did it have your name upon it?"

"Yes," I replied plainly.

"Then make your way to the classroom," he said as he stepped to one side.

I had just made my way past him when a priest came towards me walking quite quickly. In his hand by his side was a jug that I knew was for lamp oil. He brushed past me shaking his head.

Rakeen now burst out laughing. "Oh leave him be! How was he to know that he should take oil with him to refill the lamps!"

I too now laughed as I pulled my little treasure towards me and walked on.

I leaned over the table in the classroom and tried to place the box as gently as I could upon the table. This was the last movement the box could endure and as it was set down it completely fell apart. I started to sort its pieces, pulling the rotted wood from within the metal bands and placing it to one side. I lifted the plaque with my name upon it.

"Who knew to write this?" I thought as Rakeen came in.

"You wrote it," he said and came to stand beside me. "And you took your time in getting back to it."

Once again I knew not to bother asking for an explanation. In an instant I felt it related to the dream in which I saw myself with others rescuing the crystals to bring underground.

I traced over the engraving with my finger as Rakeen started to sort through the remains of the box as well. He pulled away the rest of the wood and the metal until there was just the soft pile of silk.

"That is yours to open," he said and stood back.

I saw that the silk was gathered in one place and there was a fine thread holding it together. It did not take much to break this as the thread was as aged as the wood. As it crumbled in my fingers the silk fell open. There sitting inside it was a crystal unlike any I had seen.

At first I thought it was green, then it seemed to show shades of blue. There were opaque patches of white in it as well. It was barely the size of a plum yet I could see all this in it.

I was about to ask if I could pick it up but then lifted it up without saying a word. It felt warm and that was all I could feel. This disappointed me immensely. I figured that it was so old that it must have lost its original charge or value but remembered it was no older than any other crystal that I had studied with.

"It is not the same as the others," Rakeen said softly beside me. "All you need to know is that it is yours and you found it once again. Keep it with you and when the time is right you will know to leave it somewhere to be found again if you choose."

It seems this was all I had left to achieve at the underground school. The other boxes were there waiting for their owners to find them also. Rakeen told me many men came and left without even venturing to the area which held them. The boxes though would wait for another lifetime to be found.

I asked why they did not replace the boxes as time took its toll upon them and the answer was quite simple.

"You all made those boxes, chose the crystal and placed it in the box. You even engraved your own name. No other man has the authority to alter any part of your creation as it would alter the energy that connects you to it. It would be like birthing a child but having someone else raise it—the connection would be lost," he explained.

So the boxes sat and continued to decay as they waited for their owners. I wondered how many crystals were found sitting in a pile of dust with a name plate sitting askew beside it. Indeed many would take this long to find them and some still sit there until this day.

The school was abandoned around 500AD. Well not so much abandoned as simply forgotten altogether. Fewer men were eligible to stay as custodians and even those that may have been suitable became distracted by the new religious wars occurring above ground. When the last priest began to fill the entry vestibule with sand he knew he was doing more than closing the school down. As he poured the final bucket, bringing the sand level with the opening and then sliding the cover back in place, he knew he was also helping end the era of true mystery schools.

He did not cry or even question it. As he walked away from the temple he never even glanced back once. There was no point in looking back. What had been there had served its time and consciousness. It must now move on in new ways. He lifted his face up towards the sun and smiled.

"It will be nice to spend more time with you," he said and walked on.

My final day at the school began almost as usual. I woke with the men and walked to climb the ladder to watch the sunrise. Only today I carried with me my satchel and canteen.

I sat in silence and smiled as the sun rose. When the other priests stood to go about their daily routines I bid them a simple farewell. Some bid me well and some simply smiled as they walked away. Rakeen stood in place until they all left and then came to me, taking my shoulders in his hands.

"Travel well and remember much," he said and then walked towards the entrance of the temple.

"Thank you," I called out to him.

He stopped and held up his hand as though to stop me speaking anymore.

"Never thank a teacher. Just live what they have shared with you," he said with one last chuckle as he disappeared inside.

I swung my satchel over my shoulder and walked down the stairs. The sun felt so hot even this early in the day but it was wonderful.

I had only walked about a mile when I realised I had no idea where to go. Stopping in my tracks I looked about me. After being in the caves I had lost my bearings entirely. Then I realised I had all I needed to direct me. I looked up at the sun as it made its way west and I remembered the Nile.

"Thank you," I shouted out to it and walked west. The river would be my guide—that is once I found it again. At the very least it would give me water and this would be enough for my body for now.

I wandered a bit more, my head down watching my feet which seemed to have forgotten what it was like to walk upon stones and uneven ground. My skin too had forgotten what it was like to be in the sun and I felt it begin to burn. I decided to use my shawl as a shade and was pulling it out of my satchel when I heard a voice call out to me.

Looking up I saw in the distance another man and he was running towards me, waving his hands as though I might miss him.

"*Oh Rakeen, you will have fun with this one!*" I thought and tried not to laugh as he finally arrived before me panting and doubling over to hold onto his knees to catch his breath.

Finally he was composed. "I am looking for a sch—I mean a temple. It is meant to be nearby. Have you seen anything?" he gasped.

"Keep walking east. It is there. You just cannot see it until you are right upon it," I said.

He raised an eyebrow, suddenly deciding not to trust me even though he had been the one to ask me. I knew what would assure him. I reached into my satchel and showed him the amulet.

"You have been there? What did they teach you?" he asked.

"Much," was all I would offer him. "Go now so your day will be full and don't hesitate to show your amulet. You have wasted enough time with me already."

With that I covered myself with my shawl and began to walk away.

I did eventually look back to see him standing in the same place looking awkwardly from one point on the horizon to another. I am sure he finally chose a direction—whether he made it to Rakeen's school though I will never know.

CHAPTER TWELVE

I spent another twenty years in Egypt as a student. I wandered from one mystery school and temple to the next. It became such a vocation that I actually gained a reputation as did all men who made a personal commitment to these studies. I went through schools which were known as well as those that were hidden and reserved for the elite.

These secret schools would send me invitations and they would invariably be the same. I would be sitting within a taverna or resting between classes at a school when I would be approached.

"You are Pythagoras of Samos," they would say and it was never a question.

I would nod and they would sit themselves next to me, scanning around with their eyes, checking for anyone lurking nearby. Then they would all pull out of their satchel or sleeve the same two items; a small scroll and an amulet. The amulet was always the same—a cartouche shape with those same three symbols. The scroll though would be a map with minimal markings upon it.

They would speak in a hushed voice while still looking around, giving me clues so that the map would make some sense if I chose to follow it. I would listen intently and nod when they finished.

Then more often than not I would dump the amulet and scroll somewhere along the road. I may have been hungry for knowledge but I soon could sense a false school the minute I was handed the amulet. There were many schools set up to satisfy the egos of the teachers after many of them had been expelled from the true schools. These other schools were created from anger and frustration and never taught the authentic mysteries. This I knew because if one had learnt of the mysteries then they would not set up a school. Instead these schools simply rehashed astronomy and geometry as though these alone were enough and to some they were and this was appropriate.

I had been in Egypt for ten years when I was made the worst invitation of them all. On my way to a new temple I decided to stop and sit under a tree to rest when the latest scout came to me. I had sensed him following me since the last village and part of my decision to stop was to allow him the chance to speak to me and then I could travel on without this shadow hanging behind me.

He walked towards me as though he too was just a casual traveller. Stopping to give the customary greeting I raised my hand and returned the greeting. He made as though to walk on then stopped and turned back.

"You are a long way from home," he said in perfect Greek.

I looked into his face a bit closer now and saw that he was not Egyptian at all.

"As I see you are too," I replied and it felt curious to be speaking Greek once again.

He walked back and gestured to the ground beside me, asking to be invited to sit a while. I nodded and he sat heavily, grunting as he adjusted his skirt and bent his knees beneath him. Then he pulled some bread from his bag and broke off a piece, offering it to me.

I took it not so much because I was hungry but to seem friendly which encouraged him to speak openly. I heard about where in Greece he was from, what his family was like and why he came to Egypt. So in turn I too conveyed my story, with much editing of course.

"Why do you stay within Egypt?" he asked.

"I am studying the ways of the temples here. The religion fascinates me," I answered and this was not entirely a lie.

The scout rubbed his chin and put his hand back into his bag, I knew immediately it was not for more bread and could have burst into fits of laughter immediately when I saw the scroll and then the amulet. He went into the usual spiel and I nodded along. I could not help but smile.

"You seem most amused by this. I take it this seems quite novel to you," he said slightly offended.

"No, not at all. In fact it is quite the opposite. I have been in Egypt ten years now and this process of invitation is neither new nor amusing," I said still smiling.

"Well, perhaps then I should withdraw the invitation and allow you on your way to whoever may choose you next," he spat and pulled the amulet and scroll back towards himself.

I sat and said nothing but bit my lip to stop from laughing outright. My irreverence though was not missed by the scout and his face turned red. He flung the tokens back into his bag and stood up. As he straightened his skirt he fired one last missive at me.

"You know not everyone thinks you are so clever! In fact the elders argued as to whether you were worthy of an invitation. I can now let them know that you indeed weren't!"

He walked back in the direction he had come and I allowed him some dignity in waiting until he was beyond hearing before truly collapsing in laughter.

You may wonder why I would feel the need to stay within a country for over two decades seemingly just studying the same information over and over. I will admit that by the time I had left that first underground school I had learnt everything that I needed but my thirst to know all that could be known drove me on to attend every genuine school and temple in Egypt. Given the distances between schools and that I stayed in some for up to a couple of years you can see how my time was well and truly filled.

I revered every teacher who gave me their time, even when I sensed that their teachings were off-kilter or redundant. Never dismiss anyone who shares knowledge with you when you have been the one to seek them out. It is all appropriate. If you have placed yourself in the experience then you have done so for your own gain—even if it seems to be negative at the time.

It was fifteen years into my travels within Egypt when this made itself truly known.

I had left many schools in the early years feeling incomplete. Even my beloved Rakeen, who had given me so much, still left a lot unanswered. I continued to breathe each day but it was more out of duty than a personal commitment to my expansion. Some schools did not promote the breath at all as they were solely about academic knowledge and even six months at a school like this broke my rhythm.

But it would call to me. I would be in a swirl of thoughts and I would feel that pull to slow my mind down and step into its purity.

I was in the garden of a school in the south, upon one of the islands near the place you now know as Philae. Sitting in the shade of a tree all was silent but for the lapping of the water nearby. It slapped against the shore as the Nile flowed and I was soon watching it intently.

There were little ripples as it made its way over the differing depths or was caught by a breeze. There were small waves that pushed against the rocks of the island. In and out, in and out. Nothing stopped them. I soon found my breath matched their rhythm and this drew me back into that place within that felt even sweeter having seemingly left it alone for a time.

"*Why do I forget you so easily?*" I asked of it.

I knew the answer immediately and forgot it within days. It kept coming back though, each time I allowed myself some quiet.

After five more years of this same routine of walking and finding a new school things suddenly changed. It did not seem to be my choice but it fulfilled what I knew in my heart I needed. Though I wished that I had taken my next step in a less dramatic fashion, sometimes we just need an event like this to make us let go.

Twenty-two years of shaving my head and wearing Egyptian kilts. Twenty-two years of priests with their temples and animal-headed Gods. Twenty-two years of hieroglyphs and sand that seemed to get within every space of me physically and emotionally.

I had studied with 746 teachers and priests. I had met 10,784 other students within the 427 schools and temples I resided in. Yet it took only two men and their egos to end it.

Cambyses now ruled a Persia that he inherited from his father Cyrus the Great. It seemed being the son of someone great was not enough for Cambyses and so he aimed for tremendous. Persia had claimed all of the Middle East for its own and as Cambyses rode his lands his pride swelled. He looked upon cultures and tribes that had existed for eons and were now his.

One day he rode to the southern edge of his domain and as the Egyptian border guards raised the flags that declared their hostility his eyes grew dark.

"Are you in the mood for a skirmish?" One of his generals asked. "We could just wound a few to make our presence known."

Cambyses drew in a breath as he looked down into Egypt and he shook his head.

"No, not today. When I strike Egypt it will be to take her in her entirety. There is no point in hunting to just bite at a heel when you can devour the whole animal," Cambyses replied calmly then turned his horse and led his men away.

The conquering of Egypt weighed upon Cambyses though. To capture this land and these people would leave no doubt as to his power. He had heard the stories of the Pharaohs who had claimed *his* lands and peoples for centuries at a time, diluting their culture and bloodlines. They were "clean" again of these southerners and now was the right time to return the insult that had washed over his lands and peoples.

Cambyses knew though that his army could not achieve this alone. Divided up throughout the Middle East to keep his newly occupied lands subjugated left him with just the bare essentials of an attacking legion. It was still formidable, no doubt about that, but Cambyses knew Egypt had resources that he could not predict or take for granted. He knew his only chance was to gain some sort of alliance with others of the region. So one day he called his household staff together and announced they would be travelling to Samos.

Polycrates still ruled Samos as tightly as he had when I left it. Twenty-two years had seen him reshape the mentality of the island so that it was as though it had never known any other way of being. What remained of my forefathers amazing ship building enterprise was now simply part of Polycrates' war machine as they now toiled to construct and maintain his fleet of one hundred boats. These ships ploughed through the Aegean and Mediterranean seas claiming all in its path.

Cambyses knew he needed the Greek state of Samos on his side. It was bad enough to have Egypt in her enormity as a foe, but to have another so close by as notorious and barbarous as Polycrates rightfully concerned the Persian. In his favour Cambyses knew he could tempt him with access to eastern trade routes, as well marriages to Persian princesses.

Against his favour was the fact that Polycrates already had a strong alliance with Pharaoh Psamtik, established through his father Pharaoh Amasis. Psamtik was new to the throne as was Cambyses and they both had something to prove. Cambyses knew that he had just that bit more to persuade Polycrates to join him and it was with great confidence that he set sail for Samos.

Cambyses fleet of five boats cut west across the sea with flags of peace billowing from the masts. Word had been sent that this was a visit of friendship but Cambyses needed to be sure that his intention was clear. Polycrates sent some of his generals, ministers and a phalanx of soldiers to greet them at the docks. The same docks that Mnesarchus had landed upon all those years ago and the very place he had asked for my mother's hand in marriage. Today it was a place of political bargaining.

The boats were tied while archers held their arrows tensed against their bows and aimed at the ships ready for any slip in the agreement of the purpose of the visit. The crews of all the ships were called above deck and then onto the docks, even Cambyses was escorted off his boat with arrows poised at him. He smiled and acted as though it was nothing. The indignity would be worth it if it helped him to rule over Egypt.

The swordsmen finished their search of the boats and declared that nothing was on board to infer that the King had come with the intention of provoking war. It was only then that generals yelled out in Greek to the archers and their arms finally rested back at their sides. The chief general walked towards Cambyses, placed his right hand upon his chest and bowed.

"Welcome to Samos," He said with a smirk as he stood straight.

"*Welcome indeed!*" thought Cambyses but outwards he smiled.

"It is my pleasure to land upon your shore. Now take me to Polycrates," he finished with no smile upon his face. He may be a visiting king but he was still a king nonetheless. While politeness may be needed they would not make him subservient.

When Cambyses was led into the great hall of the home of Polycrates he found him slouched upon the huge chair in which he received people. The Persian's blood began to boil.

"*First the indignity upon the dock and now he acts as though I am a gardener reporting on his crops*," he thought.

Polycrates knew he had Cambyses' fate within his hands but he also knew not to push his luck too far. He waved to someone nearby and a chair of equal size was dragged beside his. The Greek stood from his chair and gestured to the seat beside him.

"Please join me," he said both politely and with as much respect as he would ever muster.

Cambyses lifted his chin and smiled.

"*This is more like it!*" he thought as he grunted and went to take his seat.

Mad men make great bed fellows. They live within the same paradigms and this made the negotiations between the Greek and the Persian somewhat straightforward. To the common man though, the discussion would have seemed stranger than any fiction.

They outlined their current interests and hopes for the future as a farmer would assess his harvest and stores. They referred to their empires as a child would speak of his toys. Within every statement each man expressed his ego and power as though every word was a silent arrow embedding itself into the other man's land.

Though no actual weapon was wielded and no blood was spilt this was as decisive a battle as any that was waged upon any field. The thing about battles of the mind though is that no man truly knows who has won. Within politics, actions do truly speak louder than words and no two men knew this as well as Polycrates or Cambyses.

Even the handshake in agreement to end the meeting and the meal shared afterwards were laced with distrust and paranoia, with neither knowing the other's true thoughts. Much could happen within the days and weeks following even an informal pact between leaders. Only time would reveal how the alliance would play out, if it did at all.

Polycrates shook hands with Cambyses that day knowing that to undo a decades' old alliance with the huge power that was Egypt could be his demise. Even his stranglehold on the Aegean and much of the Mediterranean was no guarantee that he could survive on his own. He looked into Cambyses' eyes though and saw something that scared him.

He saw himself. He saw the hunger for power at any cost and he knew of the stories that walked with this man.

The Greek also knew the power of rumours and how a simple tale could evoke fear despite it having no foundation. He had used this tactic himself. It was a great weapon to have on your side. If the stories of the Persian were true and he did not join him then he would conquer Egypt with or without his alliance. Then Samos would be next.

If Polycrates did not maintain his alliance with Egypt and Pharaoh Psamtik slaughtered the Persian army then the Egyptians would march north and take all of Persia. This would make Egypt the formidable presence it had been under the great Pharaoh Thutmose. Polycrates potentials for trade would be quashed and Samos would then become a target of the Egyptians.

Polycrates did not sleep that night and farewelled Cambyses the next day with dark circles under his eyes. The Persian's eyes were not so different upon his waking.

They shook hands once more and kissed upon the left cheek, but neither set of lips was warm and each man felt this. The Persian boats left with no arrows aimed at them but instead heaped with fresh fruits, meats and wines for the journey home.

As the boats finally left their sights a general turned to Polycrates.

"For which direction do you say we set sail?" he asked.

"I do not know," was all Polycrates could answer.

It was another week of sleepless nights for Polycrates as he pondered the question over and over. The wrong decision could destroy all that he had established in almost twenty-five years and part of him cursed Cambyses for dragging him into his power play. This though was something he had to face to ensure his own survival and even as he sent his ships from the docks part of him still was plagued in doubt.

"It is times like this I actually wished I believed in the gods," he muttered out loud to himself. A nearby priest, called to bless the ships and pray for the men, heard him and shuddered.

A godless man is one that lives by his own rules. He can create them as he goes along in life without fear of any recourse for his actions, bar the consequences of his own mistakes. He knows that only he is to blame and as such this makes for even more weight upon his decisions.

Polycrates loved when other rulers blamed their failures upon the gods.

"Live by stories, die by stories!" was one of his favourite sayings and he watched so many men abide by this every day.

He laughed when he heard accounts of his army being met by a line of priests or that people would hide in a temple as though it was impenetrable. Polycrates tried so hard not to show his amusement as Cambyses had spoken of his conquests as driven by divine will. The Greek had looked hard into the Persian eyes when they met and all he had seen was bull-headed determination. No god can give you that. It was something you were born with and had nurtured by those around you. That was the life of a prince.

Polycrates was no prince but he was born with the determination of one. This he knew gave him the boldness to conquer as he did, with no ties either to an empire established through bloodline nor any concern as to an heir. It was all *about* him and *for* him and no-one else.

As he listened to Cambyses he saw the Persian's lust for control as motivated by his family ties and he knew this was a weakness. It would only be a matter of time before he was undone, but for now he might go along so that it would be him that brought down the Persian. Play with your enemies as though you are friends and you learn their ways in a manner no spy could garner for you. It would be worth the years it might take.

In Egypt the young Pharaoh Psamtik was in his court surrounded by generals, viziers and priests all talking at once. He sat in his throne dumbstruck as the discussion dissolved into a drone around him. Unable to even focus on one thread of the conversation he closed his eyes and clenched his jaw.

"They would never have done this to Father! Never! Why can't I control them?"

He opened his eyes wide and screamed out loud, "Silence!" and the only sound remaining was the residual echo of the voices bouncing off the stone walls.

Psamtik looked around in disgust at the men assembled before him. It had barely been five months since his father's death and he could not believe that the stable court of his father had fell into such disarray. He also knew there was only one person to blame for it—himself.

Inheriting a powerful empire was enough of a burden but having to manage these men with their separate agendas was like nothing he had been prepared for.

"The men of the court know their places and their duties well. Do not make such huge waves to begin with that you throw them out of balance. Feel into your role," was the advice his father had given him as he lay upon his deathbed.

So Psamtik made no waves. He barely sent out a ripple believing that a strong hand so soon would cause him disfavour. Unfortunately this led the men to feel that they could and should make their own decisions. There were murmurs that the new Pharaoh was too young and could not lead so each faction of the court simply began to act in their own interest with the full belief that they were doing so for the good of Egypt.

When news of Persia's expansion reached the Pharaoh and he called the meeting his father's strong and cohesive court was no more. The rabble that assembled let him know that if any attack was made then he would surely lose and this stabbed into his heart worse than the death of his father.

"No man will take what is decreed to me by the gods!" he shouted to his men but his voice faltered and they sensed it. Several even looked down to hide their smirks and within that moment every man standing in that room knew that Egypt was already defeated.

Not that any one of them dared to say the words out loud. Instead they all enacted their duties to the best of their abilities and with seeming positivity that they would in fact survive this threat. The armies planned their strategies, the priests carried out rituals and the viziers oversaw the gathering of supplies. All carried on as it would have at any other time that Egypt prepared for war.

Psamtik readied to lead his men from his capital of Sais to the eastern part of the Nile delta and a city called Pelusium. This was the closest port to the Persians and where they were expected to begin their assault when they chose to. Cambyses though knew that to cater to expectations was not the way of the successful warrior. So the Persians made their way south and then west by foot; his legion of Arabic chieftain subjugates providing his army with all the water and food they needed along the way.

As the Egyptians prepared and the Persians began to travel they both wondered where the alliance of Polycrates would land because both men already encumbered with their own self-doubt, also knew that the madman's promise wasn't good until proven.

Psamtik had sent word to Samos for Polycrates to send aid immediately and each day they waited at the harbour for the Greek boats to approach but their sails were never seen. Instead word arrived that Polycrates' ships had landed just north of the Egyptian border upon Arabic land.

Even Polycrates himself played his own self-doubt to the last stroke. His men, themselves fearing they would be slaughtered by Cambyses upon their arrival, landed at a place which might still allow them the option to retreat safely and even possibly defect back to their Egyptian alliance. This was not necessary and they soon walked side by side with the Persians.

When Psamtik heard of the betrayal his face turned red with anger.

"Get rid of any Greeks upon my soil. They are no longer welcome here!" he snarled.

This order was enacted immediately for any Greeks within Egypt could well commence their own uprising or join with the Persians as they entered the country. For some Greeks this meant their death. A door suddenly burst open would be followed by a sword to the neck before they could even realise what was happening. The closer you were to a city the greater chance that this would be your fate as you were more likely to be a trader, or retired soldier or some sort of ambassador upon the Pharaoh's land and therefore a larger threat. Those that lived simple lives were given a more humane option; to climb aboard a cart and be dumped across the border.

Of course you did not have to accept this alternative and then you too would be killed unceremoniously. But only a fool chooses death over what was in fact simply an opportunity to change your life.

So it was that as I sat within the grounds of my current school just south of where Thebes lay I was approached by five soldiers. They were young and I could tell inexperienced which was why they were not with the more senior legions preparing for battle.

"You are Pythagoras of Samos," one said to me and I knew, once again, this was not a question as quickly as I knew this was not going to lead to an invitation to another school.

Instead it was simply the signal that my time in Egypt was over and my next chapter would begin.

I was walked to a cart that was built so that it looked like a cage on wheels. The sight of it almost made me laugh as any man who truly did not want to be held captive in it could break out with ease, such was its hasty and incompetent structure. I climbed into it without any struggle or protest and saw the soldiers look to one another as I took my seat. One of them flung my bag at me and I caught it roughly, lowering it to my side.

"You do not even make fight!" the soldier snarled at me. "Egypt will be made richer for having you no longer here."

This was quite ironic given my banishment was based upon the idea that I may contribute to the Persian-Greek attack. I merely shrugged my shoulders as I looked up.

"Why make difficult that which must happen," I said and could tell that this made no sense to men who belonged to a country preparing for war.

I rested back upon the wooden bars as the horses began to pull the cart. Two soldiers sat upon the cart to drive it while the remaining three rode surrounding me. I tried not to look at them too closely as I knew they would use any excuse to beat me but as the cart bumped along and I tired of the landscape I could not help but start to take in the details of their uniforms and the markings upon the leather of their saddles.

One of them caught me staring and rode close to the cart, hitting at the bars I rested upon with the short sword he carried. It did not hurt but I reflexively jumped away from the side of the cart and turned to see what had caused this. The soldiers burst out laughing.

"Hah! So you can move when you need to," one shouted and they all laughed some more.

I decided that I had been enough fun for them for today and so I lay down in the middle of the cart, clear of any of the bars.

"Do not think you will sleep Greek!" the same soldier shouted again. "This ride is not for you to rest."

I refrained from sharing with him the dozen phrases that flew across my mind, instead pulling my tongue tight within my mouth and keeping my lips together. There were many ways to rest and few involved closing your eyes. So as I fixed my gaze upon the changing pattern of the sky with her clouds above me I decided this was a good time to breathe.

In this way a good three to four hours passed. I heard the occasional smart comment from the soldiers as well as their discussion about the impending war which eventually lapsed into casual conversation. Then the talk returned to me.

"He hasn't moved in hours," one of them said softly. "Do you think he has died?"

"No. His chest is still moving," came a reply.

"Yes, but only barely. Perhaps he is about to die," the first said again.

"I am not dead or dying," I called out plainly afraid that I would soon be prodded at like a fish to test if it survived being pulled from the water.

This bought me another hour of rest upon the cart's floor but then all the horses came to a stop. I stayed still for a moment but was too curious as to why we would have finally halted so I sat up.

We were upon the outskirts of a town that I could barely recognise but then it had been eighteen years since I had been here. I knew we were getting close to the northern areas just west of the Red Sea and that within another day we would be at the border of Egypt. I also knew that close by was a school frequented by Greeks. I slid into a corner to make ready for some others to join me.

A soldier opened the door at the back of the cart and stood to the side.

"Come and relieve yourself," he commanded and though I did not feel any urge to do so I stepped down from the cart to at least move and stretch my legs.

The soldier followed me behind some bushes but had the decency to look away as I lifted my skirt. His sword though was drawn and held ready.

"I am done," I said as I finished and lowered my skirt.

"Then get back to the cart," he said and gestured with his sword.

As we walked back to the cart I saw the other soldiers frogmarching a man towards us. His head was down and people stood along the way watching him.

"Go home Greek!" one villager yelled but everyone else stayed silent.

The four soldiers lifted him and threw him into the cart where he fell on his side, unable to lift himself easily due to his hands being tied behind him. I felt a push to my right shoulder.

"You get in too," was snarled behind me and I climbed awkwardly into the cart trying not to step upon my new travel companion.

The door was slammed behind us and locked as crudely as before.

"You can untie your friend if you please," mocked a soldier as he climbed aboard the front of the cart and flicked the reigns to get moving.

I knelt behind the other man and tried to undo the ropes. As I did I heard him whimper and looked to see his face begin to streak with tears.

"Stay strong," I whispered in Greek. "This will be over soon and we can go home."

"I cannot go home!" he replied loudly in Egyptian, drawing the attention of the soldiers and making them laugh.

I continued on working the knots in the ropes when I realised that a knife would be most helpful. My own knife had been taken on my capture and to ask for one from the soldiers would just set off another round of laughter so I struggled on. It took me an hour but eventually the ropes slipped through each other and became loose enough so that my companion could pull his hands out of them.

He pulled himself up and slid to the side of the cart leaning against the bars as he rubbed his wrists and looked around.

"Tied up like an animal!" he shouted out as he looked at the soldiers. "And why? To appease some man who cannot rule his country properly while there are men working to a greater purpose—and yet we—we are the ones who get punished."

He was rambling and we all knew it, even the rambler himself. The rest of us remained silent and allowed him the display that the soldiers had actually expected from me. When he too fell silent the trip became almost pleasant. The sun began to sink and with it the temperature softened.

As it fell dark the soldiers began to talk of where we would stop for the night.

"We are far from the next village and there is not enough of a moon to light our way to reach it safely in the dark," the leader said. "We can make camp here."

It was agreed upon and the men alighted from the horses and tied them to some bushes. They stretched, yawned and made jokes about their genitals being tender from the hours spent upon their horses. It was as though they forgot about us for a while as they gathered twigs to make a fire and unrolled their swags to make beds upon the dusty soil. I turned to my fellow Greek who had not looked up since finishing his tirade.

"I am Pythagoras. What is your name?" I said in Egyptian deciding not to test anyone's irritability at this time of the day.

"I know who you are," he sneered and slowly lifted his head.

I looked once more upon his face and the memory of our meeting ten years ago by the roadside came back to me.

"So my clever friend, you refused my invitation but it looks like we ended up no different in the end," he snarled even more and any pity or empathy I had for him was gone in a flash.

"Only one of us was dragged in shame to this cart needing to

257

be untied," I replied. "So I would not consider us to come to the same ending at all."

His spit hit me so quickly that I hardly saw him lift his chin to project it.

That was the last conversation we would ever have.

When the cart finally trundled over the border I was not sure who was the most relieved of us all; the soldiers to have finished their menial job or the Greek to finally be away from me despite the addition of three more prisoners to break up the tension of being alone with me. As we all climbed from the cart with swords pointed at us the lead soldier yelled out his final command.

"Head whichever way you choose but do not even think to cross back into Egypt. If you do you will not receive the clemency that has been shown. You will be killed with no questions asked."

It was simple and with no need of further explanation. We had been taken to a point on the eastern border, far from the impending approach of the Persians. There was a small temple nearby but I could see that it had been long abandoned, yet another symptom of the decline of the current dynasty. I stretched my arms over my head before putting my bag over my shoulder.

The other men began to walk north along the road with postures of defeat. Not allowed to shave or bathe since our capture we now all looked decidedly Greek once more regardless of our still wearing Egyptian skirts. I pulled my cloth wrap from my bag and draped it over me as any Persian would.

It was time to let all of Egypt go.

From the way my other countrymen walked I could see they were not going to release this experience too easily. They walked like men in a funeral cortege as though the path they were taking now was of a duty that they had not chosen or wanted, but was inevitable.

I began to walk behind them, keeping my pace slow so that I could avoid catching up to them and having to hear any negative talk that I imagined would be bound to happen now. We all soon came upon a branch in the road with a secondary road forming that turned even further east. The men tramped onwards north without even stopping to contemplate the possibilities that may lie down this route.

This was enough of an indicator to me that this would indeed be a wonderful option for right now, not least as it would help to make the distance between me and my adversary greater. I turned to the right and began my journey deep into Babylonia.

CHAPTER THIRTEEN

Babylonia had changed somewhat since my last visit well over twenty years ago. There was a new openness between what would be deemed religion and the mysteries. In Egypt there was still a divide between what was publicly celebrated as religion and the source of its teachings. There was still the sense that the common man could not understand the depths of the mysteries or live them as they were intended.

In Babylonia this spiritual snobbery was greatly dissolving and any separation that had been here was coming to an end. Its priests did not hide within schools, nor did they refuse anyone who came to them to learn.

"All the universe is here for every man" was the motto of these men and this was the theme of my next ten years with the Zoroastrian Magi of Babylonia.

I still had my first amulet and the ancient crystal with me, ready to pull them out should this somehow be of use but they never would be again. My name and reputation had made their way with me from Egypt and unbelievably were also remembered from my time in Babylonia before I headed south.

There were no great schools here anymore. These were now seen as relics of the past where men retreated in the pursuit of knowledge. For the magi now did not see any benefit in hiding away in religious cloisters, withdrawing themselves from the everyday machinations of society and culture. This was just a form of separation and to know yourself as well as know the universe and all it held you could not be apart from anything.

Certainly there were still places that men could travel to and lodge as they studied with the elders but they were not closed off nor were they hidden. Zoroastrianism was now something spoken of as openly as Egyptian religion and it had temples for the people to reflect within. While some chose to live it more deeply as the magi did in the hope they could reach others, most people were living part of its teachings in some shape or form.

The multiple gods that still played such an important role within the lives of the Greeks, Egyptians and some of the Middle Eastern clans were losing their hold within this land. The simplicity and clarity this

261

gave to the people was beyond measure. The more I walked this land and the more I spoke with the dozens of magi here, the clearer I felt my mind become. Once again I came to know my breath in ways I could not imagine.

The date of Zarathustra's life is still being debated. When I was in Babylonia I was told he lived "not so long ago" by every magus I asked.

"Does it matter when he lived? Or does it matter that he did and gave us his teachings?" one of them added and I had to nod. No teacher so far had been able to tell me the age of the source of their knowledge and it hadn't been important to me.

I will tell you that it was around 1000BC that he sat atop a mountain looking down upon the plains of Babylonia as it was then. Life for him up to that point had been a journey of frustration and chaos.

"There must be a way out of the turmoil that lies within the mind of a man," he said to himself continually. Years of travelling through mystery schools and temples had done nothing to answer this clearly. Like myself, he had seen glimpses of it only to have it buried within more teachings or his own thoughts.

He walked about his village when he returned home and as he looked upon daily life he saw it as futile.

"Work hard to eat so you can work harder and create children to repeat the pattern. Break from that pattern and you are condemned and vilified," he muttered as he watched the people.

So Zarathustra decided to walk. No agenda, no plan. Just to walk.

He walked for ten days with barely a sip of water and eventually came to the mountain that he would climb. Zarathustra climbed for four hours and when he reached the summit he was neither thirsty nor tired. There was nothing within his mind as he looked out upon the land he had walked. He sat for some time watching the occasional wind whip up some dust or the clouds cast a shadow.

Zarathustra sat so still that he could soon feel the pulse of his blood within his body and then even stronger was the flow of his breath. He surrendered to this sensation and was given the answer he had sought.

As he breathed in he felt everything within; the intricacy of his body, every emotion he had stored, all the feelings that shaped who he was and then washing over all this was calm. It was the peace he knew was there but buried underneath the chaos that he believed life to be.

Zarathustra breathed out. As the breath made its way out of him he imagined he could see it merge with the air around him. He saw it flow out to blend with the dust and seep into the rocks.

"This is my connection with all that is," he said to himself and from somewhere within this network of all that existed he heard the word that let him know all he had felt was true.

"Yes"

Zarathustra nodded. He knew the voice was not his own. He knew it was the voice of the one energy that was the source of every particle that was him and everything around him.

"Show me. Teach me. I am ready," he said out loud.

With that Zarathustra and the energy he would call Ahura Mazdā began their own school.

When Zarathustra made his way down the mountain ten days later there was a basket of fruit and a full canteen of water sitting beside a rock. He looked around to see if there was someone nearby but there was no-one. He knew that Ahura Mazdā had gifted this to him and he ate with great thanks. Then Zarathustra walked once more to share all that he had learned.

Out of chaos comes calm. Within turmoil there is stability. Each element has it reflection, its opposite and its balance. It is the joy of each person to choose which they will follow.

This was the simplicity of what Zarathustra shared and it was the ability he had to demonstrate this that people responded too.

"You can dive into argument with your fellow man, revelling in hostility and destruction. Or you can respect his ways and express yours. In the middle is understanding and peace. Which will you choose? How do you wish to live your life?" he would say.

The duality of everyday existence was no longer a trial or penance to be endured, Zarathustra told everyone. It was simply to help man see the path towards clarity.

"Breathe in and know yourself. Breathe out and know the universe," he said. "Do this often enough and you will see that they are the same."

When he told people that they only needed one god or creator to form their beliefs he was met with a mixture of relief and scepticism. Some were happy to now have some focus while some feared the consequences of rejecting the familiar.

"I have yet to meet ill will for my beliefs as does anyone who practises what I share," he would say. "Yet look to the kings of the lands west and south of us. Do they not continue on with their discord and destructive ways?"

It all made sense and each day as Zarathustra showed himself more of the truth of what Ahura Mazdā had shown him on top of the mountain, the more people came to him to learn. They carried the words away with as much commitment as he held for them and so the new religion grew.

When men came to him to be apostles and study his ways he was always honoured and touched. When they wanted to stay on and asked why he did not create a monastery as other religions did, he would shake his head.

"Because to create a monastery I would be asking you to separate from life. These beliefs are not about separating. They are for you to feel the connection between all that you are, all that you have been and all that you will be. Hiding in a monastery does not serve this. Nor does it serve you to miss all the joys and beauty that the universe offers to you. Enjoy food, enjoy the sensual pleasures of a spouse, enjoy fine clothing and comforts. These are all part of life for a reason—to show you the grandeur and joy of living!"

To save people the rigours of pilgrimage Zarathustra then walked to meet more people. There was never a night when he did not have a roof over his head or a wonderful meal within his stomach. The legend of his gift of fruit and water became known so that people often left these upon the roadside hoping the prophet would find them and in return they would receive a blessing from Ahura Mazdā himself. Zarathustra was always grateful and amused to find these gifts and would smile. Inside though he would wonder why they did not just eat and drink of it themselves.

Men walked with him for some days as companions and to hear him speak, while women gathered to hear him at every stop on his journey.

"Do not think you come to hear my words because I am someone so special. Know that you come to hear these words because your heart knows their truth and calls you to live them!" he would say with all the humility he could muster.

For all the greatness and majesty that Zarathustra knew he had within him, he also knew he was the same as any man or woman who stood before him. What made him different was not that he had dared to ask the questions but that he had been willing to listen to the answer. Now as he sat with people before him, he knew they were exactly as he had been upon the mountaintop. It was simply his role to pass on all that

Ahura Mazdā had shared.

So when I began to work now with the magi I too saw this humility. I saw men who understood so much yet they did not see themselves as any different to any other man or woman. They too knew that were simply channels of the information for anyone willing to listen. So they embraced me as Ahura Mazdā did Zarathustra upon the mountain.

The first thing I had to overcome was my attitude towards self-discipline. Discipline to the magi was of an entirely different perspective than I had known it. I had been shown the elements of discipline through being very particular and strict with my physical being. The restricted diet and my attitude towards sleep were all part of helping me to structure my mind and my beliefs. Now in Babylonia I had that all challenged.

I was not so long in Babylonia when I was received by the first magus just outside of the capital Babylon. His name was Erasmus with a physique as generous as his hospitality. When I arrived at his home he ran to his door pushing aside his servants to greet me as though I was a long lost child returning home. He grabbed me by the shoulders and pulled me towards him, kissing me on each cheek and then hugging me.

"Oh my! Those Egyptians did not treat you so well. I can feel your bones," he said as the hug turned into a physical examination and I felt his hands pat along my spine and then my ribs. "It is no worry for you are in Babylonia now and we will take care of you. Rest and bathe, then we will eat!"

He stood back and clapped his hands. "Come, come! Take our new friend to refresh himself!" he called out beckoning to the servants he had pushed aside.

Two of them ran back towards me and grabbed a hand each to lead me away.

"Be gentle with him!" Erasmus said and he laughed. "Can you not see how fragile he is!"

While I was splashed and scrubbed Erasmus called more servants to him. Some were sent to the markets, some were sent to invite other magi to his home and others were assigned chores in the home.

I had a towel wrapped about my waist when my bathing was done and once more the two men led me by both hands along a corridor to a bedroom.

As we stepped into the room I gasped. The rest of the home had been magnificent enough but this room was spectacular. The bed was the hugest I had ever seen and without even touching it I could see how soft it was. It was laid with the most luxurious of fabric and more was suspended from the roof to form a canopy. I started to count the colours but gave up.

Along one wall were three wardrobes, carved with such intricacy that almost defied the possibility of being made by men. Another wall housed a dresser, laid out with endless bottles of oils as well as brushes of every shape. A mirror stood atop this reflecting back to me a very gaunt man in a towel flanked by two men holding his hands.

Then I felt the towel drop. The servant to my right held the towel in his hand. He was a small man with the dark skin of someone from much further east than the Babylonian border.

"You sleep now," he said and pointed to the bed while the other man walked to the huge windows and pulled the curtains making the room as dark as it could be for the afternoon.

The first servant walked to the bed and drew back the bed cover. He pointed once more to the bed.

"You sleep now and we wake you later," he said and poked his hand to the bed as though I could not understand him.

I understood alright. To be honest I was just scared of the bed. I had never been in anything like it in my life and wondered if I might ever be able to sleep upon a stone floor or dusty ground again after having been in one.

"You sleep now!" repeated the servant and he said it louder as though this might help me understand.

"Yes, yes, I sleep now," I answered and climbed into the bed.

The two men went to either side of the bed and drew the cover over me, then pulled on each side so that it tightened over me and not a crease was within the silk.

"We go now and come back later," said the same man and pointed to the door.

I nodded and they left, closing the door behind them. I could barely think about just how much silk was hanging above me and wrapped around me when I fell asleep.

It was a deep blissful sleep. The sort that is so deep that you forget where you are and what the day is. I may have dreamt but the depth of the sleep left the images there in that realm. I was awoken by a hand shaking my shoulder.

"Wake up now," came the voice that accompanied the hand and I knew it was the servant who had put me to bed. Beside him though was not the man who helped him bathe me. He was of a entirely different stature, posture and expression.

"You wake now," said the servant and the other man rolled his eyes.

"Yes, he is awake. Can you not see his eyes are open?" he muttered and the servant stopped shaking me.

I sat up in the bed as the servant pulled the cover back.

"You dress now," he said and I saw that the other man looked over my naked body just a little slower than a servant or any man should and drew in his breath.

He finally turned his eyes to look into mine. "I am Zorbo, Erasmus' chief dresser. He has sent me to dress you for dinner," he drawled as I rolled awkwardly from the huge bed to stand before him. Once again he looked me up and down again in a way that made my skin crawl.

"I can surely dress myself," I said as I let my hand fall before my crotch. "My clothes are not so complex."

Zorbo walked over to the chair on which sat my bag while my skirt and tunic were draped over the back. He lifted the skirt between two fingers and turned it to and fro as he screwed up his nose. Throwing it to the floor, he rolled his eyes and turned to the servant.

"Burn it!" he spat and walked to the first of the wardrobes as the servant ran to gather up my now maligned clothing.

Zorbo threw open the doors of the first wardrobe and it were as though another room of materials was loaded inside it. He rummaged through piles and flicked through things hanging. Every now and then he would throw an item over his shoulder and as soon as it hit the floor the servant was there to gather it in his arms. When the servant's arms were full he would place them upon the bed.

The two of them played this out for ten minutes, moving from one wardrobe to the next, until it seemed the bed was double in height. Then Zorbo walked back to face me and once again looked me up and down. He tilted his head from side to side as he stroked his smooth chin and sighed several times. Then he put out his right hand.

"The loin cloth first," he said and snapped his fingers. Within seconds a piece of white silk was in his hands and he moved towards me.

"Step your legs apart and for goodness sake move your hands out of the way!" he said with no interest in hiding his lack of distain for being made to do this.

I had not been dressed by another since my childhood and to have another man's hands upon my body like this was most uncomfortable. Not least when he cupped my genitals to arrange them within the binding of the loincloth. He felt me squirm and I heard him sigh again. I decided to make small talk to somehow try and diffuse the discomfort.

"I see you are not of Babylonian blood. Where are you from?" I asked.

His hands stopped and he stood up straight before me. The burn in his eyes as he looked into mine was unforgettable.

"I am a dresser not a talker!" he said through a clenched jaw.

It was my turn to sigh as he continued on with his work.

It was about an hour later that I was ready. Not that it took that long to dress as a magus did but that Zorbo decided to dress and redress me several times. This, combined with his stopping numerous times to berate the servant, made the whole ordeal take much longer than I felt it should. He finished by pushing me towards the dresser.

"Sit," he said abruptly to me and then snapped his finger at the servant. "Hair. Then beard. Then oil."

The servant nodded and picked up one of the dozens of brushes before me. He had barely touched it to my hair and Zorbo left without a word. I wondered if he was going to return but realised within minutes he would not.

"Will he come back?" I asked the servant quietly.

The man shook his head in response as he gently pulled at my hair which had started to grow back its Greek curls.

"Is he always so terse or have I evoked that for some reason?" I pushed hoping the servant would open up which he did.

He looked around as though to check no-one was within the room and then leant in close as he continued to brush.

"He is a very angry man," he whispered and his face grew red as though he was telling the darkest of secrets. I nodded and smiled hoping this would encourage more but the servant stood straight again and changed the brush for another.

He faced me now and began to work on my very short and rough beard.

"Where is he from?" I asked quietly and once again he looked around and lowered his head to speak.

"He come from north one day," the servant shook his head but I nodded pushing for more and he went on. "He come to learn with other priest but was bad. Too much wine and other bad things. Priest throw him out with nothing and say bad things about him to other priests. No-one would teach him or give him food. He come here crying and Master says 'I take you in, but you serve me and prove you be good'. He been here one year and Master says he still not good so will not teach him things. 'How I be good when you not teach me' he yelled at Master one day. Master say to him, 'When you good then you know I have been teaching you.' That just make him more angry. He hates when men like you come here and Master loves them."

With that he put down the brush and then turned back to me.

"You not tell that I tell you this—please—or Zorbo do very bad things to me!" he said quietly but desperately.

"Of course. You have my word," I said and squeezed his hand hating to think just what that man could do.

The servant nodded but I could see he still was shaking a bit at the thought he had said too much. He asked me to choose some oil and I picked up the nearest bottle that was decorated with pieces of faience and nodded. He took it from my hand and shook his head.

"This is for women," he said plainly and reached for a larger brown bottle towards the back of the dresser. "This one is better for men."

With that he poured some on the ends of his fingers and then flicked it on me. The strong aroma swirled around me and it was indeed masculine. My eyes started to water as the servant placed the bottle back down.

"You go eat now," he said pulling at my hand to make me get up and leading me to the door.

Once again I was led back down the corridor which was now lit with lamps. We turned left into another corridor much wider than the one from the bedroom. At the end, huge double doors sat open with much more light coming from them. I saw one servant leaving with a jug in their hand, followed by another with an empty platter. They disappeared through a door on the left of the corridor and just as the door was closed it opened again and two servants came out. One carried a jug in a way so that I could tell it was full while another man behind him held a platter piled with food. They made their way through the double doors.

As we approached the doors I could smell roasted meats and my mouth grew wet while my stomach growled.

"You need food," said the servant quietly and he smiled.

I did indeed. My sleep had seemed to reset everything within me. I had allowed myself a luxurious sleep like nothing I had in the past twenty-five years of my travel. I had let myself be preened and adorned like I was royalty. Now to eat a feast was an apt finale to my day of decadence.

As I walked through the door my senses were barraged. Once again the room was filled with coloured cloths. They hung on the walls and draped the ceiling. The floor was covered in rugs woven with intricate patterns. In the middle of the room was a huge low round table. In the centre was a sculpture of a tree and its branches were loaded with dozens of small lamps lighting up the table. This along with the lamps that lined the walls and several lamps hanging from the ceiling lit the room brightly.

The table was filled with plate upon plate of food. There were the meats I smelt from the hallway as well as every sort of vegetable and fruit I could imagine plus some I could not have as I had never seen them before. The food was as colourful and rich as the fabrics of the room.

Surrounding the table were enormous vibrant cushions embroidered with gold thread and upon them, completing the scene, were three more magi along with Erasmus. They were as rotund as my host and dressed as elaborately and vividly as their surrounds. If it were not for their movement and laughter they may well have blended in with the scenery.

Except for their names I might not have had any means to tell them apart from each other. Each man, as well as carrying a generous belly, had a round face that blended into beards which poured down to sit upon the ledge of their tummies. The hair upon their head likewise had not seen a blade in many years and tumbled down their back. Though they wore scarves twisted about their heads to keep the hair from their eyes, these adornments themselves were so elaborate and full that, along with the beards and the hair protruding out from under the headdress, their upper bodies seemed as large as their lower.

They each sat propped up on their respective pillow, their legs crossed before them and their hands, when not reaching out for food, rested upon their knees. Each man was dressed as I was in pants which ended just under the knee, then a tunic over these that was tied at the waist and over this a loose sort of coat that gathered upon the shoulders and fell to the floor. You could pull this tight and tie it with a belt or you could leave it open and loose.

There was one thing, along with my thinner physique that made me appear different though. Each magus was dressed in tones of red; some bright like a new cherry while others were deeper like a pomegranate seed. I, on the other hand, was dressed in tones of green.

As I entered the room the men's chatter stopped for a moment.

"Yes, yes, here he is!" called out Erasmus lifting his hands in the air and waving them to summon me in further. Then his eyes looked down at my clothes. "Did Zorbo not dress you?"

"Yes he did Erasmus," I answered and instantly I understood that the dresser had once more demonstrated his badness.

"Mmph," grunted Erasmus and quickly put a smile upon his face. He hit the empty pillow beside himself. "Sit down and eat!"

I lowered myself slowly, still getting accustomed to all the extra clothing now upon me. The servant had trailed me to the cushion and flicked the coat out behind me so that I would not catch upon it. After I settled myself and arranged my legs to cross at the ankles like the magi did, I realised that he stayed standing behind me. Now that I was comfortable he leant forward close to my right ear.

"What would you like to begin with?" he whispered.

"Yes, begin Pythagoras! What can we tempt you with first?" Erasmus smiled and hit me on the arm. "There is plenty and we have all night so don't feel you have to budget your time or stomach space."

I looked up for a moment and saw that all the other men were watching me as though intrigued as to what I might choose. I noticed that each man also had his own server hanging close by to pass and pour for them. These men too were watching me. I scanned the table and by now was so hungry I could have devoured it all but my years of discipline kicked in.

"Some breads and vegetables would be fine," I said nodding and smiling for even though this might sound like a simple meal, upon this table was an array of the most divine bread and vegetables cooked in delicate spices and oils.

My servant quickly stepped between the cushions gathering one dish at a time of bread and then the vegetables. He spooned some onto my plate until it was so full it actually would have been as much as I would have eaten in a week. Then without asking he poured me some wine and stepped back to wait to be summoned for my next serving.

The magi continued to watch me and then when I began to eat looked at one another.

"No meat?" asked Erasmus.

"No. I have not partaken of flesh in over twenty years now," I answered simply and hoped they knew enough of other schools to understand this.

"Are you not even tempted tonight by this feast?" asked another magus.

I shook my head and smiled. "No. Live without something long enough and it is not something to miss or to tempt you when it does arrive."

I lied and they knew it. The smell of lamb, goat and fowl was eating at my stomach with a ferocity I had not known in years. It was as though the richness of my surrounds suddenly made me want to dive in and taste every part of what was stimulating my senses. The colours around me, the slip of the silk on my skin, the oil flicked on me—everything seemed to trigger something within each sense that wanted to have more of what it was feeling.

I did not cave though and this too was noted by the men. They continued to watch me a moment more and then they too lost themselves back within the food. Then the questions started. They wanted to know about the schools I attended and what I had learnt. I shared as best I could while respecting the confidentiality of where I had been whilst making sure not to compromise my gains or hinder my interaction with the magi.

As the wine flowed and our bellies grew full though the talk grew more casual and boisterous. A joke would be made and the laughter grew so intense that one of the men would actually fall to his side in hysterics and have his servant rush forward to help him right himself only to have him collapse again. Even with my head clear of any wine I found myself joining in the laughter so much so that I was wiping tears from my eyes. Then for a moment the talk resumed a more serious tone.

"You do know that the Persians took Egypt successfully don't you Pythagoras?" one of them asked me and I nodded for the news had indeed been made known to me. He looked at me quite seriously for a split second and within that I felt him ask me to acknowledge that I was lucky to have been exiled when I was. Then his eyes narrowed with a glisten as his smile grew once more. "Do you know what the Persians did that took such power from a land so great?" Then through his laughter he told me and the men collapsed in laughter again.

When Cambyses had looked upon Egypt the one thing that stood out to him was the temples.

"They are magnificent," he thought and within that magnificence he knew was the power he needed to undo. An army may be great but it is its doctrines and mindset which made it formidable. Cambyses knew that two archers could hit a bullseye in practice but that did not make either of them a warrior. It would be the fire in their blood that made them able to hit a man with that arrow and to be able to do such things you needed a cause worthy of breaking those parts of you that aligned with everyday morality.

Inside those temples were all the causes that shaped what

Egyptians believed worthy. Use the psyche of the religion and you undo the psyche of the people.

When the reports of his spies came back to him that the cat goddess, Bastet, was the most favoured of the Pharaoh and the northern Egyptians he smiled.

"Cats? They are making this too easy," he laughed and he turned to the generals. "Let us make an army of cats then."

So the Persians and all her allies painted cats upon their shields and the sides of the chariots so that as they marched the Egyptians would see their very own god coming to attack them.

As the magus narrated this story the men began to chuckle but I found nothing in this so amusing. I smiled with politeness anyway as he carried on. The next part of the story was what really made the table shake with laughter.

"But not only did they paint themselves they carried the animals with them," he said and held his stomach as he laughed. "Then they threw them ahead and yelled to make the cats run towards the Egyptians, making the men flee lest they harm the animals."

My stomach churned when I heard this, somewhat due to the excess of food and somewhat because in spite of the rudeness of throwing me out of their country, I felt for what might be lost to this new invasion. A part of me also knew that this story was complete rubbish.

I was right. Cambyses had been so wrong about the Egyptians. Yes, the Persians did paint their shields and chariots but they did not waste their time and energy seeking out thousands of cats. No army commander is that insane. It was not the imagery of Bastet being so repulsively blasphemed that scared the Egyptians into retreating. It was the size and power of the army that made their blood run cold.

To look out upon a sea of men that has no end to it makes any man know they are defeated no matter how that army walking towards them adorns themselves. This in itself would have been enough to secure Cambyses his legend but for the despot it was having shown he undermined the very core of Egyptian religion that was more important. For the message that he truly wanted known was that he had used the Egyptians' god to defeat them and that the only one capable of making a god turn upon its people is another god. His reputation was cemented and as he collected the crowning piece of his empire he smirked.

As he looked at the temples Cambyses knew there was no strength within their walls. The people he had conquered could continue to play with their animal gods. It made them seem so quaint now and within this he could use ridicule to show that they were doomed to his rule.

Erasmus noticed I did not laugh as the story was told.

"You do not find this amusing at all do you? I also believe that we have shown a rather coarse side to you in our being entertained by this?" he asked with a gentle smile.

I nodded as I lowered my eyes slightly uncomfortable with being at odds with my host and his company.

Another of the men leant forward and spoke now. "Do not think we find humour in war but in the foibles of religion."

I looked up and stared at him wide-eyed hardly believing that men who dedicated themselves to teaching a form of religion could ridicule another's. The expression on my face made all the men laugh again.

"Don't insult my guest with your double speak!" shouted Erasmus and he threw a bone from his plate at the other magus. This was followed with another round of inevitable laughter.

I shook my head, not in disgust or disbelief but in sheer bewilderment at what this next stage of my learning would entail. It was twelve years later that I decided I had learnt enough from the Magi and I never regretted one minute.

The next day I was woken by having my shoulder shaken by Anson, the servant who had cared for me the day before and was now my personal servant during my stay.

"You wake," he said until I opened my eyes. "Good. You sit up now."

He threw my blanket off me and I sat up letting my legs hang over the edge of the bed. I raised my arms to stretch myself and as I did this Anson leant down to a bucket of water, pulling out a cloth and wringing it. He then took advantage of my raised arms and began to wipe at my underarms, then grabbed each arm in turn washing them down. As he leant down to refresh the cloth and move on to my legs I looked around the room for the dresser. I sighed with relief but wondered if he would simply show when my bathing was complete.

"Ahh—will Zorbo be coming to dress me?" I asked.

Anson stopped twisting the cloth and looked up. Once again he had that look as though he might say something he shouldn't.

"Zorbo is gone. Master wake him this morning and tell him to leave. Master says 'you never learn to be good here with me. You learn to be good somewhere else.' It is very happy day for the house."

With that he began to wipe my legs but I could see him smiling.

"Was it because of how he dressed me?"

Anson nodded without looking up but I saw his smile grow wider.

Thankfully Erasmus did not see fit to send another official dresser and left it to Anson to help me. He went straight to the middle wardrobe and pulled out some red garments. As he laid them out on the bed I thought how peculiar that the wrong outfit last night had resulted in a man being dismissed. Men can create their destiny through many strange ways.

Once dressed, I was led once more back to the dining room for breakfast. As I walked in I thought for a brief moment that the table had not been cleared from the night before but then I could see the plates were full of fresh food and no meat was in sight.

"Come, come my friend! Eat up so we can begin," Erasmus called to me from his pillow. "As you can see I have decided to join your vision of a diet with no meat this morning and I have to say ..." he stopped and patted at his belly, "... I quite like it for this time of day." He laughed and leant forward to grab a piece of cheese and put it upon some bread.

I smiled back as I took my seat. It was indeed a delightful breakfast and I astounded myself at being able to eat the amount I did after what I had the night before. As I said there just seemed to be something about all the colours around me and the joviality of my host which made it so easy to be indulgent.

Not surprisingly I doubled in size in the first month I spent with Erasmus. Not that this made me anywhere near as portly as him but let's just say I would now more closely resemble the busts and drawings that carry my image. In truth I did feel more vigour but this was not something that was of huge importance to me. I would always have the energy to do what I needed.

We finished up our breakfast and Erasmus clapped his hands.

"Let us make way to temple," he called out to everyone.

As we stepped into the corridor another set of servants waited to greet us. Well I thought they were servants but they were not. They were students and acolytes who gathered here each morning to escort Erasmus to temple and then study with him. Most were from the surrounding area, while those that travelled to the region were billeted to local homes. They paid their rent by sharing their studies with the residents of the home and performing rites for them. In short they acted as the household's private magus.

I discovered that few students such as myself were ever invited to stay within the home of a magus. When I asked Erasmus why I had been allowed such an honour he was quite serious.

"A week before you arrived I had a dream. I saw you riding towards my home upon a camel and though you did not look as you do now, I knew it was you. As you rode towards me I heard Ahura Mazdā speak. He said to teach you the best way I could because one day you will be part of the new consciousness that we know is coming. He did not tell me how or when and that is not for me to question. I just know that I pledge to you my greatest intent to share as much as I can," he said and with that he closed his eyes and gave thanks to Ahura Mazdā.

I nodded because I knew the vision he spoke of. Erasmus had seen me with the other men measuring the unusual star. I knew this was confirmation once again that our spirit carries on beyond the limits of a body.

Days at temple with Erasmus were rich and fulfilling. That first day as he walked me up the huge rise of stairs I could feel him almost bursting with pride. He smiled so much I thought his face might split even though he puffed with the effort of the climb. When we reached the portico he stopped and held onto a column. Erasmus turned as though to look at the town but I knew he was just catching his breath and I bit my lip to not laugh.

"Yes, I am not as robust as you but this gives me opportunity to see the beauty of my home. I used to just stop and look at my feet as I gathered my breath but to look out upon the place that nurtures me and protects me is rather a nice way to start my day of work," he finished and turned to go inside the temple but I stayed and looked at my new home a moment longer.

"Come along, Pythagoras. I know you have your breath and we have much to do," Erasmus called out to me.

I took a deep breath and walked inside.

The smell is the first thing that hits you when you walk into a Zoroastrian temple. Despite having its own source of light it takes some time for your eyes to adjust so that you can see. Each temple is designed in the same way so that you begin by entering a room that although square has a circle of columns so that you initially think that it is round. In the centre is a large round pit, sunken slightly into the floor. Bursting forth from this pit is a fire that burns continuously. A rail about two feet high circles this more to protect the fire than those who come to worship.

Four columns within the rail rise to the roof, supporting the edge of an opening above the fire that allows most of the smoke to escape.

The rest of the acolytes had already made their way inside and taken places around the fire. Upon their knees they chanted out their own prayers with their eyes closed. I knelt beside Erasmus and as he began his own chant I looked around me.

It did not have the scale of the Egyptian temples nor the elaborate decorations and carving. It was beautiful nonetheless. Something of its simplicity made you understand the religion. Grandeur does not need to be elaborate. Divinity does not need embellishment. Stay true and pure and you have all you need.

The fire had nothing to do with this. This fire was said to have been born of the flame that warmed Zarathustra while he sat upon his mountain receiving the divine word. It represented the eternal presence of Ahura Mazdā and when people came before it they believed they were within his physical presence.

The fire though was not just a symbol of this God. It also showed the power of transformation.

"Anything you can imagine can be transformed by fire," Erasmus told me, "Anything! Water turns to steam. Wood turns to ash. Metals soften and can be shaped. Rocks can crack. Even your body can be turned to dust. It is the element that is most powerful."

This was also why they knew it represented their God. Submit yourself to Ahura Mazdā's teaching and you too will transform.

The fire in any Zoroastrian temple was monitored and maintained around the clock as part of this homage. If for any reason it went out this was of course seen as a bad omen and a full forty days of ritual were required when it was relit. Magi and acolytes took turns to oversee night shifts. As we arrived in the morning those that had been in temple through the night said their greetings with bleary eyes and shuffled home to their beds.

As the first prayers were finished the daytime acolytes rose and made way to a doorway between the columns on the left side of the room. Some re-appeared with ladders and others with buckets of water. The first duty of the day was to wipe away the soot of the fire. This fire may have been a god incarnate but like any god in any form it required maintenance.

Other acolytes were sent to organise the bundles of wood that many townspeople brought as offerings. Some men simply began to sweep.

"We have no servants of the temple as such. For all man is a servant of Mazdā and his home," Erasmus explained as he handed me a broom.

I began to sweep and as I fell into the rhythm of my work I smiled. Looking up at the other men, all busy with their designated or chosen chore I felt the dedication and joy they felt in being able to do this. This fire burning eternally would show me much.

By midday our chores were done and then, after a lovely lunch provided by the villagers, we made way to the room behind the one that held the fire. This was another square room with shelving along all sides full of books and scrolls. Each one in turn held the numerous writings of Ahura Mazdā and of the disciples who carried on his work in the generation after his death. A disorganised group of chairs was scattered across the floor.

"Those of you who have begun the studies of the Avesta shall continue on today," Erasmus said loudly as he looked over all of us. "Those who are newer shall come with me."

With that he walked towards a door at the back corner of the temple room. I followed close behind him and outside the door we stopped for a moment upon the rear portico of the temple. There were only three other men with us and they were far younger than my forty-one years. Erasmus glanced over us one at a time as though checking that we were all eligible for this group.

"Hmph," he grunted quietly and then began to walk down the stairs.

We all followed with no idea where we were going and not one person dared to ask. Erasmus led us through the city and the only sounds from our group were the scrape of sandals upon the dirt or the returned greeting to the endless stream of villagers who acknowledged us as we walked.

One woman ran and threw herself at Erasmus feet, crying out for help for her ill husband. We all stopped in our tracks wondering how he would react. Erasmus adjusted his feet so his belly would allow him to bend down. With one hand braced upon his knee to steady himself he stroked the woman's hair.

"All will be well. Remember your teachings and continue to make virtuous choices. That is all that can be done," he said gently but firmly then grunted as he strained to stand straight again.

He stepped around the woman and we walked on.

Our group continued to the outskirts of the village and soon we were away from all buildings bar the odd farmhouse dotted between the mountains that surrounded the village. Erasmus stopped at the base of the tallest mountain and looked it up and down intently. Then still without any words he made way to a trail that worked its way up.

In single file we followed him up the trail as it curved from side to side winding its way through the more hospitable parts of the mountainside. We were about two-thirds of the way when the trail bent to the left and as we stepped onto this part we could see a cave opening to the right. It was quite large and clearly had been enlarged by men as the debris lay scattered amongst the crags just below it. Erasmus stopped outside of it, looked down and then burst out laughing.

"Ah, I used to be able to climb all the way, but this is as far as we need to go for now," he said catching his breath. "Oh, to be young again ...." He led us into the cave but jumped slightly as he looked inside.

There at the back of the cave was a young man sitting with his knees pulled to his chest. His eyes were dark and he looked at us all as though he wasn't quite sure if we were real.

"Mobus! You are still here?" cried Erasmus. "Oh heavens! Get back to the temple to bathe and eat. Why are you still here?"

"You said you would come for me when you knew I had done enough," growled Mobus.

"Yes, well let that be a lesson that no man can decide another's fate no matter their wisdom," he joked back. "In fact, let that be a lesson to you all. The first for today—listen to your needs as no-one else can know them. Go Mobus!"

Mobus stood and swayed on his feet for a moment. As he passed Erasmus he scowled and then we heard his feet scraping back down the mountain. Thankfully he took his body odour with him and the air in the cave lightened immensely with his departure.

Erasmus took a seat upon a stone near the cave entrance and gestured for us to gather around him.

"If my body was more capable I would take you to the peak but this must suffice. It was on the peak of a mountain that our great prophet Zarathustra received the divine teachings and it was not through any accident that he did. Lift yourself above the world and you lift your soul. Rise above the chaos of society and you can see and hear with clarity. Take yourselves now to the peak here above us," he stopped and pointed upwards. "Find a place to yourself and breathe. Listen for the voice of Mazdā and listen for your own voice. When the sun begins her setting then we will return home. Go and listen," he finished and waved us outside and back upon the trail.

Once again following the trail we all made our way higher up the mountainside. The peak was a roughly level area, leaning down on its south side. Huge rocks sat upon the small plateau almost dividing it into rooms. Amongst these rocks, scraggy bushes held onto the scant soil for dear life.

The clever students quickly moved to the sides of rocks that had begun to throw shadows. Despite the gentle breeze that found its way here the sun would soon sting our skin. The last of my group ventured as far from the end of the trail as possible and I had no choice but to follow him to the opposite side of the peak where it dipped down. He headed to the left and so I took to the right and found a lovely smooth ledge to sit upon. As I sat I realised its even surface had resulted from a long line of behinds that had sat upon it. There was even a slight curve where my legs hung over the side.

As I sat now I looked out upon the plains and the village that was below us. For about the hundredth time now as I journeyed I suddenly felt all those who had been here before me and who had been asked to do the very same thing. Then for the first time I wondered about those who would come.

Remembering my task for the day I closed my eyes now. I breathed deep. I felt that calm wash of letting my mind quieten. Then I invited Ahura Mazdā to speak with me.

"Welcome my son," was his greeting and the next four hours went by as though they were a single, brief moment.

When my fellow student tapped me on the shoulder gently I opened my eyes wondering why I was being disturbed so soon. He said nothing but pointed to the sky. The bright blue of early afternoon was now the soft pink of the arriving dusk. I nodded and pushed myself up to stand.

The others had already made their way back to Erasmus and I whispered a thank you to my colleague.

"It is no matter," he said and smiled. "I too had to be summoned."

Erasmus was sitting upon his rock waiting patiently for us. The others were standing in the cave stretching.

"Ah, Pythagoras. I trust you were not just sleeping," he joked and I returned his smile.

"No, not at all my teacher," I replied.

"Good. Let us make way to temple. Unless someone would like to remain here to do more work?" he asked and looked around.

"I would Sir!" said one and he jumped forward as though to block anyone else out.

"Fine. You may stay," said Erasmus and he stepped outside the cave leading us back home. Then he stopped and turned back to the cave. "But please do not wait for me to summon you. Return of your own accord." With that he began to walk again and I am sure his giggles could be heard all the way down the slope.

When we reached the bottom of the mountain Erasmus stopped a moment and I would have imagined it was to catch his breath or allow his hips some respite. Instead he looked amongst us and pointed to the man who had called me when it was time to leave the peak.

"You! Come walk beside me," he said and waved the student to him. As we all began to walk again he asked the man, "Now tell me what you heard?"

He called each of us one by one to do this as we walked leaving me until last. We were almost at the steps of the temple when he turned and pointed at me.

"I will listen to you over dinner," was all he said before he led us up the stairs.

The heat within the fire room was overwhelming by this time of the day, even with all the doors on three sides being left open. We all knelt down to say a final prayer and though I did not know the proper words I gave my own thanks to Ahura Mazdā for his company that day. I am sure I was not the only one who was grateful when the night magi and students appeared as I could hear several stomachs beginning to rumble.

Erasmus' group did not follow him back to his house. Instead they dispersed to their own homes as we walked so that it was only the two of us approaching his. Servants came rushing forward to take our coats, while others held bowls of rose water for us to wash our hands and face.

Soon we were in the dining room again and my tongue and stomach indulged themselves once more. Erasmus asked me of my time upon the mountain and I shared as best I could. He nodded and smiled. Later I slipped into my soft bed and fell asleep with a smile for I knew that not only had I pleased my teacher but today had been a most productive day of learning.

When I heard the greeting from the energy that was known as Ahura Mazdā it was like being reunited with an old friend. I also felt someone beside me and I knew it was Zarathustra taking a seat beside me, curious as to what I would speak of and also to lend some support.

"Every time someone seeks Mazdā as I did, my heart swells," I heard him say and then he was silent.

I conversed with all things of the universe with Mazdā. He showed me the source of all that was and how it had split to make all that we know of existence. I saw that for everything that was created, an equal and opposite was also created. This he explained was necessary.

"For man to know and feel his place in the universe there must be contrast. This is the way to understand the levels of existence. This gives substance to experience. This gives meaning to your choices. Without contrast, without duality then there is no flavour, no texture and no complexity for man to walk through to know himself."

Then I was shown the chaos of existence.

"This is the result of duality," he explained.

Then he showed it slowing down. Within the swirls of contrast there were now moments and flashes of clarity and organisation.

"This is the result of pure choice," he said again and I understood beyond the words.

The gift of clarity is not something to seek outside of ourselves from teachers. It lies in how we choose to live our life. It is not found in rebounding from one side of the contrast to another. This results in more chaos.

Clarity comes from choosing a steady and virtuous path. This was the core of Mazdā's teachings and he shared that with me in such a way that it made all I had learned so far seem insignificant. Yet I also knew that if I had not learnt what I had so far then I would not have understood this moment.

Erasmus nodded when I told him this last insight. He raised his glass to me and toasted me with a blessing.

"Blessed be the one who knows that no moment of his life has been wasted!"

With that he took a great mouthful of wine, wiped at his mouth and smiled.

"My dream was not wrong was it?" he asked.

All I could do was nod.

CHAPTER FOURTEEN

The following two weeks were a wonderful repeat of this day. Sometimes I would be told to stay at temple and read in the library, and other days I might be sent to the mountaintop again. I was asked if I might like to be alone in the cave but at this time I believed my cave retreats were well and truly done with. When I said this to Erasmus he laughed so much he doubled over.

"I know, I know," he said. "I only send the young ones there as it satisfies some sort of student martyrdom in them. Mobus was not the first one I have forgotten up there. Thankfully we found him before he collapsed!"

I leant against a pillar and watched as Erasmus and the other elder of the magi performed their rites around the fire. Villagers came and went as the rites went on and it was lovely to watch them enter the temple as though they were visiting the home of a friend. Here in this temple reverence did not equate to humility.

Then it became Erasmus' turn to take care of the fire at night. This meant that his group of acolytes were also responsible.

The first night was possibly the hardest as we simply stayed on from our day at temple and as the hours wore on some of the younger ones started to wilt. I smiled as I walked and placed some more wood upon the fire. As I did so I once again thanked Thales for his discipline so early in my studies. As the sun began to rise my body too wanted sleep and was more than grateful to make its way to my big soft bed.

Nights at the temple were not just about keeping the fire burning. This was now our time to read and discuss the teachings. We did so around the fire most nights as its warmth was needed and helped to keep us awake. Then Erasmus would ask us to be silent.

"Look into the fire and see what Mazdā wants to share with you," he would say and we would stare into the flames.

We would do this for an hour or so and then talk about what we had seen. Some of us saw entire scenarios played out while others just saw symbols. None were made wrong or right by Erasmus.

"You see with your eyes in a way no other man can. This is your unique style of seeing. It is the same with your hearing. Never compare with another that which your senses share with you. It is all about what you feel from them," he said. "Now that is what you can share!"

After our last night shift we were allowed the following day to rest as we always did and the following night was ours to reset our body clocks before returning to days at temple. Unable to fall into a deep sleep I walked to my window, pushed the drape aside and peered out to the night sky. The moon was merely a sliver and, without any clouds to blur the sky, it seemed each and every star was making themselves known.

It was quite a while before I changed my focus to the garden that was outside my room and there in a clearing stood Erasmus. His back was to me and he stood with his hands clasped behind his back while he looked so high in the sky I could almost see the tip of his nose. Erasmus barely moved a muscle as he did this and with the silver light of night washed over him he could have passed for a statue.

Eventually Erasmus moved and I saw him turn to a small table to his left. He picked up a quill and scratched something onto a scroll. He then turned to his right, placed his hands behind his back as before and looked up again. Erasmus was now sideways to me and though I could not see his face so clearly I could feel the gentle way he regarded the heavens as though nothing else was of more importance. It was some time until he stepped back to his table and made more marks on the scroll.

I dropped the drape back down, filling the room with darkness again. As curious as I was I did not wish to disturb my teacher's night reverie.

All magi study the stars as did all men of knowledge and wisdom of my time. Here you measured your place in the universe. The stars marked the change of seasons and the passage of time with more detail than the rise and fall of the sun. To men of wisdom the stars showed the intricacy of all that was, all that is and all that is to come.

For the magi of Zoroastrianism the stars were much more. They were like Mazdā's noticeboard to the humans below. A change in what the night sky held would signal an omen so that meteors and comets were beacons to signal approval or disapproval as to the state of mankind. However for all the seemingly trivial or objective interpretations that a falling star may give to a man lucky enough to have witnessed it, there was a far more important reason for the magi to watch the skies.

When Zarathustra sat upon his mountain and spoke with Mazdā he was taken into the very depths of human existence. The chaos of duality and the clarity of choosing were but one layer of what mankind had shaped for themselves.

It had been a week that Zarathustra had been sitting upon his mountain when a wave of sadness swept over him. In an instant he felt every struggle of every person who had existed. He felt the pull of darkness and the lessons learned through suffering. As he imagined all the sorrow that was yet to come Zarathustra broke down in tears.

"Why do you weep?" Mazdā asked him.

"I weep for the futility of existing in a world which pulls at you. I weep for the paradise that men could have from birth and yet must wade through duality to even know it exists. Why create a world where brutality and pain exist when you could have given us a heaven and allowed us to live in beauty and grace," Zarathustra yelled out to the clouds.

"Because this is how it is," was all Mazdā would answer.

This enraged Zarathustra. He grabbed at a rock, threw it at the sky and then broke down in tears again. Exhausted now by his outburst he lay upon his side and fell asleep. Finally with Zarathustra's emotions and thoughts put to rest, Mazdā knew this was the time to share with him the future of existence.

Mazdā showed Zarathustra in his dreams the design of what was to come. There would be a time when mankind's need for duality would end. The need of opposites and reflections would no longer serve a purpose. It would simply fall away. There would be a new dawn in consciousness and the world would change. This time would be heralded by new prophets and signs that would present in ways never seen before and to allow this change to occur in itself would be a challenge.

It would happen though, regardless.

When Zarathustra woke from his sleep with this knowingness he felt relieved.

"This will be worth it," he said to the sky.

Mazdā did not give details of this era for even he knew that consciousness could and would decide this when it was ready. He simply told Zarathustra to tell the people that their commitment to choosing virtuous lives would see them rewarded. Now this makes the incentive much greater, for not only do you grant yourself a fulfilled harmonious life but you are also working for the good of all.

The paradise that Mazdā showed Zarathustra was not only earthbound. It crossed into the heavens and as all changed upon the planet the energies worked across the realms and would be felt by all who had been as well. Paradise may not always be instant but when it is attained it knows no bounds.

Every magi spoke of this future to their acolytes and congregations.

It was the reward for virtuous choice in life and a promise that every magi believed with every fibre of their being. Nothing was fruitless or done without sending an echo throughout time. The more people that attuned to this belief then the quicker the new consciousness would be born.

So each night across the lands that the magi lived, they all watched the skies. Here Mazdā would show them just when the new life would begin.

Little change shows in the night sky and the dedicated magi knew to be patient. They celebrated the comets and were in awe of meteor showers, knowing that even the smallest event was a wink to encourage them to continue what they were teaching. Though it would appear on paper to be a somewhat simplistic and unproductive aspect of the religion it was the commitment to this that five hundred years later saw three of the noblest magi find the star that did indeed herald in the new dawn.

This was the star that led them to Bethlehem.

Something in this intrigued me. So far my astronomy studies had been quite cold and mathematical. I was shown constellations and taught their measurements and placements. It was as set as the markings on any scroll.

When Erasmus invited me outside one night to join him as he did his observations I saw the stars in a new way. At first I fell into the old ways and found myself checking off the constellations I knew by heart. I noted their height and position as I had been taught.

"Stop moving your head so much," said Erasmus with a soft laugh. "Be still and look into them more."

I did this now. I focussed on one area and though it took a few moments what I was looking at began to change. The stars I knew so well remained as they were but then between them I saw more stars. They were fainter and not so sharp in definition, but the more I stayed still and looked, they then came into focus. I was no longer looking at the sky as some screen that images were projected upon. It was now something to look into and I felt the depth of what surrounded us.

I saw the movement, albeit fleeting, of small meteors beyond the constellations close to us. For a moment I even imagined one of the smaller stars was growing larger as though moving towards us. I knew now that the sky was far more dynamic than I had realised and this night time vigil to watch them was not nearly as sterile as I had first expected. It was actually quite mesmerising.

"There is much more than you have been shown or taught?" Erasmus said softly.

"Much more," was my reply.

This shaped the way I followed astronomy from then on. I would look at the skies in a new way now and whenever I did I would think of the magi in Babylonia watching for the sign they had been promised.

When I left the home of Erasmus to move on to the home of the next magi I did so with everything new. My Egyptian clothes were disposed of upon my arrival and I now wore the same attire as those who taught me. The body they dressed was transformed; the foods had filled me out, not so that I was plump, but that you would no longer call me thin. My hair grew and its Greek curls returned and my beard now covered my jaw and chin. In fact it now needed trimming.

"You are not the same man who arrived here," said Erasmus and he shook his head as he thought about it.

I certainly was not. My physical attributes now reflected the life of abundance and riches that Erasmus had shared with me. As I walked out the front door of his home he had even more to bestow.

There waiting for me was one of his camels. I knew this one well as it was the one Erasmus would give me to ride if we travelled from the village to visit other magi. He was a fine beast who stood tall and proud. When he saw me he brayed as though to greet me. Standing beside him holding his rein was Anson who smiled at me as his way of a greeting.

"This is my gift to you," said Erasmus and he waved his hand toward the animal. "All magi travel by camel. As of today I am making you a magus so you must now travel as one."

For a moment I was overwhelmed. After more than twenty years travelling by foot or the generosity of a passing cart, to now have my own means of transport was quite a luxury. I walked to the camel and stroked his neck as I looked at the beautiful saddle that was upon him then realised that along with a rolled blanket tied behind it there was a bag hanging on either side that were clearly filled. I opened the first and saw there were more clothes inside.

"The other has some food. I cannot send you off without some basic supplies. The clothes are so you can arrive at another's home clean and respectful. Do not let the dust of the road lessen your arrival," Erasmus said.

I went to him and hugged him gently. I may not have had a permanent home during my travels but this camel was going to come very close to it. The concept of travelling with supplies or luggage when you are on foot is not at all practical. Now with my camel I could actually consider having possessions beyond the means of survival. I had never felt wealthier.

"Let us not lose ourselves in emotion," Erasmus said as he pushed me back and began to laugh. "It is time for you to continue on with your journey." He pressed a scroll into my hand. "These are the men I recommend you to study with. I have sent word to each one and they will not be surprised to have you arrive upon their door. Now go and I look forward to hearing your name again someday."

Erasmus had tears in his eyes as he farewelled me and I will admit so did I. I climbed up onto my camel and reached down to take the reins from Anson but he pulled his hand back towards himself.

"He is my gift also. Treat him well," said Erasmus.

At this I protested. "No Erasmus. I have no need for a servant!" I shook my head as I spoke.

"He is not your servant. He is your student now. You know you want to be a teacher. Well, here is where you begin. TEACH him well! Now go before I make you come back inside to eat something!"

With that he turned his back and walked inside and though I heard him chuckling I could hear his crying as well. I looked down at Anson and sighed.

"Are you happy to travel with me?" I asked.

He looked up at me and a smile spread across his face. He said nothing but nodded so much I thought his head would come off.

"Fine. Let us make our way then."

Anson walked beside the camel until we were outside the city's boundary and then I invited him to join me. As he slid into place, balancing upon the back half of the saddle and my bags, I let out a slight laugh.

"You are going to have to bear with me for some days as I grow accustomed to having a companion—and to travelling in such a way," I said to him.

"It will be half the fun of getting to know each other," he said, speaking the most articulately he had since I met him.

I paused for a moment as I took in the way he had answered me. Anson smiled and looked ahead as the camel raised itself and began walking. Turning back to guide the animal I realised there was much about my student and companion that I needed to know and wondered who was going to teach who.

Anson's skin and speech had let me know that he was not a

native of Babylon, but given the extensive trade routes and selling of people into slavery it was not unusual to see such men within wealthy households. I had not asked so many questions during my time with Erasmus as it was not considered polite nor even something that had aroused my curiosity at the time. However in the first few days of travelling and seeing a whole new side to Anson it became something I had to do.

Each day he revealed another part of himself. Anson's speech became increasingly eloquent. He became more confident and outgoing, leaping from the camel ahead of me to negotiate lodgings, order food or ask directions. Anson did all this without once losing sight of the fact that he was also with me to learn.

As we bounced along between places he asked endless questions about my studies and travel. Some days would end with my throat almost raw from talking and the dust I had breathed in from the road. It was a fascinating exchange for as I retold my story I revised it. I recalled the people I admired and those not so admired. Anson's probing pushed me to recall teachings that had fallen behind others so that I was able to look at them in a new way.

Sometimes as I spoke I would trail off as I distracted myself with pondering upon something I had remembered. Anson would never call me back, simply leaving me to my reverie and knowing I would remember him in time.

At first Anson did not ask me anything, he just listened. Eventually the questions started and they were as insightful as anything an elder could have asked. We had stopped for lunch one day and ended up in a particularly passionate discussion. The language became more florid and suddenly I had to stop.

"Anson, we have travelled for only three weeks together. There is no way you learnt to speak like this in the little time you have spent with me," I said as I smiled. "I think it is now time you told me your story."

Anson glanced down and began to laugh. He looked back up at me, still smiling, "And what purpose would that serve you?" he asked.

"Because you know as well as I do that the student teaches as much as the teacher! Besides are we not friends now? I like to know all about my friends," I replied.

Anson nodded and began.

It amazed me how much our stories paralleled. Anson too was born into a wealthy family in the northern reaches of ancient India, in an area that is now part of southern Nepal. His life was comfortable and easy with endless luxuries and servants to wait upon him.

However as with the rest of the world, new ways of thinking were being born here also. To the west the mystery schools were growing stronger and evolving, while to the north throughout China there were new philosophies shaping new religions. So it was that Nepal would be the birthplace of one of the most prolific religions mankind would know. For it was here that Gautama Buddha was born.

Anson's life began just as Gautama's ended and the teachings, so new and fresh, were making their way through the land to anyone who could hear. As Anson grew he walked places that the mighty Buddha himself had. However it was not the proximity of the great teacher's life or the teachings that inspired him. It was the story of Buddha's beginning that touched something in him.

For like Anson, Gautama began his life in privilege, somewhat protected from the harshness of life. When Anson read how the Buddha escaped his palace to experience the truth of man's existence in all forms, something pulled inside of him. Anson looked about his home differently now.

"For all the glory surrounding me I knew that it would not help me know my divinity nor the beauty of the universe," he said to me.

So at fifteen years of age, with a small satchel of necessities, a heart full of trust in himself and a mind full of wisdom taught to him since childhood, Anson walked from his home. He told me he took one last look at the huge house before he walked away.

"I thanked it for being my beginning but knew it would not be my end," he said.

Anson walked west. He knew instinctively the lands here would show him what he needed. As he travelled he decided to speak only as he truly needed to, never engaging in conversation just for the sake of it. This time was needed for observation.

"When you choose silence you see so much more. It is like all other senses are sharpened. You stop making sound and then you allow more of life to come to you. I am sure that was the blessing of your breathing retreats in Egypt," he said and I nodded.

There came a time when he knew he needed to learn the native language though. Even though dialects changed from region to region he still needed to train his tongue around the new sounds. So he began to speak more and this led to amazing interactions.

Anson was invited into homes fascinated with his dark but soft skin. Women were attracted by his huge round eyes framed by long lashes while some men were drawn by his somewhat feminine attributes. Both sexes made propositions and attempted to seduce him but Anson refrained from all.

"This journey was about me. I was not going to be distracted by another's sexual needs and the thought I could satisfy them."

He had been travelling two years when he arrived at Erasmus' home. Anson knew much about the magus by this time as he had heard about him over and over. Despite this, Anson had no desire to study with Erasmus as I had.

"I knew I would learn more by living beside him as a member of his household than I would as a student. How a wise man lives shows much more about the depth of his wisdom than what he says to his pupils," Anson said.

So Anson presented himself to Erasmus and asked for a job. Well in truth he approached the housekeeper who in turn spoke to Erasmus.

"We have need for a new servant and one presents himself on the very day we decided to look for one. He is eastern though and his language is basic," stated the housekeeper to the magus.

Erasmus grunted and smiled. "Well, it appears that if we need someone and someone arrives then the solution has presented itself. If you are happy then so am I."

And so Anson was taken in as a servant. The broken speech that at first made him a novelty soon served him as a cloak. It allowed him to appear uneducated and simple so that even when he was given more responsibility he was rarely confided in.

"I was there as part of the household but never included as all the other servants were. Once again my limited conversation allowed me to observe in a way I never would have been able to as a local."

Anson watched how Erasmus lived his religion through his life over two years. He watched how the magus allowed abundance into his life without ever questioning his worthiness. Also how he dealt with servants, his wife and children in the most admirable of ways. Of course he watched too the different students who came and went as part of their studies.

"These men and the way Erasmus was with them taught me the most. He knew immediately how dedicated they were and who was simply playing with the notion of being wise. Some he took to his bosom—as he did with you—others he kept at arm's length knowing that he simply needed to walk through being a teacher with them. Then came the day that Zorbo arrived ...." Anson stopped and shook his head. "It was with that man that I learnt the most."

Zorbo arrived and stood upon the doorstep of Erasmus' home with his chin held high in defiance of all that had been spoken of him. It was Anson who had greeted him and within an instant he had felt his flesh crawl as though warning him of the man. As Anson walked Zorbo to meet Erasmus he was sure Zorbo would be turned away. Instead Erasmus took him in, albeit with conditions.

"I watched Erasmus' expression as Zorbo spoke, asking to be accepted as a student. Erasmus' face stayed so still and calm. There was neither a smile nor a frown. He was like a statue as he let that villain speak. When he gave Zorbo his answer I could have screamed but at the same time I knew Erasmus was doing the perfect thing.

Unfortunately given his background Zorbo was put into a position where I was answerable to him. He immediately used his power in every way he could. The rest of the servants would be sneered at and he would yell 'one day I will *have* servants, but you will always be one.' I suppressed my desire to laugh when he said this because once a servant chose to make fun of him and that night Zorbo raped them.

One night he came for me too but I was expecting him and kept a knife by my side. Someone with that much darkness needs to do this to people to feel safe but I know how to make myself safe from these people. He was sensible enough to leave before I was forced to use the blade.

When you arrived and he was told to dress you I somehow knew you were to be his undoing. As much as I did not want you to be another of his victims it was fascinating to see him self-destruct. When he pulled those green garments from the wardrobe it took everything I had not to say something and I know he gloated to some other servants about what he had done."

Anson stopped and sighed.

"I told you this was why he was banished but I lied. I saw the way he looked at your body and how he touched you. I knew he was planning to rape you also. It would have been the perfect way to express his anger at Erasmus' sponsorship of you while he was assigned to serve you. That night would have been perfect for him—well, it would have if you had taken the same amount of wine the others had! I knew though that the heavy meal in your slight frame would have been much the same as if you were drunk. So I waited in the shadows of an alcove in the hallway near your room and sure enough when all was quiet I heard his feet making their way to your door. I waited until his hand was upon the handle before I held the knife to his throat. 'Leave now and all is well but touch my new friend and your blood shall pour upon the floor,' I said.

Just hearing me speak in that way was enough to scare him off though the knife helped add a dramatic effect.

The next day before I came to bathe you I went to Erasmus, being careful to get to the master before Zorbo came to dress him. I told him what had happened and he was horrified. I then felt compelled to tell him of the other assaults upon the servants." Anson shook his head and I saw tears come into his eyes as he recalled this. "The look on Erasmus's face was heartbreaking. 'I failed,' he said to me. 'You knew he was bad from the start and yet I thought I could change him. I have learnt much.' When Zorbo came to dress him Erasmus sent him away immediately. He had seen me leave the master's room as he approached so he knew it had been me that sealed his fate. He even came to find me before he left just so he could spit upon me. 'I may be bad but you are a fake,' he said and I laughed outright at him."

Anson stopped now and hung his head. "It intrigues me that as to all the paths a man can choose why he would choose one so full of rage and knowingly create continual disharmony. That is the question that still lingers on with me from that experience."

We didn't speak when he finished as though we both needed some time to release the story, letting it vaporise and float off away from us. Then finally I spoke because after learning all this, there was one thing I still wanted to know.

"Zorbo revealed your truth to Erasmus didn't he?" I asked quietly and this made Anson burst out laughing.

"No, no, no! And I am surprised you think Erasmus to be so gullible! He had me pegged within a week of my arrival but said nothing. After all I was performing my duties diligently and pleasantly. He had no reason to reprimand me for anything and I believed I had gotten away with my ruse until the day of Zorbo's demise. Erasmus called me to his room after I had put you to bed that night and confronted me— well not that so much as he simply asked to hear my story. You see I could not so much be called a liar when in truth I had never been asked about my background. Much of what the household believed to be my circumstances were assumptions and conjecture. I had never been asked so it had never been denied and they all thought my poor speaking skills would not let me tell the story properly anyway.

That day standing before Erasmus undid all that—or so I thought. He had seen through me on day one and much as I had been amused to see Zorbo's fall take place, so too was Erasmus watching with interest as to how long I was prepared to play out my part within his home.

He was sitting and waiting in the dining room when he summoned me. As I walked in he patted a pillow beside him for me to take a seat also. As you know this is unheard of for a servant so I baulked and said I would stand. I will never forget how he leant forward and made his eyes wide before saying to me 'It's time to stop pretending.'"

When Anson took his seat beside Erasmus, the magus poured him a glass of wine and handed it to his servant.

"I have known there was something beyond what you presented when you asked for work in my home. I took you in as much for my curiosity as a need for a servant. It was as though Mazdā told me to take you in—that your presence would somehow serve me in a much greater way than completing the menial tasks you would be assigned. I realise today that truth was shown to me. So that I may know just how this has all come to pass I am going to ask you to tell me the truth of your life," Erasmus said and sat back waiting for Anson to speak.

Anson told his story and Erasmus wept at the beauty of it. When Anson finished he nodded, closed his eyes and then dropped his head. He stayed that way for a minute or two then lifted his face again and opened his eyes.

"You knew I was making a mistake by taking in that man didn't you?" asked Erasmus.

"I don't believe you could ever make a mistake Erasmus. Zorbo showed us all how some men are simply irredeemable no matter the support they are given," Anson answered.

Erasmus cried again at hearing this and nodded his head. Nothing disturbed Erasmus more than a man who could not choose a virtuous life. Then he offered Anson anything he wanted; money to travel onwards, a promotion within the household, even a place within the temple to study to become a magus.

"I have no need of such things right now," was Anson's reply.

"Well then all will stay as it is," said Erasmus. "But when the day comes that you do desire change then I will help you make that happen."

That day came when I told Erasmus it was time for me to move on. The six months Anson had at my side, overhearing about my travels and my studies, fired up the wanderlust within him. When Erasmus called him so that they could organise the camel and supplies for my journey Anson knew it was time to enact their agreement.

"I want to leave with Pythagoras," Anson said simply.

Erasmus paused for a moment taking in the idea of losing both his star pupil and his star servant and then nodded.

"So be it," he said.

"And that is why I was gifted to you," explained Anson.

"Well you weren't exactly a gift were you?" I said with a laugh.

"No, I suppose not, but would you have taken me on as a travel companion if we hadn't arranged it thus?" Anson asked quite seriously.

This caught me by surprise and I thought about it. I had always travelled alone—my only form of company coming from my time spent at schools and temples or the incidental contact made while on my way to somewhere else. To have someone with me, learning from me or influencing how I might make my journey had never appealed to me. In fact it had never crossed my mind to even consider it. In truth I would have said no if Anson had asked, but that was without knowing his story.

Given this, our time together was not only pleasant but fortuitous. Having him by my side made everything much easier. Other magi knew Anson from Erasmus' household and this made my standing much greater in their eyes. Even the mere fact that I had a servant with me made it known that I was not just a transient seeking opportunity wherever I went. I was seen as a man of means and purpose.

That Anson helped to create this charisma about me delighted him to no end. The list of magi that Erasmus gave to me led us the furthest east through Babylonia that I had ever been. I do believe it was also further than Mnesarchus had ever travelled. Something about this was exciting and I was glad to be heading into lands that were unknown.

What thrilled me mostly about this is that as you get closer to another region the teaching and beliefs of the neighbouring countries start to be heard. Buddhism, though well-established was still considered new and the inevitable curiosity helped its teachings travel. Men who went into the northern reaches of India and Nepal heard of the writings and the newly named practice of meditation. Though they would not follow the religion, its novelty made it a source of conversation.

As we travelled we found more and more of these men speaking of Buddhism and we also came across those who were venturing east to study it. Each time one of these eastbound men crossed our path I saw something in Anson's eyes light up and then as we farewelled them his eyes grew dark.

"You wish you were travelling east with them don't you?" I asked him one day.

He shook his head no and looked down. Then he lifted his head, looked into my eyes and reluctantly nodded yes.

"I am reminded of what I have left behind, where I started and those who nurtured me. It is of no use to feel such things as I have much more to learn with you," he said softly but his voice faltered a little.

I took in a deep breath as I looked at him. "Perhaps I could travel east with you and study the new ways just as these other men are doing?"

Anson looked at me puzzled and I am sure he thought I was teasing him.

"It will take us some weeks to get there," he said as though this was a problem.

Instead I just laughed. "I have been travelling for twenty-three years to get to *this* place. Another few weeks will hardly be a deterrent to learning something else!"

Anson joined me in laughing and nodded. "I look forward to sharing my home with you."

The journey east was probably the most pleasant time in all my travels. The land changed from day to day and I loved the softness of the people as we arrived close to India. As we rode across the border I could sense the difference that Buddha had imparted on these people immediately. It was like nothing I had felt before.

I imagined that this new religion was going to enamour me. The sense of calm in its monks and those that practised it was charming enough but as I delved into its philosophies I still found its basis almost the same as those I had already encountered. As with most others, the difference came in how the religion was lived.

I had come from magi who embraced all aspects of life in all their abundance to now sitting with monks who cloistered themselves and felt they learnt through deprivation. The use of the breath was employed with all the beauty I knew of it, even if here they imposed solitude in order for you to connect with it. To be honest some men just needed to do this in order to reduce their distractions and given my early experiences I was far from being critical of this. I just hoped that some day when I had my own school I would find a new way to approach this.

The one aspect of Buddhism that intrigued me and opened up something within me was their understanding of reincarnation. That it was tied so heavily to the doctrine of karma was another thing! As with all my studies I took what felt right and left the rest behind.

This great sense that who I was, was not something limited to my body and my current experience had been growing stronger. My breath retreat when I began my time in Egypt had been the catalyst for this. Though no-one had explained to me the visions I had seen, I had instinctively felt a connection to them that I knew was beyond that of the seers who predicted things. I knew that what I was given a glimpse of was something that was intimately connected to me; that my sense of awareness and this part of me that would become labelled "consciousness" was something that transcended the simple process of birth leading to death.

Egypt's religion had limited this to a continuation in the afterlife, where you found your way to eternal paradise or darkness. This depended on the weight of your heart, where they believed the soul resided. The Zoroastrians believed that when the new consciousness was birthed then all souls would return to live again in this spiritual freedom. With the Buddhists I found my middle ground. For with this new religion I was told that my life would occur over and over until I had learnt all I needed and lived a life that expressed it with purity. Then I could reach nirvana.

I listened intently as the monks spoke to me of this. I told them of my visions that I knew were not dreams and they nodded.

"It would make sense that you have lived many times to gain such wisdom," one of them said to me but something didn't feel right.

I was living an amazing life—born into wealth, nurtured and loved, encouraged and supported by all I met. To the Buddhists I was being rewarded for past lives of virtue. For me though, to think that my existence may soon reach a state where discovery and experience were no longer of importance just made me shake my head.

I lay in bed one night and thought about this. I considered that this may be my last lifetime and that there was nothing else to experience and within me came a great loud voice saying "No!" I knew that humanity was upon the brink of a great awakening. I was seeing it being birthed every day. The magi knew it too and watched the skies for it. I though saw it in the eyes of every man I spoke with.

My eyes grew heavy with sleep and I assured the voice within that this would not be our last experience upon the earth. My very essence ached to see the changes that were coming to humanity beyond any measure of time I could comprehend. I would return to be part of it, not through some punishment for lack of virtue nor as some resurrection as reward for morality. I would walk again someday to see the changes by my own choice.

When my time came to leave India I did so feeling complete with everything I had encountered. Not just here but with every place since I left my family. I knew it was time to go home to Samos. Even thinking these words to myself made me smile. Samos was not so much my home as it was the place I had begun. I had travelled for thirty-five years with no place to call home. In fact the closest I had come to anything permanent was my camel.

The call to return was strong. It came from that part inside me that I had opened up with the breath and I knew to not doubt or question it. If this deep part of me said it was time to return then it just was.

I broke the news to Anson as to what my intentions were. He smiled and bowed to me.

"As you wish. I though choose to stay in my homeland," he said simply.

I took a deep breath and smiled. "So be it my friend. I will miss you but I know it will serve me well to travel alone as I retrace my steps."

My return from India to Samos took me a year for I did indeed return to most of the places I had been. As I headed for home I stopped and visited most of the men who had taught me and even those who had generously housed and fed me. I shared with them what I had learnt since I saw them last and reflected upon what they had taught me.

Riding my camel I wove back through Babylonia, and across to Tyre, taking time to visit my family there as well. It was here that I was made to consider that my family upon Samos had changed as much as I had. We spoke of my parents, both now long gone and the news sent sporadically by my brothers who were still in shipbuilding. It was a grand reminder of what I had left behind and braced me for what I would find on my return.

I headed north along the coast, past the mountains of Carmel which made me smile. Travelling never made me weary in all the thirty-six years I had been doing so, but as I arrived in Miletus, the very place that I had begun, I felt a wave of exhaustion wash over me. I made my way to the first inn I could find and slept for a day.

My dreams were intense and scattered. I dreamt of people long gone such as my parents and Thales. I saw schools I attended in this life as well as many that were surely from other lives. Visions of the future came to me and I saw an amazing school filled with women and men all waiting for me to speak. Every scene was so intimate and detailed that when I woke it took a few moments to sort which reality I was actually in.

I lay upon my back and went into my breathing.

"*It's time to teach,*" was what I heard and in reply to myself I said "*Yes.*"

There were few times I was emotional in all my life. Apart from the burst of anger with the first school in Egypt, I had allowed myself some tears when I had news of my mother's death. Those two times were the only truly notable instances when my emotions made my decorum crumble. The only other time I felt I may succumb to such sentiment was in saying goodbye to my camel as I prepared to board the ship back to Samos.

As my camel was gifted to me I saw it only fitting that I should gift it to someone else. It would have made more sense to trade it for my passage back to Samos but this was an opportune time to rid myself of the last remaining coins in my purse. Instead as I rode from the inn to the docks I looked about me. I saw a beggar upon the street but knew he would not need the animal and would probably only be robbed of him.

Then the obvious struck me but time limited my ability to execute the plan. As always a solution presented itself.

I was near the markets when I saw the familiar robes of some Thales school students. Even though the crazy old sage was gone his teachings were still carried on. I approached the three young men, dismounted and introduced myself. One by one their jaws dropped when they realised who I was.

"We have heard all about you," one said with his eyes wide.

I nodded and smiled, somewhat amused by this but I decided not to get too distracted by the celebrity that had been assigned to me. Besides I had a boat to catch. I kept it simple and straightforward.

"I am gifting this animal to the school. It is my intention that it be used for students who wish to travel and attend other schools. It will be up to the elders who will be worthy of this," I said hoping to sound firm but my voice cracked in a few places.

I grabbed one of the bags containing a few small things that I would need but left the rest upon the camel. As I did this the men all spoke over each other as they thanked me or commended my generosity. I stopped for a moment before the camel and looked into his eyes. This was when I felt my emotions surge.

He had carried me so far without question or complaint. This huge beast had seen all my teachers and the sights I had in the last ten years. He had been my home, my transport and some days my only company. Whenever I looked at him I was reminded of Erasmus and his beautiful warmth and kindness. Now here I was at the end of my journey. Saying goodbye to this camel also meant saying farewell to this huge chapter of my life. How fitting that he should now go to the school that had began it all.

I swallowed hard, patted him on the neck and muttered a thank you. Then I turned and walked away as fast as I could.

CHAPTER FIFTEEN

I arrived back upon Samos in daylight and with my head held high. My reputation arrived before me. Polycrates, who once feared me, welcomed me back as a son of Samos, eager that my knowledge and experience could now serve him and his state.

I returned as a changed man to an island as transformed as I was. The family shipbuilding business, now in its fifth generation, was still focussed on building and maintaining Polycrates' warships that terrorised the sea around Samos. They still built merchant ships but these were few and far between. Private boats were not their main concern so the merchants took their business elsewhere.

"We either took Polycrates' business as our priority or we would have perished," explained Eunomus.

I nodded knowing that if they had said no then not only would the business have perished but my family may also have lost its wealth and, even worse, possibly their lives. Not once did I think badly of their decision.

Back home upon Samos I was now once again a wealthy man as you would define by material standards. Eunomos gave me rooms in our family home which had become his when our mother passed away.

"I suppose this is rightfully yours now that you are back upon Samos," he said as he took me in.

I shook my head, "It belongs to all of us but is more so yours for all your care of it."

After thirty-six of travelling it didn't feel like my home anyway. I walked about it picturing things that had occurred in my childhood but the memories seemed like I was just playing with my imagination.

I would recall something from our youth to either Eunomos or Tyrrhenus and ask them if they remembered. Invariably I would be met with a smile and then a shrug of the shoulders would follow. Neither had any investment in the past and truly no longer did I.

This feeling grew more and more as I walked the island visiting other family and friends. Even returning to the temple my father built for me was not the event I had anticipated. It was like a stranger walked about Samos.

Six months later I still felt this despite having started my own school within our temple. The students grew and as they did I began to feel more comfortable upon Samos. My choice to teach and my passion for it filled my heart. To see people so eager to come and hear what I had to share made my spirit soar.

However the local Samians were not ready for my style of teaching. I was too straight with them, presenting the materials in a manner no-one there had experienced. They wanted it padded with fables and the supernatural. This was no longer how I related to the universe and though I encouraged discussion to allow them their individual expression they would soon lose interest and made an excuse to no longer attend.

More would arrive, only to also misunderstand my intentions. I hate to say it but it seemed that what I had to share was beyond the scope of the local intelligence. This was not to say that my homeland was lacking in the ability to learn or grow in awareness. But I do believe that almost forty years of heavy tyrannical rule had numbed them. Part of me felt frustrated by this but part of me knew they were here by choice. Any of them could have left as I did.

I could have allowed this scenario to lead to a lot of anger and more frustration. However my travels had taught me much about this. When a place no longer serves you, just move on. It was quite simple. I never understood how people could live an entire life in one locale when it offered them no opportunity or expression. Yet people even in your time do this still.

So it was that only eight months after landing back upon Samos I packed my satchel and bid my family goodbye.

"This island never truly was for you," said Eunomos as he squeezed my shoulder in farewell.

"It has its place in my life," I replied. "It is just not where I must be right now."

The truth was it never would be again.

This time in my travels I headed west landing upon the mainland of Greece in pretty much the same area as Mnesarchus had when he came here seeking the oracle. As my feet touched the ground and I walked off the dock I felt someone close behind me. Turning I saw no-one but I felt him there. It was the spirit of my father walking with me. This amused me to no end and I smiled.

"*All this time I travel and now you choose to walk beside me?*" I thought to myself.

"All this time and now you choose to feel me!" came his reply and I burst out laughing as I continued on.

It seemed only fitting that I should now visit the oracles and see what they did. I went to at least seventy of them, though it was probably closer to eighty. Some were young and just starting out; some were old and well versed enough to deal with my questions and curiosity. Some lived in their family homes and received people there while some lived in caves or were housed in great temples. All were female.

What they also all held in common was the reverence and respect shown to them by the Greeks. The slightest sign of the gift, no matter at what age it was shown, was nurtured and supported. Some families did this knowing that the ability could be exchanged for money, while others did it believing their daughter to be chosen by the gods as a channel for their divine word. So this indeed gave great variation to the integrity of the oracles. Fakes were sorted out quickly so this was rarely an issue. However even the most talented oracle could be tempted to give a message that appealed to the seeker before them.

I sat before them all and asked the same questions. This helped me to gauge for myself just how connected the girl or woman was with this channel they had opened. Some days I was overwhelmed with the clarity and insight in which they told me of where I had been and what I had experienced. Other days I knew it was simply a lucky guess. Then one day I finally found a seer who was different.

Lucretias was still young; around ten years of age, on the verge of womanhood but still with the air of playfulness that makes children charming. She received people in the garden of her home where her father had built a grotto of sorts for her from roughly arranged stones. It curved around and over Lucretias like a protective cape, giving her some shade and respite from the heat.

When I arrived at her home, her mother received me and bowed. I handed her the purse we had agreed upon but she shook her head.

"You pay me afterwards. We only take money if you feel we have helped," she said and smiled. She then gestured for me to follow her and led me to the garden.

Lucretias was sitting upon a stool in the grotto. Her feet were awkwardly crossed in front of her and she picked absently at her dress. She was looking down and I could see the sweetest smile upon her face. If I had not known who she was I would have just imagined her to be a young girl daydreaming.

"Lucretias, your next seeker, Pythagoras, is here to see you," her mother said softly as we approached.

She looked up and straight into my eyes with such depth and

confidence that I had to stop walking. Her posture snapped into that of an adult and the playful smile shifted into that of someone who knows far more than they appear they should. Lucretias nodded at her mother and then at me.

"Good day, Sir. It is an honour that you have found your way to me," she said with the voice of one beyond her years.

I took my seat upon a stool that faced her in the grotto while her mother took a seat behind me. I heard someone else shift nearby and looked sideways to see a young man leaning against a pillar to the side of the garden.

"That is my son. We stay close by to watch over Lucretias. You are assured of our discretion," the mother said barely above a whisper.

I nodded understanding completely. So far I had witnessed at least ten women collapse after they had spoken and at more public places seen some oracles threatened when the message they relayed did not please the seeker.

"If you are ready and comfortable we will begin," Lucretias said and I nodded once more in reply.

The young woman closed her eyes and took a deep breath. I saw her breath go deep into her belly. With her eyes still closed she smiled so sweetly that it was like a warm invitation to join her. I too closed my eyes and dived into my breath. We did this for a minute together and then I heard her voice and opened my eyes.

"Mother, Luca, you can go. This man is no concern. Leave us," she said softly but strongly.

"Are you sure?" said Luca not lifting off his pillar.

"Yes. Very. I have never been told something so clearly in my life," she said as she looked at him and then to her mother. "Please. This is important."

"As you wish," said her mother and stood from her stool. Her concern though was palpable.

Lucretias watched them leave without any emotion on her face. When she was sure they were gone she looked back at me.

"You have been in the cave temples where the seed crystals are kept," she said and it was not a question in the slightest.

"What?" was all I could reply. This was the first time any oracle had mentioned this to me.

"They showed me. I saw you there," she said and then in detail she described to me the underground temple I had studied at.

All I could do was nod. Lucretias smiled once more and stood up. I made to stand up too but she put out her hand letting me know to stay where I was. She then walked to the back of the grotto, reached up into some crevices between the stones and pulled something out. Lucretias turned back to me and placed the object upon her stool.

It was a crystal. It was Amunite.

I looked up at her and shook my head. "Where did you get this? Who gave it to you?" I asked.

"It's mine," she said plainly and turned to pull another crystal from another crevice and then placed it upon the stool. "They are all mine," she continued as she pulled another crystal from the wall. "They always have been mine and they always will be."

When she was done she had a dozen crystals sitting upon the stool. Lucretias then lowered herself upon the ground behind the stool, sitting back upon her feet. As she arranged the crystals lovingly before her on the wooden seat she spoke, keeping her eyes upon the precious stones the whole time.

"When I was very young my mother sent me to the market to fetch some things. Unfortunately I was very easily distracted and this day a huge man with wings was standing in my path so I had to stop," she said then paused and looked up at me, tilting her head. "You do believe me don't you? Because if you don't, then there is no point in me telling you this story."

"Of course I believe you," I said with all honesty but even if I hadn't I would have said so to hear the rest of what she had to say.

"Good. So the man with wings asked me to follow him. I told him that I had to get to the market or my mother would be cross with me. He told me this was more important than my errand and that my mother would understand. So I followed him and he took me to a small cave in the side of a hill near here. He pointed to a pile of rocks and told me to lift them. I told him they would be too heavy for me and he should lift them but he said he couldn't and he would make it so I could. I grabbed the first one and it was like a feather in my hands and so were the rest.

When I had moved four of them I saw what he wanted me to see. It was a leather pouch and inside were these crystals. He told me they were mine and that they had always been mine. I had put them here to find again when it was safe.

I asked him how he knew about them and he just laughed and said we can talk about that another time. Then he turned into a bright light and vanished.

When I finally got home my mother was furious but when I showed her the crystals and told her the story she was not so angry anymore. Instead she was worried."

Lucretias' mother was indeed concerned. Here in her home her own daughter was showing the signs of being a seer. The very signs that she herself had shown as a child but had been quashed by her parents.

"You aren't clever enough to be this Daughter," her father had said and in that moment her connection to spirit was lost. As her daughter spoke about the man with wings this memory came rushing back. When her husband returned from the fields that night she spoke with a power she thought was long gone.

"Our daughter has the gift. Tomorrow I am taking her to the old oracle so that we can make sure she doesn't lose it," she said to him and her husband felt that he could do nothing but agree.

While her parents had this conversation Lucretias lay in bed trying to sleep but the vision of the man with wings kept coming to her. Then suddenly he was standing by her bed.

"Hush!" he said holding up a finger.

"Why are you here now?" she whispered to him.

"There are more things to show you," he said softly, "But I need you to be asleep."

Within seconds the sleep Lucretias had been struggling to find was upon her. When she opened her eyes she was in a room filled with people. They were all grabbing crystals from boxes and shoving them into small sacks or into their pockets. The panic and fear was overwhelming and she began to cry.

"It's alright," she heard from across the room and when she looked to where the voice came she saw the man with wings leaning against a wall. He put out a hand and she went to him, letting him take her hand in his. "I am just showing you where the crystals came from."

He then led her through an opening in the wall and they walked through the caves beyond the crystal room. Lucretias saw people living here as though they knew nothing of the land above. The scene changed now and the man with wings walked her along a tunnel which had a light glowing way ahead of where they stood.

Then they were above ground and before them walked an old woman. Lucretias looked around and realised this was the hillside near her home. The woman was going to the same cave that the man with wings had taken her.

"She doesn't know we are following her, does she?" Lucretias asked the man with wings and he shook his head.

They both stood and watched, hand in hand as the old woman took from her sleeve the same small pouch that Lucretias had found there that day. The old woman placed it in a dip in the ground then arranged the stones upon it. When she was done she sat there and wept.

"Why is she so sad?" Lucretias asked the man with wings.

"She isn't sad," was all he could answer.

Then they were back in her bedroom. The old woman was gone and only the man with wings was with her.

"Tomorrow your mother is taking you to the old oracle in the next village. Tell her everything I have shown you and tell her about me," he said.

"Who are you? Why are you showing me these things?" Lucretias asked.

"I am Raffa and I show you these things because I promised you I would," he answered and once again turned into a bright light and disappeared.

Lucretias woke the next morning feeling exhausted and when she stepped before her mother with dark circles under her eyes, her mother looked at her knowingly.

"You were busy in your dreams, were you not?" her mother asked for she remembered those sorts of dreams well.

Lucretias nodded and sat heavily into a chair so her mother could brush her hair.

"What did he tell you?" her mother asked.

"He showed me where the crystals came from—and he told me to tell the oracle today all that I have been shown and told," Lucretias said keeping her eyes down.

The mother stopped moving the brush and looked into her daughter's eyes. "Did you hear me talking to your father last night?" she asked the girl.

Lucretias shook her head in reply and her mother nodded.

"It's alright. I believe you heard it from the man with wings. Did he tell you his name?" the mother asked.

Lucretias nodded. "He said his name was Raffa," she answered and once more the brush in her mother's hand stopped moving.

"That was the name he told me too," she said barely above a whisper and then continued to brush Lucretias' hair.

They walked to the next village in silence. Her mother only spoke

307

when they approached the door of the oracle's home.

"Do not lie. She will know it if you do," was all that she said to her daughter before an attendant showed them to the oracle.

The old oracle was in her early eighties—a remarkable age for this time and seen as a reflection of the strength of her gift and the blessings of the gods upon her. She received people in a sitting room at the front of the house. The space was full of weavings hung upon the walls and strewn on the floor. Shelves and stands lined the walls and these were crammed with endless ornaments and curios given as gifts to her over the years.

The old woman sat in a comfortable low armchair, propped up by pillows stuffed with down and under her feet was another pile of the soft cushions. They were so soft and fluffy that at first it almost appeared she floated upon them.

When Lucretias and her mother walked into the room the oracle looked up and smiled at them in a way that made them feel they were family returning home.

"Welcome my dears. It is an honour that you found your way to me," she said as she smiled at them. "Come. Sit down with me and tell me what it is you are wishing to know." She gestured to the seats opposite her.

When they were settled Lucretias' mother spoke first. "I bring my daughter to you so that you may guide her. I believe she has the gift of seeing."

The oracle's smile grew wider and she looked at the mother and then Lucretias. "Indeed she does. Raffa told me you were coming. I have been expecting you." She sank back against her pillows and closed her eyes. "Now tell me all he has told you," she said.

Lucretias then spoke and left no detail out. Her mother sat by, not interrupting once, knowing that this was her daughter's moment. It was almost ten minutes later when she was done and the old woman kept her eyes closed the whole time. When Lucretias finished the old woman still did not stir nor open her eyes. All that moved was her belly with her breathing.

Lucretias and her mother looked at each other.

"Is she asleep?" whispered Lucretias.

"No, I am not," said the oracle, still keeping her eyes shut. She remained this way for a few minutes more. Then she opened her eyes, leaned forward and tilted her head towards Lucretias. "Where is Raffa now?" she quizzed the girl.

Lucretias looked over the woman's shoulder. "He is behind you, to your right," she answered confidently as she could see him as clearly as she could the oracle.

"Who else is here?" asked the old woman.

Lucretias looked behind the woman again and saw another huge man with wings standing beside Raffa. She quietly asked his name and felt the answer.

"There is another like Raffa who calls himself Izrael," she said aloud to the oracle.

The oracle nodded. "Is there anyone else?"

Lucretias could see no-one else behind the oracle but could feel someone behind her own chair. She turned around to see another winged man, though his stature and physique was gentler than Raffa and Izrael. She asked his name but while she could sense it her tongue could not form it.

"There is another smaller one, but I cannot make his name to speak it," the girl said and the oracle nodded.

"No man or woman can," the oracle said and laughed. She then closed her eyes again as she folded her hands into each other and rested them upon her belly. With a huge smile upon her face she gently nodded her head.

Lucretias looked up at the winged men behind the old woman and though she didn't see their lips move she knew they were talking to the old oracle. From behind her she could feel the third one communicating also. Then Raffa looked at her and she felt his words come to her mind.

"It's time for us to begin our work," was all he said but she knew exactly what he meant.

The old oracle opened her eyes and smiled at Lucretias. "They will come with you. This is your connection to all that is that will allow you to see for others. Work with them wisely and diligently and they will serve you, and those who come to you well."

This was all that the woman had to say to Lucretias and she told the mother to take her daughter and to return to their home. When the mother offered the purse to the woman's attendant the oracle sat forward in her chair and shook her head.

"There will be no money exchanged today. No oracle takes money for helping guide in the next generation of seers. This has been my honour," she said and then sank back upon her pillows.

Lucretias and her mother again walked in silence back to their own village. Lucretias could feel the winged men walking behind them, following them.

"You can see and hear them too can't you?" Lucretias asked.

Her mother shook her head and tears filled her eyes. "No, daughter, I cannot. It seems my time for this is long gone."

"Raffa is saying that is not true," Lucretias said softly.

The woman stopped and looked about her. "You need to tell them that it does not matter whether I can see or hear them. All that matters now is that you do. This gift is yours. This work is yours. I pledge to help you but that is my only involvement in this," she shouted.

Lucretias dropped her head. The winged men were saying much more but she would not repeat it. She knew she had upset her mother enough. Lucretias simply nodded and began to walk again.

Raffa, Izrael and the other were now with Lucretias constantly. At first she enjoyed their company but soon the steady bombardment of information they spouted overwhelmed her. Even a trip to the market with her mother was now exhausting as each person she passed sparked some message from the three winged men. Lucretias was not ready to be so open about this yet and so simply let the messages build up in her head until she felt it would explode.

It was three months since her visit to the oracle and Lucretias had not begun to receive people. Her mother would ask if she was ready and the daughter would respond with a muttered "not yet" and a shake of her head. Not willing to push her lest it might shut down her talent, the mother knew the winged men would know how to handle this. The opposite was in fact closer to the truth.

Raffa and his companions had the infinite patience of those in the ethereal realms. They knew Lucretias would begin when she was ready and if she never would be then they would simply slip away as they always did when the human broke the agreement. They held no powers to persuade or convince her of anything that was not of her choosing. So the three beings simply kept open the connection, hoping that something they had shared within the communications would eventually trigger the confidence Lucretias needed.

The connection now shifted and while the three winged men stayed near Lucretias, their words stopped. She could still feel and see them, but no longer could she hear them. Initially this was an immense relief for Lucretias. She simply woke one morning and as always they were standing at the foot of her bed, but today they were silent. Their usual instant barrage of messages had stopped.

Lucretias slumped upon her pillow and could have yelled out in thankfulness to the gods. Instead she rolled on her side, pulled her covers up over her head and fell back asleep.

The silence lasted for three more days. The men walked behind her as always but now she could receive a greeting from a neighbour and not have to hear from her entourage that the illness they were suffering would soon abate. Lucretias felt normal again and it had been so long since she felt this way that she savoured it. However the shadows behind her reminded her that she was far from ordinary.

On the morning of the fourth day of the silence Lucretias decided to tell her mother that the messages had stopped. When she saw the colour drain from her mother's face Lucretias regretted telling her. Her mother's words made her realise what was actually happening.

"They are preparing to leave. It is your choice whether they stay," the mother said and walked away. She couldn't say anything more to her daughter. To speak those words had been hard enough.

Lucretias ran out to the garden behind the house and threw herself upon the stone pavement there. She wept as much as her body would allow her then she raised herself up on her arms.

"I'm sorry," she cried out. "I'm so sorry I don't know how to do this. I'm sorry I'm scared. I don't want to be scared of this but I am."

Raffa appeared immediately by her side, kneeling upon the ground next to her.

"We know," was all he said but it was enough to change everything.

The next day when Lucretias woke, the three winged men were back to talking, but now she knew she could ask them to stop.

"Enough!" was all she had to say either out loud or silently and they would be silent, giving her some moments of normality as she walked the village. It was only a week later that she approached her mother and said the words "I am ready." Her mother simply nodded.

It was only a matter of days after this that Lucretias saw her first seeker. Not a word had been uttered to anyone about her gift and yet they found her. Her father was putting the last touches of mortar upon the stone grotto when a voice called out at their front door. The mother walked to the door to see an old man, leaning upon a staff. His clothes were in tatters and his sandals seemed to still be upon his feet by some miracle. Breathing heavily he asked the mother if he might be able to see the oracle.

"How do you know there is an oracle here?" she asked truly

puzzled.

He raised his arm and pointed to his right. "I passed three men upon the road as I travelled. They told me all the answers I sought would be here. You are a bit older than they described though."

"It is not I, it is my daughter. Wait here and I will see if she is prepared to receive you," she said and hurried back to the garden where Lucretias watched her father. "There is a man here to speak with you. Are you ready?" she asked.

Lucretias turned to her mother, smiled and nodded. The mother went to get the man while her father tidied around the grotto and placed a chair for his daughter. As Lucretias sat upon it he gently put a hand upon her shoulder.

"May the gods protect you," was all he could think to say.

Lucretias smiled. She knew she had all the protection she needed, though this did not stop her family from staying close by when someone called upon her.

Each day from then on was the same. People would appear having been told of Lucretias by three men passing them by. Then word passed amongst those who had come and of course the villagers noted the stream of travellers and strangers who made their way to Lucretias' home. Some days would see only one seeker knock upon their door, other days a queue would form. Lucretias made time for everyone and in-between she spoke with her three guides for her own guidance and learning.

One day, only a few months into her new vocation she suddenly remembered her bag of crystals. Lucretias had hidden them away in her room, stashed between clothing to keep them safe. This day though she pulled them out and emptied them upon her bed.

"I still don't really understand what these are," she said to the winged men.

"You do understand," replied Izrael. "They have done all they had to do for you."

Lucretias nodded but something within her made her believe that the crystals had not shown her all that they needed to. She walked out to her grotto and looked at the rough stones that surrounded her each day.

A vine was now delicately making its way over its curve, sending tendrils into the crevices. On the inside flowers were tucked into the gaps and small ledges of the uneven surface. Some were fresh and vibrant; others were drying and beginning to fade. Each one was carried here by a seeker as a gift.

The first flowers were brought by seekers as instructed by the three strangers who directed them to Lucretias' home. Soon it became as customary to do this as it was to offer payment upon completion of her session. Lucretias herself placed each flower lovingly amongst the stones when they arrived and would not remove them until they were so dry that they began to fall apart.

Today she took her crystals to the grotto and, as she did with her flowers, she placed them within the stones. Unlike the blooms though, she pushed the crystals within the crags so that they could not be seen. As she placed each one she felt them grow warm, as though this new home was giving them a new burst of life. Lucretias' smile broadened as she confirmed her intuition to place them here.

"Others like you, other crystal keepers, will come. They will come to you and they won't have any questions. They will come and you will know them. There will be nothing you need to do. Just welcome them and let them know that you remember your connection."

Lucretias heard the words clearly and she knew it was not the winged men who spoke them. The words came from the crystals.

When I arrived at her door she felt I was one of these people before she even saw me. As I walked in she had been speaking to her three guides asking them what they knew of me and her smile as they spoke was what I saw as I walked into the garden. I wasn't the first of the crystal keepers to sit before her and I would not be the last. Today though was different from when the others came to her.

As Lucretias looked up at me walking towards her she could see my own entourage surrounding me. Some had wings while others did not but she knew each one was there with a purpose.

"Your guides are gathering," she said to me.

I leant forward and furrowed my brow. "My guides?" I asked.

"Yes, your guides. Those from beyond who come to show you the way and protect you. I see your father and I see those with wings like my own guides," she said then stopped and tilted her head looking over my shoulder. "I also see men not from this time or that which has passed. They are here to just learn."

I sat back once more and waited for her to continue. I could sense what she was speaking of but it was so beyond that which had been taught to me so far that I could not formulate any questions of her yet. She kept looking about me and then around the garden as though different beings were addressing her. Sometimes I would see her nod before she turned to the next. Her smile never wavered.

"It's time to begin your school," she said now turning to look me in

313

the eye. Lucretias kept smiling but she shook her head as she continued, "No more seeking. No more studying. Find your students and remember you learn from them as well. Leave mainland Greece but do not go back to any place you have been to do this. Continue west." Lucretias stopped, closed her eyes and took a deep breath. Opening her eyes once more she shot me a smile and said, "One day it will seem so silly that a young girl had to tell you this but you will know that it was necessary."

It was my turn to take a deep breath now and I leant forward in my chair. I looked to each side and then to Lucretias. "Do my guides have anything more to say today?" I asked.

Lucretias let out a soft laugh and bent forward to match my posture. "They are gone. You are on your own now to do as you know you should!" She stood now and began to place the crystals back within their places amongst the stones while I sat somewhat stunned by the final sharing.

"Why would they leave me now?" I thought out loud.

Without even turning back to look at me Lucretias replied, "Because they are now part of you." She turned back to me once more. "You have spent so long gathering knowledge that you often forget what you have within you. You have been keeping these parts of you outside yourself, but when I spoke of your school and you allowed yourself to feel what that is like, then one by one they faded. They are not needed to stand outside you when you begin this new venture."

Lucretias sat down once more, smoothed her dress over her legs and wriggled into a comfortable position. I watched her once more intrigued as to how this ability to channel could dwell in someone who was still so young in human ways. Then something struck me and the irony seemed too great not to question it.

"I have one last question," I said loudly and sat bolt upright. "If I do not need these parts outside of me to do this work that is so important then why do your guides remain separate from you?" I finished by crossing my arms high on my chest.

Lucretias bit her lip as though to stop herself from giggling. She closed her eyes and took another deep breath then opened her eyes again.

"Because my dear friend, my guides are from a much higher order than the guides of most men or women. They are pure angelic beings that are not part of any person. My charge to work with them is much different to yours. I have agreed to bridge the worlds between the human and divine. Your work is to show humanity the expressions within the physical realm that reflect the divine."

The young girl stopped speaking and for a moment looked

perplexed. It had not been her speaking in that moment and the phrasing was not something that she as a girl truly understood. We had both felt it though, beyond the words and beyond the phrases. In that moment we had both created the confirmation of all that we had sensed about ourselves and what we were here to do.

CHAPTER SIXTEEN

My time on mainland Greece was well and truly done with. As the young oracle had spoken I travelled west, sailing towards the lands just beyond Greece. These are the lands you now know as the southernmost province of Italy. In my time this area was filled with Greek colonies. So yes, you could say it was a soft option for me but the heart of the matter was that this area of the world was where I felt my teaching was not only needed but where it could expand the knowledge and be appreciated.

Part of my legend has it that by the time I landed upon the east coast of Italy the news of my pending arrival saw hundreds of people there to greet me. The reality was somewhat different. There was indeed a party to welcome me but it only numbered closer to fifty. That to me was dramatic enough and perhaps it was in the tone in which I spoke of this that over the years as the story was retold, that it came to be much more.

The group was a mix of men and women. This in itself was enough to let me know that I was indeed in a progressive place that saw beyond old limits. This party reflected all that was characteristic of the southern Italian colonies. They were seeking change and expansion. When they heard that I was on my way, the rumours that my intention to start a school there did not create fear but instead excited them. Change was seen as something to accept willingly and not as a threat to their present way of life.

The men and women who came to meet me introduced themselves and offered their homes to me. I laughed when I realised I now had almost fifty places here to call home.

"I do hope your hospitality is matched by your hunger to improve your minds," I said as another stepped forward to embrace me and offer me shelter.

That night at dinner they answered this for me as completely as they could. As expected the conversation started with a barrage of questions to me. I skimmed over details to share the gist of my travels and the variety of schools. I mused upon the disciplines of astrology and geometry. However it was when I dipped into some of my favourite themes; the use of the breath, the sense of the soul's passage into other experiences, the concept of being a creator—that the fun began.

I was no longer being asked questions but was being quizzed. Each one of them leaned in forward or moved to sit closer to me so that they could contribute to the conversation. Someone would put forward their ideas and could be simultaneously applauded and jeered. This would only push the discussion on further.

Even beneath the jeers or disagreements (when they did occur) there was an immense camaraderie and respect between them. I sat back at one stage as a heated dialogue about the nature of the individual soul escalated. The past knowledge being quoted alongside the fresh and new ideas of these people was inspiring.

I knew I had arrived at the right place to found my school.

The confirmation from the oracle as to my role as a teacher sat within me both as a reminder and as my driving force. Not one day passed that I lost my sense of purpose. I will admit that there were moments in which I may have been pulled from this direction but the underlying awareness of what I was to do never abated. I knew now that my short time returning to Samos had been just that; a small delay before I gained clarity and moved on.

I arrived in Italy renewed and refreshed, determined now to truly make my place in history. Yes, I did have a feeling that my name would be remembered. It was known throughout the lands I had travelled and beyond. This was now the time to take all I had achieved so far and cement it into time so that it would live on. I owed it to all the teachers before me and I owed it to myself.

It is wisdom that keeps humanity alive and expanding. To not push the constant drive and momentum of the human mind in turn slows the momentum of spirit. When this flow is interrupted then stagnation occurs. I know that it did occur many times after my life was over but this civilisation was in not an era of regression or decay. That was why I chose to be here and even though I did not have a full sense of that at the time I soon would.

Surprisingly I did not settle into one place immediately within Italy. Here too my legs kept moving and my mind kept observing. I walked all the colonies of the south and talked politics as much as I did philosophy or science. I am not sure if it was the accumulated wisdom within me or the fresh eyes that looked upon their societies but this aspect of their lives soon consumed me.

I met with village elders as well as commoners. I asked why they accepted that someone not living within their bounds or even their land ruled their communities. For despite being mostly of Greek blood here now, mainland Greece still sent men to administer policy and gather taxes.

"Do you not wish to decide your own ways and to keep your wealth for yourselves? How can a man thousands of miles away know what is best for you?" I put to them.

It took two years and endless discussion and petition but I helped most of the major colonial communities gain independence, not from Greece entirely, but from the distant rule that limited them. As each one severed the tie from the mainland it felt like the society took a deep breath.

Inbetween the lobbying I did speak to gatherings and the crowds grew. It was the day when the local amphitheatre of the town I was in overflowed with people that I realised I needed a place built and designed specifically for my followers. Of all the places I had been I knew only one would do and that was Crotona.

Crotona was one of the first towns I visited. Its accessibility made it as appealing as the people within it. Close to the shore, it was easy to reach by boat from Greece and it was far enough south to prove the commitment of those who travelled by land.

I remember the exact moment I chose the location. I had taken some time away from everyone to sit upon a rise that looked out to sea. It was one of those glorious moments—the sun was so bright but magnificent and the light bounced off the sea. I closed my eyes and felt the sea spray on my face, carried by a light breeze. No voice gave me a message and no vision came to me to guide me. I just knew the time and place were right.

When I turned back to look upon the town this feeling did not falter. I gazed upon the layout of the town and could see exactly where I would build the school. It would be to the west of the town centre with the hills as a backdrop. There would surely be caves or outcrops for students to meditate and have retreats amongst them. It would also mean that we could not be surrounded. Secrecy and protection were going to be of some importance here.

My family wealth was still as abundant as it was at my birth. I sent word back to my brothers to send me money and it arrived in a chest carried by two trusted guards. It was my start but it was not my only means. As I began to speak of my plans for building and approached the tradesmen who would help make this happen more money soon arrived from the most unexpected places.

The richest families of Crotona sent purses to me, excited that such a prestigious school would be there amongst them.

"Make it grand!" one man said to me as he pressed the leather pouch into my hand.

Not to be outdone, wealthy families of the towns I had helped liberate also sent contributions. Some were in thanks and some I knew would be as a way to warm a place for their children. I received them all with gratitude and honour.

Then one day as I watched the land being cleared so that the building could begin, a man arrived before me on horseback. His frame and posture was striking and as he swung down from his horse every muscle made itself known beneath his skin. I did not recognise his dress. Though it was the similar skirt and tunic of most men of the east, his skirt was dyed the deepest red and the same red coloured the cord which tied his tunic to his waist.

"Pythagoras," he called out as he led the horse beside him towards me.

I stopped and looked at him as he walked. His greeting seemed to indicate some familiarity but I could not recognise him. He saw the puzzled way I looked at him and began to laugh.

"You do not know me, Sir," he said as he laughed. "Though, I do feel that I know you."

The rider had made his way from India. He was not Indian himself but from a remote region of Babylonia and worked as a messenger and courier for anyone who could hire him. This gave him money and the joy of travelling. His last assignment had been to carry a message to a magus who had made his way to India to study the ways of the Buddha.

When he had completed his task the messenger made way to an inn where he could rest and eat. He was sitting at a table enjoying some tea when he was approached by a local man.

"You are a messenger?" the Indian asked him in perfect Babylonian dialect.

The messenger nodded. "That I am," he answered.

"How far might you be willing to travel?" asked the Indian.

"As far as you are willing to pay me!" answered the messenger.

With that the Indian took a seat and from his side he pulled two purses and put them upon the table. "One is for you, the other needs to be taken to Magna Grecia," he said plainly but he watched the face of the messenger intently.

The messenger burst out laughing. "I can tell you without even opening either purse that the contents of both would not pay for my journey!"

The Indian sighed and opened the first purse, tipping it upon the table. What fell from it were not the usual copper and bronze coins but pieces of gold. The messenger fought all his instincts to gasp and reach out to touch it. He remained composed and motionless as his business side pulled him into order.

"That is a very risky cargo to trust to another," the messenger said with a smirk.

The Indian nodded. "Yes it is but I would not be sitting here before you if I did not feel you were a man to be trusted."

The gold was not the only means by which the Indian plied the man into his confidence.

"I will also give you a horse to speed your travel," the Indian offered.

This made the messenger snort outright. "A horse! My wage will all be spent on its upkeep and stabling as I travel!"

With this the Indian pulled another purse from his side. "This is for the care of the horse."

The messenger smiled and nodded, sealing the agreement.

When Anson handed the purses to this messenger he knew the gold would be safe. Like my sense in selecting Crotona, he just knew he was making the correct choice. There were no visions and no strange men giving him cryptic messages. Anson had watched the man arrive and conduct his business and just knew.

Anson had waited some time for the right person to do this. When news that I was finally building my school reached his ears he smiled and knew instantly that he would contribute. However he had no desire to leave his home ever again. Here in India he now had aging parents to care for. Anson also, like myself, was now teaching and his students pulled at him as much as his family. The arrival of the messenger was his solution.

Local men would not do. They would not know the languages needed to travel west nor the customs. Their appearance would mark them as foreigners and easy targets for theft. The Babylonian messenger with his immense physique and strong eyes sent out the signal loud and clear that he was not to be interfered with.

The element of trust was another thing altogether. Anson first had to trust the rumours of my new school that had been carried to him. Then he had to trust his instincts choosing the messenger. Anson had to believe that all would work out as he hoped and planned. Invested in this was his belief that an action instigated from the highest good could not be overturned by any force.

His trust in each phase of this donation was proved beyond measure. The next day as the messenger mounted the horse to leave with Anson watching him, he smiled and looked down at the Indian. Then he shook his head.

"Never in my life has anyone put so much faith in me. I swear to you upon my life that I will get this gold to its destination," he said to Anson.

"I know you will," was Anson's reply.

Those final words exchanged sealed the contract more than any of the discussions they had up to that moment.

The trip to find me in Crotona was like no other journey that the messenger had ever undertaken. He would arrive within a town to find lodging for the night and when he spoke of why he was travelling the mention of my name would invoke a smile. For indeed many of the towns he passed through were ones that I myself had been.

Some days he would not even make it to an inn as a casual conversation with a villager would lead him to free lodgings for the night.

"I remember that Greek and his wisdom," they would say. "Let us honour him by sheltering you."

The messenger would then not only be fed and housed for free but he would also be regaled with first hand stories and the odd myth. It became that when he was asked as to his business he no longer claimed his role simply as a messenger but he would instead say that he was on his way to see me. This in turn made for his protection as he was then viewed as a pilgrim of mine as opposed to one carrying something of worth. So indeed by the time that he did get to meet me in Crotona he was already quite familiar with me.

The messenger also arrived with most of the gold he had been handed by Anson. The hospitality he had been shown, based on my name, had proven quite fortuitous in more ways than one. When he rode into Crotona he had barely used either of the purses given to him to pay expenses. This seemed almost ironic that he should finish his job with more money than the beneficiary of his journey. It was no wonder that he had a smile from ear to ear.

When he handed me the purse filled with gold I too smiled. Not because this would cover the cost of the immense auditorium that I had planned but because I knew that news of my school and my work had made its way to the edges of the world. I expected that the greatest minds were now aware of what I was doing and this in turn would bring them to me.

I knew with no doubt in my mind that my school was going to change history. I knew that what was spoken here would remain for eternity.

I took the purse back to my private room in the home I was staying at during this time. Pouring the gold upon a table I ran my fingers through it and smiled some more. It represented so much to me; the respect of a friend, the generosity of the world to support me and the abundance to do as I wanted.

Each piece was beautiful and so I randomly chose one out of the pile. This coin I took and placed in a silk pouch that lay amongst my belongings. Within this to keep it company were two other pieces that I treasured; my amulet and my crystal.

My school was completed in six months. However when I say completed I mean that the initial buildings were finished and ready. The auditorium was ready as were a basic dormitory for students and several classrooms. Also I now finally had my own quarters to live permanently in which was momentous enough in itself.

The school would grow over the years though. As the numbers of students increased and more came from lands all over, the dormitories and classrooms expanded. Within years the school became a rambling campus that edged Crotona and almost seemed to eclipse the town. With some inevitability the school and its leaders soon dominated the area.

Perhaps you noticed I used the term leaders and not elders. I was even reticent to use that label upon my more senior colleagues at first. In reflecting upon the organization of all the schools I had attended though I knew that some sense of structure was needed. And given that much of our teaching would be about the more factual subjects -- such as mathematics, it would have been quite surprising to have a school without a form of discipline.

Now discipline is something I need to clarify with you. There are so many myths about my school and how I ran it. Once again small things were made into something much more, but even worse was the way that general knowledge of the school and its approach became distorted. Some of this was simply by means of stories losing their accuracy through retelling. However quite a lot of what was repeated was done so with quite malicious intention.

You see even with the large amount and variety of schools which existed in our time there was still rivalry amongst us. This competition was not for funding but simply for the prestige in which your school was viewed. New schools no matter how credible they may have been were easy targets and even with my reputation I know I upset many of the elders, even down through Egypt, having had the audacity to start my own school.

"It is an affront to the very nature of the mysteries," one priest declared and his fellow elders nodded in agreement.

I did not see it as such. I simply wanted to start afresh so that the wisdom could be carried on in new ways. The original schools would never understand this. So please let me clear for you some of the legends that have endured as to what being a student of my school entailed.

I had learnt so much about discipline as I attended the very traditional mystery schools. I had seen how strict rules and protocols protected the knowledge from being twisted and abused. However I also saw how it limited the students' interaction, dampened their expression and often stopped them from developing a personal relationship with the material. This was never anything that I wanted to do to my students.

The very impetus behind building the auditorium was that it was a place where anyone could speak and be heard. In fact it was this era which actually coined the very name of this type of theatre which also signifies its meaning. No student would ever feel that they could not speak what was within their being. Imagine if some of the greatest minds had never said what they were thinking or feeling. Where would humanity be now?

So one of my first challenges then was to create a balance between structure and freedom within the school. I decided that this had to start in how we selected participants. The school needed students who had a level of commitment to the materials we would share and yet were bright enough that they would contribute as well. So this became the ideal that would shape how we chose admissions.

When someone presented themselves at the school they would be interviewed and analysed in every area we could assess. Their build reflected their physical care. If they were slovenly, then they were likely to have low awareness. If their posture was poor, this would indicate poor self-esteem. Bright eyes reflected a bright mind. Negative comments in conversation showed they were limited in thinking ... and so on.

As you can imagine this might take several days but the legend that says this took seven years is just ludicrous. No school, even mine, as awesome as it was, is worth waiting seven years for. If I had done that I would have had notable students but I would have also lost some truly great ones in the process to other prominent schools with realistic admission procedures. I am still laughing about that idea of seven years but then I wonder how many amazing people heard that rumour and never bothered to come to me.

I was not averse to suggesting to many of them, as Thales had done with me, to move on after a few months. Not that I ever threw anyone out for wanting to study with me longer—and many stayed at the school until my demise or theirs. Plenty though did travel just as I had, wandering down through Egypt and across Babylonia into India. These travellers returned with the same knowing that I accumulated and were perhaps the favourite of all my students.

As much as I hated the division between older and newer students I had grown to understand how necessary this was. However when someone new came to the school and could prove their academic history by demonstrating the basics of geometry, astronomy and anatomy, amongst other disciplines, then they would be placed within the more learned groups. I knew just what it took to become skilled at all these things and to place someone back to the start of their studies would have been the height of arrogance and disrespect to a fellow seeker of knowledge.

The two groups in which I divided the students was firstly the akousmatikoi or the outer circle of listeners. The inner circle or elder students were known as the mathematikoi. It was quite simple; when you first started to study you listened to the older students until you had gathered enough knowledge to then participate. This step to the mathematikoi did take at least two years but the belief that new students were not allowed to talk until that time is entirely false.

Brand new students were advised to converse as little as possible and also encouraged to take part in cave retreats in complete silence for up to forty days as a maximum. I advocated the value of silence in getting to know yourself and the truths within but to keep someone from speaking for months or years would be barbaric.

That length of silence is detrimental not only to the spiritual and mental aspects of a person but it is also harmful physically. There is only so long before the vocal cords and the muscles of speech would atrophy. Silence is an invaluable skill in the practice of meditation but speech is crucial in communication and expression. To close one of these off entirely for the benefit of the other is plain foolish.

Also there was no period in which students had to prove themselves worthy of actually meeting me. Certainly there were times when I travelled back to Samos to visit family or to other places to speak of my teachings but when I was at Crotona I greeted new students and walked amongst the classes the same as anyone else did.

I truly hate the way I have been made to look as though I was aloof or distant from my students. This was an unfortunate by-product of being a celebrity. For you see it was the philosophers and scientists that sat alongside the political leaders and were known for being the most notorious and noteworthy of our time. If there had been gossip magazines I would have made a cover or two. I was venerated as much as I was lambasted. Thankfully the praise far outweighed the criticisms.

Much the same as being a celebrity in your present time raises one above ordinary people, so too I was elevated above the common man and then beyond even that. In ancient Greece being a celebrity catapulted you straight to superhuman status. In other words you became god-like and as is the way of a god created by humans, I had to have certain qualities. Thus this image of me as a distant, harsh and controlling man was simply how men of my prominence were seen and regarded.

Vegetarianism remained one of my most ardent values for many reasons. Firstly this was cost efficient. Vegetable patches and fruit trees did not require the care or cost of keep that animals did. As at Thales' school, students spent time amongst the kitchen gardens even when we eventually hired gardeners specifically for this task. This was a place to commune with nature in a unique way and to understand the energies that go into the foods we eat. It also helped them appreciate that which was upon their plate each day.

We did not require shepherds to take flocks grazing. Also we did not have to deal with the smells and hygienc issues of having animals in our care. Vegetarianism kept life simple. We also did not need to have the brutal energies of butchering within our school. That no blood was ever split upon the grounds of my school was something I will always be proud of.

The concept of reincarnation did play something towards this but it was an adjunct to my more core principles of vegetarianism. I still maintain, as Thales did, that abstaining from meat had significant effects within the body as much as it did upon the general lifestyle taken to nurture it. The digestive system worked with ease; from the teeth not needing to chew so much, the stomach not needing to produce so much acid and the bowels finding it easier to eliminate.

If a student did wish to partake of some meat they were not banished or looked down upon. They were simply asked to do so off campus and out of the nasal trajectory of their fellow students. Breaking rules was forgivable but to lead others astray as you did so was not. I remembered my deviation when I was at Thales' school and how much I taught myself in doing so. You can only tell someone so much. To truly feel and understand a concept they have to experience it. Rules introduce the concept, but it is the personal commitment which bridges this into experience.

Let us address some other stupid enduring misconceptions of me while we are upon the subject. I never told people to not touch white cocks or to leave something upon the ground if it were dropped. The sheer lunacy of such things is beyond belief and, I would hope, also beyond those with the slightest of intelligence. That these silly comments cannot be explained or supported should have been enough for modern historians to dismiss but alas they are repeated through the fear that they will omit crucial elements of history.

As we all know now, history is as subjective as gossip. It all depends on who says it and when it is said that the basis of its credibility is staked.

Along with the precepts of vegetarianism there was another principle that I was so glad the school embraced. This was the equality of the sexes upon campus. During our time this was considered incredibly progressive because as you might know this was not a time when women could speak publicly. That is not to say that women could not be active in business or influence politics, just that they could not do so in an open way. It was done through the men of their family or through marriage.

Egypt had shown me that this could work. Many of the temples I studied in had female teachers or priestesses alongside the men and I had always loved this balance. I believed that to exclude women you dismissed a whole other dimension of thought and philosophy. Besides it was natural for men and women to coexist as such.

Segregating the sexes into roles was completely unnatural despite that some were suited to one over the other. Now that may seem sexist in itself to say such things but some physical traits did just make one sex more suited to certain tasks. Intellect though is the great leveler of the sexes and every man knows this. To attend my school your gender was of no relevance and the admissions procedure was designed not to be influenced by this factor in any way.

It was of great benefit to the school that we did because we had some truly amazing women come to take part in our studies. It was also of great benefit to me personally as it was this policy which brought my wife to me.

Until this stage of my life the idea of marriage had simply been that—an idea. It was something I had thought about but was also something that never seemed to eventuate. As is the life of the traveller and seeker of wisdom; the concept of having a relationship seemed to conflict with what I was doing. Much like my father, Mnesarchus, I also simply had not met a woman who could make me feel that such an endeavor was worthy of my energies.

This is not to say that I did not have some intimacy in my life. In many temples I studied the sacredness of sex and felt the true joys of physical interactions with others. I also studied the beauty of pleasuring myself which I found, like vegetarianism, kept life very simple and respectful.

There was often the craving for the emotional intimacy as well but I knew this was just a conditioning of society and the result of temporary feelings of inadequacy. I was always quick to remind myself that I was complete and needed no other.

However when I met Theano and grew to love her, I knew this was not about needing someone to fulfill a part of me. It was neither an attempt to achieve the role of husband that society had decided for me nor was it to have a woman to provide me with children. It was that I finally met a person who I felt worthy of being called my partner. Her mind and soul was beyond compare and as I spoke with her I realized she needed me as little as I needed her. It was a perfect partnership.

Theano was twenty-four when she arrived at my school from her hometown nearby. The building work was barely completed. In fact she arrived as we were all sweeping out the last of the dust.

"Might I help?" she asked before she even broached the subject of joining the school.

I looked up from my sweeping. "You may but I do not think that there are any more brooms to use."

"Then perhaps I might take yours and free you for something else?" she said with a smile.

I handed her my broom and stepped back, watching her intently as she began to swing the broom and push the dust outside. She was definitely not of Greek parentage even though she spoke it clearly. Theano's features were as Italian as they could be and women of this pure descent were rare this far south within the Greek colonies.

"As you suggested I will go now and attend to other matters. Thank you again for your help," I said and turned to leave.

"Oh, can you tell me where I will find the mighty Pythagoras when I am done?" she called out behind me.

I spun back to face her, trying hard not to laugh as I answered but could not help it. "I am the mighty Pythagoras. Who might you be?"

Theano gave a quick giggle turning red as she did then looking straight into my eyes she said, "Why, I am the mighty Theano."

She bowed her head and I bowed my back.

"Well mighty Theano. I shall be in my private rooms. I look forward to hearing more about you," I said, bowed my head once more and left.

I smiled all the way back to my rooms so much so that one of the builders called out to me as I passed, "You seem most happy with how things progress, Sir."

"Indeed I am. Indeed I am," I answered.

When Theano walked to my school she did so as an independent woman. These were few and far between in this time and unfortunately most women gained their independent status through tragedy or misfortune. Then again that is all about the perspective that one wishes to take.

As with most women Theano had been arranged into a marriage that her parents approved of after she was deemed worthy to be chosen by her spouse-to-be. He had been a man much older than Theano, by at least ten years but this did not worry her so much. What worried her was the inevitable boredom that would come from the monotony of running a household and pleasing her husband.

Not that Theano had great ambitions to do much else as there were few options for women in her village. So she smiled politely as preparations were made for the wedding. The smiles continued on through her wedding day and even following the grunts and heavy breathing as her marriage was consummated.

Months passed and she did not conceive. This caused concern with her husband and family but not so much with Theano. Each monthly bleed was a relief as it staved off any addition to the boring life she was committed to. There was one advantage to the marriage that she did enjoy though and that was her husband's library of scrolls.

Her husband, for want of a better term, was a failed scholar. I use the term failed as in that he simply gave up on his studies to run his family's vineyards and olive groves. Marriage for him had also been another duty and this small woman with searching eyes that shared his bed confounded him. Now to make it all worse she could not bear him the heirs he needed.

The husband's solace was his scrolls. Each night with a lamp he would read them over and over. Not so much to review the knowledge that he feared he would lose but as he sat and unrolled the parchments he could forget he was a farmer and return to being the student he so loved being.

One night Theano wandered into his study as he read.

"What are you doing?" she said and though she was not loud the husband still jumped in his seat.

Looking up he sighed as he was pulled back to the real world around him.

"I am reading about astronomy, my dear," he said plainly and looked back down.

"Really? I did not know you knew such things," she cried out as she walked quickly to beside his chair and looked over his shoulder. "Read it to me. Teach me," she said and leant in so close he could feel her breath against his cheek.

"Fine! But get another chair so you do not crowd me so. I can barely see the writing before me," he huffed.

Theano slid a chair close beside him but leant over anyway. Her husband looked at her and took a deep breath. "Are you ready?" he asked and Theano nodded.

This began something quite beautiful between them. Previously they grasped at finding things to make conversation but now their time together was filled with discussion on what was held in the scrolls. Even though their ability to conceive still plagued them, somehow now it did not seem such an issue. Theano and her husband found in each other

330

something more satisfying.

It was only three years into the marriage that the husband fell ill and passed away soon after. Theano wept for the loss of their friendship while behind her the man's family sneered at the fact that no heir remained to claim his property. As was the custom of the time, all that he owned returned to his blood and Theano was told to pack her personal belongings and return to her family.

"Might I have his scrolls?" she asked tentatively of his brother.

"Certainly. They are as much use to us as farmers as you were to him as a wife," he mocked.

Theano was not hurt by his words. She knew she had been as much of a wife as her husband had truly needed.

When Theano returned to her home her mother wept loudly for a month. This was as much as was needed to fulfil the socially accepted requirements for mourning. When the month was complete though her tears would not stop for now in her home she had a daughter not only widowed but one that had proven to be barren. No man would come to ask for her now. Each time the mother thought of this her tears flowed again.

Men did come to ask though. They were men whose wives had died and who had children and homes needing care. For those with their heirs in place a barren woman was not a liability. Instead she was someone guaranteed not to die in childbirth.

Theano refused them all. That was the one joy of being a widow. For although she was within her parent's home once again she no longer was theirs to marry off.

Her mother would cry as each man was turned away and then she would plead through her tears, "Why? Why? Why?"

Theano would just sigh. "I would rather stay here and attend to you and father in your old age than to some brats from another's womb," she finally said out loud one day.

The mother stopped her sobbing when she heard those words and nodded because that indeed made perfect sense.

Soon the men stopped calling and Theano came out of her personal mourning for her husband. She finally was brave enough to unpack the scrolls from the boxes in which they were carried to her home and then she arranged for some shelving to place them upon.

Then each day, when she completed her chores, she sat and read. Theano found scrolls which her husband had never shown her. These were the ones with mathematics within them that was beyond the simple geometry he had shared with her. He had been too shy as he did not truly grasp them himself.

When Theano first looked upon them she too was overwhelmed. She realised they had been beyond her husband and this made her smile.

"I'll work them out for the both of us," she said out loud.

This indeed she did. What at first seemed to be a jumble of numbers and symbols eventually fell into some semblance of order. Then as Theano studied them more they made perfect logical sense. The more she studied the mathematic scrolls her hunger for other material to study grew. So she began to seek out the men who studied the discipline.

At first she was laughed at when she approached them, partly due to her sex but also due to her youth. She then tried another tactic.

"My husband sent me," she would say and explain he was just too busy with business to collect such things. Even she was surprised at how easily this line worked upon the old men she called upon.

She would return to the men with questions and by the time they had figured out her ruse they didn't care, succumbing to teaching her openly. Theano's mind kept up with whatever they presented to her. She was a natural mathematician and her teachers knew it. It was one of these men who told her of my new school being started in Crotona.

"You need to be there. He is taking in female students and you will show him just what a female mind is capable of," he said.

I did need her here at my school and she did indeed show me not only what a female mind was capable of but what any mind was capable of when committed to learning.

We were married a year after her arrival when I was fifty-eight and she just upon twenty-six. It was a huge difference I know but to us our ages were just numbers. And, to a mathematician, all numbers are beautiful.

Theano's barrenness during her first marriage was soon proven to not be of her physiology. Together we had three daughters, Damo, Arignote, and Myia, and two sons, Mnesarchus and Telauges.

After all the years as a lone traveller it was wonderful to spend my final years surrounded by my own family.

CHAPTER SEVENTEEN

The first group of my students, drawn from the original welcoming crowd as well as those, like Theano, who made their way to me in the early days, became my school's elders. I did not appoint anyone to this standing unless they could impress me not so much in what they had learned but in that they had minds willing to push the boundaries of what was known.

There is a fabulous legend that this elite group even killed one of their own when an argument erupted over the discussion of a new numerical concept. I regret to confirm this as true.

It became my passion, as the oracle had shared, to make the mysteries of the universe accessible to man through mathematics. Within mathematics you could show the patterns within life all around you—from the swirls of a fern frond to the predictability of the stars. When you could see all of this then you could understand where you as a unique creation in your own right, fit within it all.

This passion transferred to my elders. Now I use this term in a new way and just to highlight that these were the men and women I trusted most for in fact they were my equals. Most of the breakthroughs in theorems were as much due to their expansion as it was my own. Really anything that is credited to me should in fact be credited to the school as an educational entity and not only to any one person.

We pushed mathematics to its limits. The auditorium which had been built for the purpose of lectures and for individuals to share new insights was often the scene of loud, dramatic debates. There was always a moderator appointed to keep things in order but we soon realized that the powerful discussions moved as much energy and inspired even more progressive thinking than a sedate pondering session.

One day though all of this became too much. One of my elders, Hippasus, had been exploring the squares of numbers and then, as a balance, the square roots of numbers. He had not gone so far into this exploration of square roots when he struck upon something. Hippasus had gone no further than the number two.

The excitement as he came upon a new realization was that feeling we all had when we unlocked something new or saw something in a new light. Hippasus flew from his desk screaming out with joy. This was not something highly unusual at the school yet it still attracted the attention that he hoped for as any elders or students who heard him came to see what was the cause of his outburst.

"Get everyone to the auditorium!" he yelled as he passed them.

So anyone who was free gathered at the auditorium. They came in and found a place as Hippasus wiped clean the huge slates behind the speaker's podium. He was still breathing heavily from his run through the school but also from his own excitement. I arrived and took my place, front and centre, as I always did.

"Begin, Hippasus!" I called out when I was settled.

Hippasus turned and faced us all. He had an audience of only thirty that day due to classes being still in session as well as some cave retreats being held. I was most thankful for this turn of events when I heard what Hippasus had to say.

He picked up a piece of chalk and began to write a number upon the slate. Beginning at the very top left corner he kept writing and writing until he filled the board. Hippasus didn't utter a word and we all kept silent too. Then finally another elder called out.

"Are we just here to watch you write? Could you not have just circulated a scroll?" Dymas shouted at him.

Hippasus turned and smiled at Dymas. "No. I could not have because no scroll could contain this," he said as he pointed to the slate. "This number has no end nor does it have any discerning pattern. It is infinite and without any laws upon it."

There was impenetrable silence when he finished speaking. Within those words Hippasus had undone all that the school stood for. He had found an irrational number; a number that could not be expressed as a simple relation between two other numbers. A number that did not reflect the order of creation.

I stood up and looked at the people who had gathered. "All akousmatikoi will leave," I said plainly and stayed standing until they rose and left, making sure that only my elders and experienced students remained. Then I turned to Hippasus. "Wipe the slate clean and take us back to the beginning of this."

So Hippasus did, explaining that he had begun to play with square roots and upon the very first one that required a fraction he had decided to explore it as much as he could. That it was the number two was something Hippasus had found intriguing and amusing.

"Such a simple number and yet within it we have this immense complexity," Hippasus said with a grin.

No-one else was smiling. I could feel my heart pounding and didn't know quite what to say. At the back of the gathering one voice found some words.

"You should have gathered the elders privately and not run

screaming like a madman, gathering even the freshest minds to hear such things. This is something that needs much thorough consideration before being made public."

It was Hippostratus and he spoke in a slow measured tone that reeked of anger.

"Hippostratus is right. This is not something to be spoken of beyond even the most senior mathematikoi until we have explored it further," I added. "Besides you may be wrong. Your calculations may be incorrect or misdirected."

This last statement was punctuated with grunts and soft calls of agreement. However from what I had seen I knew his work to be correct. I did not let go of the hope that one of the others, or even myself, might find some way to settle this within our model of teaching.

Three months passed and we still had no way to disprove what Hippasus had found. Sleep was lost and debates grew more heated. I could see no way to resolve this. The constant discussion on the matter as well as the private visits from my closest elders made my mind reach breaking point. I decided there was only one way for me to find a solution. I decided to take a cave retreat.

"Really?" said Theano when I told her.

"Yes. Not because I am lost but because I know this is the best way to see through to the answer. Besides, the men are beginning to wear upon me. I need some time away from the constant barrage of their arguments and personal agendas," I explained.

Sitting high up on the hillside within my cave I thought of the oracle in her handmade grotto and smiled. Suddenly I wished I had brought my crystal with me. I reached beside me and picked up a small stone.

"You will do for the time being," I said, wrapping my fingers around it.

It did not take so long before I had the clarity I sought. I slipped back into that place of solitude and reflection like one does a favorite piece of clothing. By noon of the very first day I walked back down the hillside to the school with my solution. As I walked I realized I still had the small stone in my hand. I laughed as I flung it down the slope ahead of me.

Slipping back into my breath with no sounds around me was a delight. There was no colleague to engage me and no sounds from my children. It was almost like the life I now had disappeared for a while and my youth seemed to come back to me.

With my eyes closed I imagined that I was that young man first making his way across the sands in his search for wisdom. Suddenly I had a vision of Egypt. I was standing upon the Giza plateau with the pyramids before me. There was an old priest standing before the Sphinx and through the glare of the sun I saw him wave me towards him.

When I approached he disappeared behind the Sphinx and I followed him. When I found him again he was standing next to a large hole in the ground. He waved me towards him again and, when I was beside him, he pointed down into the hole.

A ladder rested inside the hole and it looked exactly like the one I had climbed down into the underground temple school. This time I did not need to climb down though.

I looked up at the man and said a simple thank you. As soon as I did the scene dissolved and all I could sense was my breathing. That was when I decided to return to the school.

I called my senior elders together and told them my revelation.

"Hippasus, I am sending you to Egypt. I think it best you present this to the mystic priests and see what they can illuminate for us on this subject," I said and then nodded.

The elders though were not impressed. Hippostratus spoke first in the usual slow and calculated drawl that he always used to discuss the matter. "Who is to say that he will just return saying that he is correct."

"Yes," agreed Dymas. "He could just travel until he convinces someone to agree with him."

Hippasus sighed and rolled his eyes. "Well then why don't one of you go then?"

"Because when we return proving you wrong, you will accuse us of the same!" spat Hippostratus.

I held up my hand signalling that enough had been said.

"All three of you will go. Leophron, you have been quite neutral upon this," I said pointing to another elder. "You will join them to keep some balance. I do trust though that you will remember that you are educated men and not gladiators going into battle."

The four men sailed for Egypt the following week. I watched the boat leave the dock at Crotona and as it grew smaller something twisted inside me. The look this put upon my face remained until I returned home.

"Were they fighting already?" Theano said when she saw my expression.

I shook my head, "No. Despite this being of best intentions I have just realized this may not go as I hope." There was no other way to put the feeling into words.

The four of them travelled as though they were not a group of any kind. Leophron, already sick of the whole debate found a place upon the boat where he could be apart from the others. Unfortunately he was not attuned to sailing so he soon turned white and became nauseous, not making him the best of company.

As he bent over the rail of the deck to vomit for what seemed like the hundredth time he cursed the number two out loud. A sailor nearby screwed up his nose, assuming he had heard wrong.

"That was indeed what he said," assured the captain when the sailor repeated his words. "These are men whose lives revolve around their love of numbers."

"He didn't seem to speak of this number with much love," said the sailor and they both laughed out loud.

Hippostratus and Dymas made an excuse also to create some space between themselves and Hippasus. They spent the trip huddled together and muttering between them.

"All we have to do is stand back and watch his theory come undone," Hippostratus said to Dymas as his colleague nodded.

Hippasus' theory though did not come undone.

The four men walked the streets with some cohesion. They discussed and agreed upon directions to travel and the more mundane details of the journey with ease. Hippasus had the sense to not discuss the cause of their venture without necessity. Any tension that could be avoided would only make the trip flow and help it end sooner.

I had given them strict guidelines as to which schools to consult. They arrived at the first one within a day of stepping off the boat and handed a letter of introduction written by me to the elders. I did this to ease the beginning of any work they would do together as well as hopefully avoid any initiation process.

It worked and the letter would see them ushered into private rooms where Hippasus would begin to speak of his theory while Hippostratus and Dymas would sit with their arms crossed. Leophron, overwhelmed to finally be in Egypt and with the mystics, watched the Egyptians' every gesture and expression as though he had never seen a human before.

At the first school Hippasus finished and the priests looked at one another.

"I am surprised he sent you to us and not to Babylon," one said slyly.

"Our Master had a vision. He was told to send us to Egypt," Hippasus answered and beside him he felt Hippostratus stiffen in his chair.

Both the priests' expression fell from their face.

"What exactly did he see?" the second priest asked.

"He was shown the chamber under the Sphinx," snapped Hippostratus. "You are aware that he attended *EVERY* temple and school in Egypt, are you not?"

The same priest turned to Hippostratus, his face red and his jaw clenched.

"*EVERY* priest in this land is aware of that. That does not mean that four men arriving in our temple sent by him are privy to *EVERY* piece of knowledge we have to share," he said back with small flecks of spit flying from his lips as he spoke.

Both priests stood up now and the same priest that had been speaking pointed to Hippasus and then Leophron.

"You two shall come with us!" he said and then pointed to Dymas and Hippostratus. "You two shall wait outside."

"Oh no, no, no!" cried out Hippostratus, jumping up from his chair. "We shall all go with you!"

"You will do as I say or I will send you all away and notify every school and temple in this land of your incorrigibility. No-one will receive you! Even if you had a letter from your beloved Zeus to vouch for you," he snapped back.

Hippostratus grunted and left the room after one last glare at Hippasus. Hippasus knew it to be a warning and he dreaded facing the two banished men when the meeting was completed.

The two priests and two Greeks made their way down a corridor and turned right into what was the temple library. This was an immense long room lined with shelving as well as having free standing shelves jutting out from the walls forming small alcoves. The second priest walked towards one of these alcoves and took down some scrolls, while the first priest gestured to a table and chairs, inviting them to sit.

Eventually all four were settled around the table and the first priest unrolled a scroll. Upon it were the same calculations that Hippasus had been working on. Hippasus took a deep breath.

"So my reckoning has been correct? There are numbers that have no limits. You know this also?" Hippasus asked.

Both priests nodded and looked at each other. The second priest now spoke, "This has been known for centuries. What it means, well that is what we do not know."

"But I am right? This needs more contemplation then?" Hippasus continued and the priests nodded. "Why could our colleagues not be here to hear and see this?"

The first priest shrugged his shoulders. "I did not like the angry one, and the other smelt as though he had not bathed in weeks. I don't want men like that near our scrolls," was his honest explanation.

Hippasus and Leophron looked at each other and fought every impulse to laugh out loud. Their desire to chuckle though subsided as they walked back down the corridor to face the others. When they were outside they could see Hippostratus and Dymas standing a little way off from the temple.

"I will tell them," volunteered Leophron.

"Thank you," replied Hippasus.

With this Leophron quickened his pace so that he was ahead of Hippasus. He kept picking up his speed so that he was almost running by the time he reached the other two.

"He is right! He is right! He is right!" Leophron shouted as he ran past them and kept going.

Hippasus stopped where he was and dropped his shoulders as he sighed.

As expected, Hippostratus and Dymas were not impressed by the news or with Hippasus' description of what occurred in the library. They sulked back to the inn as they gathered their thoughts. With Leophron reunited with them they discussed what would happen next over the evening meal.

"We need to go to more schools to confirm this," said Hippostratus firmly.

"But I saw the scrolls! The calculations are exactly the same!" protested Leophron.

"And what if these priests are as deluded as our friend?" Dymas suggested as he waved his hand at Hippasus.

Hippasus did not respond to the jibe. He knew there was no point. In fact he wanted to see more schools as well now they were here. If one had the beginnings of information about this theory then others may have more.

"Pythagoras did not give us a list of schools if he did not see any merit in visiting them all," Hippasus finally offered. "Besides, Leophron, shouldn't we make the most of our journey while we are here?"

"Well it is a nice change from Crotona," admitted Leophron. "And we can spread word of our school."

With that the four men agreed to continue on through Egypt. School after school confirmed all that Hippasus had put forward to us at Crotona. The consensus was so evident that Hippostratus and Dymas finally conceded.

It was on the boat home that it all fell into disarray.

The boat was way out in open water, far from any shore and night had just fallen. Leophron was once more hunched over the rails at the back of the ship wrestling with his nausea while the remaining three stood to one side discussing how they would share the results of the trip with the school.

They agreed that I would be most impressed at what they had confirmed. When they moved on to how it would be shared with others was when things became chaotic once more.

"We cannot share this beyond the mathematikoi. We don't even understand it completely ourselves and we have seen the ancient writings of it with our own eyes," stated Hippostratus.

"Don't you see that is why we must speak of it? If we keep this wrapped in scrolls like the Egyptians have then the knowledge cannot expand. What if a new mind arriving right this moment at Crotona could suddenly see through the complexities of this?" Hippasus argued.

Dymas shook his head. "Hippasus, don't you think there is a reason the Egyptians have not spoken of this with many. Even our great leader, with all the wisdom and intelligence he possesses, did not have this shared with him while he studied amongst them. That in itself must tell us this concept is not something to be discussed with all men. Please, my brother, look at this is a grander way! This has the potential to undo all that is being achieved at Crotona."

Hippasus shook his head defiantly. "This has the potential to progress mathematics beyond our imaginations. I will not hide this information any longer. When we return to Crotona I will leave the school and speak of this freely as an independent mind. I do see the grand view of this and I do not understand the fear that the rest of you are succumbing to." With that he turned and walked to the edge of the boat and looked out to sea, confident his point had been made and his agenda was clear.

Hippostratus was upon him before Hippasus knew what was happening. There was barely a struggle and Dymas would later confess to others that it was as though Hippostratus' physical abilities took on supernatural powers. With one clean movement, Hippostratus grabbed Hippasus and flung him overboard.

Dymas ran to the railing but there was nothing he could do. Hippasus was nowhere to be seen in the dark water and even if he could see him, to dive in would have seen his demise as well. Dymas could do nothing but stare incredulously—first at the sea and then at Hippostratus whose chest heaved with short breaths.

"He had to be stopped, Dymas. He just had to be," he muttered.

Dymas looked back out to the water but he knew Hippasus was long gone. The boat was moving quickly across the sea and even if he had re-emerged above the surface he would not be anywhere near them by now.

Leophron still fighting the urge to be sick looked up and saw that only Hippostratus and Dymas were upon the deck. He had not heard Hippasus short cry before he hit the water and the silence that came from the other men now was a welcome relief to him.

"Oh good, they have stopped fighting," he thought and leaned back over his rail.

The next morning when Hippasus did not seek Leophron to ask as to his nausea, was when Leophron became concerned. He let go of his beloved rail at the back of the ship and walked clumsily around the deck looking for him. Instead he found Dymas sitting upon a bench toward the front of the boat. Dymas looked up at him and Leophron gasped at the state he was in. His colour was indescribable and beneath his eyes were circles so dark that it was as though he had rubbed coal upon his skin. Dymas held his stomach as though he was easing some pain.

"Oh dear. It looks like you have developed the same distaste for sea travel that I have," joked Leophron.

Dymas did not reply. He turned his head to look where the boat was going as he tightened his hold upon his belly.

"Have you seen Hippasus? It is not like him to not be above deck by now," asked Leophron.

Dymas shook his head. "He is gone," said Dymas barely above a whisper.

"Gone? Did you say gone?" Leophron leant down towards Dymas in the hope of hearing him clearer but Dymas could speak no more and began to shake.

Leophron was confused and he could tell Dymas would say no

more. He looked around the deck and saw Hippostratus climbing up from the sleeping quarters. Despite his queasiness returning as the boat surged over another wave Leophron fought it back and walked quickly to Hippostratus.

"Where is Hippasus?" Leophron called to Hippostratus, who dropped his eyes as soon as he heard the name. "Where is he?" repeated Leophron and now his voice spoke with urgency.

Hippostratus looked up and nodded towards the ocean.

"What do you mean?" Leophron now shouted but as he spoke the words he realised just what Dymas' words and Hippostratus' nod meant. His nausea now overcame him and it was not from the movement of the sea. Leophron ran to the side of the boat and dry retched over the railing.

Behind him Hippostratus muttered the same words he had said the night before to Dymas. "He had to be stopped."

The atmosphere was heavy for the remainder of the journey. The crew had not witnessed Hippasus' demise but had gathered the events from how the remaining three interacted. Hippostratus was well avoided by every one of them. Dymas and Leophron soon decided this was best as well.

Each of the three dreaded arriving at Crotona and facing me. So on that final day of the voyage as they approached the dock it was no surprise that Dymas, his eyes dark and his voice heavy, walked up to Hippostratus and declared, "You shall explain *EVERYTHING* to Pythagoras!"

Hippostratus nodded. He knew his actions and their consequences were no-one's responsibility but his own. As the gangway was dropped down for the men to disembark, Hippostratus braced himself for our meeting.

Their return should have been a triumph. Their fellow students should have greeted them with cheers and hugs. Instead when only three of them walked back through the gates of the school they were met with gasps and whispers. The few who did venture to ask anything were met with blank stares and silence.

I waited for them in my personal salon. It would be best to hear the news of their journey in private before we presented anything to the rest of the school. When only three of them walked through the door it took me a moment to realise that one was missing.

"Where is Hippasus?" I asked looking to each of them in turn.

Leophron and Dymas dropped their heads. Hippostratus though looked me in the eye, took a deep breath and began.

I listened. I took in all the news of their time in Egypt. I nodded

342

and smiled at what they achieved. Then Hippostratus told me of what occurred on the return voyage. My eyes grew wide. Hippostratus finished with the same words he would always use to explain his actions, "He had to be stopped."

"Is this true Leophron?" I asked.

Leophron looked up and his eyes were red. "I was not witness to the actual—event," he replied with his voice trembling.

"Dymas!" I said not only as a question but in hope I would not hear the same answer.

Dymas looked at me and I saw now just how dark his eyes were. He nodded and though he opened his mouth he could not speak. I held up my hand letting him know I knew enough.

I looked back at Hippostratus and wondered whether he was expecting to be praised or admonished. I could do neither. Instead I looked down, reflecting how not even one lamb or rat had been killed at my school yet now this had happened. Without saying a word I stood up and left the room. I went outside and leaning on an olive tree I bent over and vomited.

The confidentiality of the specific details about the events surrounding Hippasus' demise were thankfully well-kept. However the rumours and gossip that spread about his demise did not help with the overall image of the school. I demanded that no-one from the school speak of this publicly and they conceded as any loyal followers would.

I assigned Leophron to now continue Hippasus' work and he did admirably. When he stood before the mathematikoi and stated the truth of irrational numbers I felt that he did it as much as a tribute to Hippasus as he did for the good of mathematics and universal wisdom.

CHAPTER EIGHTEEN

Mathematics was in everything and I was determined to show humanity this although our work was not all about such things that needed to be shown in numbers, lines and curves. In fact the greatest way I achieved this was through music. If it were not for me you would not have music as you know it today.

Sound was never thought of as something determinable nor something that could be explained. It just was what it was. I knew there was something within it that was far from intangible.

I had experienced the beauty of toning. I know that in essence, toning goes against all modern rules of song and music. It does not have any form placed upon it by the constraints of melody or rhythm. Toning is pure creative expression and this is why it is such a powerful tool in meditation and self discovery.

The sort of toning I had experienced thus far was not something I wished to study further. There really was nothing else to pursue with it. Like the breathing, its simplicity was the key to its efficacy and its exploration was as individual as the student's appearance.

No two people ever have the same experience with breathing or toning. That is why they are such beautiful tools to work with. They continually evolve as humanity and consciousness does. I instinctively knew this and to put anything down in writing or to even teach them as some sort of discipline would be redundant within years. So this left music as the other significant way in which sound worked its way through consciousness.

From the very early days of the school we played with music as a healing art. It has been recorded that I would play something similar to a lyre over people who were ill. There was no discernible tune as such as it was more about the vibration than how the ear translated the sound to the mind. To be honest a screeching cat may have sounded more appealing than much of the noise that we made around these poor sick people. However this worked in some way with many and for others it even seemed to accelerate their demise.

Theano hated this therapy. "Perhaps they died to escape the sound!" she said to me one day and it made me think about this some more.

"The word harmony is used for music as well as in general terms about life for a reason, Pythagoras. The more soothing the sound, then perhaps the more soothing the energy. If you create random sounds then you get random energy and random results. That cannot produce healing energy in any way," she stated.

"Yes, but what about the intent behind it," I argued as I thought about all the times I had watched or experienced toning.

Theano laughed. "Really? You use "intent" as an argument? Perhaps next time I do some calculations I shall forget all the mathematics I know and simply write numbers with intent!"

I nodded as I stroked my beard. Theano was right, but then she rarely spoke without having her thoughts clear. I knew now that I needed to find within music the laws and language that we had for numbers within mathematics. I found the answer in the most unlikely of places.

It was a few months later and I was walking through what was the industrial area of Crotona. This is where you found weavers, painters, shoe smiths or anyone else who could do for you what you couldn't. I had no business to complete on this day I was just wandering for the sake of some gentle exercise. It was nice to do so amongst the bustle of tradesmen, even if I had wandered here simply by chance.

As I walked towards the blacksmiths I smiled. I could hear the steady rhythm as the blacksmith hit against his anvil shaping something. Then another rhythm joined in, though the sound was different. The sound of the two together was quite like music; a high clang and then a lower clang. Sometimes the rhythm of one would speed up so that you heard one sound twice before the other. Then a third rhythm began and this note complemented the first two.

The sounds danced around each other with absolute beauty and I realised this was the harmony Theano spoke of. I picked up my pace until I was at the blacksmith's shop. This was a large space with one side wide open to allow their fires to ventilate. The chief smith looked up as I stepped towards his shop front. He bowed his head to greet me as he stopped striking at his anvil.

"Good day, Teacher! How might I help you this fine day?" he asked me with his big grin.

I returned the smile and replied, "Might I just watch you and your men work for some time?"

The blacksmith nodded and pointed with his chin to a seat at the side of the work space. "You should be able to watch safely from there," he said.

As I turned my back to walk to the seat he looked at his workmates, raised his shoulders and grimaced. He had no idea why I could possibly want to observe them and the high esteem in which I was held at Crotona didn't give him the option to question me. They went back about their work as though I was not there while I leaned forward in my seat watching them closely.

I stared as they hit the anvils once more hoping to now see just what it was that made these sounds so appealing together. I wondered if it was the quality of the material they were working or the angle in which they struck upon the anvil. I looked at the size of the hammer and knew this had to be part of it. Then I turned my attention to the anvils and saw what I knew was my answer.

Standing up I waited for the men to stop striking before I called out to them.

"Might I take a moment to measure the anvils?" I asked.

The chief blacksmith was now totally confounded and, try as he might to hide it, his face showed it. Nonetheless he walked to a bench, picked up some wooden rulers he used to measure and handed them to me.

I did not take long to collect the numbers I needed. Then I thanked the blacksmiths and left, so lost in thought that I didn't explain my actions.

"Do you think he is preparing to open his own smith shop at the school?" one of the blacksmiths said.

The chief blacksmith shook his head and laughed. "Oh I doubt it. Who knows? Perhaps today, here in our humble shop, we have helped the great Pythagoras to make history with some new wisdom!" He walked to his main anvil and bent down. "What mysteries have you been hiding from me?" he said to it quite seriously and then dissolved into laughter with his workmates joining him. "Come let us return to our mystical anvils!" he said and they went back to their work smiling.

I walked back to the school so engrossed in the measurements I had just gathered that I did not notice anything around me. Subsequently I offended several people in not returning a greeting and fed the myth of my elusiveness.

I could sense what was within the numbers but I knew it would not be entirely clear until I could see it plainly upon paper. When I finally had the numbers written down it was so obvious that I could hardly believe no-one had determined this theory sooner.

Each anvil was in perfect proportion to the other. Their sizes divided into one another making complete and whole ratios that matched not just between the adjacent sizes but from the largest in relation to the smallest. It was all about proportion and relation. Immediately I knew how this would transfer to music.

Music became my focus for the next year. This was ten years into establishing the Crotona school and my elders were suitably prepared to teach the main disciplines of mathematics without me. All of my children were born and the oldest were now well into their education. Damo, my eldest, had taken to trailing me about the school whenever she could get away from her tutors.

"Why can't I just learn from you?" she argued one day.

"Because my dear you need to learn your basics. My time now is best spent in gathering new wisdom so that when you are adult you can then expand upon this. You see, little one, you are part of an important chain, but you need to start with the small links," I explained.

My explanation only made Damo want to stay by me even more. She decided that following me was the best way to see firsthand just how one discovers new things. It was never a problem having her around. She would sit quietly and truly observe. In turn I would delight in quizzing her or asking for her insights.

When I started to explore music I dived into expanding what I had already observed about proportions. I set up nails and strung thin strings between them, setting different distances between the nails. At one point I had a huge table with over one hundred different lengths of strings stretched between the nails. I walked back and forth plucking at them in different patterns listening to the change in tone.

It became something of an obsession, so much so that some days I would walk out of the rooms I was working in and the tones and sounds would still be ringing in my ears. Theano and others would be dragged in when it got to that stage so they could listen with fresh ears.

"You are certainly on to something. You just need to pull it into some form," said Theano as she bounced our son Mnesarchus upon her hip.

So I revised what I was doing and decided to make things simpler. I removed half of the strings and focussed on the shortest fifty strings. This was more realistic as it reflected more closely those found on instruments.

Damo came skipping into the room one day with that look of triumph she always carried when she could spend time with me.

"Ah Damo," I called out and opened my arms to give her an embrace. As she hugged me I lifted her in my arms and walked once more to the table.

"How are your studies, Father?" she asked.

"Slow, but I am sure I will find my answers soon," I replied and placed her back down on the floor.

Damo ran to the edge of the table and began to pluck at the strings. I sat down and watched her play for a while, thankful for some distraction. She continued on, up and down the table, one string after the other. Then she plucked every second string, then returned to the smallest string and began again but this time plucking every third string.

As I looked at her doing this I was at first amused by her playfulness but then I realised she was not just playing. Damo was quite decidedly working through a succession of increasing intervals, comparing the tone of the notes in relation to each other in as many ways she could. Her small hand reaching the strings from a different angle to that which I did was also setting off different sounds.

Unable to reach too far beyond the nails at the end of the table Damo plucked them just next to where they fixed. This gave the sounds an entirely different quality to the way I made them sound when I reached halfway into them. I continued to watch her, as suddenly I was hearing new qualities in the sounds and how they related to each other.

Damo continued on with her playful research and I saw in her face a look that was familiar but could not place. I studied her for a while longer and realised she reminded me of the young oracle I visited all those years ago and the look upon her face as she spoke with her guides. As I looked at Damo though I knew no-one was speaking to her. She was entirely present and focussed upon what she was doing.

When I told Theano of this later my wife just laughed. "And now you know what I see when you are working on something!"

I couldn't help but smile as Damo repeated pattern after pattern. Then she did something I had never considered—she plucked two strings at the same time. Once again she started picking at strings that were adjacent and then she chose them at various intervals til her hands could not reach further apart.

Then she finally stopped and looked at me. "Papa, I need your help. Come and do this with me so we can see what sound patterns are made with more than two strings."

So I stood by Damo and we pulled at three strings and then four. Damo shook her head at this last combination.

"Four does not seem right. Three is a better sound."

She was right.

After that day I finally pulled my research into the form that Theano had said I needed. I devised the first musical scale and the concept of chords. Damo and I together formalised the exact lengths and ratios which gave the most harmonious tones and even redesigned several instruments to fit this.

The first time we heard one played was a revelation. Theano put her hand to her heart declaring, "Now that sound would heal anyone."

Theano, along with my elders Damocles and Phyltis, developed the very first versions of sheet music and with this development music was changed forever.

It seems an anomaly that someone looking into the science and mathematics of an art could transform it but this is what I did. The bridge between expression and that which can be stated upon paper in black and white has never been one of long distance. It just takes an open mind to see that they are closer than you think.

Never look at science or geometry and see something that is simply cold and formulated. Never look at art and assume there is no physics or chemistry involved. To believe that emotion and that which is physical have no connection is the simple greatest mistake a human can make in understanding their experience.

Everything is connected.

Everything.

CHAPTER NINETEEN

My school progressed on and I lived to an age few men at this time did. I was in my early eighties and celebrating just over twenty years of the school at Crotona. My eldest daughters were now into womanhood and were making developments in psychology and philosophy, feeling they were complete in their studies of mathematics.

My sons followed in the ways my own father had set out for me. They studied hard and were able mathematicians and philosophers.

Mnesarchus though never fit into the model of our school well. Some days it was as though it was my own father within his body; there was an innate intelligence but it was not one to be bound in a classroom or applied upon scrolls. It was the business world that made my son content in actually using his wisdom. He left Crotona when he was sixteen to make his fortune on the mainland of Greece.

Telauges, my eldest son, grew up intrigued with my stories from my days travelling. I lost count of the times he would corner me in the evening and ask me to tell him a story before he went to bed. Then he would spend the night dreaming of his own adventures. I was not so surprised that when he turned eighteen he asked that he might travel to Egypt to study with the priests as I did.

"But son I have told you all that they shared with me," I reasoned, not so much to dissuade him but to test his resolve and make sure he was clear on what he wanted.

"I want my own experience, Father," Telauges said with such certainty that I could do nothing but give my blessing and send him on his way.

I remember bidding him farewell at the dock at Crotona with a weird feeling within my chest. It was not the pull that comes from the concern of a parent for a child. It was a sense that my son's trip to Egypt was of something more important than mere studies.

Two years later when we heard no more from him I knew this to be true. His last message had been a simple one.

"I am well and continue being received with great respect by the schools. I have been invited to a small temple further up the river. I was gifted an amulet with the most unusual hieroglyphs as part of this invitation...."

I did not need to know anymore to know Telauges was heading to the underground school of the crystals. This was one story I had not told him or anyone else. This was the most secret and sacred of the mystery schools and as a past student I was bound to protect it.

When I thought of my son being found worthy to attend it I almost felt tears in my eyes. It had been many years since I had set my eyes upon my amulet and crystal but the day we received Telauges message, I went to the place I kept them hidden and removed them from the pouch. I traced the hieroglyphs on the amulet and imagined Telauges looking down upon his own amulet.

"Learn from them well, my son," I said as a quiet prayer and blessing for him.

When the boat left Telauges in the mud on the bank of the Nile River he looked around and cursed me.

"Damn you Father!" he cried out loud, realising this was one place I had left out of my stories.

As his feet squelched their way on to the dry land he began to laugh. He washed his feet just as I had and then pulled out his map from his satchel. Telauges looked at the map, then his surrounds and once more began to laugh. He rolled up the map, put it back in his bag, took a deep breath and then walked the way his instincts knew were right.

Telauges made straight for the temple, finding it in half the time that I had. There upon the steps was a priest and he waved to my son when he saw him. When Telauges was close enough to hear he called out a greeting.

"Good day, traveller. Might I invite you inside and out of the heat of the sun," said the priest with a grin.

Telauges nodded, deciding to play along for a while just to see what would happen. As I had experienced the priest made small talk for a while and Telauges joined in. Then when his curiosity to see the true school could not be contained anymore, Telauges pulled out his amulet.

The priest nodded and waved his hand, signalling to follow him behind the altar where he lifted the cover for the entrance into the school. Telauges looked down into the glow and shook his head.

"Oh, you do not want to enter?" asked the priest.

"Oh my, I certainly do," he answered with a laugh. "I am just amazed that you can keep this place as secret as you do."

"Well there are many ways in which we do that, and when you are finished here you will understand not only how, but why," responded the priest.

When Telauges made his way to the bottom of the ladder there was a group of priests waiting to greet him. He was startled to see that most of them were his age or barely older and he stopped short when he realised this. To their left Telauges saw the oldest man he had ever seen in his entire life. This priest was hunched over and leaning upon a walking stick. He shuffled forward and tried his best to stand as straight as he could.

"See, I told you all he would be here in time," he said and lifted his hand in Telauges' direction. "Good day, my son, I am Rakeen."

The same priest who had taught me was still there and ready to teach my son. Rakeen took Telauges to the crystal room just as he did with me. Then that night Telauges too dreamt of how the crystals were taken underground. He woke the next morning with a sense of knowing something more than just what the dream held.

Rakeen knew Telauges was my son the moment he looked upon his face. Word had travelled that a son of Pythagoras was in Egypt and Rakeen had prayed that he would come to his temple to learn. However Telauges' timing made his arrival all the more incredible. For you see the temple was in a time of changeover. This was when the old priests handed the temple over to the next generation of guardians. Telauges' timing was far from coincidence.

As each new guardian arrived, was given the wisdoms and then accepted their role, an elderly priest would cross over. This had occurred over the space of just a year. Such was the process so that the new guardians would all begin at around the same time. When several months passed and no new recruits appeared, the young priests were concerned for Rakeen. They feared that his advancing age was not going to afford them the time for someone else to arrive.

"Let us go and find someone," begged one of them.

"No!" shouted Rakeen and he hit him with his walking stick. "If you cannot have some faith in the process now with your young mind what hope does this place have! We shall wait and all shall occur as is necessary and proper. It always has and it always will! We have word of someone on their way. Now, be patient!"

Telauges arrived the next day and Rakeen began his education as he always did. No matter how synchronistic his timing or how suitable someone appeared to take on the role of guardian, there were still basic procedures that needed to be fulfilled.

My son had been there for just over a week when he was told to have a day to himself. Telauges nodded and went to his private room to meditate and write. Then he heard a whisper from the corridor and he was sure the voice called his name. He stood and went out into the hallway but could see no-one. Telauges turned and was about to go back into his room when something flickered in the corner of his eye.

It came from way down the corridor, past all the private rooms and at the end he had never been to. Telauges looked down into the darkness here to see if it might appear again and it did. First it showed as a flicker and then it slowed to a steady glow, eventually growing brighter. Telauges made his way towards the light.

As I had done over fifty years before him Telauges entered into the vestibule area. This time though it was fully lit and he saw the two doorways facing him. Telauges walked straight towards the one on the right and entered the room that was filled with the decaying boxes. This too was lit and upon a chair in the centre of the room was Rakeen.

"I apologise for the gentle nudge in getting you here, my son, but time is pushing on," said Rakeen.

Telauges looked about the room at all the shelves lined with boxes. There were more gaps here now since I had taken mine.

"Please take a closer look," Rakeen suggested.

As he had done with every step regarding this temple Telauges walked directly to the box whose plaque had his name upon it. Unlike most of the boxes though there was another word underneath his name. That word was "Custodian".

Telauges knew immediately what this meant and he broke down in tears.

Rakeen sat patiently and allowed Telauges his emotions. When he saw the young one had gathered himself he tapped at the seat next to him with his walking stick.

"Sit and we shall discuss all this," Rakeen said softly.

I cannot share with you any details of their discussion. I can tell you it took two hours and more tears were spilled by both men. When they finally rose from their chairs the agreement was solid; Telauges was now a custodian.

"I want to send word to my family," Telauges said to Rakeen.

"There is no need. Your father will know," Rakeen replied and smiled.

He was right. I did know.

Rakeen crossed over to the afterlife three days later. He was one hundred and four years old. The new custodians wrapped him in a sheet and took him to a burial place in the desert where they knew the sands would mummify his body as beautifully as any mortician.

When they finished Telauges looked up at the sun and thought of his family. The ache when he did this would soon not be so sharp. His duties and the fulfilment of teaching would replace it.

Back in Crotona it edged on eight months that we had no new word of Telauges. Though I had no concerns and repeated this to Theano, one day I found her crying. I said nothing at first but walked away to our bedroom. When I returned I had in my hand the amulet and my crystal. I took her by the hand and walked her to a lounge.

"Theano, there is one story of Egypt I have not told you ..." was how I began.

CHAPTER TWENTY

Time wore on and as it did the school became as much of a political force as it did an educational movement. We were glorified and vilified. Many of my elders created their own reputations. The story of Hippasus' demise reinforced the myths of secrecy and elitism which made us hated by those who could not understand what we stood for.

As my physical age advanced and still more students came to my school I began to be seen as someone who was unstoppable. This brought out great fear in those seeking power in the colonies. Even though we had gained autonomy, the mainland still watched us closely.

There also began a sort of tension between the colonial states around Crotona. Our philosophies carried to many of them but it was the town of Metapontum that embraced them like no other. It grew to almost rival Crotona for the amount of men and women there who had studied with me and who lived our lifestyle. Other states watched this and worried their towns would soon follow.

I was now in my late eighties and while this was not entirely rare it was certainly not common. The whispers that I may be immortal began. This fed fears that I could eventually take my teachings everywhere. My followers were known for their passionate preaching of our philosophies with many travelling to other countries to spread the wisdom.

Schools enduring over centuries were not unknown but what made us different was our size and influence. Myself and my elders were also known as powerful politicians and as a combined force we had shaped the ways of Crotona. As with any political movement this can only remain for so long before an opposing force will challenge it.

It did not begin within Crotona but in the city states surrounding us. They saw our ideas take hold in Metapontum and wondered when they would also be overtaken by the Pythagoreans. So it was from towns like Sybaris that our opposition arose. They would send men to spy upon us at Crotona and they planted seeds within the minds of the regular Crotonian leaders.

Even though we tried to maintain the equilibrium that we had always known here, the unrest soon escalated. It began as heated arguments when political meetings were held. Suggestions and reforms that any Pythagorean put forward usually would have been accepted. Now they were met with derision and cynicism and we would return to our homes defeated and debased.

"This cannot go on like this," I said to Theano after one such

357

meeting.

It didn't but when the change came about it was for the worst.

Several of our male students were beaten while out walking through the town. During the night slaughtered animals would be left at our entrances.

"*Senseless acts,*" I thought to myself but I knew the message they were trying to send through such things.

New students stopped arriving and I wondered what was being said of me and the school beyond the colonies. Even worse I had to consider if these men and women travelling to us were stopped in other ways.

I looked at my children and was thankful my sons were no longer here as I was sure the violence would soon target them. Part of me knew my daughters and wife were safe but the thought of what might be done to them in place of a beating made my heart race.

Everything seemed to settle down for a while. We avoided the political meetings, happy to relinquish this involvement for the sake of the school and its teachings. This withdrawal though did not satisfy those who were against us as it just seemed that we hid in our secret world. This only fed their paranoia as now they could not openly keep informed of our activities.

So it was that one night a dormitory was set alight. It only took one man to sneak in and begin the fire but it was enough to scare us all. Thankfully no lives were lost and we were able to put it out before it spread to other buildings. It was signal enough though that we were no longer welcome.

I stood the next morning and watched the smoke curling up from the ruins of the building. I thought about rebuilding immediately to show the perpetrators that we were not that easily stopped but I sensed how this would just increase the severity of the attacks. Instead I called a meeting to announce the dissolving of the school.

When everyone was gathered I broke the news and it was met with tears and anger.

"How dare you submit to their thuggery?" one man yelled out to me.

"Is this the strength we are being shown? To surrender all that we stand for?" shouted another.

"This is not about submission or weakness. This is about knowing when change must come about," I reasoned. "Look about you. Look! Who among you would you be happy to see die? Who of you would be happy to die?"

"I would gladly die for the sake of wisdom," cried out Bryas.

"Then you die a fool," I yelled back. "To give of your life for any reason or cause is not an act of strength. It is merely a ploy of ego."

I then instructed people to return to their hometowns.

"This is not the end of the school. This school was never about the location or the buildings. It was about the people who came to learn. Continue to learn, continue to share and the school lives on," I choked as I spoke the words.

Then I went to pack with my family. I had decided we would leave for Metapontum as soon as possible.

"Are you sure we will be safe there?" asked Theano as our three daughters looked on.

"Yes, I am. I can feel it is right. Besides I have been advised that they are ready to receive us." I exaggerated this somewhat. I had received a letter when the trouble started to brew, but that had been months ago. In truth I was going on my instincts that this hospitality would still be shown.

Thankfully my instincts were correct. I sent word ahead of us and when we arrived in Metapontum we were received with cheers and warmth.

When I left my school at Crotona it had been over twenty-five years since I began there. This was the greatest time that I had ever been in one place. Even though I spent two decades in Egypt I had moved from town to town with a year being my longest stay.

I looked over my shoulder at the school as we rode away on the carriage. You would imagine this to be an incredibly hard thing to do, wondering if I would return and what would become of this place. It was not so difficult.

I did not see a place that had been defeated. It stood strong and defiant in the Italian sun. I had created the first entirely new school in centuries. It had educated hundreds of men and women. We had found new theorems and refreshed ancient ones. Even without knowing the permanence of some of our teachings I knew that what we had achieved affected humanity for evermore.

No, it was not sad to leave such a place. I rode away in triumph.

The words I had said before my school at that final meeting turned out to be prophetic. I didn't truly end the school. I simply left the buildings which housed us.

Now settled into Metapontum I continued my studies and teaching. Students still came from as far as India and the southern parts of Egypt.

No longer within the formal constraints of a school I simply taught anyone who arrived.

The malignant talk of our oppressors in Crotona helped keep the flow of students to an amount I could handle at any given time. The spread of teachers throughout the colonies and across to the mainland also dispersed the student population. It was soon only the die-hards who felt they needed to actually see or speak to me. This didn't make them any more or less dedicated than those who found and studied under one of the elder Pythagoreans.

I sometimes believed that the dissolution of the school as we knew it was for the best. I was even glad that it had occurred during my lifetime and through my direction. If I had died and left all in place as it was then it may never have changed. Some days I saw the blessing in having been "forced" from Crotona.

Other days my anger would begin to swell. I would pine for my beautiful school as it was in its glory days and ache as I thought of the auditorium filled with voices. I would get lost in thinking about what might have been discovered if we had continued on all working together in the one place. Now here we were, all scattered to the wind and going in our own directions.

The two contradictory feelings would pull at me continuously. I knew there was only one way to soothe this—a retreat.

When I told Theano this, she bit her lip and smiled. "My darling, you forget your age. How will you climb a mountain to do this? Let us keep the house quiet and you can do your breathing here," she suggested.

I shook my head in annoyance. "I am far from frail!" I declared.

This was true. I was now eighty-nine and I did not need a walking stick or assistance for anything. Certainly I tired sooner than I used to but that was no sign of frailty.

"Let him go Mother," said Arignote. "He will probably just end up sleeping."

"I agree," said Damo. "We can always sneak up and check on him anyway."

Theano liked this last idea. So she came to me and asked how she might help me prepare.

"What food can I pack for you?" she asked.

"Just some bread and one canteen of water," I replied for I could still survive on basic provisions when I did a retreat.

The day I left for the retreat Theano shadowed me out of town. She followed at enough of a distance that she wouldn't be sensed but I knew she was there. Our daughters had warned me. So I left her to play out what she saw as caring for me and to be honest I did want her to know where I was. Part of me was prepared to die during this retreat and that in itself actually worried me.

In my entire life I never once contemplated ending my own life. Not even for that brief flicker of a moment that most humans will experience sometime in their life. I was asked once to imagine my death and the thought of doing this was so foreign to me that I faked my answer to satisfy the teacher. This inability to consider death made me wonder if somehow I had indeed found a key to being immortal.

However since the end of my school and moving to Metapontum the thought of when and how my life would end kept seeping into my thoughts. I had the recurring sense that it would be instant and this made me think the ones who drove us away from Crotona would come and attack me here. Then my paranoia would abate and I would assure myself that I would only die suddenly as I would never let an illness drain life slowly from me.

This swaying back and forth of thoughts about the end of my life only fuelled the see-sawing thoughts about the demise of my school.

So I walked away from my home to the solitude of a hillside, appreciative of my younger wife's concerns lest I was simply heading towards my timely death.

I did struggle up the hillside, thankful for the small trees that lined the way as they gave me something to rest upon as well as steady myself as I walked. Suddenly I remembered that first mountain I climbed on my way to Egypt. I was only twenty then. Now almost seventy years on I was still climbing in the hope to learn something. All that had changed was my body, or so I thought.

Theano watched me from the bottom of the hill and I was tempted to stop halfway to turn and wave to her but I didn't. This was not the time for any sort of teasing.

About two-thirds of the way up I found an ideal place and I almost laughed. It was no cave by any means. Instead it was a simple curve into the hillside, with plenty of room to sit and enough enclosure to shield me from the weather. For a moment I thought I was back on mainland Greece and sitting before the young oracle in her grotto.

Just like her grotto there were rough rocks jutting out of the wall. Something made me walk to the wall and reach into the spaces around them. I was not surprised when I pulled out three crystals, all from different places. What also did not surprise me was that one was identical to the one that waited for me at the crystal school. The other two I put back into their places.

"Your owners will arrive eventually," I said to them and laughed.

I turned and faced outwards, looking down on Metapontum and in the distance I could see the blue of the ocean. Taking a deep breath I lowered myself, slowly, down to the floor of my grotto.

"Let us begin," I said to no-one and everything.

I began what was to be my last retreat in the manner that I always did. I simply breathed deep into my belly. There was no need to form a question or to visualise anything. All I had to do was move into my feelings and all would be revealed.

By this age and with the accumulation of experiences I had doing this I knew not to expect anything in particular. Sometimes I would hear things while other times I would see things. There were even the occasions where I would seem to just sleep. It was not a deep sleep but what I saw and heard was like being in a dream state. Yet I was aware of my surrounds completely.

Today though was different again. The one element that all my retreats held in common was that I was given insight to move forward. To me this could translate as seeing ahead into the future, for want of a better explanation. This time I was taken back in time.

I realised that it had started during the climb up the mountain. That flashback of my climb up to the cave of the toning group had been the beginning of my meditation. I should have known that my retreat began the moment I left my home but this had never occurred to me before. It always seemed I should be within the cave or refuge before it started.

Now as I breathed I was taken back even further. I saw my time with Thales then the scene changed to the walk south and once more I was seeing the glisten of that light that called to me. Then I was in the cave surrounded by the sounds of toning. I could not help but open my mouth and begin making my own sound.

Theano was still at the base of the mountain when I started. Reluctant to leave, even though she saw that I had safely found some sort of grotto, she stood at the base and stared upwards. When she heard the sounds I was making Theano began to cry. She sat down upon a rock and wept for several minutes. Then she stood and looked up the hillside one last time.

"Come home. Please come home," Theano said softly. With that she turned and walked back to the village.

The rest of my day was filled with more reminiscing. I stood over the table and watched the dissection at the Moschus school. Once more I was within that small room in Egypt, breathing for hours on end. I saw the crystal library underground and could hear Rakeen laughing at me. A fire roared before me and I saw a circle of magi around it.

Each key moment of my journey played out before me in a way that let me see how perfect and complete each experience was. Then I felt a huge wave of awareness and knew how they were all connected. I now knew how together they were much more than simply a human life.

I opened my eyes and sighed as I took a deep breath. It was night now and though I was ready to go home I knew it would not be safe to climb back down the hillside in the dark. I pulled out a blanket from the bag I had carried with me and lay it down on the ground. Upon my back I looked out at the sky and saw the stars twinkling.

"*I wish I had spent more time with the stars,*" I thought to myself. "Oh well, perhaps in my next life I will," I said out loud then fell asleep.

My sleep was not filled with dreams and though I heard some animals scratching nearby they did not disturb me so much either. Just before dawn I sat up to watch the sky begin to light up and regretted I had not placed myself to see the actual sunrise. Instead I settled for seeing Metapontum slowly reveal herself from the shadows and the ocean start to sparkle again.

When there was enough daylight I slowly made my way down the hillside to return home.

Theano and Arignote were on their way to check on me and we met on the road as I walked. Arignote ran to embrace me but Theano stayed where she was. I could see dark circles under eyes and now tears filled them. She could not speak and just shook her head.

"Are you not happy to see me and know my retreat is complete?" I asked her.

Theano now nodded and though her tears still fell she now began to laugh.

"I may be slower at most things, but at least I am still quick to perceive what I need to hear," I said.

Then with my wife holding one of my hands, and my daughter holding the other, we headed for home.

This retreat experience signalled many things to me. Firstly that

I did need to reflect on my accomplishments and this in itself set off a new phase for me. During my time at the school I had resisted creating a library of all we had discovered or expanded upon. This may seem quite foolish to not document all that we did and this unfortunately was a product of the paranoia that had cost Hippasus his life.

With nothing recorded there was nothing of value to steal from us. Information could not be taken in the form of a scroll to be studied elsewhere. This meant our students' minds were the only system of storage. In order to know it all completely and thoroughly they needed to spend upwards of six years with us. By this time they had so much respect for the teachings as well as the disciplines of the school they had no interest to take the knowledge away to be presented somewhere else.

Now I decided was the time to make some permanent records. This insight triggered by the retreat tied in with the second issue that it raised for me—what legacy was I going to leave?

When I contemplated this my immediate answer was "the students and their passing on of the knowledge." I also knew that this was not to be the only way. I needed to write things down in my direct words and with my own wisdom infused upon the parchment. This is not because I did not trust those who would follow me. It was just that I knew firsthand how information became diluted and reshaped by another's methods. Even the way they chose to live could alter how they shared information.

I thought back to the crystal school in Egypt with its beautiful books. Every generation of custodians taught the same words with the same respect and honour. I could not guarantee this for my teachings. What I could guarantee was that there would at least be some lasting evidence of what I stood for.

So I began to write and on the days I could not hold my quill so well, Theano or one of my daughters would help me. I started with my work on geometry and we marked out diagrams that are still used now. My beloved theorem of triangles was captured on parchment and when I looked upon its finished drawing I wondered how future students would take to this.

If you had told me then that thousands of years later, in schools across the world, children would be taught this I would have burst with joy. If you had added that my theorem would be accepted just as we formalised it I would have been astonished to know that we had explored all there was to know about triangles.

The one thing I could never subscribe to was that knowledge had no possibility to expand any further. I never once believed that I had found the answers to everything. I also never believed that I had ever discovered the final solution to any theory. My school and my teachings were a marker for humanity. They were a step within progress that had been solidified so that it was now a platform to build upon.

If you asked me what I hoped to be known for it would not be that I am seen as a man who knew all there was to know. It would be that I am remembered as a man who helped humanity move forward. That was my only wish for what I had achieved.

CHAPTER TWENTY-ONE

My retreat did not quell this sense that my end was impending nor should it have. A man approaching ninety is far closer to death than he is to birth. This is not an age for grand plans. It is a time for resolution. Reflection also calls to you at this age but I saw no point in this after my final retreat. I looked ahead. That was all that made sense to me now.

Unlike other phases in my life I had no direction to take. My body expressed its limits to me in ever increasing ways and I submitted to this willingly. I knew when there were things that could not be fought. I could no longer walk so easily to the temples and join the locals in prayer, nor could I sit too long to receive any students making pilgrimage to me.

My days were filled with reading and some writing as I remembered something else to record. I would occasionally receive a visitor from Crotona asking for some political advice but I would wave my hand and send them away. Even my passion for such things had faded since leaving.

The new peace I found in Metapontum enveloped my life in such a way that anyone other than my wife and family seemed agitating. Some of the elders who followed me to Metapontum would still want to engage in heated debates and would gather to do so around me. That was when I would pretend to sleep and they would slip out as soon as they noticed.

Everything slowed down around me and I felt everything slow down within me also.

I began to see figures around me that I knew were not of the human realm but did not speak of them lest I be considered senile. When they came I would just breathe and be thankful they did not speak in words with me.

One day there were three of them—huge males with wings. I did not know them by sight but knew them by sense. I returned their smiles and then they were gone.

At that exact moment over on mainland Greece, a woman smiled and tears fell from her eyes. The oracle, now a mature woman, looked at me through the eyes of her guides and said her farewell.

Some of these energies would spend days with me while others would provide only a glimpse of themselves. Some were from the past and others I imagined from the future. I was thankful my real visitors were less each day else my mind could not have coped with the traffic through my home.

One night I finally confessed my visions to Theano. She sighed and made no expression.

"Do you think I have begun to lose my mind?" I asked her.

Theano shook her head. "No, I think your mind has just finally slowed down. It has worked hard and fast for over ninety years. It deserves a rest," she replied as she stroked my cheek.

My end was not tragic or dramatic. As with the rest of my life this too has been subject to myths and legends. I will tell you the truth.

I was not killed by the hands of another. I was not chased to my death nor did I surrender myself to being killed instead of walking through a bean field (as yet another enduring fallacy claims).

I was ninety-four when I passed away. The idea that I could have even contemplated running from an attack is ludicrous. That someone would have needed to stab me with a knife to end my life even more so. It would have been far simpler than that to rid the world of me. In my now fragile state even a grandchild sneaking up to playfully scare me sent my heart into spasms.

No, my end was far gentler than this. It was quite beautiful.

I woke up on one of those days where my legs were not so stiff and my back not so tired. These mornings always signalled a day of joy for me. The sun was shining and there was calm within my house.

I ate my breakfast with Theano as we did every day. We made small talk; speaking of our children and their families. We spoke of events in the town and what vegetables in our garden were ready to pick. It was a lovely time together.

When we rose from the table Theano asked me, "What will you do today?"

I smiled, "I think I shall go for a walk."

"Alright my love," she said as she left the room. "Just don't go too far."

I didn't make it too far. I wandered to the outskirts of Metapontum where a wheat field grew almost to my shoulder height. I watched it sway in the breeze and brushed my hand across the top of the ears that were now full with their seeds.

It would turn gold soon and then it would be cut away to be made into food. Then a new crop would be sown.

"*The beauty of life is never ending,*" I thought.

Suddenly I felt so tired. I lay down upon the ground and looked up at the ears still swaying in the breeze.

"*So beautiful .....*"

This was my last thought.

As the breeze caressed my face I released my last breath into her. She carried it away as gently as a mother would a newborn child.

It was Arignote who found me. Theano sent her to find me with the excuse it would soon be time for lunch. She could have come to look for me herself but that feeling of concern she held for me most days was amplified today. Theano feared the worst and she could not bear to face it. She knew Arignote could and she was right.

When my daughter found my body next to the wheat she did not scream or cry. Arignote slowly lowered herself to sit beside me and smiled upon my form. Then she gently reached out to stroke my face.

"Where have you gone on to now?" she whispered to me.

No matter how many times we separate from our bodies at death, each time seems like it is the first. We never grow accustomed to it and it is always with an initial shock.

When I slipped from this life though, there was not the heavy pull of my body. It was instant so that suddenly I looked upon myself lying in the field and wondered what had happened. Even as I gazed upon my body I decided to convince myself that I was simply deep in a meditation. However when I made the decision to return to my body and wake, it just would not happen.

Then Arignote arrived. It was when I saw her reaction and heard her words that I realised I was dead.

"I wasn't ready!" I cried out to anyone who would listen.

I knew this was not true though. My work was done. My life was complete.

I watched as Arignote called out to some farmers nearby and saw the expressions on their faces as they looked at my body. One of them mouthed a prayer, then kissed his hand and placed it upon his heart. The men then lifted my body and took me to a cart they had nearby. Another took off his tunic and covered my face. It was a small gesture but one I appreciated.

Then slowly they walked me home.

Theano collapsed against the doorway when she saw Arignote walking alongside the cart with the farmers. She did not cry or go into hysterics for which I am thankful, but she could not deny her genuine grief to lose me.

Arignote ran to her. As she hugged her mother they finally let themselves weep.

"He went in peace, Mother. He went in peace," Arignote whispered to Theano through their tears.

Theano and Arignote were soon joined by Damo, Myia and their daughters. Together all the women prepared my body. I was washed and dabbed with oils. Then they draped me in white clothing.

The men of my family carried my body to the parlour of our home and laid me upon a low lounge in the centre of the room. Then the entire family sat around to acknowledge the life that had been. There was silence for some time, aside from an occasional sigh, the rustle of someone shifting in their seat or the muffled sobs of someone as a memory evoked some sadness.

Theano turned her gaze from my grey face and looked about to the faces of our family around her. She looked at each one of them; her three daughters, their husbands and the twelve grandchildren who now filled her home. In some she saw my eyes, in others the curve of my nose or the way their hair made curls just as mine had.

Theano smiled and silently thanked me for each and every one of these people in her life. She thought back to before she had met me and could hardly imagine that another form of her had existed. Theano leant forward and smiled.

"Have I ever told you of the day I met your father?" she said to all within the room.

"Yes you have, Mother," replied Damo. "But, please, tell us again."

So Theano did and when she finished Damo told her favourite memory of me. When she finished Arignote's husband spoke and when he finished another story from another family member was told. The room filled with warmth and humour. As they spoke these stories, my death seemed not to have occurred.

Theano looked at me as she heard yet another story that made the room echo with laughter.

"You'll never be truly gone," she said quietly.

However I already was. I watched for a while longer as my tomb was prepared and my funeral took place but I was ready to move on the moment my body was prepared.

When I let go of my body in this life, my personality remained with it. I did not take one shred of it with me into the ethers. I freed myself as I knew I would. The sense that once you relinquish your physical ties with a life that you are then free to move on to the next incarnation was exactly what I experienced.

The emotional ties were all that remained. As I saw my family speak with joy of their time with me those too dissolved. The curiosity of what would follow kept me a few days longer but as I walked with the cortege to my resting place this was fulfilled. My pallbearers' hands were still upon me when I separated myself from this existence.

I did not watch as Damo vowed to protect my scrolls. This she did until her own death when they were passed onto the new leader of my school. I did not see the school in Crotona re-establish with the pledge to never be involved in politics again. For that I would have cheered as loud as I could.

I saw nothing more of what would come because now I simply wanted to move on to what was next for my soul.

My soul played with existence in every way you can imagine. I chose lives of honour and glory, then ones of malice and treachery. I returned as kings, queens and slaves. I knew what it tasted like to abuse and be abused. The rich tapestry of human existence offers countless opportunities and infinite potentials. My soul ached to experience every colour and texture it possibly could.

I went back to my past and was my own grandson while I was Pharaoh. Then I travelled so far into the future I cannot even describe where and when it was. It was all amazing.

Then something seized me. It was a call from within as clear as anything I ever heard with human hearing. It was my divinity, my oversoul, my truth.

"Enough. The time has come," it called to me.

I understood what this meant. It was time to stop playing with life as I would a toy. It was time to delve into my true calling. The time had come to be the teacher that my very essence knew it wanted to be.

Pythagoras had been a teacher in a glorious way that sent lasting ripples throughout consciousness. In his life I had heard the call and did it in a human way. Now it was time to do it in a divine way.

I sent my essence out into the expanse of consciousness that does not know time or space. I felt into where I was needed. Then it was as though I was shown a flicker of every lifetime I had played with. I saw the lives where I had connected with this calling and realised I was being offered a chance to live those times over again with a new awareness— an awareness that would be much greater than I could ever comprehend as a human.

My oversoul though knew just what this new awakening within me would express and how it would connect with humanity.

Instantly I knew which life I would start with.

My next life would allow me to witness the dawn of a new age. This was the era that the Zoroastrians had known was coming and I would help usher in.

I sent my soul in close to the lands of Babylonia. It was here I would return and begin my life as Balthasar, one of the three magi who would welcome the prophet Yeshua to humanity.

It was possibly the grandest life I would ever lead.